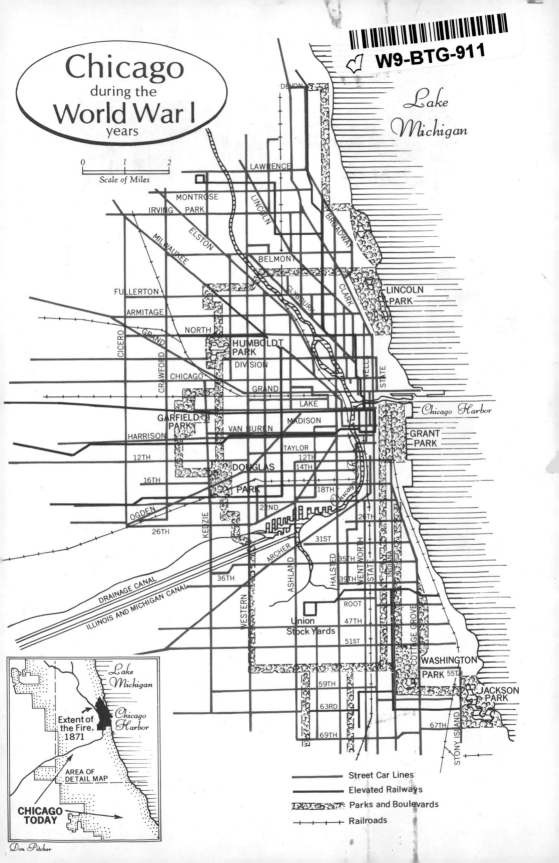

Chicago during the World War I years

Scale of Miles
0   1   2

Lake Michigan

W9-BTG-911

DEVON
LAWRENCE
MONTROSE
IRVING PARK
ELSTON
MILWAUKEE
LINCOLN
BROADWAY
BELMONT
CLARK
FULLERTON
LINCOLN PARK
ARMITAGE
GRAND
NORTH
CICERO
CRAWFORD
HUMBOLDT PARK
DIVISION
CHICAGO
GRAND
PLYMOUTH
WELLS
STATE
LAKE
GARFIELD PARK
MADISON
Chicago Harbor
HARRISON
VAN BUREN
GRANT PARK
12TH
TAYLOR
12TH
DOUGLAS
14TH
16TH
PARK
18TH
OGDEN
22ND
26TH
KEDZIE
26TH
ARCHER
31ST
HALSTED
35TH
WENTWORTH
STATE
INDIANA
36TH
39TH
DRAINAGE CANAL
ROOT
47TH
WESTERN
ASHLAND
Union Stock Yards
COTTAGE GROVE
ILLINOIS AND MICHIGAN CANAL
51ST
59TH
WASHINGTON PARK 55TH
63RD
JACKSON PARK
67TH
69TH
STONY ISLAND

Lake Michigan
Chicago Harbor
Extent of the Fire, 1871
AREA OF DETAIL MAP
CHICAGO TODAY

——— Street Car Lines
■■■ Elevated Railways
▨▨▨ Parks and Boulevards
+++ Railroads

Don Pitcher

CHICAGO

1860-1919

BY STEPHEN LONGSTREET

THE PEDLOCK SAGA

The Pedlocks
Pedlock & Sons
Pedlock Saint, Pedlock Sinner
The Pedlock Inheritance

The Lion at Morning
The Beach House
Remember William Kite?

HISTORIES
The Wilder Shore (San Francisco)
Sportin' House (New Orleans)
War Cries on Horseback (Indian Wars of the West)
We All Went to Paris—Americans in the City of Light
Chicago 1860–1919

THE ARTS
The Real Jazz Old and New
Complete Dictionary of Jazz (Paris—in French)
A Treasury of the World's Great Prints

PLAY
High Button Shoes

BY STEPHEN AND ETHEL LONGSTREET
Man of Montmartre
The Politician
Geisha
Yoshiwara
A Salute to American Cooking

with illustrations by the author

STEPHEN LONGSTREET

CHICAGO

1860-1919

DAVID McKAY COMPANY, INC.  NEW YORK

To the memory
of one who first suggested this book
To
Theodore Dreiser

CONTENTS

BOOK TWO—GROWTH OF A CITY

BOOK THREE—ROGUES AND CITIZENS

BOOK FOUR—HOW TO SEIZE A CITY

BOOK FIVE—SOCIETY UPSTAIRS AND DOWN

BOOK SIX—SODOM BY THE LAKE

ACKNOWLEDGMENTS

Much of this book is the result of personal conversations and note-taking with old Chicagoans, material collected over the last thirty years, and whose help I have acknowledged in the introduction. I have also used extensively the collection of John Ross—rich in letters, documents, and journals of the West and Middle West— and on whose collection of prints and photographs I have based a great deal of the drawings that accompany the text. I have been aided in the matter of changing fashions by Helen Wurdemann, Director of the Los Angeles Art Association.

For solid documentation I have thanks to offer to the National Archives, the Library of Congress, the Chicago Historical Society, the Chicago and New York Public libraries, the Newberry Library in Chicago, the files of the *Chicago Tribune, Chicago Sun-Times,* and *Chicago Daily News.* There are also files and stray copies of newspapers which have long since silenced their presses. Various historical societies in Illinois, Ohio, Indiana and Michigan have also been of help. The quoted section on the Everleigh Sisters is from *Nell*

Kimball, Her Life as an American Madam, By Herself (New York, 1970), used with permission.

It would take up too much space to list all the books, magazines, newspapers, pamphlets, and manuscripts that were examined in the study for this book. The following lists some of the major titles that helped.

ABBOTT, WILLIS J. *Life of Carter H. Harrison* (New York: Dodd, Mead, 1895).

ADDAMS, JANE. *Twenty Years at Hull House* (New York: Macmillan, 1910).

ANDREAS, ALFRED T. *History of Chicago* (Chicago: Andreas, 1884).

ATKINSON, ELEANOR. *Story of Chicago* (Little Chronicle, 1911).

BANCROFT, EDGAR A. *Chicago Strike of 1894* (pamphlet).

BLANCHARD, RUFUS. *Discovery and Conquests of the Northwest with History of Chicago* (Chicago: Cushing, Thomas, 1881).

BROSS, WILLIAM. *History of Chicago* (Chicago: Jansen, McClurg, 1880).

BROWN, G. P. *Drainage Channel and Waterway* (Chicago: Donnelley, 1894).

CASSON, HERBERT N. *Cyrus Hall McCormick* (Chicago: McClurg, 1909).

COLBERT, ELIAS. *Chicago: Historical and Statistical Sketch* (Chicago, 1868).

COOK, FREDERICK FRANCIS. *Bygone Days in Chicago* (Chicago: McClurg, 1910).

CURREY, J. SEYMOUR. *Chicago: Its History and Builders* (Chicago: Clarke, 1912).

Fergus Historical Sketches of Chicago. (Chicago: Fergus, 1876–1896).

FLINN, JOHN J. *History of the Chicago Police* (Chicago: Flinn, 1887).

GALE, EDWIN O. *Reminiscences of Early Chicago* (Chicago: Revell, 1902).

GOODSPEED, E. J. *History of the Great Fire in Chicago and the West* (New York: Goodspeed, 1871).

History of World's Columbian Exposition (Chicago: Chicago Record, 1894).

HUSBAND, JOSEPH. *Story of the Pullman Car* (Chicago, 1917).

Inter-Ocean History of Chicago (Chicago, 1910).

JETER, HELEN R. *Trends of Population in the Region of Chicago* (Chicago: University of Chicago Press, 1927).

JOHNSON, CLAUDIUS O. *Carter Henry Harrison I* (Chicago: University of Chicago Press, 1928).

JOHNSON, ROSSITER. *History of World's Columbian Exposition* (N.D.).

KARSNER, DAVID. *Eugene V. Debs: Authorized Life and Letters* (New York: Boni and Liveright, 1921).

MAYER and WADE. *Chicago: Growth of a Metropolis* (Chicago: University of Chicago Press, 1969).

MOSES, JOHN, and KIRKLAND, JOSEPH. *History of Chicago* (Chicago: Munsell, 1895).

MURPHY, JOHN E. *Railroads of Chicago* (Chicago, 1911).

PLUMB, RALPH G. *History of the Navigation of the Great Lakes* (Washington: U.S. Government Printing Office, 1911).

QUAIFE, MILO MILTON. *Chicago and the Old Northwest* (Chicago: University of Chicago Press, 1913).

Reminiscences of Early Chicago; Introduction by Mabel McIlvaine (Chicago: Lakeside Press, 1912).

SHEAHAN, JAMES W., and UPTON, GEORGE P. *Great Conflagration: Chicago, Its Past, Present, and Future* (Chicago, 1871).

STEAD, WILLIAM T. *If Christ Came to Chicago* (Chicago: Laird and Lee, 1894).

SWIFT, LOUIS F. *Yankee of the Yards* (New York: Shaw, 1927).

WALSKA, GANNA. *Always Room at the Top* (P.Y., N.D.).

WASHBURN, CHARLES. *Come Into My Parlor* (Knickerbocker, 1939).

WRIGHT, JOHN STEPHEN. *Chicago: Past, Present, and Future* (Chicago: Western News, 1863).

Stormy, husky, brawling,
City of the Big Shoulders.

CARL SANDBURG, "CHICAGO"

INTRODUCTION

People of respectability tolerate things here which are perfectly shocking to the moral sense of respectable people elsewhere. Men, reckless of public opinion, and women, regardless of feminine delicacy, are continually creating social sensations . . . The painted woman drives an elegant equipage paid for, perhaps, by some prominent citizen; whole thoroughfares are given over, nay abandoned, to bagnios and brothels.
JOHN J. FLINN (*1871*)

A big city is not a little teacup to be seasoned by old maids. It is a big city where men must fight and think for themselves, where the weak must go down and the strong remain. Removing all the stumbling stones of life, putting to flight the evils of vice and greed, and all that, makes our little path a monotonous journey. Leave things be; the wilder the better for those who are strong enough to survive, and the future of Chicago will then be known.
THEODORE DREISER, THE TITAN

It was my meeting again Theodore Dreiser—that fighter against sexual puritanism—in California in the early 1940s that first planted the idea in my head of writing the neglected story of the great city of Chicago, that section of its unquiet history that ran from the start of the Civil War to the end of World War I. A period overshadowed by later decades, the books on the Capone mob rule, the many volumes on the so-called Roaring Twenties and Desperate Thirties.

We used to walk in the then-still-crisp white sunlight of Los Angeles, and Dreiser would talk of the Chicago he had known before the turn of the century, with its insatiable, clamorous hunger for sensation, and his knowledge of its later aspirations and prowling precarious life up till 1914. He spoke of what pleasures, violence, drama it had contained, what drive, power and cruelty it had shown, impulses both primordial and artistic. He had captured it in his personal volumes about the struggles of his youth in Chicago, and best of all in two now classic American novels, *Sister Carrie* and *The Titan*.

In the first book, he told me, the growing city of the eighties was still Slabtown in part—and gilt brick Victorian, too—the world of a country girl brought suddenly in contact with a sensual, busy existence, a society in perpetual corruption. The second novel was the climax in the life of a ruthless grabber and wheeler-dealer, the avarice of a baroque redundancy, a life based on the true facts of the financier, Charles Yerkes, who stole and plundered and fornicated and made the city of Chicago bow to his wishes. A parvenu and thief of genius.

Dreiser was in his last years, but some of the fire of the creative artist using raw material outlining an isolated American phenomenon still smoldered in him, helped, one must admit, by alcohol. ("Underneath my table is a bottle of Gordon's Gin—a siphon of seltzer. Life is difficult and I must keep up." Dreiser, in the 1920s, to H. L. Mencken.)

It was, then, in the 1940s, I began to collect the material, the surface splendor, appearances both destructive and of moral ambiguity, that became this volume. Carl Sandburg, too, was part of the California scene for a time. We were working together on some government wartime project that used writers (badly, it turned out). After the committee meetings, Carl would lean back in his chair and toss back his lime-colored fringe of hair and talk of Chicago as it had been before the First World War—the world of the Pullman strikes, Haymarket riots, gowns by Worth, and music by Offenbach and the first riverboat jazz. Some of what he remembered also went into my notebooks.

The third figure of early Chicago I knew was Ben Hecht, fighting a plague of ennui, yet eager for the big money. It was no secret that he often hired young authors to aid him in his film writing. I was one such youth, in the mid 1930s, who, having adapted his and Charles MacArthur's play, *The Front Page*, as a radio series, was invited to meet Ben at New York's Algonquin, then the hostel for a group of now near-forgotten columnists and journalists who made literary and gossip sounds. Ben hired me to spend some weeks working on a Goldwyn film he was writing. From this employment there developed many years of talk about Chicago as it had been for a very young newspaperman. Ben's Chicago is a Kierkegaardian vision, half fantasy and half the Katzenjammer Kids—much frosted over with the grotesque jeweled prose he took such pride in. But it was gay *Angst* (he called his last book on Chicago, *Gaily Gaily*). When his facts could be checked, much of it was a valid history of the streets, its characters, and some events that might have been lost but for his strong nostalgia for his beginnings as a young writer of the Chicago Renaissance and its hoodlum setting.

Upton Sinclair, whom I visited in Pasadena, was also helpful. And so were talks with Clarence Darrow and Edgar Lee Masters. But the solid content of this book is the result of years of research, of burrowing in old newspaper files, collections of private letters, court records, and the manuscript volumes of early journal keepers and amateur historians, the reports of commissions and reformers.

Limiting myself to the Chicago between the two great wars—1860–1919—I was free to focus on that period when the city was taking on a certain ambitious color, producing besides the histories I used of gamblers, whores, great merchants, industrialists, even murderers, its own novelists, poets, little avant-garde magazines, such as Margaret Anderson's *Little Review*, even arty theater groups eager to struggle with Ibsen and early Shaw. There were wild painters and wilder sculptors, Satanic cults, followers of Aleister Crowley. And a special brand of journalism full of fury and gory details, based sometimes on the truth. But spiced with the imagination of reporters and editors who decided on what would be readable and excitable to a city given in part to Baudelaire's idea, "the tragedy of being human."

That the city was ravished even while attempting culture with its opera house, museums, traveling ballet companies, and symphony conductors made for a ferment of progress and regression. There was a struggle to make itself respected, even in the smell of the giant stockyards, the horrors of the packing houses that in 1906 produced Upton Sinclair's novel of Chicago, *The Jungle*. A book that knotted the nation's stomach in nausea, to the author's regret, rather than touching its heart at the dismal conditions of the slaughterhouse workers.

It is this mixture of good and bad, of fury and hope, the enigmas and paradoxes of this great city on the lake that are the material for this story. Of how it was once—who was there, and how it reacted to such bizarre events as the Great Fire (did Mrs. O'Leary's cow start it, or not?). Could one leave out the Everleigh Club, the most famous luxury brothel in the world, or the native American pattern that Lincoln Steffens saw as the perfected political corruption by those masters of vote stealing, graft, and influence peddling, the ward bosses, Bathhouse John and Hinky Dink of the Levee?

Ambiguous and strange as much of the text may seem, there is no fiction in it, no imaginary dialogues, and wherever some shaky sources could be checked, I have done so and left out much that was mere myth or legend. There was enough actual history, salacious, incoherent amusement, and *tableaux vivants* solidly documented to fill the book.

In the past, most books telling the Chicago story, or part of it, have been divided into two kinds—those that praised its great merchant princes, its packinghouse kings, the society of the Potter Palmers and their friends, and the books that were dedicated to digging out the vice, the lives of the madams, the gamblers, the sad stories of whores, and the corruption of the city by political bosses. Often these were not factual. Here I have tried to combine both facets into a fuller, truer telling of the history of a city that mixed its top and bottom layers more than most writers have admitted.

I have attempted balance, to be fair, and have written from all available material to be found, published, often unpublished. Everything is based on facts.

I have had access to two private sources. One is the scrapbook, a sort of history of Chicago, made up of notes and jottings of a self-educated man, Edward Bronson, who for over forty years was a streetcar employee in Middle Western cities, first as a driver of horsecars and then as a motorman. He came to America after the Civil War from Macroom, in Ireland, which he identified as "being part of the Macgillycuddy Reeks." In 1912 he moved with his family to California, and is survived by a grandson who gave me permission in 1952 to work through the mass of undigested material. Some of the pasted-in clippings are undated and unidentified. In the text I have indicated the material that comes from the Bronson scrapbooks.

Elliot Paul, in the 1940s, gave me some clues to a history of Chicago he planned to write and never did.

Miradero Road,   STEPHEN LONGSTREET
California

BOOK ONE

THERE WAS A BEGINNING

1

GROWING PAINS

This is a frontier town and it's got to go through its red blooded youth. A church and a WCTU never growed a big town yet.
GEORGE WELLINGTON WHEELER, CHICAGO LAND SELLER

That the nation was headed for a civil war was clear to many in Chicago by 1860—events moving with the force and shock of a hemorrhage—but it was a city busy with its own rush toward bigness both in pork and crime, in business and in vice. It was clear that what it needed most for its safety was a nonparasitical police force. Mayor John Wentworth was starting his second term in 1860. "Long John" Wentworth demoralized, some thought, the existing police by hiring and firing men at his own discretion.

An early unnamed historian wrote sadly . . . "he left large districts of the rapidly growing city at the mercy of the criminals who infested Chicago in shoals. . . . The force under Wentworth toward the close of his administration had been reduced to a captain, six lieutenants and about fifty patrolmen, and it proved to be entirely inadequate to meet the demands made upon it."

When the legislature vested all police control in a board of police commissioners, Mayor Wentworth fired the entire police force.

It took twenty-four hours for the board to reorganize a new force. But it was never a very healthy organization; it lacked resiliency and was short of men. It remained inefficient and was given to the taking of graft and payoffs from Chicago gamblers, madams, and criminals. The tragic implication was "you couldn't trust the police to be on your side."

Long John Wentworth had appeared on the Chicago scene in the late 1850s—he never explained why he came west—three hundred pounds of him all arbitrary energy, six foot seven inches in his bare feet. (In his youth he had enjoyed promenading barefoot on public streets.) He was a graduate of Dartmouth, had been a member of Congress at twenty-one, and had moved in and out of the mayor's seat since 1857, ready to tackle the sublime, the insoluble, when in 1860 the new party—the Republicans—were gathering in the city, and the talk was of Abe Lincoln, the lanky man who had said of Long John, "He knows more than most men." Long John could only agree: his ego was bigger than a mountain; he could outface anyone, even royalty.

The Prince of Wales was also in the city that year of destiny, 1860. Victoria's Bertie was a sensual little chap full of vitality and audacity, not yet the gross hedonist, the bearded, large-paunched satyr that ravished and jollied the grand courtesans of Paris and had Lily Langtry as a mistress. Long John welcomed the prince in frontier style, introducing him from a balcony to a gathering crowd.

"Boys, *this* is the Prince of Wales! He's come to see the city, and I'm going to show him around. Prince, *these* are the boys."

Some might have felt this was rather crude. But Long John had no respect for local press opinion. In his conflict with publishers, neither side spared the other "abusive language nor epithets of questionable decency."

Long John was for scientific progress—he brought the first working steam fire engine into the tinderbox wooden city with its uncleaned, littered alleys, stables, and barns. The firemen rebelled and rioted against the "damn tea kettle on wheels," and Long John had two hundred fire fighters arrested for "disorderly conduct."

When merchants ignored the mayor's warnings that he was going to enforce the law against illegal-sized signs and street obstructions, one clear night he brought in men, chains, and teams of horses and pulled away and carried off *all* the signs, posts, awnings, and displays. They could be recovered by the paying of a fine, but could not be erected again. He was not a mayor given only to campaign clichés.

Chicago was a gambling town, and the houses of chance ran wide open, protected by the police and aldermen taking bribes. Long John led a raid on Dave Burroughs' fine place on Randolph Street, and hauled off all the furnishings and jailed sixteen men. He refused to accept bail from anyone doing business under a city license, which he said he'd withdraw. The gamblers spent a night in jail with drunks and petty crooks. Most gambling houses closed down for a while. But soon they were busy again.

The notorious Sands section was a place of whores, pimps, petty thieves, pickpockets, depraved shows of women mating with animals, saloon fights, and mean groggeries where the customer often was murdered for a little gain. Long John schemed on how to wipe out the rabbit warren of decaying buildings that was the Sands.

A big dogfight had been arranged between a dog owned by Dutch Frank, and an animal raised to ferocious power by a Market Street butcher, Bill Gallagher. On the day of the fight, all the able-bodied hoodlums and barroom loafers, gamblers and thieves went off to witness the dogfight at the Brighton racetrack. Long John rushed into the Sands with huge wrecking crews. Nine shacks and dwellings were pulled down, while the women and boys left behind began to loot the remaining houses and dives, grabbing clothes and bottles, smashing what couldn't be carried off. The celebrated fire engine came up and tore apart two more houses with streams of water. After the wreckers had left, three more houses burned down; it was assumed they were set afire by their irked inmates who did it "out of spite."

The *Chicago Tribune* spoke of the Sands's destruction, of "the vilest haunts of the most depraved and degraded creatures in our city . . . literally 'wiped out,' and the miserable beings who swarmed there driven away. Hereafter, we hope the Sands will be the abode of the honest and industrious, and that efficient measures will be taken to prevent any other portion of the city becoming the abode of another such gathering of vile and vicious persons."

(But the whores and the gamblers and the thieves merely

packed up what was left, stole a few horses and wagons and transported themselves and their bundles across the Chicago River to fouler rookeries.)

Thousands of drifters, criminals, folks of low morals of both sexes came into the city, also dandy gamblers dressed in the best of flashy attire, madams in diamonds, with pearl earrings, and their collection of prostitutes. In the 1860s they overflowed, went into the suburbs of Lemont which became Smoky Row, and Cicero, already tough, but not yet notorious as it would later become. So many shootings and knifings took place at Peter Schlapps' Dutch Gardens that the press insisted it was "peopled by a set of riotous, untamable, half savage rowdies."

The South Side took in the refugees of the Sands, who set up brothels, saloons, grog cellars, gambling dives, and shady lodgings where a man could be murdered in bed for his clothes. Below Madison Street from the river to the lake, it became "untenable for decent folk." Embroilments and tumults were normal, and womanizers, drunkards, gamblers made up a passing parade.

The heart of the vice activities was the corner of Wells and Monroe streets, a criminal germ-culture growth called Rodger's Barracks, set up and run by one Rodger Plant, who called his resort "Under the Willows." Actually, there was only one dog-tormented willow tree that survived the travail and rowdy jubilees.

One of the renters of space at the Willows was old Mary Brennan, superchampion pickpocket and shoplifter, who daily drove her own cart and horse to the center of town where the big stores were, and came back at nightfall with a load of loot. She was a female Fagin running a school for young children in training to steal, grab purses, and empty pockets. She showed her faith in her crime academy by enrolling in it two of her own daughters. She rewarded her star pupils by giving them pennies for candy when a fat wallet or gold watch was brought to her. Her mercantile instincts were as good as Marshall Field's—and she had less overhead.

The Willows missed nothing in the line of crime from procuresses, to premises where lured virgins were gang-raped and sold to houses; homosexual prostitutes existed there, also assignation rooms were for rent, besides secret chambers for the hiding of plunder, and as hideouts for thieves and embezzlers on the run. Whores paraded nude, or in froufrou swishing taffeta petticoats, batiste gored corsets, and open kimonos.

One of the habitués of the place was "Speckled Jimmy" Calwell, safecracker, burglar, who introduced the ploy of gagging and binding victims with court-plaster tapes. (Speckled Jimmy is also listed in police history as the maker of the first bomb used in Chicago, which infernal machine was discovered on a Blue Island horsecar track.) He also carried a pistol.

> *Oh you pass my door, you pass my gate*
> *But you can't pass my 38*
> —BANG BANG. FOLK SONG

Master of all this domain of decay and vice was a tiny Englishman, a native of Yorkshire, Rodger Plant, who weighed less than one hundred pounds. He was a wild, reckless, bantam-sized fighter when armed with pistol, bludgeon, dagger, and his own sharp teeth. He ritually watered his one ornamental willow tree with a mixture of rum and water. The only person not in fear of him was Mrs. Plant (*if* the union was ever made legal with benefit of clergy). She bulked up like a loaded river barge, at 250 pounds, and when angry with Rodger, would hold him up in the air with one arm and spank his bottom with the other. She ran the whores in black cotton lace stockings working on the premises, between producing young Plants, fifteen young criminals being littered by her over the years.

The Plants, unlike some criminals, knew when to retire after about ten good years: like the quality, to an estate in the country, and here Rodger lived as a "patron of the turf and otherwise blossomed out into a pattern of respectability." However, talent ran in the family, and in a later Chicago *Black Book* listing owners of dishonest vice-ridden premises, there it set down Rodger Plant, Jr., as owner of three saloons and two whorehouses, and Kitty and Daisy Plant, madams of brothels next door to each other on South Clark Street.

Crime knew no color bar in the 1860s and, later, vice no segregation. Black criminals were entrenched in Shinbone Alley, from Adams to Quincy streets, near Wells, and ran over into shacks on

Chicago's Patch, by Chicago Avenue, to become Conley's Patch. Conley's Patch was dominated by a huge, soot-black woman, the Bengal Tigress, who enjoyed a fight, took strong drinks—senega snakeroot medicines—beyond counting, and when she came tearing along in one of her shrieking, berserk fits ready for battle, doors were barred, windows iron-shuttered, lights put out. She twice tore apart shacks with her bare hands as if they were firkins of butter. The police avoided her until one of her prolonged rampages became a menace to the entire neighborhood. Then four cops moved in on the Bengal Tigress and clubbed her into submission with the vigor of the "Anvil Chorus" of *Il Trovatore*. When sober, her trade was finding very young girls for lake sailors.

The Civil War was to make the Wells Street dives and saloons run by Ben Sabin, Tim Reagan, and Andy Routzong hangouts for army deserters, bounty jumpers, strong-arm bandits of military supplies, and general rowdies. The state bounty paid for enlisting in the army—three hundred to four hundred dollars—made careers for many men who enlisted and deserted a dozen times under various names in different regiments.

The Till Eulenspiegel of the bounty jumpers was Con Brown, who began as a youth stealing horses, but was ready for any kind of criminal activity. Drink turned him murderously insane. Con may well have been the record-breaking bounty jumper of the Civil War. He enlisted and deserted over twenty times and earned eight thousand dollars in bounties. (When imprisoned he escaped five times by bribing the jailers, and enlisted three more times.)

In 1865, Con was sent to Joliet prison, escaping six times in three years; as an escape artist he seems to have been a bad hider-outer. Three years later, Con Brown tried to cut the throat of one Pete Boyle in a Smoky Row saloon. Instead, Boyle killed him.

These hoodlums, thieves and brothel keepers, harlots, had no class and knew it, no quality of the ballet-like grace of the underworld pictured in *The Threepenny Opera*. That kind of color and life was reserved mostly for the important gamblers who were the tony aristocrats, the glamour of the semiunderworld. They seemed to live in an anchored serenity, distracted, aloft. Many a tinhorn tried to pass for a big-time gambler, wore flawed jewels and flashy clothes, but fooled no one on the wide side.

2

THE RAIL SPLITTER AND THE WIGWAM

An honest election, under democracy, is an act of innocence.
GIL ROBLES, SPANISH STATESMAN

On May 16, 1860, the city of Chicago had been the scene of a national political convention. The newly formed Republican party, chaotic but hopeful, was about to nominate a candidate for the Presidency. The setting was neither glamorous nor neat. On Lake and State streets, where had once stood the Sauganash Hotel, there was now a huge wooden shed—it could hardly be called anything else—which had been nicknamed "The Great Wigwam." The city boosters with a tendency to stretch things a bit were vague about how many people it could hold: "Ten to twenty thousand . . ."

The steam cars were bringing in delegates, a collection of tobacco-chawin', linen-coated, straw-hatted individuals from the canebrakes, citizens of the river bottoms, the village squires. And from the East, men in fancy waistcoats, city fellows carrying carpetbags, a flask of bourbon in the back pistol pocket. New Englanders with chin whiskers and dyspeptic expressions, Abolitionists, merchants, bankers.

There was much talk in hotel lobbies around the spittoons and cigar stands about this Rail Splitter, Abe Lincoln, "the dirtiest storyteller on the frontier . . . the smartest galoot that ever trimmed a city slicker in a courtroom, sharp as a new-honed axe." Some said forty thousand Lincoln men, consuming sow belly, collop greens, beefsteaks, fruit pies and not saying no to a drink "to cut the morning slimes . . ." were in town.

Everyone for Lincoln wanted to know what did Judge David Davis think, he who had ridden on the circuit with Abe, and was now talking up the candidate in the Tremont House Hotel, where there was a continual parading of hobnailed cowhide boots and spitting, the lighter tread of Eastern dainty leather, and the smell of good cheroots. The Whigs were as good as dead, and the Abolitionists, watch out, were just plain fanatics; only the Republicans were for the people.

The party workers drank potent high-proof whiskey, the serious, more reserved delegates gathered at champagne dinners to try to plan the action for their potpourri of new Republicans hell-bent to nominate somebody.

William H. Seward was the man to beat, the man with the real big money, headquartered at the Richmond Hotel on Michigan Avenue and South Water Street. A candidate solidly nested in brass bands and banners; and everyone, the folk talk of rivertown men said, so full of sly, la-de-da Eastern manners, "why butter you'd think wouldn't melt in their mouths."

Judge Davis went his own cautious, careful way. Packing in his delegates early at the Wigwam, seeing the tall farmers, the sun-baked cattle drovers, small-town boys, tanners, crossroad blacksmiths, heads of large families, backwoods folk *and* too many lawyers, besides the steamboat men, all primed to nominate. (Several hotels had cannon set up on their roofs to celebrate with blasts of victory gunpowder, and it was hoped they wouldn't blow some of the town apart.)

The Seward delegates and party workers, arriving at the announced time, found themselves kept out of the already packed Wigwam. All seats seemed taken by the Western mudsills and clodhoppers, the village iconoclasts and the country bully boys. The accredited Seward delegates made it inside, shoehorn style. But most of the Eastern party workers who had been primed to stampede the place for William Seward were left outside; standing room maybe was the best a few of them could get. Judge Davis had a rational skepticism about trusting anyone east of the Blue Ridge.

Still, William Evarts, the big New York City lawyer, did a bang-up job nominating William H. Seward with the proper high-flown prose and all the Judaic-Christian virtues. What Easterners could get in cheered and howled for Seward, but the big mob of his party workers were marooned outside, and the ovation did not stir the blood. Confusion and disarray hit the Seward men. These country jaspers for Lincoln were no fools.

It was lawyers all the way ("if they were lazy and smart they read law"). Norman B. Judd, legal dignitary of Chicago, "sharp as hound dog's scent," nominated "the Illinois Rail Splitter, Abraham Lincoln of Springfield!" The yell that went up, the jamboree shouting, was like a prairie hurricane against the pipsqueak wind for Seward. Said Henry S. Lane, governor of Indiana, of what followed: "It wasn't a shout. It was worse than a shout. It was an unbridled shriek . . . unearthly . . . made the Wigwam quiver . . . made a cold sweat come out on the brows of the New York delegation."

(East against the West was the name of the game. The old corny rallying cry that was to carry down to today's political conventions: the mythology of the honest pioneer West against the effete Eastern Establishment, an extraordinary resilient slogan to impress the simple and the dim-witted.)

First ballot in the heated, dusty Wigwam in a babel of voices: Seward, 173½, Lincoln, 102. Needed to nominate, 233. Now the deals set in. Lincoln had ordered his people to make no prenomination promises; Judge Davis, with magnanimity, made promises; Pennsylvania was offered a seat on the Cabinet in exchange for its delegates. Over came Pennsylvania to Lincoln.

On the third ballot, the clerk cried out over the rising din, Lincoln had 231½—just one and a half votes from nomination. Ohio sensed the poignant moment to make history, changed its vote, and it was Lincoln all the way. Loud voices began to cry out to the city from the roofs, "Abe Lincoln nominated!" On top of the Tremont House Hotel, the cannon fired a hundred rounds of gunpowder. Telegraph clerks, huddled over their chattering keys, sent the news to all corners of the nation. The Eastern Abolitionists shook their heads sadly. "He'll let the Southerns have their way. He is too weak, too uncouth, too simple-minded . . . doesn't see the wickedness of the slaveholders. They'll outwit him." In the West, the Northwest folk said, "He sees slavery is morally wrong, but he isn't going to persecute the South on that account. All he'll do will be to preserve the Union . . . that's what we want."

The telegraph had tapped out the news to the waiting Lincoln in his home in Springfield. He knew the seriousness of the moment. He was also one of the most skilled political generals in American history, hardened by personal frustrations, a mystical, dark, melancholy man. His image today is so distorted by myth, by pallid historical novels, that there is blocked from us the shrewd, calculating, remarkably able man hidden in a clown's lugubrious humor. He was neither the plaster saint, nor the gorilla, nor the baboon the South insisted on, but a shrewd manipulator of public opinion, erratic, petulant at times, masked in stoicism. Capable of harsh measures to save the Union (how many today know that during the war he did away with trial by jury, and habeas corpus?).

It is hard for us to see his prognathous country simplicity, merged with a catch-as-catch-can country lawyer in a stovepipe hat, often crude as a ripsawed plank; a man who could answer a Chicago lady reporter who was to ask if running for office was tiring, "I haven't had time to shit or shave."

The popularizers of history have done little to remove the festooned, bespangled legend about him, begun in that Chicago hall. (It was H. G. Wells who was to remark, "It wasn't John Wilkes Booth who killed Lincoln, it was Carl Sandburg.")

Certainly that May night of 1860, in that hour of nomination, there was already an uneasiness, a premonition of fearful times ahead. Some delegates prayed on their knees, some went touring the saloons, some took advantage of being far from their families to visit the more popular brothels. Gamblers dealt cards for many a delegate or party worker; it was morning before some made it to a hotel or boardinghouse bed. The Wigwam was a shambles, the banners tattered, badges discarded along the curbs or left in hacks and carriages, or by some in a whore's bed. The more serious, the fastidious, brooded on the incipient rebellion on the horizon.

Chicago, that summer of the usual campaign disorders, followed the words of the nominated men as best it could. The curse of the modern distorting and bought media, television and radio, the transmitting of photographs by wire, or being able to print them (woodcuts were the best there was) were still not there to distort or to sell a candidate like a stuffed turkey. Lacking, too, as yet, was money by the millions from special interests, although the perfectibility of man did not exist then any more than it does now. No matter how the ward bosses, the political hacks did their business, in those times it was mostly the people speaking their choice—not advertising agencies, theater makeup artists, doctored documentaries, or oddly contrived polls. Political corruption in Chicago was, as elsewhere, a stock in trade.

In November 1860, in the city's tacky mud, thousands of the "Wide Awake" marchers, in oilcloth capes and glazed caps, paraded the streets carrying coal-oil torches, hooting it up as the slow election returns came in. Other marchers carried rail fences decorated with lanterns and pictures of Lincoln in a newly grown beard.

It was a three-cornered fight. Lincoln, Stephen Douglas ("The Little Giant"), the choice of the Northern Democrats, John C. Breckenridge, the darling of the Southern Democrats. The splitting of the Democrats elected Abraham Lincoln. (He carried Chicago by a five-thousand majority, the state of Illinois by nearly twelve thousand.) It was Chicago, its packinghouse, slaughterhouse, stockyard workers, its clerks and hack drivers, the middle class in its belief in the Union, their cumulative effort, that held the state for Abe Lincoln.

A half-million youths, all across the nation, had followed Chicago's idea of the "Wide Awakes," filling the streets in their caps and capes, their torchlight parades. It was a kind of petulant shape of things to come. For in half a year, many of those Chicago young men who had seen their candidate win would be marching again, in blue, in some agony of apprehension, with rifles on their shoulders, moving out of the city to camps, from the camps to the raw Mississippi at Vicksburg, devastating the Virginia valleys, joining the concentrations of brigades along the Potomac, and some to face the final brutal push through the Wilderness under a man named

Grant, as yet a former captain who had been seen a few times on Chicago streets, shabby in a worn military uniform. Disgraced, Grant had been dismissed from the army service as a drunkard, reduced to peddling kindling wood by the barrel, trying to clerk, or run a hard-scrabble farm.

The cannon from the rooftop of the Tremont House also went off to war.

3

CHICAGO GENESIS

And the earth was without form, and void.
GENESIS I:2

Just how did it come about that in 1860 there was a Chicago waiting to nominate Abraham Lincoln, a city with convention facilities and the sound and fury hinting of coming events? For, from that date on, Chicago was not to be stopped in its growth, its wild and caterwauling career as a city with a flavor and color of its own. It could in some ways claim it began the Civil War, for a man less earnest and serious than Lincoln in the White House *might* have been more lax in his principles, and the war itself avoided—but Lincoln *was* nominated, and the city was turned into a supply depot of rations, gear, and men.

It had begun as merely an unpleasant area of wild America—some bogs and sloughs on both sides of a river inhabited by muskrats and rather tasteless fish. The great lake was often higher than the riverbanks, and so for several months much of the land was underwater. Wild rice grew in the channels, sandbars and drift muck, old trees uprooted, choked the river's mouth to the lake. Even then,

17

no gentle smells held the riverbanks where grew the reeking skunk cabbage, also known as the wild onion, among which lived collections of polecats and other noisome varmints. Even the various Indian tribes eyed each other with misgiving and trepidation.

To all this section of land the Indians gave the name of *Checagou* or *Chickagow*, meaning *Bad Stink*. From the sound of this Indian term of a nose-holding gesture came the final corrupt version we call *Chicago*. Two small settlements first existed, one at the Forks, or Wolf Point, of the river that saw its first citizen in 1779: a black, one Jean Baptiste Point de Saible, who put together a rough cabin. A few miles south, four or five miles, in 1803, a weather-bleached farmer named Charles Lee cleared a bit of a farm at a place that became known as Hardscrabble. The same year, Fort Dearborn was put up by the army in some unstable transitory phase, on the south side of the river (a site that is now near the Michigan Avenue bridge). Soldiers began a life of indigenous boredom, squaw-chasing, and drink.

Other people drifted into the region—a half dozen—and among them was a doer and a boomer named John Kinzie, who was also a silversmith and Indian trader. Come spring of 1804, he bought out De Saible, and the land of a French Canadian named Le Mai. It began to look like a permanent settlement with chimney smoke on the wild horizons. The North Shore village of Wilmette took its name from an early settler, Antoine W. Ouilmette (spelling was still Elizabethan out in the wilderness).

John Kinzie is given credit as being the true founder of Chicago, building himself, as his daughter-in-law was to record, the luxury of a dwelling, a "low building with a piazza extending along its front, a range of four or five rooms. A broad green space was enclosed between it and the river, and shaded by a row of Lombardy poplars. Two immense cottonwood trees stood in the rear of the building. A fine, well-cultivated garden extended to the north of the dwelling, and surrounding it were various buildings." It was not urban sophistication, but the solid setting of a family with a deep responsive chord to the landscape.

All this grandeur seemed in danger when, in 1812, Indians, as allies of the British, burned down the fort, massacred the twenty-six soldiers, murdered twelve male settlers, also twelve children and two women, and went off with their scalps. The Kinzies ran for it, but as Indian agent, John Kinzie's house was spared the flames. He was back in 1816, as timbers went up for a new Fort Dearborn, even if old stabilities seemed lost, and pioneer women eyed the calico peignoir of an officer's wife.

The two Beaubien brothers, made for legend, soon appeared to settle in the district. Jean Baptiste "Squawman" Beaubien sired twenty half-breed children, organized the first Chicago debating society, was the colonel of the county militia, and the fort stood, double-shotted with grape and round. Brother "Jolly Mark" Beaubien fathered twenty-three children, was a champion fiddler fool, whose fame and folk tunes spread wide and far, while he ran a river ferry and a tavern, and served drink to officers in gold-laced hats and epaulets.

That some progress was called for was seen by President James Madison, who in 1816 had demanded a canal to connect the Mississippi and Lake Michigan. For years the canal talk went on in Washington—sponsored by Nathaniel Pope, territorial delegate from Illinois, that Pope who is credited with stealing Chicago (which most people then thought was in Wisconsin) and adding it to the state of Illinois when it was admitted into the Union in 1818. Cook County was named after another stump-speaking, fat-cat politician, Representative Daniel P. Cook, who could make the eagle scream with the best when he made an open-air speech. By 1829 the canal was being financed by the Michigan Canal Commission, and in 1833, Congress was pork-barreling a fund of twenty-five thousand dollars to make a harbor at Chicago. Stephen A. Douglas and Jefferson Davis, then an army officer, locked horns over the harbor site. Douglas was for the mouth of the Calumet River below Chicago, among the wild yaw trees and deer licks. Davis stood firm for the Chicago River site.

Davis won, and two five-hundred-foot piers were erected for a new channel, aided in time by a flash flood that swept everything clean before it.

The schooner *Illinois* sailed with cheers into the new harbor, and now it was time for the canal. But first a surveyor, Jim Thompson, was asked formally to plat out a town, a town to be called Chicago, on land that held shanties, muddy lanes, crab apple trees, and freakish bypaths. This task was done by 1830, and it was time for the land lawyers, the street-frontage boomers, and the auctioning off of lots, eighty by a hundred feet, to begin. They were going at prices from forty dollars to seventy dollars; talk of progress was as slick as slippery elm salve.

Thompson's map didn't take in too much land, just about three-eighths of a square mile. Chicago was incorporated on August 5, 1833, as a town, bounded by Madison, Desplaines, Kinzie, and State streets. There were twenty-eight voters, many in the peltry and beads trade, and they elected a board of trustees, who voted to keep down "nuisances, gambling and disorderly conduct; to prevent fast driving and enforce police regulations; to license shows, control markets, take charge of the streets and sidewalks, and to protect the town against fire."

You could still eat elk haunch and shoot wolves, but it was a growing town, and soon, in two months, had a population of 150, so the trustees extended the city limits to Jackson, Jefferson, Cook, and Ohio streets. More area was added from time to time to town land —even Fort Dearborn itself when it was abandoned in 1836, and the soldiers went west to eat their bugoo cornmeal mush with blackstrap molasses. Naturally taxes were in the politicians' minds, and selling of certain rights to run ferries (fifty dollars a year), collect tavern licenses (seven dollars a year), all to pass through sticky fingers at times.

Tax rates at first were half of one percent on city land. According to town records, there were taxes on "pleasure carriages; on distilleries; on all horses, mules, and neat cattle above the age of three years; on watches, with their appurtenances; and on all clocks." Time was indeed money in early Chicago.

The first hotels mentioned in old letters were Wentworth's, the Green Tavern, the Sauganash, and the Green Tree. Travelers with carpetbag portmanteaus found them "all together too dirty for comfort," dirt, drink, lewdness, greasy cooking, and corn-husk pallets being early-day comforts.

The Sauganash was named for a Potawatomi Indian chief, who was also known as Billy Caldwell. (The hotel later was burned down, in 1851, on its corner and in its place was run up the Republican Wigwam from which Abe Lincoln was to be nominated for President.)

A traveler's picture of a Chicago hotel in 1835 is rather grim. "Near the north end was a bar counter useful not only to receive the drinks, but umbrellas, overcoats, whips and parcels. The west end of the bar was adorned with a large inkstand placed in a cigar box filled with No. 8 shot, in which were sticking two quill pens. . . . At the other end of the counter were a dozen or more short pieces of tallow candles, each placed in a hole bored in a 2 x 4 block, fortified by sixpenny nails. . . . Under the counter was a large wooden bootjack and a box containing two old fashioned boot brushes and several pieces of hard, raw tallow, black from application to stogas [boots]. There was also a collection of old fashioned, perforated tin lanterns. . . . There was also to be seen the indispensable tinder box, used fifty times a day, at least, for lighting pipes, when the old, rusty bar stove was taking its summer vacation. . . . The ablutionary arrangements were exceedingly primitive, consisting of tin wash basins, soiled towels, small mirrors and toothless combs. Several dishes of soft soap were arranged along the back of the water trough. Though pretty strong for washing the hands of a 'tenderfoot,' it was in great demand after greasing the boots or applying tar to wagon axles. . . .

"In the middle of the room, standing in a low box filled with lake sand, was a large stove used in winter to good advantage, not only for the warmth imparted to the room, but for furnishing hot water for toddies, shaving and washing as well. . . . We were called to supper by a large bell, which was rung by our host. . . . In the dining room were two tables, the length of the room, covered with green checked oilcloth, loaded with roasted wild duck, fricasse of prairie chicken, wild pigeon pot pie, tea and coffee, creamless, but sweetened with granulated maple sugar. . . . These furnished a banquet that rendered us oblivious to chipped dishes, flies buzzing or tangled in the butter, creeping beetles" (Bronson Scrapbook).

Early historians of the town of Chicago, with realistic candor, gave it no high marks for beauty or comfort, just "scattered shanties over the prairie south, and a few rough, unpainted buildings had been improvised on the north side between the old Kinzie home and what is now Clark Street. All together it was . . . a most woebegone appearance, even as a frontier town . . . did not show a single steeple nor a chimney four feet above any roof. . . . The buildings of the fort were low posted and none of them exceeding two low stories in height. Approaching the village by land from the south, one would see on emerging, a good stretch of level grass, the lake on the right, woods along the borders of the main river, and, lying on the background of the green woods, only a thin cloud of smoke from the shanty chimneys, a line of almost indefinable structures, and the flag over the fort, if it was flying. A brown path, where the grass had been trodden out, led to the fort, and another, better trodden and wider, led across the prairie towards the Forks. As for buildings . . . Posts placed in the ground at the corners, and at proper distances between them blocks were laid down singly or in cob-house fashion. On these foundations were laid, and to these were spiked, standing on end, 3 x 4 scantling. On these sheathboards were nailed, and weatherboards on the outside of them; and lath and plaster inside . . . because of this system of building, Chicago got the name Slab Town."

GROWTH OF A CITY

I 'spect I grow'd. Don't think nobody ever made me.
TOPSY, IN HARRIET BEECHER STOWE'S UNCLE TOM'S CABIN

Mudtown was another favorite name for early Chicago in the 1830s. Its mud was notorious for deepness, stickiness, color, and smell. A private letter said: "Stunk like original sin, clung like piglets to a sow's dugs . . ." Quagmires took over unpaved streets, and board sidewalks were few. Many stories were told of "No Bottom Here" streets, and of signs set up by wits announcing "Short Way to China," "Right Road to Hell." The best-remembered story is of a man sunk so deep in street mud only his head and shoulders showed. Asked if he needed help, he answered, "Hell, no. I got a horse under me."

By the late 1830s, plank streets were in use downtown, but no one thought much of how the sewage and garbage were to be carried off. For the town was often below lake level, and gravity couldn't do its drainage work. An engineer—some said he had been drinking Indian whiskey—claimed the only thing to do was to jack up the buildings and put twelve feet of hard-pack grading under them and on the streets. *Something* had to be done—so it was tried.

Twelve hundred acres of the town were so treated, buildings jacked up, *every* structure in town, beginning in 1855. The job took five years, and many a drunk fell to his death or broke limbs staggering between the lifted and yet unlifted parts of the street levels.

The biggest problem was the brick Tremont House Hotel, a tall, majestic six stories of ostentatious class. And set on a mud site, 180 by 60 feet. It couldn't be lifted up, everyone said. The bricks would just come apart of contrariness. But a young, fox-faced, eager fortune hunter, George M. Pullman, offered to lift the whole hotel eight feet straight up and "not crack a windowpane." He set big jacks under the structure, got twelve hundred men to stand by and take a half turn on the screw jacks on every command. Not only did Pullman accomplish the tricky lifting of the Tremont House Hotel, but guests in residence there at the time—if they didn't look out of the windows—were not aware of what was being done. (Pullman was later to perfect the railroad sleeping car and go down in industrial history as the meanest cause of big, bloody, workers' strikes in the nation. He had all the charm of a carnivorous jungle plant, and a genius for making money.)

Chicago remained an Indian trading town for some time, and rough bridges were built over the river to bring the hostiles into town for trading in pelts and products in exchange for whiskey and geegaws, and finally for betrayal. The latent antagonism to the true native American remained a Chicago tradition.

The Indians were Chippewa, Ottawa, Potawatomi, who had in the treaty of 1833 signed away all rights to any claims to their lands and holdings. A million dollars in goods were to be paid to them, but Indian traders and wily booze sellers stole most of it. The Indians were made drunk and cheated so that they kept very little for selling all their lands east of the Mississippi. There was a final Chicago Indian ceremony (among hangovers) when the Indians and some half-breeds moved away to promises of land on the northern Missouri. Several Indians had been killed in drunken fighting at the fete, and a real black bear was run to ground and slaughtered at the corner of Jackson and Market.

With the Indians done out of their land and rewards, Chicago became one of the main inland ports for the snake lines of wagon trains moving west. Early histories speak of the hundreds of west-crawling wagons, ox handled, moving through, with Chicago as a seething, prodigious background. Speculation, higher prices, skinning the pioneers, became almost a Chicago trade. Land speculators, tall-hatted bankers, chomping on seegars, land lawyers writing claims filled the streets, and the wagons kept coming and going, full of hope, or in cantankerous humors. "Hotels and boarding houses were always full, and full meant three in a bed sometimes, with the floor covered besides. Many of the emigrants coming in their own covered wagons, had only them or a rude camp, hastily built, for home or shelter. All about the outskirts of the settlement was a cordon of prairie schooners, with tethered horses between, interspersed with camp fires at which the busy housewives were ever preparing meals" (Bronson Scrapbook).

The lake, too, became a highway: no "vessel arrives that is not crowded with emigrants, and the stage that now runs twice a week from the East is thronged with travelers. The steamboat *Pioneer*, which now performs her regular trips to St. Joseph, is also a great accommodation to the traveling community. Loaded teams and covered wagons, laden with families and goods, are daily arriving" (Bronson Scrapbook).

Discrepancies in character and honesty separated the dupes from the rogues. A fast-writing lawyer could make five hundred dollars a day writing land titles. Every day millions of dollars in land values changed hands. Farm lots, city frontage sold added up to millions of dollars. Everyone who had wooden stakes, a hammer, and greedy ways could mark out lots, set up in business, make himself plats of towns and cities that existed only in the spinning minds of the promoters. Lots changed hands almost daily, each time at higher prices. The whole territory was soon, it seemed, nearly marked out by stakes. "If you had sense enough to eat soup with a spoon, you were smart enough to get rich." Land was money. Land was hope. As the interior became settled, "the mania for land speculating spread throughout the newly-settled country. . . . Chicago became the mart where were sold and resold monthly an incredible number of acres of land and land-claims outside the city . . . located in all parts of the Northwest . . . farming lands, timber lands, town sites, town lots, water lots, and every variety of land-claim or land title known to man. . . . Town lots were platted, often without any survey, all over Wisconsin and Illinois." Another Chicagoan wrote, "the prairies of Illinois, the forests of Wisconsin, and the sand hills of Michigan, presented a chain almost unbroken of suppositious villages and cities. The whole land seemed staked out . . . peopled on paper. . . .

"A tract offered in 1833 for $5,500, sold in 1836 for $100,000. Forty acres of Chicago lots . . . at $400 for the tract in 1833, brought $200,000 in 1835. A parcel sold for $20,000 in 1835, refused $500,000. Gurdon S. Hubbard, Indian trader, bought two lots on La Salle Street for $66.66, sold them for $80,000. He and partners paid $5,000 for eighty acres on the outskirts. Three months later, buyers paid $80,000 for half" (private letter).

William B. Ogden, of upstate New York, arrived in Chicago to look at a piece of land which a relative had bought for a hundred thousand dollars, sight unseen, most of it deep in water, a waste of bogs and sloughs. "You have been guilty of the grossest folly. There is no such value in the land and won't be for a generation." Ogden, no fool—he had the indispensable quality of seeing the main chance—stayed on. Three months later, he sold one-third of the swamp for the original hundred thousand. He became the richest real-estate operator in the city's increasing momentum. And an early follower of the frontier philosophy, "If you can't lick 'em, join 'em."

By 1837, the Illinois Legislature made the Town of Chicago into the City of Chicago, its total area being a good ten square miles. Ogden, the swamp peddler, was elected Chicago's first mayor, and the counting of heads showed 4170 humans in residence, and over five hundred structures, not counting the outhouses. There was also a courthouse, a jail, of course, for the feeding of courthouse trials, a firehouse, ten taverns or inns, five churches, and between eighty and ninety shops. Also two newspapers, gamblers, and a promising underworld of thieves and whores.

Of course there were business panics, too, and hard times while waiting for good times, so folk grew gardens on overpriced lots, and accepted illegal scrip issued by the city when cash ran out. Still the wagon trains passed, more people stayed on, and by 1840 the population was tripled. (Seven years later there was even a convention of three thousand rooting, tooting delegates from eighteen states, and Chicago was launched as a convention city, "wide open and no impeccable standards"—private letter.) A year later came the first railroad and the first ship through the canal. By 1855, ten railroads terminated there, and eleven branch lines were active with pigs, grains, and home hunters in the West. The population was eighty thousand, there were sixty miles of sewers and more were needed. There was a busy cadence on four miles of docks and piers and at night the yellowish glow of gas streetlights.

All the time Chicago was growing up, crime was keeping pace with it—an active underworld was also maturing, making satisfactory progress of its own. The first crimes had been merely selling whiskey to the Indians by French-Canadian trappers. Now the usual early English traveler came to make his notes of the local crime scene . . . "horse dealers, and horse stealers,—rogues of every description, white, black, brown and red—half-breeds, quarter-breeds, and men of no breed at all:—dealers in pigs, poultry and potatoes . . . sharpers of every degree; peddlers, grog sellers, Indian agents and Indian traders of every description . . . betting and gambling . . . the order of the day" (newspaper clippings).

To the traveler the town seemed to be held in some demonic possession, demanding games and action. There was lots of gambling, and besides whiskey drinking, whoring also was a town industry. Dean Caton, later a judge, was one of the first lawyers in town, setting up office to serve scallywags and businessmen on a barrelhead in the street at Lake and Wells. The fine for running a whorehouse was set at twenty-five dollars at first, then the price was raised without diminishing the number of brothels. Wells Street between Jackson and First was the red-light district, and the tarts in trade were surrounded by institutions called tippling houses, groggeries, hot sheet hotels, liquor groceries. Crime was on the rise even as new phaetons and carriages appeared: holdups, street battles, rioting, wrecking of saloons by blacklegs, rowdies, and loafers. Said someone, "Chicago is made up of dogs and loafers." Hardly true, as land sellers, merchants, manufacturers, and meat-packers were already beginning great careers.

The first man legally hanged was a young Irishman named John Stone, accused of brutal rape and murder of a farmer's wife, the evidence being some of his shirt left in the fingers of the done-in outraged victim. On July 10, 1840, John Stone, aged thirty-four, "ascended the scaffold," reported the *Chicago American*, "dressed in a loose white gown, and with a white cap upon his head, as is usual in such cases. He evinced much firmness upon the gallows, under the circumstances, and in the presence of the spectators (among whom we regretted to see women enjoying the sight) he persisted to the last in the assertion of his innocence—which declaration was publicly made in his behalf by the Sheriff, together with his acknowledgement, as requested, of the satisfactory manner in which he was treated in the jail. . . . The Rev. Mr. Hallam, Isaac R. Gavin, Sheriff, and Messrs. Davis and Lowe, deputies, attended the prisoner on the scaffold. The Sheriff seemed particularly affected, even unto tears. After the beautiful, solemn and impressive services of the Episcopal Church for such occasions [*sic*] had been performed by Mr. Hallam, and the appropriate admonitions bestowed, the death warrant was read by Mr. Lowe, the knot adjusted, the cap pulled over the face of the prisoner, and he was swung into another world. After he was hung until he was 'dead, dead,' a wagon containing a coffin received his body, which was delivered by Drs. Boone and Dyer, pursuant to the order of the court, for dissection. . . ."

So the town had its share of hoodlums, rowdies, con men, pickpockets, burglars, footpads, gunmen, garroters, sneak and horse thieves, even a gang of counterfeiters. All this while some decent folk imported repoussé silver toilet sets, used monogrammed towels, and had music boxes that played "Le Parlate d'Amor."

By 1857, for the first time, the police wore an insignia of office —leather stars—and carried loaded canes, batons, and signaled to each other with a rattle, until the shriller whistle was introduced.

Reformers passed a Sunday closing law for saloons, and a firm prohibition act was set to be voted on by the citizens in June 1855. The Irish, the Germans, and the Scandinavians began to march in protest to protect their tippling hours, and drink, rather than, to quote from a meeting, "submit to this outrage upon their rights." American bars on the South Side remained open, winked at by the police, but German beer gardens and Irish saloons were shut down. Rebellion was in the air. Called the "Lager Beer War," it was reported: "The saloon keepers had collected their friends on the North Side, and, preceded by a fife and drum, the mob, about five hundred strong, had marched in solid phalanx upon the justice shop, as many as could entering the sacred precincts. After making themselves understood that the decision of the court must be in their favor if the town didn't want a taste of war, they retired and formed at the intersection of Clark and Randolph streets, and held possession of these thoroughfares to the exclusion of all traffic. Crowds gathered from all sections of the city, friends and enemies."

One hundred and fifty special deputies were sworn in to aid the police. The mob of a thousand armed men rushed into battle. Firing of weapons began by both sides facing each other; clubs and knives also were used, and, after an hour's mixed action, the attackers retreated. For all the firing, only one man was dead, a German named Pete Martin who had wounded a deputy, George Hunt, having blown off his arm with a shotgun blast. Militia with cannon were ordered up—but no trouble came. Patrolman Hunt was voted thirty thousand dollars for loss of his arm.

The riot had one result—*all* prohibition laws were defeated by a good majority, and saloons appeared safe from the piety and parched hopes of the temperance forces (who were not seriously to menace legal drinking habits of Chicago until Prohibition came after World War I).

When Chicago housed the Republican nominating convention of 1860, it was big with hope and enterprise, a city full of excitement, looking for form and direction, testing the rules of fatality and chance in a troubled nation. It had sixty hotels, at least a dozen of which were of some taste and proud of their service. There were six theaters for the respectable folk, eighty ballrooms and dance halls humming with waltz tunes. Nearly forty newspapers and publications existed for a population of ninety-three thousand. (Compare this with our own dismal record in multimillion populated cities that today often support only one major daily newspaper.)

The crime record of early Chicago was also impressive: "fifty three burglaries in one week," said one police report. There was a good ghoulish business going on in digging up bodies at the Old Catholic Burying Ground, and selling the cadavers to the medical students.

There were many fissions in the city's social pattern. Among them, the Prairie Queen on State Street, which offered uninhibited dancing, erotic shows of Dionysian degenerate detail, dogfights, and a monthly prizefight, bare-knuckle style, for the pay of two dollars a fight and, for the winner, a free bed with one of the house whores. In one gay night's doings, in a house on South Water Street, a harlot kicked over a lighted lamp in a lewd dance step, and the resulting fire took twenty-three lives, and did half a million dollars in damage. Such losses were impressive to some and pointed to a growing city.

5

GAMBLING FEVER

A deck of cards is the Devil's bible.
CAMP-MEETING PREACHER

Even Mark Twain—a grand Mississippi River pilot at the time—admired the fancy-dressed gamblers who worked the cities of St. Louis, New Orleans, and spent their vacation time in Chicago, often losing their gains at dice, faro games, roulette, and other devices in the Chicago gambling establishments, playing expressionlessly, dressed impeccably, waistcoats laced in gold chains.

The best-known gamblers came north during the war years from Natchez, Vicksburg, the Delta, came via the Gothic, tall-chimneyed steamboats, paddle wheels churning, black, pitch-pine smoke pluming up while the pilot stood on the Texas deck, a cheroot glowing between his lips, and blacks with white gloves served the quality their mint juleps and lady drinks. The gamblers filled the plush seats of the steam cars entering Chicago. (The city had so many of the gamblers, because, for all their Southern sympathies, going to war for the Confederacy seemed just a bit foolhardy to men who knew how to figure the odds; one could get killed.) Chicago, too, was a ripe plum for plucking. It was a town busy with wartime profiteering, carried on in gold coin; eagles, double eagles, easy money, fast money from land deeds, bank notes—money looking for the action. New millionaires backed by farm pigs that went to slaughter, more condemned beef packed in brine, hardtack already filled with weevils shipped off to army camps. The richer men grew, who had never been so rich before, the more most wanted to spend to prove perhaps they were vehemently alive.

The gamblers showed them how to enjoy getting rid of their profits. Writing a history of the 1860s in Chicago, Frederick Francis Cook referred to the Southern gamblers selling the Southern side of the war "among the unthinking younger generation about town . . . went far in giving the impression that Chicago was a hotbed of disaffection. Indeed, so far did this Southern gambling influence extend, that of all the resorts for men-about-town, the Tremont House was about the only place where one invariably heard outspoken Union sentiment. And while there was among all classes (the German element excepted) a goodly number with more or less avowed Southern sympathies, it was the gambler who above all gave an extraordinarily aggressive tone to the local opposition to the war."

Both the local gamblers and imported tricksters found Chicago splendid prey during the war years. Paymasters, officers, and men, back from battles with unspent pay, played cards—and young men going back perhaps to die went seeking excitement. Women and whiskey were not enough; the human system had its limits of endurance. But gambling did not pall or weaken one like drink and whores. Lady Luck fascinated all. So army contractors, pork packers, new fortunes, real-estate sharks, the praying-mantis shape of sharp lawyers in their tall hats, all came to fill hundreds of Chicago's gambling houses. For the poor grifter and the tattered soldier, any plank could be a poker table, and any street shyster could handle a pack of soiled cards or rattle a pair of dice. Even those citizens of a Podsnapian respectability at times got wartime gambling fever.

The really impressive gambling establishments were on Hair Trigger Block, Randolph Street between Clark and State, and Gamblers Row—Clark Street from Randolph to Monroe. The newspapers cried out that the district was "so contaminated by these execrable vagabonds that respectable persons avoid them as they would a cesspool."

Yet some respectable persons bragged of being known or taken by the most famous of the gamblers: George Trussell, Cap Hyman, John Brown (not the one of Harpers Ferry), Watt Robbins, and Frank Connelly, who ran the place called the Senate, the most luxuriously furnished of any gambling house beyond Saratoga: juniper-scented candles, a clavichord; St. Louis (always pronounced St. Lou*ie*) sent up Gabe Foster and Ben Burnish to deal cards. Survival was a problem at times. James Watson, known as Sir James, was killed by White Pine Russel who dealt faro; Jim Elliot was killed by Jere Dunn; John Sutton died in a Clark Street saloon.

Gamblers led precarious lives, no matter what their standing in the pecking order. Dave Stanley was low class, a burglar, thief, pimp, and small-time gambler. But Theodore Cameron was high class, serving wild game, poularde Normande, le coq au riesling, and wine suppers to his patrons at no charge. Cameron made a million dollars in eight years, and left town nearly broke. Gamblers usually were victims of other gambling establishments, suckers for faro, the wheel; going against the house, they no sooner had lost all than they were back to plucking pigeons. But when they had it, they loved to spend; they hung their shady women with jewels (and often borrowed them back when they had a bad run of luck).

Did the glamorous gamblers, the kingpins of the profession, cheat? Most of them could, with skill, prudence, and decorum; some of them did.

CHICAGO TO ARMS

The Civil War should teach us the necessity of avoiding wars in the future.
GENERAL U. S. GRANT, MEMOIRS

For all its rowdy, busy life, its crime and its business activities, Chicago had come alert when Fort Sumter was fired on. Chicago was known in the South as a "nigger loving town," and the place, among its other deficiencies, was where once had terminated many lines of the Underground Railroad that moved runaway black slaves into Canada. (In 1860 there were fifteen hundred free blacks in the city; and as for escaped slaves, once, at least twenty a day were aided by the Chicago Abolitionists, who put the runaway chattels across the border.) Stephen Douglas, with loud immediacy, had called the city "Abolitionist Chicago."

Mobs of proslave groups in the clogged center of the city had tried to break up his night meetings by singing, "We won't go home 'till morning!" One night at a meeting, Douglas yelled back, "It's Sunday—I'll go to church and you may go to hell!"

In 1860 against Lincoln, Douglas got most of the Irish vote, as he was against the bigots who wanted to "protect their jobs" from the foreign born. The Irish were discriminated against, seen as comic apes with clay pipe, a shillelagh, and a huge appetite for whiskey. "Hit him again, he's Irish" was a popular Chicago saying, and signs reading *No Irish Need Apply* were found by some seeking work. The self-indulgent American democrats saw nothing wrong in the comic Jew, the watermelon-eating, chicken-stealing black as subhuman prototypes. But when Lincoln's call came to preserve the Union and join the fight, an Irish brigade was formed, and Congressman John A. Logan, whose folks had come from "the ould sod," was made a general.

War fever ran high in the city—like some compulsion gratified—the businessmen saw profits, the criminal element saw a boomtown for whores, gambling dives, and the spending of soldiers' pay. But in the main, the enlisting and shouting were done by boys and men who were behind Lincoln's defense of the Union, no house divided. In the first ten weeks, thirty-eight companies were formed, thirty-five thousand men enlisted. All sorts of uniforms were designed—the male peacock in his glory. Most striking were Ellsworth's Zouaves in embroidered jackets, wide flaring crimson pants pushed into white leggings, and a tasseled cap to top it all off. The ladies, in tiny hats on enormous chignons, flaring skirts, cheered them on their way.

The local Jews raised a company, as well as the Germans, farm lads, city boys. Camp Douglas, named after The Little Giant, who had died after shouting support of Lincoln's battle against the South, began, in the dust and chaos, to take the shape of a proper army base. The town's banks offered Governor Richard Yates half a million dollars for the war effort; their interest rates were more deadly than the Gatling gun.

Camp Douglas consisted of sixty acres at Cottage Grove Avenue and Thirty-fourth Street, and was in use all through the war as a training ground and a prison. Here in disease, boredom, madness, ten thousand unlucky Rebels were packed in a stockade of board walls. Many died of illness, neglect, and the confining, unsanitary environment. Disintegration of the prisoners caused little sympathy in the city. Southern prisons like Andersonville were worse.

As the first horrendous battles raged, soon the state had seventy-three thousand men under arms. Before the last call to attack was sounded, Illinois had given over 231,000 men to the armies of the North. Few men were drafted in Chicago, and elsewhere most of the well-to-do hired substitutes. Chicago had a population of a hundred thousand in 1861, and yet sent fifteen thousand men to war. Only fifty-eight were draftees. By war's end, every third male in the city had enlisted in the army. While the saloons and brothels were busy, and the frenzy of speculation saw millions made in pork and deadly preserved beef and shoddy gear, the citizens held two great fairs for aiding the ill and wounded soldiers. Five hundred thousand dollars were collected.

Wartime was boom time to Chicago—near the war's end it had a population of nearly 170,000. The grain market for army and navy bread, and horse fodder was soon shipping out sixty-five million bushels a year. Cyrus McCormick's reapers were busy snorting, racking over the planted prairies. (Lincoln's Secretary of War, Edwin Stanton, put it perhaps *too* strongly—perhaps not: "Without McCormick's invention . . . the North could not win and . . . the Union would be dismembered." The Confederacy never understood logistics as well as the North did.)

In Chicago, in wartime, drinking, fornicating, rioting, the burning of saloons, the wrecking of whorehouses, the shooting of over-aced gamblers might cause excitement, but it was nothing to the wild speculation in land, in futures of lard, hog bellies, in offerings of real estate, barrel staves, horse-soldier saddles, dealings in cotton bales smuggled through the lines. The solid citizens, the sharpers, shysters, green goods boys, all speculated; the confidence men speculated, bakers, meat-packers, all saw their schemes and deals pyramid while the blue and gray slaughter went on in distant Virginia and along the Potomac, at Vicksburg, Shiloh, Brandy Creek. "Business?" a Chicago broker once said. "Business is other people's money!"

Men who had come to Chicago in worn boots and shabby clothes were, in 1863, driving matched bays in splendid carriages. Jobs were plentiful and Canadians came streaming across the border to get the higher wartime pay of piled-up silver dollars or the green bills called "shinplasters." Sparkling wine, as well as Chateau Latour and Saint Emilion, were drunk—and bourbon, of course.

Near the end of the war, the city's population had gone up seventy percent, but the property values, praise the Lord, were up ninety percent. Money brought a need for show, and those who made the biggest piles began to think in terms of mansions and castles. By 1863, the stretching town needed room, so twenty-four square miles were added to the city, over six thousand new buildings went up at the then high cost of nearly five million dollars. (It should always be kept in mind that, up to World War I, money was worth often ten times what it is worth today.)

Ruttish appetites for show-off spread. What had been little streets, almost none going a couple of miles beyond the city, were, by war's end, stretched out to three miles past the center of town, with the half a dozen main ones just seeming to go on beyond the horizon. The smell of horse litter and livery stables was everywhere. Blacksmiths slaved from dawn to dark, and ferocious swindles in horse and mule sales took place.

The wooden shacks were going down on the best and the busiest streets. Wooden sidewalks downtown were replaced with stone slabs. Cast-iron facades in almost libidinous detail decked banks and office buildings. What fine art cast iron could be, said builders, when poured cherry red from the furnaces into molds to take on the decor of nude goddesses, horns of plenty, flowers, or Egyptian motifs, Greek columns, Roman cornices. It was the splendid Age of Cast Iron in bold dimensions for a clientele who liked mass.

Behind the heavy, solid safety of the walls, bankers puffed stogies, pulled on their side-whiskers, and established a Chicago Clearing House, supported the new Chamber of Commerce Building at Washington and LaSalle streets and the Board of Trade: fourteen hundred members. Grain shipments by 1866 were sixty-six million bushels, and hogs almost beyond count. Profits turned heads like some erotic intoxication. No wonder the fancy saloons served so much fine rye whiskey with the proper beads, under the yellow gaslights. Courtesans danced on tables and diamonds sparkled on waistcoats imported from London, butter-gold watch chains in place. Stovepipe hats were piled on mahogany hall tables of the gambling houses and bordellos, while banjos played songs of victory.

None of the city's important men of business went to war. Marshall Field, Philip Armour, Gustavus Swift, Cyrus McCormick, and others of wealth and/or political power mostly took advantage of their age. And the bounty system took care of the rising casualty lists. Cook County, dominated by Chicago, paid three hundred dollars on the barrelhead to any man who enlisted to fill the quota. This was raised to four hundred dollars near war's end. When there was talk of conscription, rich men hired others to fight for them. It was legal to do that. Bounty brokers were busy, and bounty jumping became a trade. The brokers filled the army's needs at a good cash payment, and the jumpers made a business of signing up and deserting, and signing and deserting again, signing under other names in other regiments.

(In the South, as Chicagoans pointed out piously, a man who owned six or more slaves in most of the Southern states was also freed from going to war. No wonder some troops on both sides marched into battle singing, "It's a rich man's war, a poor man's fight.")

The overworked railroads brought hogs and steers and wheat and other supplies into Chicago, but also brought drifters, vagabonds, hard-eyed killers from the West, Bowery hoodlums from New York, bedraggled whores, and just no good types of all kinds, looking for the main chance. There were confidence men, green goods boys, counterfeiters, madams, stock boosters, pickpockets, safecrackers, thieves, and homicidal types.

Crime took over entire districts. The Rodger Plant establishment cast its shadow over Wells and Monroe streets, where the prostitutes collected, under the bland deceptive name of Under the Willows. Rodger believed in advertising and had had the window shades of his bordello gold lettered: WHY NOT? A madam in a red-lacquered carriage spoke of an elegant clientele for transitory pleasures.

Horse racing was one way to drain off surplus war profits, and also have a good excuse to be out in the open air to see the nags trot. Most famous gambler, or notorious, was George Trussell, once a bookkeeper in a Chicago bank who became an owner of a gambling house. He also had his eye on good horseflesh, and was half owner of the wonder horse Dexter, the Man o' War of his day. With a rider named Budd up, Dexter had done a wonder mile in two minutes, eighteen seconds. Besides the war news—most of it as usual false—the newspapers carried stories of racing results, of horses like Dexter, Medoc, Cooley, General Butler. By war's end, the Chicago Driving Park was the place to be seen in new duds, with new loves, new fortunes, followed by busy pickpockets. Gay parasols revolved in dainty gloved hands, as bodies in whalebone corsets went by, dragging the trains of whores and society wives. It was hard to tell them apart until one saw the painted faces. But one couldn't be sure who "touched up" amongst the strident femininity.

George Trussell was more than a mere ex-bank clerk with an eye for horses. He was a man who had a military bearing, a grand tread, hawk-eyed, a proper stance, "might have stood for one of Remington's Indian fighting cavalry officers . . ." (newspaper report) all without ever having been a soldier. Society accepted George as a charmer even if a rascal, and a man of good, strong, silent power to him, with an ability to size up winners, and often give a tip from the feedbox to a close friend.

His mistress, Mollie Cosgriff, also known as "Irish Mollie," had come to town a decade before from Columbus to become a chambermaid at the American House. But had, she admitted, soon lost her virginity. Trussell's own background was a mystery. Some said he was a "shrewd cunning Yankee from Vermont," others shrugged and said the bastard was sired in Cook County. It was known he had been fired from his bank job for playing faro, a sport, it seemed, reserved by those institutions only for bank presidents and their boards. It was back in 1860, and he was then twenty-seven. He opened a popular gambling house with other partners, but by 1862 he had two busy gambling houses of his own, one on Randolph Street, another on Dearborn Street, paying off protection graft by "accommodating the police most munificently" (newspaper item).

His charm remained strong, when sober. But he was a mean drunk, always looking for a roughhouse brawl when loaded with prime sour mash. Another bad drunk and mean when in alcohol was a gambling-house owner, Cap Hyman, an English Jew. But some said he was actually the heir of a Southern plantation fortune, *or* related to a great Eastern merchant family. One could take one's choice. Gambling Chicago asked few questions of a man's past. Cap liked gunplay and shooting up the ceiling while in his extroverted mood, and people, if they got in the way. (As one newspaper put it: "Shooting people up at the most trifling provocation, is becoming altogether too prevalent in this city.")

Hair Trigger Block, where the gamblers and their painted women gathered, had a propensity for evil and danger. It was a favorite street for George and Cap to go gunning for each other. Actually they were capricious, lousy shots, and street signs and barroom mirrors took the most damage. So the shooting sprees went on, and yet neither man was hurt. It took Mollie to do that. Her remarkable copious body and the silver tone of her ribald laughter made her the goal of every young man with money trying to be either a sport or a dandy. Soon Mollie was seen in rich white moiré, in fine carriages, sipping Beaujolais in red velvet dining rooms. One result of a fast life was the birth of a child, father unknown; she was sent away to school in South Bend to be educated, "unaware her mother was notorious," as one newspaper put it. When Mollie became the official mistress of the dashing George Trussell, the romantic dream of a prostitute's heart, she had reached the top, an event that could only be celebrated by her becoming the madam of a luxury whorehouse on Fourth Avenue.

Perhaps George was fickle, sexual victory became mundane; perhaps the busy trade at Mollie's place—there was so much detail in running a proper parlor house—irked George. So the romance cooled, discontent grew, the epicene pair took on cruel tones toward each other.

The night the Driving Park Track was to open, Mollie, dressed to the nines, went hunting George on Gamblers Row. She faced him in an ornate saloon, but he made the mistake of mocking her, gave her a shove toward the swinging doors, then began to drag her out. Mollie pulled a pistol from somewhere in her fine clothes, put it to his side, and shot her lover. He ran into an alley, she fired again, then got in a last shot in Prince's Livery Stable. As George lay there, dead eyes staring at the startled horses, she fell across his body lying in the hay, crying out, "My George, my own dear George! He's dead!"

He certainly was. A jury of men-about-town, or admirers of a grand courtesan, gave her one year in Joliet on manslaughter, but gallant Governor Richard Oglesby pardoned her before she could be locked up.

(George Trussell's estate, among other things, was "five gold watches, two diamond pins, one revolver, one single barrel pistol, five hats . . . twelve pair cassimere pantaloons . . .")

A much more important death by pistol shot must be recorded. On May 1, 1865, Lincoln's funeral train with an entourage of mourners and sycophants entered Chicago on its way to the body's final resting place, Springfield. There had been one addition. Marshall Field had put up money for George M. Pullman to finish the first of his new parlor cars. It was suggested by Mr. Pullman that it would be desirable for Chicago to add that new car to the funeral train, even though, as it proved, many bridges along the route would have to be widened to accommodate the fat Pullman car; it was good advertising, and no one saw the reprehensible travesty this made of the sad journey.

First came a pilot engine, then the engine and train carrying the body, both decked with huge enlargements of the features of the martyred President. Black drapery and silver stars were draped over the engine boilers. The train came to a stop on the lake edge of the pilings of the Illinois Central Railroad. The *Tribune* reported a miracle, awed by the fact "the stormy waters of Lake Michigan suddenly went calm as they felt the need for silence . . . imperative necessity of the mournful occasion." Members of John Wilkes Booth's profession, the actors of Chicago—and the managers—decided to close the theaters for the event.

As the coffin was carried to the Court House, three dozen schoolgirls went ahead, scattering flowers along the way. The Court House doorways and windows were draped in black, and the body of Lincoln lay there in state for a day and a night. A hundred and twenty-five thousand people moved slowly past the coffin in disquieting tribute to a greatness they were already aware of. Most remembered Chicago had nominated him at the convention that sent him to his destiny.

7

THE MADAM WITH THE WHIP

*The highest thing a woman can do for a man is to come within his range
at the right moment.*
KIERKEGAARD

After the death of George Trussell, shot by his love, Irish Mollie, the
racing world did not have to wait long for its next murder. Just two
weeks after Mollie cried out that her dear George was dead, a big
race with two favorite horses was run. The horses, General Butler,
with driver McKeaver behind him in the sulky he was pulling, was
racing Cooley, a fine trotter, his reins held by a famous horse handler named Riley. It looked like a real close race, two sets of finely
matched animals and drivers. In three heats it was a tie. The fourth
run should show a winner. Twilight had come down, and the race
was run in a dusk like dark pollen falling. As the two horses and
drivers came out of the shadows into the sight of the judge's stand, it
was clear to all, with a crying out of horror, that General Butler was
running with no one in the driver's seat.

Back a ways, on the dark section of the track, they found poor
McKeaver, his head crushed in like an eggshell by a thrown rock. It
was one way to prevent a favorite from winning a race, if some

gambler group had bet heavily on Cooley. Only the rock that had meant merely to stun had killed. The judges had to call all bets off. The dubious coroner's jury could only report the murder of McKeaver as "by persons unknown."

Cap Hyman, like most gamblers, also had woman trouble. His mistress was "Gentle Annie" Stafford, a holy terror, a wildcat of a woman who loved with a minimum of subterfuge. Cap had treated her to the ownership of a whorehouse, and a fine place it was. Many patrons remembered it at 155 North Wells Street. Gentle Annie, *not* so gentle, was also *not* so slim. She was pointed out, with pride, to visitors to the streets of sin, as "the fattest cathouse madam in town."

Gentle Annie learned a lesson from poor Mollie's fatal shooting of a lover. For while Mollie had called herself Mrs. Trussell, no marriage lines were in evidence; Gentle Annie decided she had to have those damn lines. Cap, a born bachelor and a logical positivist, kept repeating he wasn't the marrying kind.

One September day in 1866, Gentle Annie came roaring into Cap's gambling house on Randolph Street, carrying a mule skin-

ner's long and dangerous whip made of rawhide. Banging her way up the stairs into his office, where Cap was trying to catch some sleep on a satin sofa, Annie brought him back to life with a few swipes of the whip in her hefty arm. As he yelped in pain, she drove him ahead of her down the stairs and into the street, expertly whipping him like a top as he ran, he crying out in his agony. A mule whip is a deadly weapon. It took a few more solid hints and punishment, and in a few weeks Cap Hyman saw the advantages of a good healthy wife. The wedding was magnificent, the best of the underworld of madams and gamblers, ponces, confidence men, safe-crackers being present, some from as far away as New Orleans.

At the wedding, sumptuous and wild, Cap announced he and the bride were going to run a tavern and high-toned roadhouse, a place of opulent hedonism, at Sunnyside, then outside the city, but now North Clark Street and Montrose Avenue.

The opening of the tony roadhouse was like a Fourth of July celebration, even if it was a crisp snowy night with sleighs out. The best people of both worlds—the lower and the upper—attended. The police captain, Jack Nelson, city and county officials, and politicians were present. The press sent its best social reporters. Of the happy couple's own set present were madams of the town's best whorehouses. And acting as hostesses were Gentle Annie's own girls from where she served as madam. Thirty of the best exotic odalisques. One redhead claimed a fine family background and a knowledge of world literature. She amazed one male guest seeking her favors by asking:

"Who's your favorite poet? Now mine's Lord Byron."

Cap knew how to run a press conference, long before today's publicity firms gave them polish. He got the boys into his office and set out the booze.

"I'd like you gentlemen of the press to understand that this affair will be straight to the wink of an eyelash. All the ladies are here on their honor, and Mrs. Hyman will see to it that nothing unseemly takes place."

Frederick Francis Cook, who was there as a reporter for the *Chicago Times*, noted that "all the rest of the little formalities that distinguish like functions in the haut monde were strictly observed. Yes, the make-believe was quite tremendous."

After the reporters had been sent back to Chicago, the guests were free to express their own peculiar idea of fun. The party ended in a free-for-all fight at dawn, after case after case of champagne. Cap Hyman shot out the lights, Gentle Annie chastised madams for distributing business cards, and half a dozen girls were upstairs for trade. The redhead was still perhaps inquiring, "Who's your favorite poet?"

The hopes of the newlyweds, so ebullient and extravagant, were doomed to failure. The Sunnyside roadhouse, for all its innate possibilities, lasted less than six months, and Cap and Annie came back to the city, to the gambler's deck of cards and the strumpets' rallying call, "Girls, gentlemen callers!"

Cap Hyman, a year later, suffering no doubt from the Old Ral (syphilis), also called Big Casino in underworld circles, went into a full mental breakdown and died insane on the West Side, Gentle Annie Hyman, loyal to the last, holding his hand in his final hours.

Happier sporting citizens and clowns were two gamblers on Hair Trigger Block, Al and George Hankins, who ran a house of extreme simplification. They were, however, streaked with superstition, omens, magic gestures. Opening their shop for play, they burned an old shoe every day for good luck, and set a pinch of salt and pepper on every player's chair seat to bring him bad fortune. If anyone really began to have a run of luck at the brothers' tables and games, Al and George would come running up with a shaker in each hand, and begin to spray salt and pepper on the head and shoulders of the too-heavy winner. It certainly made for a loss of tranquillity. As their house averaged winnings of about fifteen hundred dollars a day, there might have been something in their hoodoo-making shaking. If some winner objected to the rhythmic pouring of salt and pepper on his person, the house bouncers stood ready to give him the heave-ho out into the street. Unsuperstitious sports, who weren't too neat and dainty, went on playing.

BIG MEN

God made man, and man made money.
ANON.

Marshall Field was one of Chicago's many sincere materialists. He said: "As a rule, people do not know how to save." And coming from his five feet nine inches, thin but regal frame—he walking straight, blue eyes clear, no boozer—he was listened to. He was an impressive man, his hair and moustache prematurely a polite French gray; the only elegance of dress he permitted himself as a merchant giant was waistcoats a bit on the daring side, but never vulgar; he was never one for ostentation or self-indulgence. An admirer said Field could pass as "some foreign Prince or diplomat." Not a talker, some called him "Silent Marsh." His employees, to whom he was fair, if not generous, called him a great deal more.

When he opened his newest store in 1872, the city was thirty-five years old, Field, thirty-four. The *Tribune* exploded into pride, describing the event: "The attendance of wealth, beauty and fashion was something unparalleled in Chicago history . . . long lines

of carriages filled with the cream of the avenues. The attractions were unusual—a dry goods store in a marble palace."

Others might say mean things of the city, but not Field. There was Frederika Bremer, a Swedish writer and visitor, who had just seen early Chicago and written in disenchantment and petulant prose: "Chicago is one of the most miserable and ugly cities I have seen in America . . . very little deserving of its name, 'Queen of the Lake' . . . rather a huckstress than a queen . . . the city seems for the most part to consist of shops . . . it seems as if . . . people come here merely to trade, to make money. . . ."

Field would have agreed to the last part of her perverse picture. There is no record that Frederika understood American big business and its *get* and *go,* but she must have visited a Field store.

After all, a city named after the Illinois Indian word for *great* or *big* as some claimed, or as some others said meaning merely *skunk* or *wild onion* in Chippewa, deserved some credit for pulling itself up into marble and cast iron from a mere Fort Dearborn set down in the river mud in 1800. Marshall Field was the symbol to many of pride in Chicago. Others, however, saw Chicago in the image of Gentle Annie, the wild and savage madam of a luxury whorehouse where the profligate sports and rich of the city and their guests laughed loudly, copulated cheerfully, and didn't give a damn in their tippling or lechery about the city's reputation for the number of pork barrels or yard goods sold in marble halls. The extremes of response to the city ran from pride and forbearance to the hell with it.

The first mayor, William Butler Ogden, had set the seal on what to seek in the city. "When you're dealing with Chicago property, the proper way to do it is to go in for *all* you can get . . . and forget all about it. It will take care of itself." Field knew that to be true. After all, by the late 1840s, 105 smoking, roaring trains were grinding and shaking in and out of the ornate city depot. And the new Field store made the country folk from the butterwood and cocklebur farms "let their eyes bug out." Six stories high, Corinthian columns, faced with white marble hacked out of the hills of Canaan, Connecticut, at the price of $105,000. (The *Chicago Times* had to admit it was "Architecturally the most perfect and imposing building in the country . . . as well as being better adapted to the dry goods business.")

Certainly it helped dress Chicago, give it some silken tastes, some feel for style—offering cashmere, scented soaps, hoopskirts, balmorals, ladies' cloaks, perfumes. Daring hosiery: striped, lace inserted, even silk ones as sleek as any courtesan's of the Second Empire. And all those grand mirrors, full length; dare one primp, even partly undress in front of one? State Street, the heart of the Chicago shopping center, took great pride in Field's. As for Marshall Field— he watched everything. "I believe in reasonable hours for everyone, but *close* attention during those hours." No sitting down in any place for the help. He launched, in time, several thousand broken and flat feet, a limping politeness of service—"the customer is always right." (Said to have been corrupted by Gentle Annie in her brothel to "The customer always comes first.")

If Marshall Field was the placid merchant with noble ideas, and an eye on the money till and later the cash register, Cyrus Hall McCormick was the volatile-tempered Mr. Bang, the massive, angry-faced individual who felt the entire world could be a foe, except for that large segment of it that bought his farm reaper. He had a nervous, hair-trigger temperament that exploded into grudges and rages, not a calm inch to him for all his six feet, his ruddy complexion, and a beard like a lion's mane. Existence was singular and secretive.

His pants were size fifty-five, his best weight was 215 pounds. His favorite food—as loved by him as his scrolled mahogany bedends—was milk and mush, boiling hot mush and cold milk—a huge bowl of it to start the day; and later at supper, let the roast be bloody and large with the potatoes tucked around, and the cherry pie big as a washbasin. He was a ravenous feeder in a day of big eaters with no queasiness, as calories were unheard of and cholesterol unnamed. He was a Virginian. No matter that most of his life was spent in Chicago. He was born in 1809 in Rockbridge County, Virginia, the first of eight children. Parents were both Dutch-Irish. His mother, with a demeanor of decorum, raised a flock of peacocks, and was proud of a carriage that boasted folding steps like that of the best gentry. The McCormicks, some Virginia people said, "Cut it high on the hog."

"I loved best the old fashioned pinks," said Cyrus McCormick of Virginia flowers, "because they grew in my mother's garden in Virginia." The big man could actually weep real tears, produce a plaintive dirge, at the mention of Virginia and the Shenandoah. ("The most beautiful name in the American language": William Faulkner in conversation with the author.)

McCormick was at his most sentimental at a banquet given for Chicagoans in exile from Virginia. "I may say of Virginia, as David said of the city of his love: 'If I forget thee, O Jerusalem, let my right hand forget her cunning." He was much given to such rhapsodic solipsism.

There is no record he did anything for Virginia in a material way, just praised her. He was only twenty-two when he put together a practical farm reaper in 1831. Actually, he only invented the idea of the main wheel operating the gears. The other features came from many places: the side draft, the vibrating knife, divider, reel, fingers, the grain platform. Just so the Wright Brothers made a practical flying machine, Edison, a working motion-picture projector.

By 1847, McCormick had a factory in Chicago, and three years later he was turning out and selling sixteen hundred reapers a year. By 1858, he was also making a million dollars a year. He fought off other inventors' claims, sued at the drop of a word, and loved lawsuits. Once Abe Lincoln was the lawyer in a case against him, and won. He hated Republicans like a plague from then on.

McCormick made up his own patent laws and took them to court. Edwin Stanton once remarked, "His claim seems to rest on the notion that *everything* in the reaping machine belongs to McCormick that is not the subject of some other successful monopoly." McCormick felt that monopoly, like virginity, could be lost.

His ire against railroads for some reason—most likely shipping costs—brought on lawsuits that took years to settle. When one of his family lost a trunk on the New York Central, valued astonishingly at thirteen hundred dollars (by the owner), the railroad sent a check as soon as the complaint was presented. "We sure don't want any lawsuit with a McCormick." The Pennsylvania Railroad was not so smart. McCormick filed a claim that lightning had destroyed some luggage while legally it was in the protective hands of the railroad. McCormick fought the case for eighteen years. And at last, twenty-three years after the McCormick luggage brought down the lightning, the Pennsylvania gave up and paid off, defeated by that awesome magisterial quality in the man.

McCormick was too busy in the factory and courtrooms to marry early—but he got around to it when he was forty-nine. Nancy Folwer was twenty-six, from upstate New York. Every morning she read at table from the Scriptures, while the children had their hot mush and cold milk. Five of the brood survived the diet of Bible and mush to maturity. One senses a household of stern patrician benevolence.

The Civil War made McCormick millions as wheat and other crop needs took more and more reapers—all he could make. But for his Hawk-dominated times, he was an amazing Dove about the war. In 1864 he wrote to the *Chicago Times*, in a letter that could have been written in the 1970s: "We have no choice but to stop the war, declare an armistice and consider terms of peace. . . . Another Republican President elected and the country—the Union is lost. The Democratic Party only can—and it will—save it." With hindsight, we can imagine how his temper would have flared today when every major twentieth-century war has been declared by the Democratic party in office.

For the good of the nation, he announced his candidacy for Congress. The *Chicago Tribune*, in its usual inconsistencies, called him, "poor white trash of Virginia."

McCormick cried out at such dastardly irregularity of behavior. "*Stop* my subscription to the dirty sheet at once."

McCormick was defeated when Lincoln, running for reelection as a wartime President, swept in most of the Republican ticket with him. Abroad, however, they appreciated McCormick; Napoleon III made him a Chevalier of the Legion of Honor. McCormick sent the emperor a silver-plated reaper in return.

The biggest yearly event among the farmers was known as Field Day, when McCormick backed his machines against the best of his competitors. Field Day fairs were held all over the country, wherever a good stand of wheat was ready to harvest. Whole steers and sheep would be turning on the barbecue pits, hot sop sauce splashed on, whiskey bottles, hard cider on hand. Most often the McCormick machine won in such categories as time, neatness, and sturdiness. The only problems, as the Field Days grew more popular, were the betting, the drinking of local still-made whiskey from jugs, from a pail and dipper. The bigger the crowd at these hoedown Disneylands, the wilder the doings. Only a randy, shouting camp meeting could match them. Booze-filled farmers would finish off a wheat field in a McCormick reaper, then go hell-for-leather after standing corn, groves of young fruit trees, flocks of hens. Tugs-of-war took place, two reapers attached by a steel chain, trying to see which reaper would fall apart first. McCormick got tired of sending specially reinforced machines for these tugs-of-war contests; this, and the rude behavior of the country mobs, in time caused him to suspend Field Day and eliminate his personal beatitudes and blessing to harvest events.

By the time he was selling ten thousand reapers a year in the 1870s, he was also involved in fantastically expensive lawsuits, much of his profits from his sales going into patent litigation. It is ironic that the great McCormick fortune came not from the reapers (by 1884 he was selling fifty-five thousand a year), but from investments in the proper kind of real estate.

All his life he saw justice in the terms of Jehovah's thunderbolts. Long before Freud, he had discovered the Herr Doktor's principle. "Accept yourself for what you are and make use of it."

He paced his own Aubusson carpet in his temper—owned no oil paintings of satyrs and nymphs so popular among the rich. Instead, the McCormick Hall at the Presbyterian Theological Seminary got nearly a half million of his money. Charles Yerkes, the Traction Trust head, called McCormick "an insufferable prick" (Bronson Scrapbook note).

THE STOCKYARDS

All flesh is grass.
ISAIAH 40:6

The Civil War really made Chicago Big Town. It also, with no delicate subtlety, made the stockyards. In four years the war added seventy percent to the city's population, and best of all for the real-estate speculators, nearly one hundred percent to property values.
Taxes, those gifts to the raffish assemblies of greedy politicians in
City Hall, rose four hundred percent and even in those pre-Parkin-
son's Law days, the city, in its gyrations and transformations, managed to spend all of it, and more.

There is some truth in the city's historians' statements that the
slaughter of pigs, steers, and sheep did as much to win the war for
Lincoln as the great battles. The Union was fed its meat rations in
large part by Chicago. One-third of all the hogs killed and processed into bacon, ham, and lard in the West—nearly a million—
was moved through Chicago in one three-month period. (The
proud title of "Porkopolis" was taken away from Cincinnati and
given to Chicago.) As the war progressed murderously, or simmered
into stalemate in its own great slaughter, it was clear to the pig bro-

56

kers and beef packers that a huge new stockyard was needed, not the surviving pattern of scattered yards all over the city that served the various butchers. Independent yards were hard to deal with, prices could not be controlled. So a stockyard trust or cartel was the solution. The switching of loaded animal cars to so many yards was too costly. Pigs had to be processed with the mechanical precision of a drill team, to keep up with the demand.

The answer was the Union Stockyards, and capital stock was offered. Two million dollars was at once subscribed among the packers and the nine railroads that ran into the city. It was built to the southwest of the city on a square mile of land, four miles from downtown Chicago—but not far enough to keep away the smell. It was outside the city limits, and, it was soon too clear, two feet *below* the river level.

But if the packers would do nothing to see that their workers were well housed and fed, the hogs got royal treatment. Over thirty miles of sewers were put in—a Herculean task—to drain the site, to turn bog and quagmire into dry firm land. To protect the hooves of the animals, streets and alleys were paved with wooden blocks. The 345 acres of the stockyards were made into a model animal settlement. By Christmas Day, 1865, a time when toy cattle gazed at the Holy Family in wooden models of the famous stable, the Union Stockyards were opened; no one ever took credit for opening the great slaughter of the animals on the day accepted as the birth date of the Son of God.

In the first week, seventy-five thousand pigs, twenty-one thousand steers, twenty-two thousand sheep, and two hundred horses were led to the killing pens. But while they lived at the stockyards, they drank pure artesian well water from a bore that went down a thousand feet. The humans of Chicago had to make do with filthy lake water that made Chicago scarcely endurable, poisoned with the filthy slush miscalled water. But then, overlooking Dean Swift's advice, people could not be processed, smoked, barreled, and shipped out at great profit to feed the Union armies and the rest of the population.

Traffic at the vast stockyards was regulated by one thousand workers, servicing each railroad's thousand feet of unloading plat-

forms—where double chutes unloaded top and bottom compart-
ments of cars containing arriving hogs and sheep.

All this did not help the accumulation of bad smells in the city,
or create a better system of sewerage. It merely added seventy-five
miles of sewer lines of revolting slaughterhouse offal which poured
their filth into the river which in turn poured into the lake from
which the city drank its water from a wooden inlet just six feet from
shore. Diseases of the alimentary canal—called locally the miseries,
trots, wind colic, flux, shakes, river fever—killed off the weaker citizens and many babies. The wise drank good steam beer, keg lager,
cider, buttermilk. The European immigrants brewed wine, and the

rich imported springwater, while the drunkards had the laugh on all, for they feared water like Old Scratch himself.

The reek that came from such places as Garlic Creek was dreadful, and as the war produced more factories and killed off more pigs, when the wind was right, the odors of the stockyards and packinghouses could not be filtered out by scent held to noses or closed doors and windows.

The position of health officer was invented, consisting merely of one appointed policeman, and most of his duties were collecting bribes from the worst offenders. (The *Tribune* described the water the city drank as it came from the river, as "Black, with a shocking odor . . . greasy to the touch.")

Pumps were put to work to reverse the flow of the river, but the factories and slaughterhouses kept gaining, so soon an epidemic of erysipelas filled the town with dead, and fears of a plague, the blame going to the foul Garlic Creek. In March of 1864 it was decided to dig a tunnel five feet square, twenty-six feet down, and extend it two miles into the lake where it was hoped the water was cleaner. The crib that sucked in the water was anchored down with forty-five hundred tons of stone to withstand the winter's lake storms. Three years after the start of digging at the foot of Chicago Street, fairly clean water was being pumped into the 164 miles of Chicago's water mains. Some people even began to take baths, for three million gallons a day were added to the usual quota of water recorded on the meters; but the bathtub was hardly in fashion. Those who bathed usually used a washtub.

But still the stench of the slaughterhouses, the smell from the stockyards could not be eliminated, and men like Philip Armour and Gustavus Swift grew to enjoy the smell—or rather the profits it meant—the more of *it*, the more hogs and steers were being shipped in, poleaxed, more rows of carcasses drained, cut up, smoked, pickled in brine, barreled, and shipped out. They were, these packers, not men who read Samuel Johnson: "Pigs are a race unjustly calumniated. . . . We do not allow him time for his education; we kill him at a year old."

The packers' own homespun philosophy was more that of the Ohio farmers: "Feed a pig, and you'll have a hog."

(On July 11, 1971, the newspapers reported the end of the historic Chicago stockyards:

EMPTY—*Weeds grow between vacant pens*
of Chicago's historic Union Stockyards.

FAMED STOCKYARDS IN CHICAGO TO CLOSE

CHICAGO (AP)—Chicago's historic Union Stockyards, a major arm of the livestock industry for more than a century, will go out of business Saturday.

No special events have been planned for the demise of the 345-acre tract.

On Saturday, for the first time in 105 years, the stockyards will stand empty of livestock as a result of the moving of packing plants closer to farms and cattle ranches.

The Union Stock Yards and Transit Co., owner of the yards, cited a steady dwindling of livestock receipts in recent years as the reason for closing the yards. The company said their operation is no longer profitable.

This week members of the Chicago Livestock Exchange announced formation of the Chicago-Joliet Livestock Marketing Center to replace the Chicago yards.

It will be ready for operation in temporary facilities near Joliet, 35 miles southwest of Chicago, on Aug. 2.)

10

VICE TOWN

Vice ran riot in the Chicago of provision shops, groggeries, hardware stores, lawyers' offices, brickyards, slaughterhouses, tanneries, soap and candle works, in spite of all the large families, many churches, picnics in parks, and the sporting life.

And while it would always be a city of vice and industry, a mixture of depraved slums and strange politics, for some it would become in time a poem, by one Will Carleton:

> The rich and voluptuous city,
> The beautiful thronged, mansion decked city,
> Gay Queen of the North and the West . . .

One saw at times the seekers of pleasures—women in stylish dress squired by men, hard-cheeked with an enormous quid of chawin' tobacco . . . while dancing the polka and the redowa, resting from the music, between swallowing charlotte russe de la reine and pyramids d'Espagnol, patties of quail and prairie chicken, even a boar's head.

61

While a later age with brutal talent was to find that crime paid best when based on illegal brewing of alcohol, drug selling, and organized gambling cartels, Chicago, in the two decades after the Civil War, found that prostitution was the business that brought the biggest returns—perhaps because so many respectable people owned the properties where it thrived. Also because both the police and city officials all were eager to claim a share. So the madam, the whore, the pimp were the city's most serious problems. Decency experienced a great dislocation as thousands of loose and immoral men and women flooded Chicago during the Civil War. The peddling of women's bodies seemed the easiest way of making a living for these vagabonds, criminals, and the professional prostitutes, mixed with willing, part-time amateurs. (The *Chicago Journal* in times of a less permissive use of language called these women "the withered rose leaves of society," which neatly evaded the sociological background and the problems.)

Later, after the Great Fire, the whores and pimps and their criminal friends were as active as ever, almost like those pine cones that wait for a forest fire to help them burst into life. It was also a Victorian puritan society that felt prostitution was needed, but even so *must* be kept in the dark. Ladies whispered that the male animal in lust was a bit too profane for decent wives, and young men *might* menace virgins. So there must be this sexual cesspool at which to slake undischarged physical passions. But always the fact of prostitution had to be ignored, hidden unobtrusively, if possible. The trouble was vice went in for loud noise, gay parties, and even advertising. Whorehouses, saloons, assignation places led directly to the usual ward alderman, a hustler who cared only for graft and votes. So the whole process of commercialized vice, like the Mafia of today, led to connections with city officials and respectable people who somewhere got a cut of the vice action. Rapaciousness made many strange partnerships.

During the four years of the Civil War, it was roughly figured that the town supported about two hundred whorehouses, not counting the services available in the back of saloons or in other enterprises. Two thousand prostitutes, full time, were on street and house duty. In 1867 they were arresting 1,670 women and 542 keepers or owners of the establishments or enterprises. A yearly arrest, or maybe two, was good for grafting police and officials—it showed what could be done if payment was not made. Criminology was simply in most cases boodle-seeking from the depraved (police records).

Besides Shinbone Alley and the Patches called Conley's and Chicago's, houses of ill fame were clustered on Franklin, Wells, Clark, State, Sherman, Dearborn, Van Buren, Adams, Congress, Polk, South Water streets, and in between. Blue Island, Fourth and Chicago avenues were also in the pudenda trade, with a spot here and there for the libertine seeking *le vice anglais:* pederasty.

Streetwalkers, "Gamahucher specialists," were every place accosting a john, or mark, as a prospective male was called. He would be approached with great boldness and with a description of what could be had in perverse delights. Not only was the male passerby in danger of being faced off by a painted whore, but she might be working with a holdup artist, pickpocket, confidence man, or crooked gambler. As for the police on these streets, a newspaper said that "a policeman was seldom seen—outside of a saloon."

Parlor houses were for bacchanalian orgies, a little more protected and neat. The first finely finished luxury brothel, The Mansion, was created during the war by Madame Lou Harper, at 219 Monroe Street, where high prices prevailed, and high-bosomed tarts worked at erotic games and techniques beyond what was described as "Mama and Papa fucking." Madame Harper's trade was rich young men: lawyers, businessmen who liked to see the girls in classy evening gowns, elaborate coiffeurs—girls who had last names and were not just Alice or Maude or Jennie, but were introduced as Miss Brown, or Miss Glory. The Mansion had no red light outside its door or oversized street numbers. Madame was a shrewd innovator—just a good, solid, golden oak door and a polished brass plate,

MISS LOU HARPER

There was no drunken brawling on the premises or dirty talk, and favorite guests were slipped a card reading:

THE MANSION
219 MONROE STREET
TWENTY BEAUTIFUL YOUNG LADIES

Ostentation and opulence made pleasant atmosphere.

It wasn't likely any house of the period was as grand as Lou Harper's. Still, there are good comments on the girls at Kate Anderson's Senate, at Rose Lovejoy's where a huge whore called Mountain Nell sang sad songs and, doubling as a bouncer, threw out unruly guests. Madame Annie Stewart was on Clark Street, and there in 1868 while playing a friendly game of euchre and drinking several bottles of wine in her bedroom with Police Constable Marcus Donahoe, she swore he was cheating her at cards. She got a pistol from under her pillow and drilled the police officer dead. However, Madame Stewart, when brought into court, had fellow officers on hand to testify the dead constable's fingerprints had been clearly seen on her throat, and it was pure self-defense. Judge Erastus Smith Williams nodded—stern, perhaps facetious—and ruled that Madame Stewart had not "forfeited her rights to self-protection by resorting to the disreputable life of a Cyprian."

The Great Fire was to destroy the biggest, meanest, toughest brothel in the city when it burned out Ramrod Hall, a huge one-story building on Quincy Street near Wells. Madame Kate Hawkins kept the harlots in line there with a mule skinner's whip, which she enjoyed using among the thirty inmates—fifty in a busy season. Drink was the troublemaker—everybody, girls and guests, was usually looped, and sluggings and robberies of customers common. The police cooperated by clubbing a wild whore into calmness for the madam, or tossing out a customer who claimed to have been robbed and wanted to fight.

The interior of the Ramrod was wrecked in March 1871, when a whore named Mary Woods said she was "leaving to be married and become an honest woman." Madame Hawkins found this cold solace—losing a fine hooker—and reached for the whip, but the other tarts, pimps present, and even customers joined in the fight. Furniture was broken, bottles were used as clubs, and when the cops got there, the place was a shambles. The wedding of Mary Woods, if it ever took place, was not reported in the newspapers.

Low dens for salacious amusements were run by Jennie Standish on Wells Street, and by Belle Jones on Clark Street . . . which proudly announced the fact they presented for fornication the oldest "dones" (whores) in the world. Nellie Welsh and Mollie Morse were said to be nearing seventy and still actively on duty. Images out of the world of Hieronymus Bosch's paintings are suggested.

The Great Fire wiped out most of the old haunts of the prostitutes, but they soon had new ones—districts for their naked *tableaux vivants,* with names like Satan's Mile, Coop Holler, Bad Lands, Dead Man's Alley, Hell's Half Acre. Most of these sections of the city were on the South Side, bracketed between Wabash Avenue, the Chicago River, and Van Buren and Twenty-second streets.

Two hot spots of working hustlers in the business district during the 1870s were in the Bryant Block between Randolph and Dearborn streets, and here the notorious streetwalker Waterford Jack held court.

The Bryant Block got space in the *Chicago Times* as "a nest of harlots . . . the police regard the assemblage of women in this structure as one of the worst crowds in the city, and now and then reports reach them of orgies held there that would seem to indicate that ancient Sodom and Gomorrah have phoenixed themselves somewhere in the neighbourhood."

Lesbians, dildoes, "nameless ecstasies," flagellation, *soixante-neuf* are mentioned in a private report. Also most shocking to some in Chicago, mention of the use of a bidet.

Peoria Street had the New Era Cigar Store (and a wooden Indian outside), a shop run by Mamie and Eva Welch who were keen businesswomen, who saw to it that with every order of two dollars' worth of tobacco, smoking or chewing, the customer got a half hour in the back room with either sister, or a foursome could be arranged. No information is given as to who minded the store at such times.

Often, as records show, the pious churchgoer did not mind being in the harlot-selling trade. Alderman Jacob Beidler had a churchgoing, hard-praying family, but he owned the notorious Noah's Ark on West Washington Street near Halsted. It had once been a fine residence of three ornate stories, but under the alderman's ownership, it sheltered two busy saloons, twelve whorehouses. The once large rooms had been partitioned off with drapes into small spaces, just room enough to place a cot, a basin of water, and a towel. A guest was charged twenty-five cents for one sexual session, thirty-five cents if he was dainty enough to want to take off his shoes.

Two sisters here had a surefire way to make a bit extra; while the guest was coming to climax, tightly held in the arms of one sister, the other banged him on the head with a cosh (blackjack) or club, after which they went through his pockets and tossed him out onto the street with a headache and a lump on his head. It was not a place given to art nudes by Bouguereau, or music by Offenbach.

The wildest, biggest brothel at Noah's Ark was a black joint where about twenty blacks, high yellows, and beginner browns wore white tights and green blouses that hid nothing above the navel. The owner was suspected to be one Diddie Briggs, who had a branch cathouse on Halsted Street. Her star attraction there was Julie Johnson, a genuine midget who did sexual encounters—for watching Chicagoans—with a huge male partner three times as tall as she was. A woman named Del Mason did musical accompaniments on a piano at Diddie's. Del weighed in at three hundred pounds and was married to a black crook and hard case called Joe Dehlmas, also known as Bill Allen.

Joe (or Bill) seemed to have gone berserk in November of 1882, for he murdered one black, nearly killed another, and when a policeman tried to arrest him that night, he killed the cop. Joe hid out in Diddie's cellar. His mistake was when he gave the midget entertainer, Julie Johnson, a nickle to buy him a newspaper. She told the police where he was hiding, and sold the coin for two dollars to a gambler named Mike McDonald as a good-luck charm. It was observed by one pimp, "It was Joe's fault for being able to read, and wanting newsprint."

A policeman named Mulvihill started down to the cellar to grab Joe, but the black man shot the policeman dead. Soon two hundred Chicago cops began to stake out the killer. A lynch mob of underworld shady characters began to gather. Some said there were ten thousand of them armed with pistols, rifles, and pitchforks from livery stables. A black man killing a white man was doomed by frontier tradition.

At three in the afternoon, Joe was cornered by a feedbox in a yard off East Kinzie Street, and killed by a police sergeant. The body was taken to the Desplaines Police Station. The mob, wrongly informed that Joe was still alive, gathered with cries of "Get a rope! Lynch the sonofabitch!"

Police got the body in through a window, and the mob grew

meanly menacing, ready to rush the station. A history of the Chicago police recorded that "balked of its prey, the crowd became frenzied and threatened to tear down the station. Threats and promises were all in vain, and a serious riot seemed inevitable. Chief Doyle mounted the wagon and assured the crowd that the Negro was really dead. They hooted and yelled, shouting that the police were concealing the man and encouraging each other to break in the windows. . . . The body was stripped and placed on public view, and the mob were satisfied by a simple glance at the dull, cold face. All the afternoon that line moved steadily along, and the officers were busily occupied in keeping it in order. The crowd increased rather than diminished, and until darkness settled down they were still gazing at the dead murderer. After dark a flaring gas jet at the head of the body brought it out in strong relief, and all night long the line of curious people filed by."

The body of Joe was on public exhibit for two days. Del Mason, the big piano player, refused to accept her husband's body for burial.

"Hell, I wouldn't give no dollah to help bury that stiff!"

Little Cheyenne and the Bad Lands were dangerous neighborhoods. Nearly every building was a saloon, whorehouse, dance hall, or some kind of dive. The women paraded in the open, half-dressed, exposing breasts and legs through kimonos, skirts that were well above the knees. Big Maude, a black giantess, ran the Bad Lands. The Bengal Tigress, some said, was "like a kitten to Big Maude . . . when Maude was rarin' for fighting."

Dark Secret was the name of Big Maude's brothel near Twelfth Street. Her girls were mulattoes, often called *metisse, negrillonne, caloclos*. For two bits a man could get laid, have a bed for the night, and, if out of line, get beaten up. Dives would normally rent for $40 a month, but during the Columbian Exposition, the World's Fair, were raised to $125. "Black Susan" Winslow ran one such dive, and so many men were robbed there the police decided to arrest her. The problem was that Black Susan weighed 449 pounds, and no door or window was wide enough to pass her through. She had entered the place years ago—thinner and younger. Detective Clifton Wood Woolridge backed up a patrol wagon to the dive, sawed out the door and two extra feet of wall. Then a plank ramp was built from the opening to the wagon. A rope was tied around the huge hips of Susan, attached to the two unhitched horses, and the cry was "Giddup!"

The horses put their shoulders to their collars and, with a rush, out came Susan on her rump, screaming, for the rough-sawed lumber was putting dozens of large splinters painfully into her bottom. Susan stopped resisting, got up, and peacefully entered the patrol wagon.

(Cheyenne, Wyoming, called by the press the "toughest of Union Pacific rail-end towns," was honored in having its name taken for the Little Cheyenne vice district of Chicago.)

MR. ARMOUR AND MR. SWIFT

Hog Butcher for the World.
CARL SANDBURG, "CHICAGO"

Business at the stockyards never stopped, even for vices. As one of the kings of the packinghouses, Philip Danforth Armour was a solid, churchgoing, hardworking man who never entertained whores. He was thickset, living simply but well at 2115 Prairie Avenue. He was always up at five every morning, breakfast at six, down at the office at seven, driving himself in his Goodart buggy. In an interview for the press he said he liked to get down to work before "the boys with the polished fingernails showed up." His rules for success were simple: "Waste no part of the cow or pig; most men talk too much; most of my success has been because I kept my mouth shut. . . . I have no other interest in life but my business; I don't want any more money. . . . I have more than I want. I do not love money. What I love, is getting rid of it. . . . What other interests can you suggest to me? I don't read, I don't take any part in politics." The truth is a little warped and muddled in his statements. His workers starved on their meager pay, died of poisons in his chemical smokes, cursed the day they were born. His force in politics was great; with Marshall Field, the newspaper publishers, the bankers, he got the Chicago he wanted, and the latent hostility of the poor and the exploited.

Armour's philosophy was simple. In a press interview, he said: "I always have a great respect for facts. If there were fewer theorists in the world, there would be more successes. Facts can be discounted in any bank, but a theory now, it's hardly worth a look. Stick to facts. . . . I believe life is all right. . . . Everything is good and coming out satisfactory." (As for God and his ministers— "They would preach better sermons if they included more of Armour's sausages in their diet.") Education and ideas? "My culture is mostly in my wife's name. . . . God did not overlook me."

The simplicity of the human potentiality of these gross, hard-working men explains their stern, perverse behavior. The Civil War made Armour richer. He did not go to war, but he felt a brother being killed in battle balanced his account with the nation. Such was God's way. He was not a man to question the validity of creation. Pork prices, hogs pickled in brine were forty dollars a barrel. But Armour figured, *what* would they be when the South had to give up? He began to sell short (pork for future delivery) as Lee fell back and Grant's butchery bloodied the wilderness. One newspaper reported that to pork brokers Wallace & Wicks, Armour said, "I'll sell a thousand barrels, delivery in two months." "Mr. Armour, pork is going to sixty dollars a barrel. You'll want your thousand barrels back then." "I'll deliver that pork, and maybe at eighteen dollars a barrel!"

He continued selling on future deliveries. Pork fell to thirty-five dollars. Union victories broke the back of the South. Sherman's bummers had marched to the sea. Pork prices took a great tumble. Armour, selling short, selling pork he didn't have, and delivering pork when it dropped in price, made nearly two million dollars.

Slyly he would explain his dealings: "I have never speculated, as ordinarily we think of the use of the word. I have invested because you see I believed it was the best thing for me to do." Asked if he ran his business on sentiment, Armour answered, while the pigs ran grunting by to their death, "My friend, I never could run it on anything else."

He appears to have been more of a humorist than the press gave him credit for.

Sentiment, then aggressive drive *and* hard, alert work. When a rival packer got down to the stockyards at four in the morning to bid on fresh hogs coming in, Armour got there at midnight. When his rival met the hog trains out of town, or bought directly from the farmers' hog pens, Armour invited the rival to lunch and found him a clean-living man. "He's all right, he drinks only tea."

Armour came to an understanding with the clean-living tea drinker. "I make mistakes, sure, but I don't give encores." He dabbled in railroad stocks. When the St. Paul Railroad looked good at sixty-five dollars a share, he bought four million dollars' worth of stock, and watched it climb to ninety-five dollars a share. It was, for a habitually self-centered man, his form of sport. "I don't go to the theatre and clubs . . . and enjoyment at home does not wear me out. . . . I'm in bed at nine every night. . . ." Unlike some other rich men of Chicago, he meant in his own home. He'd as well have hugged a python as a whore.

Armour's great hatred—driven with aggressive rancor—was the mention of his packinghouse rival, Gustavus Franklin Swift. "I have ordered a rule posted . . . that anyone who refers to business and says we ought to do so-and-so because Swift is doing so-and-so, will be shot . . . even without a court-martial trial." To him, Swift was the turkey buzzard in the sycamore, seeking to peck out his eyes.

Swift was not the gambler Armour was on the Chicago Board of Trade. Gustavus Swift said of Armour: "He is a born speculator." Swift, unlike the bull-muscled Armour, was a lean six feet tall and weighed much less. A New England farmer's son, born in 1839. Unlike most youths, who dream of becoming firemen or engine drivers, Gus Swift had from an early age the ambition to become a butcher. He wanted to take his portmanteau and go to New York and try for a career with meat cleaver and trimming knife, bone saw and chopping block. His father pleaded, "Don't go, Gustavus. Stay here at home and I'll buy you an animal to kill, and you can start a meat market business for yourself."

He could not resist his father's kindness. Soon he was buying pigs and selling them in his markets in New England, spreading out the delivery of carcasses, hocks, tongues, prime cuts. But his dream was Chicago with its huge stockyards and its annual millions of pigs, steers, and sheep. Heaven was a vast slaughtering universe, and by the time Swift was thirty-six, he went west to the Mecca of meat—to Chicago, went with a New England wife, Annie Maria Higgins, who hated such sinful things as theater, and in the huge family bed suffered for Eve's sin (with an apple) and bore Gus Swift eleven children. Mr. and Mrs. Swift were both of yeoman stock— that solid standard ancestry.

(Swift, however, was shamelessly, madly in love with his wife. To admire her more, he would often sit her on top of his meat icebox.

"Gustavus! Don't be silly. Take me *down* from here."

"Now you know, Annie, I like the looks of you up there."

Gossip was that he once arranged some inner beef organs in the shape of a Valentine for her. But this is not true, Edgar Lee Masters told this writer.)

Chicago suited him as much as Annie did. "Chicago is the finest city for the moderate, natural, average man . . . in which to live. The New Yorker who says Chicago is a city of luxuries is probably one of the constantly growing number who are insatiable in their greed for the softer things of life. . . . I do not go in for luxuries myself."

For all his zeal for conviviality, he certainly didn't spend money with any ease. Like multimillionaire Collis P. Huntington on the West Coast, who said, "Nobody will ever get rich picking up the quarters I drop," so Gus Swift, too, believed in the simple life. He housed his family in a nondescript house down by the smelly stockyards, corner of Emerald Avenue and Forty-fifth Street, and later in life refused to see it was unfit for a very rich man. Annie insisted they move to something impressive, and to avoid a family schism, they trekked to Ellis Avenue where Swift was shocked by one of Annie's demands. "Drapes *and* lace curtains! We're not going to have any of those fool things!"

Annie's firm, melodious answer rocked him. "You had better find someone else then to live with you in *your* new house."

A crisis, Swift thought; but he demanded one small victory. "Very well, but I don't have to have them in *my* bedroom, do I?"

One wonders if the Swifts shared the big, double, Victorian bed of the period, or if Swift slept plainly and alone?

His personal love of the city remained, even after the new drapes and window curtains; they must have been on his mind when he said, "Chicago is good enough for me. I can spend my money fast enough *here*."

Apparent trivialities he built into large things. He would often inspect the foul sewerage sludge that ran from his packingplant's outlets on Bubbly Creek—in rubber boots he'd root around in the mess, and hell would have to be paid by any foreman who let a bit of grease escape into the muck and rot that was polluting the streams and rivers around Chicago. He took aggressive pride in wasting nothing—by-products he turned into knife handles (beef bones); even hair went into something (felt).

He took notice that shipping frozen beef east had been done in a hard winter of below zero. He thought of plans to ship frozen meat east *all* the year round, a man for all seasons. In 1879, he found an invention called the Tiffany Refrigerator Car, and sent in it—through the summer heat—a carload of dressed beef headed for Boston.

The railroads refused, however, to build refrigerator cars for Swift; it would, they felt, hurt the business of their other shippers, Armour, Morris, Allerton. Besides, live steers and hogs shipped east made bigger freight charges. A boycott of dressed refrigerated beef was set up by the Railroad Trust. (It was an age of trust; the Ice Trust, Gas Trust, etc.) But one line, the Grand Trunk, was not in the cartel, and dying on its rails for lack of business. Swift made a deal with the line, and dressed beef became so popular and in such acceptance in the east, soon *all* the packers and all the railroads out of Chicago were running long lines of refrigerator cars. Rubbing other people's ideas together often passed one for a thinker and maker of progress.

Swift, in austere simplicity, hated the idea of repairing anything in his plants. He felt workers were loafers, and would just stand around if they didn't have tasks like slaughtering, cutting up steers, and packing. He had one solid rule for his managers when reviewing the potential menace of repairs: "Whenever you see a lot of mechanics at work any place you are in charge, *fire* 'em!'" (press story).

He was moderately malicious at office meetings; when all his executives voted *yes* on something, he would then usually vote *no*, and the nos have it! "You voted as you thought I would. Well, I pay for real opinions, not for you saying what you *think* I think."

The Chicago packers were great speculators, Armour more so than Swift, but all gambled in pig flesh by the barrel. Salt pork was the national dyspepsia-producing dish. Packers and brokers often formed a syndicate to exploit their knowledge. In 1879, they bought pork at eight dollars a barrel and unloaded at the end of the year, in a shortage caused by their actions, at fourteen dollars, making two million dollars in that one turnover. In April, they contracted for 350,000 barrels at ten dollars, sold them at eighteen dollars, and made seven million. It was a ruthless exploitation of that part of the nation that needed a cheap food supply, and as on the wheat market of Chicago (as recorded in Frank Norris' novel, *The Pit*), false shortages were created by special dealings that raised prices for the poor and the middle class.

The *North American Review* for August 1883 wrote of the Chicago meat-packers' schemes in a story by a reporter, Henry Demarest Lloyd: "This is the communism of the [packers'] syndicate . . . and it is the only communism that the United States has yet produced. It is the code of honor among wolves that no high-minded lamb will squeal."

No, the commodities exchanges, the brokers, and, of course, the victims, the lambs, didn't squeal.

Some of the money went into the aspirations to social status: building of impressive mansions, even if Swift, unlike most of the syndicate, held out the longest and protested against drapes and lace curtains, too many wardrobes holding women's garments of percaline, indienne merinos, and coiffeurs *en coque*.

The newspaper, *The Inter-Ocean*, wrote when the Potter Palmers began to build their castle: "The age of Pericles seems to be dawning in Chicago," although there is no record the ancient Greeks had much interest in pork packaging or cornering the wheat crop.

BOOK TWO

GROWTH OF A CITY

12

"THAT DREADFUL MR. YERKES"

I wish I could go to America if only to see that Chicago.
OTTO VON BISMARCK, IN 1870 GERMAN NEWSPAPER REPORT

The subject of this section—Charles T. Yerkes—aimed for more than winning at dice. When in his last years I would sometimes walk the streets of Los Angeles with Theodore Dreiser, he would often recall his cherished memories of Chicago when he was a very young man there. He would speak of those who grabbed the city and held it for ransom during that decadent *fin de siècle*. "The dives and the whores and the pimps, the saloon drunks, the sneak thieves and the footpads, all were the vigorous prey that the police and the courts, the aldermen at City Hall, lived off, making them pay boodle and graft. And the police and the courts were under the eyes of the ward heelers, like Bathhouse John and Hinky Dink, and big-time thieves of City Hall, the state political setup, the fast Irish talkers with the big cigars and the yellow flawed diamond tie pins. Yes . . . But what they all worked for really were the true rulers of the town; all nearly snow-white pure, with big mansions, fancy carriages, and the best horses. Also pious words of advice, they being churchgoers, and splendid social creatures—but close to the dirty

79

money. The rents from the whorehouses, and stealing of the street-car routes and El trains, shady deals in gas and waterworks stocks; the banks they owned that took the notes of the pork packers, the packinghouses, the big department stores; all that that was part of the whole pattern of Chicago—from top to bottom—a gaudy circus, beginning with the two-bit whore in an alley crib."

I quote this speech of Dreiser's from notes I made one day after a walk we took. For to me, Dreiser was the best historian an earlier Chicago ever had. He wasn't fooled by the shallow surface readings most journalists gave it. He bored deep, struck for the jugular. He knew the top fancy livers, the biggest boodle hunters, the men in hammer-tail coats, and the dwellers in the fancy mansions, as well as he knew the fast-talking salesmen, the *lumpen* middle class, the lonely girls in rented rooms.

His favorite Chicagoan was one of the most brilliant thieves, Charles T. Yerkes, an art and woman collector, arrogant as a French king. Dreiser, in 1912, had put him into his great novel *The Titan* as Frank Cowperwood, who lived by the code that "All life was . . . the strong preying on the weak." In time, Chicago rode Yerkes' trolley lines, his El trains, bought his gas and power, and in a hundred other ways furnished Yerkes with millions for more women and more paintings, more mansions and the very good life. The novel is a masterwork of understanding of larcenous detail, a fictional re-creation of a man through imagination by a realist, a writer-materialist with edges of a despairing mysticism, much like his subjects. As Dreiser once explained Cowperwood/Yerkes in a newspaper interview: "The capacity of life varies with individuals. In the main the vast majority are comparable to spindling under-growth or grass. Here and there in this jungle which the will to live has produced are giant trees, sequoias, banyans . . . by and large, the financial type is the coldest, the most selfish, and the most useful of all living phenomena. . . . Often humorless, shark-like, avid, yet among the greatest constructive forces imaginable; absolutely op-posed to democracy in practice, yet as useful an implement for its accomplishment as for autocracy."

So the real Charles Tyson Yerkes, Jr., was as interesting as his fictional shadow. He shocked that pious bore, Marshall Field, by admitting he bought ward heelers, aldermen, state senators, the way he bought neckties or practiced *haute cuisine*. (Field, whose great department store also took special city favors, was shocked by Yerkes. Field was an honorable, fair-dealing man, but he shut his eyes to the true turn of events.)

Even among the robber barons of the nineteenth century, Yerkes was an amazing American product. His daring had the quality of a Medici pope cutting Protestant throats for the greater glory of God. Yerkes showed skill, were it the dubious franchises of watered stock (in one batch of $118 million of securities he offered, $72 million were water based, or of no value) or hiring court bailiffs to bribe jurors to bring in verdicts against victims of trolley accidents in damage suits. (Knut Hamsum, the later Nazi novelist, worked on one of the Yerkes horsecars in the 1880s.) Yerkes' boldness was outstanding. He bribed anyone who had something to offer. One alderman took $100,000 in cash and $111,000 in real estate to give Yerkes votes for a bigger trolley steal:

With women, Yerkes' charming side was paramount. And there were many women, often in pairs, to his involvement and obsession. It was his infatuation with Sue Grigsby *and* her daughter, Ermilie, that broke up Yerkes' second marriage.

He was a prisoner of his own uniqueness; he detested solemnity and the minutiae of domestic life. In business he combined cajolery with menace. Yet, in a sense, in his seeking of material power, there was malaise bordering on despair—as if he were aware *this* was all. He lacked all forbearance, compassion, humility. He belonged to those persons on the Chicago scene admitting *homo homini lupus,* man is wolf to man, who were talents, debauched talents, but talents, even geniuses. They made a Chicago, impulsive, capricious, vehement, but never dull. They never grasped the full understanding of their experiences, not even in contemplation long after the events.

Marshall Field, at good markups, tried to give value for what he sold. Yerkes, frank about his methods, said in a news story: "The secret of success, is to buy up old junk, fix it up a little and unload it on some other fellow." When he addressed Chicago businessmen at a swindle-loaded meeting to take over some of Chicago's assets in land for the World's Fair of 1893, he put it on the line. "Let us take the land . . . and apologise later."

Marshall Field had to be led from the meeting speechless with outrage.

Yerkes continued his scandalous private life with women, seduced, bought, disorientated, used, discarded. Details were known, but few dared publish them. When one Chicago newspaper was about to print some juicy details of aberrant sexual conduct, Yerkes went calling on the chief editor and banged his cane hard on the man's desk in barely leashed resentment.

"I . . . inform you that if you publish it, I, myself, personally, will kill you for sure. Good morning!" The editor went into near imminent collapse. The material was not printed.

Yerkes—acting the part of a social anthropoid—was no slum or ghetto brat grown tough. He was well born, in Philadelphia in 1837. His father was a solid Quaker, president of a bank. Charles, however, avoided formal education, dropped out of high school at fifteen, and even as a boy was active in small businesses. At twenty-two, he had his own stockbroker's office. Here he antagonized another stock issue specialist, the contemptible Jay Gould, who was called "the most dishonest man in America." Yerkes went dabbling in high-grade school bonds Gould wanted for himself. Yerkes speculated in Philadelphia bonds and overextended himself when his banking and stock house crashed as the result of the panic caused in part by the Great Chicago Fire of 1871—its heat waves even reached Philadelphia. Yerkes had the use of some of the city's bonds, and he misapplied the funds as collateral. It was a common practice, and in normal times he would have made good the borrowings. But in a panic year, Yerkes, aged thirty-four, drew a two-year, nine-months prison sentence. He was pardoned after a year. It completed a total alienation of the man from an acceptance of the social order.

He made some sort of a comeback, but for Yerkes, Philadelphia, his wife and six children were no longer the same. Domesticity and a known prison record irked him. He got a divorce, married again, but was always a chaser of the billowing skirt, hunter of the easy women, the flesh beyond the veil of appearances.

In Fargo, South Dakota, Yerkes did poorly in land speculation and public utilities. He moved on to Chicago and there his spectacular career moved into high gear, even if all the money he brought with him to Chicago was forty thousand dollars. Rancor and belligerence and nerve soon inflated it to a great fortune.

He now knew how to manipulate city land and public utilities, invite men with conceit and arrogance to help share the loot. Chicago was greedy and was growing and had a rich layer of people who liked to speculate and Yerkes had the programs for them. Chicago had a vast population that needed transportation by trolley and El train, that wanted to cook with gas, and light their houses with it. These needs, with the help of bribed politicians, could be raised in cost, yet always appearing to be *for* the public good. It was myopic illusion all the way—to call *stealing* service.

By 1883, Yerkes was doing so well he had the fashionable firm of Burling and Whitehouse draw up plans for a sixty-thousand-dollar stone pile of status at the corner of Michigan Avenue and Thirty-second Street, and in the popular Gothic style. He and his wife attended all the fashionable balls restricted to the best people mumbling banalities in mild insouciance. The *Tribune* reported, "The loftiest minds of the west were there," if one thought of great minds as being Mr. and Mrs. George M. Pullman, the Marshall Fields, the Potter Palmers. Yerkes saw them as shop owners, hotel-keepers, meat-packers. No poets, writers, scientists were listed as guests.

Yerkes' direct mind acted like a dagger sinking into flesh, with no handicaps or inhibitions of morality. He wanted the North Chicago Street Railways whose networks of tracks filled the North Side. For $1,750,000 he got it. His backers were two Philadelphia sharp-shooters, P. A. B. Widener and William L. Elkins. Yerkes was a fine front for these two pirates; Widener on his death left the greatest estate ever recorded in Philadelphia; Elkins, a mere thirty million dollars. Widener was a good teacher to Yerkes, and once frankly told stockholders at an important meeting, "Vote *first* and discuss *later*." (As a teen-ager, Widener had made sixty thousand dollars selling rancid mutton to Lincoln's armies. At the same time, J. P. Morgan was selling condemned army rifles to the Union forces, rifles that usually exploded, wounding or killing the soldiers firing the weapons. Most of these businessmen, including John D. Rockefeller, J. P. Morgan and others, were by law, as official records show, permitted to hire for three hundred dollars substitutes to go fight the war for them. Yerkes had splendid teachers.)

Widener, besides seizing and exploiting the streetcar lines of Chicago, Philadelphia, Baltimore, Washington, Pittsburgh, also collected paintings of madonnas; he cried real tears when viewing his best Raphael. Yerkes faced his art collection with a psychological toughness, no tears.

Dreiser told me he had a theory why rich thieves collect valuable art. "Show me a very rich man who collects high-priced paintings, and I'll show you a crook of great skill who is trying to lather his dislike of himself by buying expensive beauty. Like an ape eating a rose."

Soon Yerkes was running the Chicago West Division Railroad Company for the two Philadelphians. Yerkes helped put together The Peoples Gas Company (an ironic title) made up of various Chicago gas companies' stock. But when Yerkes gave a twenty-three-thousand-dollar fountain to Lincoln Park, he had it lit by electricity, not gas. When the University of Chicago's President William Rainey Harper hinted the school would like a high-powered telescope, Yerkes was the proper amused parvenu and ordered the school to build "the largest and finest telescope in the world. . . . I'll pay the bill." The Yerkes Observatory at the college is almost the only memory modern times have of his name. "Perhaps," Dreiser once mused, "he wondered if man could ever seize the universe."

Yerkes traveled in his hunt for women, and in New York built himself a Fifth Avenue mansion for one million dollars. He bought a bed once used by the king of the Belgians for eighty thousand dollars. (Asked a wit at the Chicago Club, "What's the mattress stuffed with, pubic hair?") Yerkes spent fortunes for Oriental carpets, and while most rich men were buying suspicious Corots, and battle scenes, and nudes with ice-cream behinds, Yerkes boldly marched into the house of Durand-Ruel and for sixty-seven thousand dollars bought Turner's *Blue Lights and Rockets*, a revolutionary picture; it gave Yerkes a sense of individualism—his taste against the other money bags.

Yerkes borrowed heavily to play the market, and in 1896 his enemies among the Chicago rich were happy to see he was overextended and his stock holdings, with accelerating intensity, dipping badly. A meeting was called in P. D. Armour's parlor, the meatpacker—himself a stock plunger—being the leader of the hounds who were trying to pull down this Philadelphian upstart and jailbird. Like Swift and Field, Armour did not play with gay ladies in lobster palaces, or private dining rooms, or trade a loan of beautiful female bodies for diamonds and pearls. These pioneer merchants lacked Yerkes' sensual challenge and fulfillment. They remained loyal to their prim bovine wives either out of fear or Christian piety, chased no draggle-tails or blowens. As a Levee madam of a fancy brothel once put it, "Their balls are just solid gold, *nothing* else."

The talk in the Armour parlor—the men in their light summer attire—as they waited for Yerkes to show up, was simple. The banks that day—of which they were the major stockholders—were calling in *all* the Yerkes loans. Bankruptcy was the only way Yerkes could turn. What would his fancy whores think of that when he was stripped clean?

Yerkes came in—he appeared cheerful, brushed, well tailored, swinging his cane. His amused glance roamed the parlor, looking over his creditors.

"Well, well, gentlemen, this is the damned biggest collection of straw hats I ever saw at a funeral."

The room was filled with a precarious equilibrium tilted against him. Yerkes got a few cold smiles, the smiles of men who didn't gamble as high with their capital and didn't take unorthodox risks as big as this fellow. Yerkes seemed unimpressed by their icy front on this hot summer day. He faced them, rocked back on his heels, as if aware of the rapacity and intrigue that had made *their* fortunes.

"Looks like I'm no good. Already busted, eh? A bad egg, a menace to conservative business, and all that, eh?" (None of this dialogue is invented—several full reports exist.)

"Yes, Yerkes, that's it, you are," someone said.

"My loans will be called? My stock sold tomorrow?"

"That is right."

Yerkes seemed in an almost amused cataleptic state. "All right. Go ahead." He came alive with a rasping sound. "You want a selling of stock, you want the damnedest exhibition of stock selling you ever saw in your lives? Go ahead. But . . . if the Stock Exchange doesn't close down, *your* banks all will."

He had them and they suddenly knew it. What horrendous misjudgment was this? *If* Yerkes sold out his holdings and all the holdings of Elkins and Widener he controlled, he would ruin the exchange, ruin all of LaSalle Street. Yerkes, they now remembered, had a great, grinding power; they had passed over the fact *he* was the Traction Ring, and the ruin of that would panic the city, bring mobs into the streets, cause a desperate run on their banks. They had been pernickety and querulous . . . too sure of victory.

Marshall Field, as Yerkes went cheerfully out, looked at the white faces in Armour's ornate parlor and heard the ice tinkling in the lemonade glasses. His careful Yankee soul was not too happy at the usual methods of stock manipulation, for all his years as a great merchant. ("Merchant Prince," the *Tribune* called him, and he hated it.)

Field sighed: "Mr. Yerkes is not a safe man. You ask for my advice. Such action as we proposed will cause a panic. Yes. People will not understand it. My advice, gentlemen, is let Mr. Yerkes alone." He had an afterthought: "Mr. Yerkes will come to his own bad end."

They were all tightfisted, rock-hard businessmen, but in many ways honorable, even if self-righteous. They cut corners, of course, in dealings, winked at certain details of the business scene. But Yerkes' direct mocking methods were not theirs. They had an austerity, a dryness. Yes, Yerkes, if the God of Sunday school existed, would have a bad end. But now in an intolerable situation, they agreed to extend Yerkes' loans as the only wise course possible to them.

Charles Tyson Yerkes, Jr., had been sure they would kowtow— he shared with Dreiser a hard, materialistic view of society and man. . . . One must strip away the unessentials from the core of one's life, both men felt. Outwardly, they believed, we live actions needed for existing in nature. We invent what we call human conditions outside of nature's indifference to us. On top of nature we create moral items, create moralities, social patterns. We try to transcend the basic brute; so man becomes an inventor, he expands natural realities and dimensions. He conceives a history of himself, he makes investigations called science, and his fantasies become the arts: music, poetry, painting, literature—also great fortunes.

It is a harsh philosophy that Yerkes (and Dreiser) had—but was made livable by hedonism. Both Yerkes and Dreiser were fantastic womanizers, sensualists of stature. This extended their acceptance of the world as a place where we are *what* has happened to us. None of us is here for specific, unexchangeable purpose; we *are,* that is all. . . . So one's ambitions can be devoted to tangibles such as money, power, sexual gratification.

13

HOW TO STEAL A CITY

God gave me my money.
J. D. ROCKEFELLER, THE NEW YORK TIMES, 1907

So Yerkes, almost ruined by his stock market losses and in danger of bankruptcy, avoided it by the skin of his teeth. He continued unchanged—pushed actively the building of Chicago's elevated railroad system, the best-known section being the Loop which encircled the rich business section, and so poured thousands of employees and shoppers into that part of the busy city every working day. Yerkes did not have any personal feeling of pride in a greater Chicago, only as it served his ability to make money, gain power—"have 'em by the short hair." He got the rights for his projects by buying up the city and state governments, then had the projects put into work by one of his strangely organized construction companies, whose costs were astronomic. The padding of estimates of costs was fantastic. Yerkes expected what he paid out to aldermen to come back to him. "Greasing their palm" was the expression, and rich men had little trouble having their personal property tax fixed, assessments at *very* low figures.

Yerkes had a large racing stable, a collection of rare jewels, a lavish mansion, a palm garden, an art collection later sold at nearly eight hundred thousand dollars, a library of rare books. All this was assessed for tax purposes by the council at only $1,337! No wonder Mr. Dooley was cynical about elected officials and governing bodies. "Th' proceedin's was opened with a prayer that Providence might r-remain undher th' protection iv th' administration."

Yerkes' specific quality was making things work. He controlled most of the contracting companies or got fabulous kickbacks for granting contracts. Meanwhile, if any councilman showed any interest in the skulduggery involved in building the El lines, the trolley extensions, the gas mains, Yerkes could usually manage to show the politician a great deal of "green goods"—cash on the tabletop—to cause sudden blindness as to public affairs. Yerkes liked to settle bribing in amity and complacency.

He knew, as always, how to water stock. The capitalization of his North and West Side transit companies, in ten years, went from eight million dollars to nearly sixty million, over thirty million more than the actual cost of the equipment and the plant values.

Yerkes' real problem was that his city franchises had limited time to run—in 1895 his trolley lines in the city, in eight years, would go from his control. Owning the state government in Springfield, or nearly so, Yerkes began to try to get a series of what were dubbed "Eternal Monopoly laws," from the legislature. They would give him ninety-nine-year rights. Governor John P. Altgeld, one of the few honest governors the state ever had, turned down Yerkes' bribe of a half-million dollars in cash to let the gigantic swindle go through. Yerkes, instead of being angered, sincerely praised the governor: "I admire *that* man."

Two years later there was a new governor, and Yerkes nearly got what he wanted. He lost the Eternal Monopoly laws by a narrow margin. Giving up in Springfield, he had a local law passed granting the city of Chicago the right to give him directly what he wanted. The governor, a man named John Riley Tanner, signed the bill. The cost to the Traction Ring, directed by Yerkes, was set at a half-million dollars.

The Chicago newspapers, hardly with clean hands in their own support of their own schemes, and strange advertising, tore into Yerkes. The *Tribune*'s Joseph Medill led the pack. "The press of

Chicago has no favorable regard or respect for a fellow who uses Chicago as a milch cow, and who takes the butter and eggs to New York . . . who grabs franchises in Chicago and uses their excessive profits to erect a palace in New York crammed with pictures, statuary, bric-a-brac and luxuries of the most costly kind."

None of the papers printed the fact that Chicago holier-than-thou businessmen, most of whom held huge blocks of stock in the streetcar systems, would also increase their profits by the new law.

But first Yerkes had a big problem—the new law, the Allen Law, would have to be signed by the mayor, Carter Harrison, Jr. (He would be elected to five terms as mayor.) In 1897, he was, at thirty-seven, serving his first term when Yerkes began to lay plans to get him to sign that streetcar system grab, which would bring the city not one added penny in income.

Mayor Harrison made his purpose clear. "If Yerkes can pass any ordinance over *my* veto, I'll eat my brown fedora."

Yerkes—a patient carnivore—came to City Hall to court the mayor. The wary mayor, however, always had a third person present so Yerkes could not claim he had paid over a bribe. Yerkes could lower his dignity when he wanted anything very much, a woman or a law. He showed up at the mayor's home on Schiller Street. Here he felt he could put his proposition to the mayor privately, directly make his cash offer to get the mayor to forget his stern order of "no streetcar franchise for over twenty years."

The wary mayor had his wife and brother listen in from a staircase. Yerkes, feeling they could talk freely, put it directly on the line with Mayor Harrison. "Mr. Mayor, what do you want, anyhow?"

"Mr. Yerkes, you may not mean by that query what I think you mean. If, however, I construe your question correctly, let me say there is not enough money on God's green footstool to induce me to vary my position in the slightest degree." Stage dialogue—but to the point.

There was most likely more to the conversation than was later reported. Yerkes had a biting edge to his tongue. Whatever else was said, Yerkes now knew it was a fight to the death; if he failed in getting the Allen Law passed, he was finished in Chicago as head of the Traction Trust. There might even be a new deal for the battered trolley rider: a cheaper fare, cleaner cars, heat, true heat, in winter. There was no end to the horrors of change that could take place. Yerkes began to spread money in deeper layers at the City Council. The mayor fought back after Alderman A. Lyman of the Second Ward brought the Allen Law to the City Council. The mayor began to address huge, citywide meetings, explaining the true meaning of the law. He was backed by the editorial fury of the Chicago newspapers. Former Governor Altgeld supported him, as did the Municipal Voters' League, one of those reform forces that begin with large hopes and end in time in bleating defeat.

Reform groups began to gather, actually carrying hangmen's nooses, symbols of the desired lynching of the City Council *if* it passed the Allen Law. The mayor, too, carried a noose onto the speakers' platforms at all mass meetings, and the crowds would yell, "Hang 'em! *Hang 'em!*"

On the night of December 19, the scowling, worried aldermen voted down the Allen Law. Yerkes could read the signs. He left his four-million-dollar mansion, sold out all his holdings to a group run by his old partners Elkins and Widener, and his stocks in elevated road bonds and other contracts to a group in which Marshall Field was active.

On LaSalle Street, in the brokers' offices, the talk was that Yerkes had left Chicago with thirty million dollars. Yerkes was not through with public transportation. He began talk with the London banking firm of Speyer & Co., about building the London Underground. When at last he died in 1905, Yerkes' fortune was down to little over a million. As an eager voluptuary, he had spent millions on women, on great houses, rare rugs and paintings, on fine living. His love affairs became legendary, and his life was fantastic to the end. He was never impressed by the *arriviste* society he had found in Chicago and other American cities. He saw little opprobrium attached to bribery. But the streetcars, the gas that lit and cooked, these served many needs as the city's business increased as more people could come into the heart of the city to shop.

Yerkes manipulated the visible and the tangible, watched the frenzy of speculation, a well-turned leg, conquered willing, yielding women; these victories to this pirate of genius were more important than the abstract ideas of pragmatists, the deep thinkers, the God seekers.

He was no isolated phenomenon in Chicago or America, a land where opportunists and parvenus were to build the material solidness of railroads, mines, factories into a great nation, even if one without true spiritual depth.

Still, those who feared Yerkes—the Chicago merchants, businessmen, meat-packers—were in agreement with those parts of his philosophy that saw the main chance, never the shadow for the substance, the word for the thing, the appearance for the reality.

Aggressive materialism made a fabulous nation, raised by shrewd innovators, manipulators. The core of Charles Yerkes was a freedom from pious cant, the eyewashing appeals to God, the banal moralizing of a Field or a Carnegie or an Armour, a Rockefeller. His way of life to these men smelled too much of brimstone, had nihilistic qualities of destructive, demoralizing naked strength.

The most solid fact that soon came out of Yerkes' leaving Chicago was that the streetcar and El service would *not* be improved in any way, no matter *who* ran or controlled them. Edgar Lee Masters expressed best the hopelessness of trying for reform in Chicago. Once lifting a glass of bourbon about an election coming up, he offered a toast. "Throw the rascals in."

WICKED STREETS

The wickedness and piety of Chicago are in their way marvelous.
SCRIBNER'S MAGAZINE

Giant black women with no subtle variations seemed to dominate the Little Cheyenne district vice trade. Hattie Briggs was not the largest, being only 220 pounds and a mere six feet tall, "black as a licorice stick," who went about in a long crimson cloak, a queen of licentiousness. As boss woman of a whorehouse and crooks' hangout on Clark Street near Polk, and an annex on Custom House Place where a girl cost twenty-five cents, the true game she played was really robbery. Hattie would grab a guest, bang him against the nearest wall once or twice, go through his pockets, and toss him out. She loved violence as an itinerant revivalist loves hellfire.

Love came to Hattie at last, even if she was "as ugly as anyone could imagine" (newspaper clipping). Willie Smith was young and feisty, of no importance, a small-time black chiseler and thief, but Hattie bought him a saloon as her fancy man, and did him up fancy, too, as her carnal darling. Tall silk hat, a larrikin in lavender pants. Yellow shirt, white waistcoat, electric blue coat, and patent-leather shoes with white spats. There were diamonds on Willie's shirtfront and on his fingers. He sported a gold toothpick tastefully behind one ear. Willie was followed around by a messenger boy in livery, who delivered messages Willie wrote with four colored pencils to officials at City Hall. Hattie felt Willie was worth it all. Proudly she said she'd end up "owning all the houses and saloons in the city and elect Willie mayor and do away with the police force . . ." (newspaper clipping).

Willie, with dalliance as his only task besides stud duty and bed passion, had delusions of grandeur. One night in 1892, when one "Ginger Heel" Paine, Hattie's brothel assistant, was being arrested by a detective, Willie stepped in, using force. The police retaliated by sending a score of cops to raid Willie's saloon, and fought a knockdown battle with two dozen of Willie's gang. The place was wrecked, the saloon license taken away, and Willie was fined a hundred dollars.

Hattie, too, was on the police bad list now, and, with pockets full of blanket warrants, the police were arresting her day and night, a dozen times every twenty-four hours. Hattie knew when the hoodoo sign was on her, so she got a big van and moved her furniture, drabs, and bobtails *and* Willie, over to Smoky Ridge and arranged new payoffs not to be molested.

Locomotives and long trains of cars and cattle and freight carriers ran wildly through parts of Chicago on the street levels. Pacific Avenue was a besmoked, dangerous street, and from the ever-present big engines it was called Biler Avenue (the closest Chicago's underworld came to pronouncing *boiler*, as in steam boiler). It was a mean street of mean brothels full of bawdy baskets (whores), and when one of Jennie Williams' girls committed suicide, she left a note, "Please bury me in my silk dress and bracelets."

The police themselves invested in vice-rich property, and Mike C. Hickey, the superintendent of police, owned the building where Dan Webster, a black, ran a big gin dive and whorehouse on Biler Avenue . . . "an infernal hell hole . . . the rottenest, vilest, filthiest strumpets, black and white, reeking with corruption." So said the *Chicago Times*. Dan felt this press notice unfair; as he said, he paid well for political protection and wasn't the head of the police himself his landlord? The Police Board tried Hickey for strange

dealings in rents, but he was acquitted by the board, as "he could not possibly know the character of his tenants." It was hinted that some members of the board were themselves owners of rich, vice-stained properties.

Carter Harrison, Sr., five times mayor of the city, himself, the *Times* had pointed out in 1877, "owns the entire block (on Harrison Street) between Clark Street and Pacific Avenue. On the corner of Clark, and running west to the middle of the block, stands a hotel. The other half of the block is occupied by four or five ordinary frame houses. One is used for a lager-beer saloon, another for a restaurant, still another for a tabacco store, a fourth as a hotel on a small scale, and right among these, as snug as a bug in a rug, Our Carter has allowed a number of gay damsels to nestle down." The only answer was the harsh cry of train whistles on Biler Avenue.

No district was tougher than Hell's Half Acre, enclosed by Polk, State, and Taylor streets and Plymouth Place. Every building was given over to whoring, drinking, lewd shows, gambling dives, cribs, and hot sheet hotels for assignations. No policeman dared walk alone there, and no evangelism and revival howling could tame it.

In the seventies and eighties its prime attraction was the Apollo Theatre and Dance Hall, where the most shocking masked balls took place—voyeurs' delights—given for the benefit of the whorehouse professors, the piano and banjo and fiddle players. Masks, and *all* clothing came off at midnight, as women screamed and visitors from the West announced they were "watered with buffalo milk and weaned on whisky" (newspaper quote).

In a passageway, Dead Man's Alley, nearby, black tarts did their business in the bodies of abandoned hacks and coaches. It was also a divvy point for robbers and the swag, and a spot ideal for holdups and footpads. Razor bucks worked here, slashing at strangers. One Black Bear (real name Henry Foster) ran a gang from Dead Man's Alley. Black Bear was a muscle brute who grabbed and beat the victim, but the brains of the outfit was a little, hickory-tough black girl, Minnie Shouse, who did the business of getting rid of the loot to some crass fence. She had a record of arrests, three hundred in six years. Bail for various charges could run up for her to twenty thousand dollars, but the bail bond people felt she was trustworthy. She was aided by dishonest cops—who would threaten the victim for "unlawfully screwing a whore"—and if all else failed, she would even return part of the booty to avoid jail. She did finally get a year in prison for robbing "a hick from the sticks," and Black Bear, missing her guiding hand and sense, murdered a saloon owner and in quick time he was hanged.

Custom House Place was next door to Hell's Half Acre. From Harrison to Twentieth Street on Custom House, the best known red-light section in the nation, was run wide open. (It held its right to that fame until Storyville came to pinpoint the sporting houses of New Orleans.) Custom House Place had *everything*: luxury parlor houses and the filthiest cribs full of scabby slommocks (harlots).

In a press interview, Detective Clifton Woolridge gives us a picture of Custom House Place when later it was busy during "the inrush of *hommes moyens sensuel,*" during the Columbian Exposition of 1893, when "day and night women could be seen at the doors and windows, frequently half-clad, making an exhibition of themselves and using vulgar and obscene language. At almost all of these places there were sliding windows, or windows that were hung on hinges and swung inside. These swinging or sliding windows were used by the women to invite pedestrians on the street to enter these places and also for the purpose of exhibiting themselves. Extension fronts were built to many of these houses from which a better view could be had of the police and pedestrians.

"All of the houses were equipped with electric bells, and a sentinel whose duty it was to watch for the police and give a signal to the inmates, was stationed at each end of the street between Polk and Harrison . . . fifty to one hundred women lounging in the doors and windows in this one block at one time. The habitués of this place embraced every nationality, both black and white, their ages ranging from eighteen to fifty years. The costumes worn by these people embraced every kind known to the human race, from that of the Hottentot to the belle of the ball. Some were in tights, some having nothing on but a loose Mother Hubbard, made of some flashy material which resembled a mosquito bar, through which the entire form of the woman could be seen. Others were dressed as jockeys, while others had no sleeves in their dresses. The waist was cut so low that their bosoms were entirely exposed, and some were dressed almost exclusively in the garb which nature gave them when they were born. . . . In these houses could be found every low and demoralizing phase of life that the human mind could think of."

When moral objections were made that young boys were seeing all this desirable flesh on display in cathouse windows, and were being led to seek comfort and release in indelicate ways or even with whores, the mayor at that time, George B. Swift, in 1896, ordered the sinful houses to paint over their windows and keep them latched. It was a crass presumption that youth could be kept from nature's scheme for them by a paintbrush.

Mary Hastings ran the most depraved house in the district, and she paid off the policeman on the beat with $250 a week, free girls, food, and drink. She also paid large sums to the captain of the Harrison Police Station, the inspectors, and the ward bosses. She objected to the high cost of protection, and a police captain told her to stop her ricky-tick protest: "Why, goddamn you, what are you made for but to be plundered?"

Mary held *outré* circus nights to prove her proud slogan: any sexual game of degeneracy or perversion could be performed by her girls. She often did her own recruiting of these talented girls, or worked with procurers, favoring girls thirteen to seventeen, often innocent girls brought to Chicago on promises of decent jobs. Details are rather revolting as to how these girls were gang-raped, often all night by a half-dozen black studs in a room, and brutalized to accept prostitution. Mary Hastings often sold them elsewhere, priced at fifty to five hundred dollars each, according to grade, age, and looks. In 1895, one wretched girl escaped from her house and five others were rescued by police. Mary ran away to Canada, skipping her bail. When she came back, the date of her trial was bounced around by political pressure until 1897; by that time, witnesses had been bought off or run out of town—and the state had no case against her.

Mary had turned over her holdings and house to Tom Gaynor, her fancy man. When free to do so, she tried to take over again. Tom threw her out of her own whorehouse, paying her off with two hundred dollars to get out of town. She went to Toledo, a victim of fickle love abandoning an untenable position.

15

THE PALMER HOUSE AND OTHERS

I was a stranger, and ye took me in.
MATTHEW 25:35

Chicago's first pioneer hostels were log cabins where vile food, soaked in grease, was served out of a spider skillet, followed by raw whiskey to restore the vitality, and the corn-husk pallet for sleep contained insect life. As the city grew, the tone of comfort was given to visiting by the new hotels' posh and plush.

Just two years after the Great Fire, at the corner of Monroe and State streets, Potter Palmer, in November 1873, opened the Palmer House, "guaranteed fireproof" and advertised as THE PALACE HOTEL OF THE WORLD. It had been the fancy design of John Mills Van Osdel, done in a style French enough, in its cloying adoration of royalty, to have frightened Louis XV out of his mind by its gaudy detail. The beds were comfortable, the service good, and there was a chef who could do more than singe, burn, or destroy. Visitors bugged out their eyes at the splendor of the hotel.

Rudyard Kipling saw it "as a gilded and mirrored rabbit warren . . . a huge hall of tessellated marble, crammed with people talking about money and spitting about everywhere." Mr. Kipling was to live long enough to hear Mr. Calvin Coolidge declare, "The business of America is business." There is a flavor of hostility in Mr. Kipling. He did not like Americans, and a Vermont brother-in-law was to horsewhip him on a country road, so one suspects his heightened ire at the use of the silver gaboons (also called spittoons) is a bit unfair, as he goes on maligning Mr. Palmer: "Other barbarians charged about in and out of this inferno with letters and telegrams in their hands, and yet others shouted at each other. A man who had drunk quite as much as was good for him, told me this was 'the finest hotel in the finest city on God's almighty earth!' "

Chicago certainly wasn't the "Injah" of Rudyard Kipling with its sahibs who found politics contemptible—downing their stingers at the Simla club, very stiff upper lip and stout fellah. When Kipling's prose on Chicago was published, Clarence Darrow is said to have remarked, "No wonder the sun never sets on the British Empire; God doesn't trust it in the dark."

But Kipling's sour report did not harm the Palmer House; it was the full symmetry of a dream to its builder—and it inspired awe in the guests seeing the 225 silver dollars imbedded in the barbershop floor, the 200 square feet of mirrors reflecting the barbers at work, and over all the yellow gaslight that gave it the look of a naughty Lautrec poster from Paris. General Grant not only had his beard terraced in this barbershop, called The Garden of Eden, prop. W. S. Eden, but the general wore a bit of a path in the rich hotel rugs on his way to the service of one of the bars.

Potter Palmer was no shy lily about speaking well of his hotel. "Most of the palaces and hotels of Europe are made up of disjointed buildings erected at various times and of mixed architecture . . . lacking in perfect form and well defined taste. The Palmer House is a realization of an era of magnificence and luxury in architecture and appointments of which the older builders knew nothing" (newspaper quote).

Certainly the Palmer House style was unknown to the Medici, the Hanover palaces, or the castles of the Bourbons and the Hapsburgs. Flush toilets held the Western country visitors spellbound by their roaring sounds. The Grand Dining Room, to tempt jaded appetites or gross feeders, was a copy of the Potsdam Palace of the German crown prince. There was an Egyptian Parlor that suggested sibyls, oracles, and the opera *Aida*—also the interment of a mummified king of ancient Egypt. The staircases were Carrara marble, the mirrors Venetian, unique chandeliers (again Egyptian), but burning Chicago gas not Nile palm oil. Everything seemed of extraordinary proportions.

All this cost money, three and a half million dollars, and some said Potter Palmer had gone completely berserk. By today's standards of high-priced but very poor food in grand Hilton-type hotels, the cost of really fine meals at the Palmer House seems absurdly cheap. Yet Cyrus McCormick, the reaper king, insisted for his family a special rate when dining there. Mr. Potter Palmer sighed but agreed, stating however, "seventy-five cents does not pay me the actual cost of the dinners." One wonders what a ten-dollar meal would be like at the Palmer House.

The words FIREPROOF were picked up by other hotels which weren't. (Neither really was the Palmer House by modern standards.) Mr. Palmer took newspaper space in the *Tribune* to call the lie to the other hotels' claims.

A CHALLENGE TO THE KEEPERS OF HUMAN TRAPS

After venting his rage at their claims, he then offered a challenge. "I hereby invite such unscrupulous people to build a fire in the center of any chamber or room of the Palmer House proper . . . the furniture, carpets, mirrors etc., to be undisturbed and the doors and windows remained closed for one hour. If . . . the fire does not spread beyond the room, the party accepting his invitation is to pay for all damages done and for the use of the room. If the invitation is not accepted . . . I purpose, with the consent of the Underwriters of Chicago, to make the test myself."

The Underwriters, of course, as expected, said *no*, and the competitors in the hotel business were wise enough to know such an extravagant stunt would pay off only for the Palmer House.

The rival hotels were Second Empire in style, or improvisations of it, with fancy mansard roofs; best examples, the Tremont House Hotel and the Sherman House (the latter said to have been named after General Sherman, who was quoted as saying, "If I owned Hell and Texas, I'd live in Hell and rent out Texas." He never maligned Chicago in such a fashion.)

A close rival of Palmer House was the Grand Pacific, set uniquely on the edge of the financial district bounded by Clark, Quincy, LaSalle, and Jackson streets, sacred to the dollar with almost religious exultation. It was favored by the railroad kings and stock market aristocracy, Jay Gould, William Henry Vanderbilt (he, when told people objected to the rough travel on his New York Central, shot back, "The public be damned").

Mr. John B. Drake, owner of the Grand Pacific, was susceptible to quail, pheasant, venison, canvasback duck, antelope, and even now and again, buffalo hump or a bear steak. The grand wild game dinners at the Grand Pacific had the Chicago gourmets and gourmands rushing into the dining room when Drake announced that a few carloads of riddled game had just come in.

Nor was the game merely served on wild rice and with truffles; it became part of the table decor. Stuffed animals, grouped as in life, stood or crouched among the wine goblets, the silver salt shakers. Birds, rabbits, squirrels posed in dramas and waited for animated feasting. Remembered are such groups as "The Coon at Home," and the heartrending "The Lost Fawn," recalling the wild with a tenderhearted grace.

People would pay for fine food, but it had to be worth it and not *too* fancy. C. V. Bemis failed at the Richelieu Hotel, on Michigan Avenue, when he tried to outdo the other posh places. One went to dinner at Mr. Bemis' past a hundred-thousand-dollar art gallery, was blocked a bit on the way to the dining room by Larkin Mead's statue, *Columbus Pleading Before Isabella*. When at last one sat down to eat, the press reported that the very plates were those "that Napoleon ate off."

C. V. Bemis was just too fancy. As one unnamed gourmet put it (he sounds like Lucius Beebe): "What did Romanoff-Beluga caviar, terrapin à la Maryland, crepes Suzette, pâté de foie gras, Dry Monopole or Veuve Clicquot, Steinberger Kabinett, Spaet und Auslese of the greatest vintage years . . . signify to palates educated to prime roast beef washed down with Mumm's?" Yes indeed? Hardly nothing to people who had come from homespun jeans to a silk top hat in one generation.

A few hedonists like Charles Yerkes might take a well-shaped, hourglass-figured lady for the foreign cuisine, the Clos Vougeot and

Château d'Yquem Lur-Saluces, but most of the rich Chicagoans, be they merchant princes with residual puritan guilt anxieties, kingpin gamblers, or bawdy-house madams gay with carnal anarchy, mostly preferred a porterhouse steak or a cut off the rare roast beef —and champagne meant Mumm's Extra Dry. It was easy to say Mumm's, and it got results.

On Adams Street there was the best Chicago had—the grand restaurant of H. M. Kinsley, who didn't make the mistake of too much French sauce, or menus in strange languages. For the cultural elite or the moneybags, his solid silver soup tureens held good American dishes, and his oysters came by rail express on beds of ice from the East Coast. If you gave a fine top-drawer party in Chicago and were anybody at all, you *always* had H. M. Kinsley to cater, and none other but Johnny Hand's orchestra to play.

As for the cafés, roadhouses for the sporting bloods of the *opéra-bouffe* world, these too were available. But what a grand hotel sight it was to see Lillian Russell, Lily Langtry, move in majestic grace through a hotel lobby's Peacock Alley, at the Palmer House or its top rivals.

No wonder Mark Twain said, "I'd rather see Lillian Russell naked than General Grant with all his medals."

There is no doubt the great hotels gave the city a taste of the amenities of good living, mixed with blatant eccentricities. The city had no use for any habitual austerity and saw itself eager, loud, and original, and it sometimes produced the language to match its vision of itself.

Once I was walking with Theodore Dreiser along a Los Angeles street—in his last days—and his thoughts turned to his memories of Chicago as he once knew it; he began to recite for me something from one of his novels: "The city of Chicago. This singing flame of a city, this all America, this poet in chaps and buckskin, this rude, raw Titan, this Burns of a city! By its shimmering lake it lay, a king of shreds and patches, a maundering yokel with an epic in its mouth, a tramp, a hobo among cities, with the grip of Caesar in its mind, the dramatic force of Euripides in its soul. A very bard of a city this, singing of high deeds and high hopes, its heavy brogans buried deep in the mire of circumstance."

"What's that from?" I asked.

"Take Athens, oh Greece! Italy, do you keep Rome! This was the Babylon, the Troy, the Nineveh of a younger day. Here came the gaping West and the hopeful East, to see. Here hungry men, raw from the shops and fields, idylls and romances in their minds, builded them an empire crying glory in the mud."

I said, "Isn't it a bit overripe?"

"Here was the negro, the prostitute, the blackleg, the gambler, the romantic adventurer par excellence. A city with but a handful of the native-born; a city packed to the doors with all the riffraff of a thousand towns. Flaring were the lights of the bagnio; tinkling the banjos, zithers, mandolins of the so-called gin-mill; all the dreams and the brutality of the day seemed gathered to rejoice—and rejoice they did, in this new-found wonder of a metropolitan life in the West."

He stopped reciting and grinned. "Guess from where that is?"

Later I found the lines in his novel *The Titan*. But he had either forgotten or skipped some of it. It is not a fair sample, for mostly the novel is under firm control, marvelously narrated and free of many such outbursts of gaudy, steamy prose.

16

THE MANSIONS AND THE MASTERS

Them as has, gits.
AMERICAN PROVERB

In an attitude endemic to a growing society, men marry and have wives; wives, if men make money, want to show it, a phenomenon that is a boon to builders. So many of the overt mansions that rose along the lakefront, and in the fashionable streets, were the result of nagging, insisting wives. ("What! no porte cochere?") Husbands, as they clipped their dollar-cigar ends with golden cutters, and patted their ten-course-dinner-grown paunch, often agreed, and so there arose mansions, châteaux, Regency shapes and Gothic, Grimm's fairy tale *schlosses,* all the agony and blueprint concupiscence that could be put into stone in the form of battlements and turrets. It made the city seem important to look at these domains of great wealth in special settings. People stared at the palaces of the Medicis of pork, the residences of dry-goods kings, creators of buttons and notions empires. And all knew the city was powerful and important, to have such houses where the occupants ate crêpes à l'orange in flamed Hennessy Three Star, and Lobster Mornay.

107

The builders of these abominations on fancy lots did not agree with Mr. Emerson: "Whatever events in progress shall go to disgust men with cities, and infuse into them the passions of country life, and country pleasures, will render a service to the whole face of this continent."

But wasn't Mr. Emerson "some kind of a prune-faced parson"? No, build where it will show, in the city—and get your money's worth. After all, wasn't it as someone said, "The chicken is the country's, but the city eats it"?

It was not that some fine designers of buildings were lacking, just that too much size and weight were wanted. Firms like Adler and Sullivan designed great brick mansions with mansard roofs on Lake Park Avenue at North Shore Avenue, Bellevue Place. Lake Shore Drive was *the* avenue for the rich, a drive facing the already polluted waves of Lake Michigan, and railroad tracks pushing in to break the sleep of millionaires at rest between satin sheets. Robert Todd Lincoln, entrenched as a corporation lawyer, built big (log cabins were for mudsills). There was the huge Romanesque pile designed by H. H. Richardson for the grocery king, Franklin MacVeagh.

But the talk of the town—a guaranteed sensation—was the Potter Palmer erection, that Gothic horror that is still standing at the corner of Lake Shore Drive and Banks Street. The Boston architect, Ives Cobb, with incisive pride, said nothing was as chic as "the English battlements style." The turrets were granite hauled from Wisconsin. (The habit of buying entire European castles, first employed by William Randolph Hearst, was not yet thought of, and London Bridge had not yet been moved to a dry riverbed in Arizona, or the gutted Cunarder, *Queen Mary*, berthed as a tourist attraction in California.)

The Palmer drawing room was *all* Louis XIV. Seeing it, the French fortune hunter, the Count de Castellane, who captured Jay Gould's hairy daughter Ann (and fifteen million dollars) wasn't impressed. The press reported that he called the Potter castle "abominable." One guest, with no ironic tongue, only admiring gush, exclaimed, "I have been in palaces of crowned heads . . . but not in Brazil, not in Russia, shall you see such taste. . . . It is a throne room fit for Liberty herself." Mrs. Potter didn't decline the role of Chicago's queen—among her court.

On the North Side, on Astor Street, judges and lawyers built grandiose only in Romanesque. On Pearson Street were châteaux, on the corner of Michigan and Huron was the three-story, Joliet marble Taj Mahal of the boss of the Chicago and Northwestern Railroad, Perry Smith. It had a staircase of imported ebony encrusted with gold; the dining room was made native with deeply carved panels of prairie animal life: ducks, rabbits, squirrels, and sage hens.

A *Tribune* reporter lost in wonder, and not up on his historic periods, wrote, "The style is Greek Renaissance, with proportions of Italian palace architecture." But the winner of remorselessly bulking up stone at great cost was the mansion of Cyrus Hall McCormick. It stood with no recherché modesty on Rush Street, the most massive, insinuating design of the firm of Cudell and Blumenthal, and done in pure sandstone in the Second Empire style of Napoleon III.

Wilson Mizner once said of the McCormick palace: "The interior decor would have caused a Beverly Hills decorator to have chewed off his fingernails in envy and tossed him into a perfumed fit." (Mizner, in times of hunger, married rich women and hocked their old masters—but he did see the homes of the great new rich—at least once.)

There were *two* McCormick libraries in the new house, even though McCormick and his family were not much given to reading books. The grand library was done in ebony, inlaid with silver; the master library was also ebony trimmed in walnut with lambrequins of raw Chinese silk. The music room held a whale of a piano of rosewood and satinwood, the dining room rested in deeply carved mahogany, dominated by a Gobelin tapestry (real or a fine imitation). The eyes of the guests were always directed upward as they dined, up to the fresco on the ceiling. Some said it was doubtful if it was a true *fresco*, "most likely only done on canvas." It was a picture that showed in full colors the insignia of the Legion of Honor awarded to the host—in the midst of some golden sheaves of wheat. All dominated by a McCormick reaper, the source of all this splendor. McCormick was said to have rejected a painting, offered him, of the *Madonna of Torre Annunziate*.

There was a two-hundred-seat private theater upstairs. Here, while McCormick looked his seventy-one years, a party was given on May 24, 1880, to celebrate the coming of age of Cyrus Hall McCormick II, with what one newspaper called a *soirée musicale*, featuring the *Rustic Wedding* by Goldmark, and a heavy repast catered by Kinsley. The only deprecators were the uninvited.

The older McCormick suffered from carbuncles, and enjoyed major lawsuits. He was always taking sulfur-bath cures and, as usual, suing someone—railroads for lost trunks, inventors who had dared to invent harvesters of their own.

The man who made modern farming possible, who in the end ruined the small farmer who could not invest the thousands of dollars needed for farm machinery, the man who made the big wheat-growing combines, the huge farms easier to work, was also in the main responsible for the great Dust Bowls, those disasters that blew away the topsoil of so much of the Middle West in the Depression years. Greedy men harnessed his machines by the regiments, in rows, broke the sod that held the Great Plains, broke open the earth with bull-tongued plows in endless columns, and set the harvesters to take in crops grown on grazing land once held by small farmers. (Those who were to flee westward with Steinbeck's Okies and had their homes tractored down. Chicago saw many of these refugees later, creating great slums of festering, bigoted, poor whites, and welfare-supported blacks rotting into nihilists, in part victims of the machines that McCormick made.)

McCormick was seventy-five when he was dying. When asked if he wanted anything, his last words were said in a serenity of detachment, "I want nothing now but heaven." Perhaps, as one minister remarked about his burial, "he hoped to plow and harvest the fields of heaven."

The Marshall Fields, too, found they had to have festive events in their mansion on Prairie Avenue. In 1885, the heir, Marshall, Jr., was seventeen, and daughter Ethyl, twelve. A Mikado Ball was decided on for the young folk, Gilbert and Sullivan being found "clean and Christian" by the churches of Chicago. The social satire, the melody-coated savage bite at all pomp and power, at tradition, and the Victorian age were usually lost on most people who adored the works of Gilbert and Sullivan as exquisite and ludicrous.

The Field house was turned into "A Japanese Wonderland," hardly the Yoshiwara courtesans' and gamblers' world of Utamaro, Sharoku, or Hokusai, but a Chicago version that pleased the four hundred young guests who danced to the non-geisha waltz tunes of Johnny Hand, and ate, not sukiyaki, but the healthy dishes in the collation of the excellent Kinsley, the *only* proper caterer of the best affairs. A Japanese print and ceramic collector, the painter James McNeill Whistler, was commissioned by Field, in London, to design the jeweled favors presented to the young ladies.

But the Big Store was Marshall Field's main interest. As one of his longtime managers put it, "Marshall Field's whole life was a serious one, no frivolity, fun or levity." Like so many rich men who rose from ordinary stock, he seemed not to have been a strong influence on his children. Gustavus Swift, the meat-packer, was stern with his brood of sons, saw great dislocation in simple things. "No young man is rich enough to smoke twenty-five-cent cigars."

Field's son and heir, Marshall Field, Jr., long after the party, at the age of thirty-seven in 1906, was to die mysteriously of "a serious bullet wound." A press notice was prepared that Marshall Field had died "from a shot from his own revolver while getting ready to go hunting in Canada." There are still men in Chicago, once hard-boiled journalists and men-about-town, who insist he died in one of Chicago's fanciest brothels, shot by a whore—the Everleigh Club is usually mentioned—and the body smuggled out to be found at home in his room, "an accident while cleaning his gun." The version of the family doctors and business associates of the senior Field are suspected as merely statements to soften the blow for the family. If there ever was evidence for that brothel story, none seems available today.

Marshall Field had an old age of loneliness, heir dead mysteriously, the first Mrs. Field long an invalid in exile in the south of France. Field would sit in his office, the door half open. Here, Peter Funk, one of his old faithful salesmen, found him one day, silent at his desk. Said Funk, "Marshall, you have no home, no family, no happiness, nothing but money."

Peter Funk was wrong (we shall take up later Field's last romance). Marshall Field just then had all he ever really wanted, the Big Store.

What was the private life of people who respected Field? Police records, newspapers, keep us fairly well informed of the life of the bordellos, gambling houses, and the criminal doings. But the social pages of the daily press give us very little reality of what "the quality" or the upper middle class was actually doing, besides dressing up, giving teas and parties. What they were *expected* to do can be found in a series of advice-giving books from the middle of the nineteenth century until 1914. These pretty well set up a standard of behavior. They had titles such as *American Family Keepsake, How to Behave, Etiquette for Ladies, Young Men's Guide.* They went into edition after edition, some for fifty years, and still turn up in Chicago's secondhand bookstores.

Just how much of the advice was taken? *The Manners Book* states: "Getting married, please observe, isn't the sole object of society, however important." Other guides inform us: "You may have great trials and perplexities in your business . . . but do not therefore carry to your home a clouded brow. Your wife may have had trials which, though of less magnitude, may have been as hard to bear. A kind, consoling, and tender look, will do wonders in chasing from her brow all clouds of gloom."

"The husband should never cease to be a lover, or fail in any of those delicate attentions and tender expressions of affectionate solicitude that won him his 'heart's queen.' It is not enough that you honor, respect and love your wife. You must put this honor, respect and love into the forms of speech and action."

As for the wife: "Never act contrary to his inclinations. Receive his wishes with attention, and execute them as quickly as possible. Apologize promptly, and in an affectionate manner, if you have allowed yourself to run into an ill-humour."

The man-trap for the unwary male was always set, and some of the publications that advised the young man offered sage advice. "Many a man has foolishly entered upon a flirtation—been drawn into an engagement and compelled to marry against the strongest repulsion. . . . Whole circles of relatives sometimes join to surround a victim, and drive him into the trap set for him . . . if you make a mistake, the moment you suspect it . . . Have no nonsense about it. Apologize . . . express your regrets, make any amends in your power . . . do anything but marry."

In ink, in a book by a Mr. Alcott (*Young Men's Guide*), on one page is written, "To John from his father, May 6, 1876." It is a text for the man who wants a wife who could keep house. The advice is direct and without mercy; as to whom to marry and how to treat her—"never fear the toil to her. Exercise is good for the health. Thousands of ladies who idle away the day, would give half their fortunes for that sound sleep which the stirring housewife seldom fails to enjoy. Overindulged girls play music . . . waste paper and ink in writing long half-romantic letters, or read novels. Servants! For what! To help eat, drink and sleep. . . . Look at her shoes. If they are trodden on one side, loose on the foot, or run down at the heels, it is a sign of the slipshod."

Jane Swisshelm, in *Letters to Country Girls*, advised against imitating the female city grasshopper . . . "hundreds of girls in every large city, who parade the streets in feathers, flowers, silks, and laces, whose hands are soft and white as idleness can make them . . . lounge around reading novels, lisping about fashion . . . thumping some poor hired piano until it groans, and putting on airs to catch husbands, while their mothers are toiling and boiling in the kitchen."

17

DEADLIER THAN THE MALE

Every girl if she only knew it, is sitting on her fortune.
NELL KIMBALL: HER LIFE AS AN AMERICAN MADAM

If the Chicago press in its lingering parochialism was hard on the harlots and the madams (even if the reporters, editors, and publishers might be either customers or owners of the places), there was another kind of press, weekly newspapers, what might be called "for the trade." In the late seventies and eighties, a man named Shang Andrews was a publisher of gossip sheets that under various names were the forerunners of modern columnists of desecrated gossip, like Walter Winchell, Joyce Haber, and others. A few choice samples of Shang Andrews:

> *Chicago Sporting Gazette*, August 4, 1877:
> Whatinell has become of little drunken May Willard?
> Lulu De Vere, the child courtesan, has removed from Goodrich's to the Hotel Costello.
> French Mary, 678 State Street, take a tumble, and don't send to respectable houses for girls, for you know that no ladies board in your low rum shop.

Chicago Street Gazette, September 8, 1877:

Lulu Lee, the little streetwalker, has gone into a house to endeavour and reform herself, but we think it will prove a failure.

Lizzie Allen has put on her fall coat of veneer and varnish, and she is now the finest looking woman in Chicago.

Chicago Street Gazette, September 22, 1877:

Lottie Maynard should not be so fresh with other girls' lovers, or she will hear something to her disadvantage.

The legend that all whores were driven to a life of sin because of poverty, seduction, or brutalizing by ponces dies hard. What can one say of Caroline Victoria, Buffalo, New York, bred from a well-off, normal, middle-class family with all the right moral slogans, and the solid background of folk well aware of their virtues and bourgeois graces? Yet as "Carrie Watson," Caroline Victoria was part of the most vicious depraved life of Chicago, catering to licentiousness, fetishism, the perversity of all desires.

She was eighteen and had claims to virginity when she went to see Lou Harper in 1866, when Madame Harper's Mansion was *the* bordello of Chicago. Carrie made a good house girl when Lou saw the merits in this youngster with a reverence for whoring—and it was soon clear this was another grand madam in the making. For two years Carrie did her best not only to be liked, but well liked. Then her chance came. A certain madam had to leave town over the killing of a policeman on the premises, and Carrie took over the leasehold and the girls at 441 South Clark Street. She changed the beds and furniture and most of the girls for a more susceptible respondence from the best males in town.

She was going out only for the top tony sporting trade, carriage gentry, steady rich guests, wanted nothing to do with just any walk-in trade. She had taken on a lover, Al Smith, a saloon and gambling-house owner. But when the Great Fire spared her house, she bought it and installed a new lover: Sig or Sigmund Cohen was the operator of a fancy gambling house on South Clark Street. Carrie felt adaptability was essential to life—and she adapted to men.

Sig's place was impressive and over it hung a huge sign:

DIAMOND BROKER — OPEN DAY AND NIGHT

Carrie and Sig seemed to be a happy pair, and the *Street Gazette* noted of the lovebirds that Sig "was the happiest sheeny in seventeen states." (People were not yet touchy about ethnic banter.)

In 1873, Carrie and Sig did the brothel over, five parlors for the guests, twenty bedrooms with a hostess in each, exotic enough to bring any normal, lusting male to a panting climax, even a bowling alley in the basement for those having surplus energy to work off. Rugs, paintings, lamps, and fittings were of the best, three musicians played loudly or softly as demanded, silver wine buckets, golden goblets were the rule—ten dollars a bottle for a girl in a heavy chignon—no matter *what* it said on the wine label. There were usually about twenty-five mopsies working for Carrie, well dressed in black lace, fully corseted, in silks. Some claim that Carrie owned a parrot that stood on a stand in the hallway and greeted each guest with, "Carrie Watson's. Come in, gentlemen." Maybe so. But for twenty-five years Carrie's was the place for the rich sports to go down the line, to cavort with the lovely inmates of what was spoken of as "the best place in town." A French visitor wrote home to an uncle, of Carrie, *"une vivandière des faunes."*

Carrie was a clotheshorse and an ambulating jewel case in public, being driven through the city with a select few of her girls in one of her white carriages, four soot-colored horses, well curried, a tall-hatted black coachman handling the reins. Carrie herself, ablaze with diamonds, adjusting the girls' sunshades so as not to ruin their complexions. Sarah Bernhardt is said to have told Carrie, "I have been among the great lovers of my time."

Shang Andrews wrote, "In all the world, there is not another Carrie Watson!" But Carrie has left no written memoirs. She was well liked and admired by many.

Even the reformer William Stead, in his *If Christ came to Chicago*, had a good word for her: "Carrie Watson is a smart woman, said to be liberal in her gifts to the only churches in her neighbourhood, one a Catholic just across the way and the other a Jewish synagogue which local rumor asserts is run rent free owing to Carrie's pious munificence. This is probably a slander, but its circulation is significant as proving that Carrie Watson can be all things to all men."

Another madam who rose from the ranks of *filles de joie* was Ellen Williams who came from Milwaukee, but was known in the flesh trade as "Lizzie Allen" when at eighteen she came to Chicago in 1858, perhaps, like Carrie, a virgin on arrival. Her Vassar was Mother Herrick's Prairie Queen, and soon Lizzie graduated to the Senate. By 1865, she was her own boss in a three-girl parlay on Wells Street. Then she built a fine place on Congress Street, where about thirty beautiful harlots, mostly under eighteen, were always on call, their main assets—perhaps their only ones—were looks, youth, and skill at their work. Old men recalled them years later as dazzling careerists. Unlike most madams, Lizzie for some time avoided a fancy man in her life, but in 1878 a man described by the mayor—a rounder, we fear—as an "imposing looking rooster." The rooster was Christopher Columbus Crabb, who clerked for Marshall Field at the honest salary of fourteen dollars a week.

Crabb left Field's to handle the various parcels of rich real estate Lizzie owned—lots and over a dozen houses. One foiled project was the lovers' proposed building of a twenty-four-room mansion on Lake View Avenue; the police said no to a whorehouse in such a fine residential neighborhood.

The two of them did build, in 1890, a $125,000 house at 2131 South Dearborn Street. That house was to be taken over by the Everleigh sisters who were to make American bordello history and enter the courtesans' Valhalla as running "the most celebrated banging shop in the world."

Lizzie died in 1896, leaving everything to Crabb; some estimated her fortune at one million dollars. When Crabb died at eighty-three, he left a tangible estate of nearly a half million. Lizzie Allen was buried properly in Rosehill Cemetery, and a tombstone was erected, by Crabb it is assumed, with the letters:

PERPETUAL EASE

There is a story that some men who had known her intimately as their favorite houri and odalisque, while high on whiskey from

Bathhouse John's saloon, visited the grave and inscribed on the tombstone:

PERPETUAL ORGASM

No documentary evidence exists of such editing, but it was a favorite story at the Press Club (Elliot Paul).

18

THE GREAT FIRE

I hear the alarm at dead of night,
I hear bells—shouts—I pass the crowd—I run.
WALT WHITMAN

Legends never die. They have a spurious immortality. No matter how often they are refuted, they spring back bigger than life. Mrs. O'Leary's cow did *not* kick over the lantern and so start the Great Chicago Fire. No matter, the general population will always believe in the cow story. It fits their operatic version of life. It all goes back to the O'Leary barn back of the house at 137 De Koven Street on the West Side of Chicago. Here on a Sunday, October 8, 1871, there lived in three rear rooms of the house at that address the family of Patrick O'Leary, laborer, a pick and shovel man, available for anything else that needed muscle. There was his wife, Catherine, and their five children. A bit crowded, one would say. Poverty is compacting. One of the boys would grow up to be "Big Jim" O'Leary, one of the most successful professional gamblers of Chicago. But on this dry, windy night, the rains long, long overdue, young Jim was just one of five, raucous, barefooted kids of a poor Irishman sunk in the fatalistic lethargy that things would not change much.

Besides children, Mrs. O'Leary, a feisty, harassed woman, kept in a two-story shack out back a calf, and five cows which she milked dry every day, peddling the milk from cans with a horse and wagon, also kept in the barn with a lot of loose hay. It was not a neat, inviting neighborhood, given over as it was to many shacks, leaning wooden fences, and the discards of the poor never fully cleaned away: boxes, old lumber, papers, and odds and ends of uncleaned stables—all this rubbish ready for a fire, all as combustible as the oil in the house lamps.

That Sunday evening, one "Peg Leg" Denis Sullivan, a drayman with a wooden leg, came to visit his friends the O'Learys, but found they had turned in and gone to bed, the seven of them in their three small rooms. Mrs. O'Leary had hurt her foot in some way, and it ached. Perhaps it was the weather that made it ache. Not a drop of rain, saints alive, since July 1, and the earth parched by drought, and the newspapers saying the woods up north, in Michigan and Wisconsin, were all afire, so sometimes the soot of the

burning would come as far as the city, also carrying the dirt of the prairies, they too burning. Mr. O'Leary and Sullivan discussed this condition of dryness for a bit. They were simple men and could identify or show interest only with the more spectacular events of their time.

It was about 8:30 P.M. when Sullivan started for home, walking toward Jefferson Street, then stopping to fill a clay pipe, and sitting down on the curb to enjoy a smoke. The suggestion is he and O'Leary may have had a jug of poteen and had a few sips. As he held a match to his tobacco, hiding the flame from a strong rising wind with cupped hands, Peg Leg saw glowing flames coming from the O'Leary barn.

Yelling the cry of "Fire! Fire!" he rushed for the barn and got hold of the calf whose hair was on fire, and which he beat out as he lugged the bawling, struggling animal to safety. Rushing back to get out the other creatures, his wooden leg was trapped between two slats in the board floor. Unstrapping the leg, he hopped out, and he just managed to save himself from the flames, he, singed and smoke-colored, still yelling the alarm.

Soon everyone was up and about in howling exasperation—as the wild wind sped the fire faster than the devil could run. It kept spreading and growing wilder among the alleys and shanties, cottages, barns, and stables. All were dried out by the prolonged drought. Everything burned: the shingles, sap-laden pine boards used every place, the tarred roofs, all fed the flames.

The Fire Department that night was not up to snuff. It was undermanned and had been fighting dangerous daily fires all that hot dry summer, and well into the rainless fall. There were only two hundred firemen in the city, seventeen fire engines and eighteen bits of other apparatus to carry ladders, and the forty-eight thousand feet of hose. Those were the figures on paper. But some hose carts and engines had been put out of action at the recent fires. And one-third of the hose was worthless, worn out or burned out. And never a sign of rain.

The firemen had answered nearly forty alarms that week, and the men were tuckered out. The day before they had fought for fifteen hours against a $750,000 fire on the West Side. Now this hot windy night the thing began badly; the O'Leary fire among the slobbering snouts of singed cows was promptly reported to the watchtower on the Court House. But in the mix-up, the lookout sent out not any of four fire companies that were closest to the fire, but instead alerted one a mile and a half distant. The gale came on steadily from the southwest, as flames spread and the fire engines bumbled around. People began to flee in dishabille, in hastily donned pants and kimonos.

Just after midnight, the fire jumped the Chicago River and entered the South Side, taking over the new eighty-thousand-dollar stables of Frank Paralee's Bus Line, then went on to harry the whores, pimps, and barflies, pickpockets and street robbers out of the dens in Conley's Patch and Shinbone Alley—"bare-assed, half-dressed, you never saw anything like the bitches in tulle and lace and their fancy men running and knocking each other down, grabbing at each other's bundles and yelling like goddamn cats in heat all the time."

Mobs were rushing about elbow to elbow over the West Side bridges and hooting in terror through the tunnels, everyone panting and looking for strayed old folk and lost children. Down before the fire went Gamblers Row, Hair Trigger Block, then, turning, the fire went rampaging through the business district, taking over in red destruction factories, hotels, theaters, public buildings, the newspaper plants, everything in its path; rafters were falling, sparks got in people's hair; in streets already the smell of cooking horseflesh and butchers' steers. And teams sending sparks from iron shoes as they ran in panic along the cobbles, urged on by merciless whipping. Glass shards were underfoot, and now and then some shawl-covered hysterical woman was stomped underfoot. From windows people made distraught, compulsive gestures then hurried to the street.

Early Monday morning the flames were across the main part of the Chicago River into the North Side, sending seventy-five thousand people running, driving for their lives, the flames moving "as fast as a man could run." Nearly fifteen thousand acres were burning out, fourteen thousand buildings going to ash, just under five hundred might be spared—smoked up and charred. Going were the waterworks, the pumping station on Chicago Avenue, lost the new Chicago Historical Society at Ontario and Dearborn. The city was creating more tragic history than it could consume. (Lost was the original draft of the Emancipation Proclamation by Lincoln, but to survive there would be a flask of alcohol containing a tapeworm.)

The *Chicago Post* kept reporters active: "The people were mad . . . they crowded upon frail coigns of vantage . . . fences, high sidewalks, propped on wooden piles which fell beneath their weight."

Looters were everywhere; hoodlums, whores, saloon bums, drifters, footpads went to work in the flames. Saloons, houses were broken into, homes invaded. Carriages, teams of rearing horses and drays were taken over and loaded by pilferers. Drinking began, furniture was dragged through the streets. People smashed windows with their naked hands "regardless of the wounds inflicted, and with bloody fingers rifled till and shelf and cellar, fighting viciously for the spoils of their forage. Women, hollow-eyed and brazen faced, with filthy drapery tied over them, their clothes in tatters and their feet in trodden-over slippers, moved here and there—scolding, stealing, fighting; laughing at the beautiful and splendid crash of walls and falling roofs. . . . Everywhere dust, smoke, flame, heat, thunder of falling walls, crackle of fire, hissing of water, panting of engines, shouts, braying of trumpets, wind, tumult, and uproar.

"The brute creation was crazed. The horses, maddened by heat and noise, and irritated by falling sparks, neighed and screamed with affright and anger, and roared and kicked, and bit each other, or stood with drooping tails and rigid legs, ears laid back and eyes wild with amazement, shivering as if with cold. Dogs ran hither and thither, howling dismally. Great brown rats, with beadlike eyes, were ferreted out from under the sidewalks, by the flames, and scurried down the streets, kicked at, trampled upon, hunted down. Flocks of beautiful pigeons, so plentiful in the city, wheeled up aimlessly, circled blindly, and fell into the raging fire beneath. After midnight, the Court House was on fire, three hundred and fifty prisoners released from the jail, broke into a jewelry store and looted it" (Bronson Scrapbook).

"The terrors aggregated into an intensity of misery, the thieves, amateur and professional, dropped all pretense at concealment and plied their knavish calling undaunted by any fears of immediate retribution. They would storm into stores, smash away at the safes, and if, as happily was almost always the case, they failed to effect an opening, they would turn their attention to securing all of value from the stock that could conveniently be made away with, and then slouch off in search of further booty. The promise of a share in the spoils gave them the assistance of rascally express-drivers, who stood with their wagons before doors of stores, and waited as composedly for a load of stolen property to be piled in as if they were receiving the honestly acquired goods of the best man in town. . . . The scenes of robbery were not confined to the sacking of stores. Burglars would raid into the private dwellings that lay in the track of the coming destruction, and snatch . . . anything which their practical senses told them would be of value. Interference was useless. The scoundrels . . . were inflamed with drink, and were alarmingly demonstrative in the flourishing of deadly weapons. Sometimes women and children, and not infrequently men, would be stopped as they were bearing from their homes objects of especial worth, and the articles would be torn from their grasp" (Bronson Scrapbook).

Wrote a reporter, Alexander Frear, "Dearborn Street as far as the Portland Block was full of people all the distance, swaying and surging under the reign of fire. Around on Lake Street the tumult was worse. Here, for the first time, I beheld scenes of violence that made my blood boil. In front of Shay's magnificent dry goods store a man loaded a store-truck with silk, in defiance of the employes of the store. . . . I saw a ragamuffin on the Clark Street bridge, who had been killed by a marble slab thrown from a window, with white kid gloves on his hands, and whose pockets were stuffed with gold-plated sleeve buttons. On that same bridge I saw an Irishwoman leading a goat that was big with young, while under the other arm she carried a piece of silk. Lake Street was rich with treasures; and hordes of thieves forced their way into the stores and flung out the merchandise to their fellows in the street, who received it without disguise, and fought over it openly. I went through the street to Wabash Avenue, and here the thoroughfare was choked with all manner of goods and people. . . . Valuable oil paintings, books, pet animals, musical instruments, toys, mirrors, and bedding, were trampled under foot. Added to this, the goods from the stores had been hauled out and had taken fire; and the crowd breaking into a liquor establishment, were yelling with the fury of demons, as they brandished champagne and brandy bottles. The brutality and horror of the scene made it sickening. A fellow, standing on a piano, declared that the fire was the friend of the poor man. He wanted everybody to help himself to the best liquor he could get; and continued to yell from the piano until someone as drunk as himself, flung a bottle at him and knocked him off it. In this chaos were hundreds of children, wailing and crying for their parents. One little girl, in particular, I saw, whose golden hair, worn loose on her back, had caught fire. She ran screaming past me, and someone threw a glass of liquor upon her, which flared up and covered her. . . .

"The city was patrolled by two thousand special policemen, four hundred of the regular force, six companies of Illinois militia, four companies of troops of the United States Army, under the command of General Phil Sheridan. He ruled Chicago under martial law. Seven men setting fires were shot, another stoned to death by a mob at Fourteenth Street and Fourth Avenue. A few women firebugs were captured. In some places the fire reached temperatures of 3000° F."

When the Great Fire roared through the city, far-off newspapers had headlines:

CHICAGO IS BURNING UP!

Allan Pinkerton, one of those hired to protect the incinerating city, posted this directive for the treatment of looters.

KILL THESE PEOPLE BY MY ORDER,
NO MERCY SHALL BE SHOWN TO THEM,
BUT DEATH SHALL BE THEIR FATE.
ALLAN PINKERTON—PINKERTON'S POLICE.

Pinkerton, the ruthless, successful defender of property. Protector of railroads, and banks, strikebreaker, with his own goons and killers. Pinkerton was a man of direct action, if the price was right. His forces had been present when Grant was nominated in 1869, at the Crosby Opera House, for the Presidency. "The millionaires of Porkopolis slept better knowing his forces were for hire" (Chicago Historical Society).

(One of the crimes caused by the Great Fire was to be a poem written by Bret Harte:

CHICAGO, THE GREAT CONFLAGRATION

Blackened and bleeding, helpless, panting, prone
On the charred fragments of her shattered throne
Lies she who stood but yesterday alone.

Like her own prairies by some chance seed sown,
Like her own prairies in one brief day grown,
Like her own prairies in one fierce night mown.

(It was Carl Sandburg's opinion that "Harte was drunk when he penned these lines.")

19

THE FIRE CONTINUED

Fireman save my child!
A POPULAR SONG

At midnight the evening the fire started, the mayor, Roswell B. Mason, had sent panicked messages out on the telegraph wires to St. Louis, Milwaukee, Cincinnati, asking to hurry all the fire-fighting equipment they could spare. *Chicago is burning!* Flatcars were loaded with fire-fighting apparatus and freight cars headed for Chicago on open rights-of-way, signal lanterns swaying in the night, switch towers alerted.

The fire had spread as the moon came up, a ghost moon seen through veils of smoke, and there was talk of backfire, or a firebreak of some kind. On the Great Plains, settlements in danger of a roaring grass fire had often saved themselves by setting a counterfire to meet the onrushing one. Why not try the same thing in Chicago?

An alderman, retired, James H. Hildreth, came forward with the suggestion of blowing up buildings facing the major morning blazes. The first try of blasting powder was a failure, as attempts to blow up the Union National Bank merely shattered its windows.

General Sheridan also wanted to try blowing up structures, but an ironic situation developed with singular intensity, it seemed. Hildreth had *all* the gunpowder kegs and the general none at all: a powderless pariah. And Hildreth wouldn't give up any powder to the troops. Why the army in its inadequacy had no gunpowder in its armories was not explained.

All the prisoners in the jails were now free, and acting in most cases "very criminally," all free except some murderers who, in steel handcuffs, were led to the lakefront and told to soak themselves while the city turned into a fiery charnel house.

The Grand Pacific Hotel, just finished, no guests as yet, all six stories of sandstone, its glass-roofed carriage court (and the elevator, called "a vertical railway to connect all floors"), crashed down in flames. Another new hotel about to open, the Bigelow, with its art gallery, Turkey red carpets, carved rare wood furniture, also was consumed. The Tremont House burned for the fourth time in its inflammable history, and the manager, John Drake, left in a hurry, carrying the contents of the safe and some pillowcases full of the hotel's best silver. Drake was not a man to panic. He viewed the world with a basilisk stare.

Drake was also a man who kept his head, so passing the Avenue Hotel on Congress Street, as yet still untouched by fire, he entered and approached the distracted owner-manager with a startling offer to buy the place, right then and there, the whole threatened shebang—holding out one thousand dollars in cash from the Tremont safe as a down payment. The deal was made, a hasty bill of sale and deed written out in the lobby, witnessed by some fleeing guests. Drake picked up his pillowcases of silver and went on toward his house, feeling he had a fifty-fifty chance of having a hotel when the fire was over. (He won—but had to insist on his bill-of-sale rights with a pistol.)

The temperature of the fire was amazing. Cast-iron columns two feet thick were reduced to molten nothing, wheels on streetcars were melted down to the hubs, the tracks turned into agonized steel snakes thrashing about. All once highly held safeguards turned to derisive failures. FIREPROOF was a dirty word.

The word FIREPROOF was never again to be believed in Chicago. "Fireproof" walls and "fireproof safes" lasted a few minutes before being consumed. Oil and paint barrels, buckets of inflamma-ble fluids, grease kegs, firkins of leaf lard, butter kegs, all exploded like a later age's Molotov cocktail. Shay's Dry Goods Store was looted of its huge stock of silk by someone loading Shay's own deliv-ery dray and driving off.

To defy looters, Chapin and Gore's, the high-toned liquor and eating place, hired men to roll several hundred barrels of fine whis-kies, ryes, and bourbons, down to the lakefront. A few dozen barrels didn't make it all the way. Many of the mob were drinking every-

thing that looked alcoholic. Firemen often had to hose down the crowds that fought to get at the free beer and booze. Greed seized some, profiteering took over. Men with wagons and horses were demanding hundreds of dollars to haul records, business material, or household goods to safety. It cost one bank a thousand dollars to get a wagon to carry off a half million in currency to safety.

On the river, the masts and riggings of ships were burning in tarry smells—some of the wooden underpinnings of bridges were beginning to burn. Railroad cars of the Chicago and Northwestern, standing like dun elephants in line in the North Division yards, included hundreds of kerosene tank cars. Suddenly they went up like land mines, sending great gouts of fireballs boiling crimson into the sky. With the waterworks gone, and their pumps, too, the only water available for the fire engines had to come directly from the river, and there was a desperate shortage of hose, and many burst with excruciating regularity.

Among the "fireproof" buildings lost were those of the *Tribune* and McVicker's Theatre. Wabash and Michigan avenues were piled high with household goods, trunks, the contents of hastily emptied stores. Looters moved like grasshoppers over a cornfield, eating away at the piles of furnishings, clothes, bottles, bolts of cloth.

The ball park at the end of Washington and Randolph streets, on the lakefront, was full of refugees looking at the end of their tether—soot-covered, burned in patches, smoldering rags around them. Some with bundles they had been able to grab. Others nearly naked. They sat mostly in shock, children crying, people kneeling, crucifix in hand, others with a bottle to their lips. Some were disobeying the one policeman on duty and burying their silverware and other treasures under the sod of the baseball diamond, the law shouting, "Don't be defacing the playing grounds!"

On the Sands, once holding the dives of the criminals and the prostitutes, all the draggle-tails, blowens, pawky baskets, the gamblers' dens and groggeries, here, too, now many of the well-to-do sat in nightdress, shawls on heads, the nightshirt much in evidence (for the pajama had not yet replaced that decent one-piece garment). People had carried off strange items from their homes: great pier glasses, carved beds in sections, rolls of rare carpeting, files, boxes of family and business papers. Some dragged dogs on leashes, carried birdcages. Sparks still fell and many rare rugs smoldered, burst into flames, and fell away in fragments. People attended to needs of nature where they could. ("Harold held up an Indian blanket and all the children made peepee"—private letter).

By Monday, the numerous lumber mills and wood storage yards on the riverbanks had burned, and many people who were dunking themselves half in the water had to flee again to keep from being asphyxiated by the black, billowing smoke. Some people pushed chairs and sofas into the river and sat with just their heads and shoulders in sight. ("We looked like the damned in Doré's pictures of Dante's *Inferno*"—private letter.) Some folk soaked knee deep in water for over fourteen hours.

Lincoln Park presented a macabre sight. Old graves had been in the process of being emptied, the contents moved. Now in the opened graves and behind stacked gravestones, whole families were sheltered. Sparks fell all the time, and in the waters of the park lagoon, people doused themselves with buckets to keep their garments from burning off their backs. Drowned rats sailed about.

Fireballs advanced before the actual main body of the flames, on the hurricane-heated winds that lifted houses on the North Side and blew them into fragments.

The servants of the rich had been busy burying the contents of the well-filled mansions. Oddly enough, some dozen pianos were buried in gardens. It is hardly imaginable that the great grave needed to bury a concert grand could be dug in a night and then covered over. Several family silver collections—heirlooms—even if buried, melted together into strange masses of silver taffy.

The Chicago Club, the exclusive nest of the rich, "did not expect God would strike his best supporters, and the builders of his churches" (private letter). Members were having a champagne breakfast while the city burned, and they toasted their defiance of the fire to stop Chicago from its potential growth. The fire entered the club just as they lifted their glasses, and the members ran for it, carrying wine bottles of the best years and filling pockets with the fine Havana cigars, not forgetting the club's celebrated red satin lobby sofas, which, a member remembered, were carried in grandiose hurry down to the lake "like the bodies of dead English kings."

Fashionable Terrace Row, Michigan Avenue, from Congress to Van Buren streets, turned to ash. People filled passing carriages and wagons with their household treasures, and often—too trusting of an honest face—never saw them again. Looters began to enter houses hunting clothes—putting on three or four suits, or dresses one over the other. One man, bulky with clothes, topped by a hunting jacket, was sent cheerfully on his way by the owner. "Well, you might as well have them as let them burn." Less generous hosts seized their guns and threatened to blow off heads.

For the records, the last house to burn, just twenty-five hours after the start of the fire in the O'Leary barn, was a doctor's residence on Fullerton Street, breaking into flame at 10:30 P.M. At midnight, a rain began to fall, not heavy but enough to soak the charred ruins, the surviving roofs. By four in the morning, the Great Fire was out, but for glowing pits of cherry red coal in the cellars of houses no longer there.

The Great Fire, as it was called from then on, was to be the most disastrous until the San Francisco earthquake and fire of 1906. Chicago's fire in twenty-four hours took 250 lives, officially, but many more were never reported or their bodies never found. Five hundred dead would be a figure closer to the truth. Three and a half square miles were burned out totally, nearly one hundred thousand people were left without shelter. Seventeen thousand, four hundred and fifty buildings were destroyed. In money value, and the estimate may be too low, losses were believed to run to two hundred million dollars.

The Reverend Granville Moody, in self-righteous sternness, blamed God; the Lord, he preached (as reported), having decided to cremate the city because the vote had gone against closing the saloons on Sunday. "It is retributive judgement on a city that has shown such devotion in its worship of the Golden Calf."

If not Mrs. O'Leary's cow, and if one did not accept God's guilt—in a state of shocked outrage—as the firebrand against Sabbath whiskey and beer, how *did* the fire start in the O'Leary barn? Both adult O'Learys swore affidavits that no member of the family had gone to the barn that night, had not been near it after dusk.

And no lamp had burned in their three rooms when they retired.

A neighbor who lived in the front part of the house swore, as she crossed herself, "Before God as me witness, nobody went out to get the milk."

The most likely origin of the fire was one given years later by "Big Jim" O'Leary, who said the fire was started by some boys he didn't know, smoking pipes and cigars in the hayloft of the barn. Hardly the avenging angels of the Lord in a time when God protested more the defiling of His commandments.

For some citizens, the material loss took precedence over the human loss. Others revealed their pathetic heartbreak. Whatever newspapers could be hastily put together and printed ran such items as: *Henry Schneider, baby, in blue poland waist, red skirt, has white hair. LOST.*

James E. McLean, head of the Customs House, found that his U.S. government vault was not fireproof, and a million and a half dollars were gone to ash. Congress had to pass a special act to prevent this sum being taken out of McLean's salary.

(Some student figured out the Chicago Fire burned out areas twice as big as the Great Fire of London in the reign of Charles II, and the Moscow burnings during Napoleon's invasion, put together.)

Five thousand special Chicago police were sworn in to prevent looting, but some of them joined in picking up what they could, unable to resist unsublimated greed. There was no supply of metal police badges on hand, so they wore a bit of white cloth that a boys' press had imprinted with the one word, POLICE.

The sale of whiskey was forbidden as the fire died down (but there were enough bottles and kegs undamaged in the ruins to keep those who wanted to stay drunk until delirium tremens came). Bread prices were fixed, and army tents were set up to house burned-out families. Crushing paroxysms of despair began to lift; life-affirming impulses took over. Help came in special trains from all over the nation's big cities. Help came, *except* from Atlanta, where a newspaper editor, with nauseating cant in print, brought back the tune of "Marching Through Georgia." When an appeal went out to that state for aid, he wrote: "We owe it—some of my friends and I—to the implacable temper of Chicago troops during the war, that we are now exiles, impoverished and struggling . . .

without a single heirloom sacred to our past affection spared us . . .
a Chicago soldier tossed into the flames the likeness of my mother."

General Sheridan, who hadn't marched through Georgia, declared martial law in Chicago when the mayor asked him to. The
governor, John Palmer, as one letter writer put it, was "a jackass
who put his pride of office above human needs," objected to the
mayor calling out the army; *that* was the state's right. But in the
end, all protocol and moral imbecility were observed, tempers
calmed. Citizens began resettling in the ruins, one real-estate man
putting up a sign:

W. D. KERFOOT
ALL GONE EXCEPT WIFE, CHILDREN AND ENERGY.

Soon nearly six thousand temporary structures were doing all
kinds of business, from sowbelly to reclaimed bricks, and plans went
ahead to build ten thousand buildings at the cost of forty-six million
dollars. Whiskey peddlers, gamblers, brothel madams were not slow
to join the boom: 2218 saloon licenses were issued in a hurry. John
J. Flinn, in his history of the Chicago police, recorded that more
than food and clothing were rushing toward the damaged city in a
convergence of human vultures. "Every train load of strangers contained a large percentage of disreputable characters. Gamblers,
bunko-steerers, confidence men, sharpers, and criminals of every
description arrived in shoals."

It was soon clear something had to be done against a renewed
crime wave, and early in 1872 a Committee of Seventy was organized to put down crime *and* get laws to keep the city from being stolen by the politicians fattening on the rebuilding. In the end, the
dry bigots who wanted to close saloons and stop people drinking
grew very vocal; "their reform idea was that if the saloons were
empty on Sunday, God in radiant confidence would be in his
heaven, all would be right with Chicago" (private letter).

In September, sixty-two businessmen, led by the head of the
German Savings Bank, Henry C. Greenbaum, issued a call to a
mass meeting. "Never was there a time in the history of Chicago
when there was less security for person and property than now. . . .
One jostles the elbow of a murderer at every angle of the street, and
yet the law seems powerless to bring the evil-doers to justice. The

police are weak and their leaders inefficient; juries are uncertain
. . . not always incorruptible. . . . There is hardly a day but that
the body of some victim is lifted dripping from the river, his gaping
wounds like those of poor murdered Duncan, having each a tongue
that calls out loudly for revenge. . . . The sad recurrence of cold-
blooded murders in our midst cannot longer be allowed to pass un-
noticed by our citizens. The people of Chicago must demand that
murderers shall be hanged" (newspaper report).

The meeting was held at the Board of Trade Hall on September 12; several hundred prominent folk came, cheered Henry
Greenbaum's idea, "There should be no prison sentences for murderers. The only way to protect society against such criminals is to
hang them." A Committee of Twenty-five was appointed to aid
"the prompt arrest, speedy trial, and sure punishment of criminals."
It reported that "unfortunately the city is infested by a very large
number of professional thieves, burglars, gamblers, prostitutes and
roughs. Chicago, great in everything, has seemed to offer an alluring field for those gentry to come to ply their vocations and revel in
their coarse appetites."

However, again the dry forces felt the only true solution was *no
Sunday drinking,* and it was clear to Mr. Greenbaum (a drinker of
beer and Rhine wines) the whole reform movement was a waste of
time in any fight against crime. He resigned and went to a German
beer garden to forget. The owner of the *Tribune,* Joseph Medill,
holding the mayor's seat at that time, felt the pressure of the fanatics and did order the closing of Chicago's three thousand saloons on
Sunday. But the rapacious criminal element did not get the message; crime continued as before.

In the next election, the temperance groups marched into saloons, flopped to their knees, offering messages to God to let Him
help saloon owners and barmen to see the light. One wit suggested
"He could have turned the beer and hooch to drinking water, but
missed the chance." The drys lost the election, and the City Council
at once signed the ordinance reopening the saloons to drinkers on
Sunday. Mayor Medill resigned his term of office after only six
months, offering a muttered "plague on both your houses."

So passed in prurient vituperation the hopes of any serious reforming of the city after the Great Fire.

20

STYLES OF SPENDING

No young man is rich enough to smoke twenty-five-cent cigars.
GUSTAVUS SWIFT, MEAT-PACKER, IN A PRESS INTERVIEW

It was always open season for taking a crack at Chicago. In 1865 *Leslie's Weekly* found the city full of "broken down adventurers, real estate sharks, fast men . . . fast bags . . . Every man owes five times the amount he can pay and is considered a 'poor cuss' if his collateral don't [*sic*] foot up to a hundred thousand. . . . Everyone from your bootblack to your hack driver . . . puts on real estate airs." Up to 1900, visitors who wrote about the city commented on the fancy hats and garish gowns of the *nymphes du pavé* from the best bordellos, on the promenade with their fancy men on their arm, often flash gamblers from a "high-toned game."

For a more respectable gratification, there was an almost yearly event, "The Final Farewell Concert" of Ole Bull, the famous Norwegian violinist. He had begun the habit of final *finals* in 1855, returned for "one farewell concert" in 1857, "a positive farewell," and then "one last" concert in 1868, 1869, 1872, 1877. Buffalo Bill, with his Wild West Show, also kept making his "last appearance" in Chicago, from time to time. It had no disquieting effect on the box office. "It's hard to say good-bye to Chicago" (Al Jolson).

There was wild dancing, obscene indecent dancing in the dives of Chicago; however, for the polite, well-off families, the Bournique Dancing School was the place for one's children and for oneself to learn in tranquillity the ambiguities of the schottische, waltz, polka, and the Chicago quadrille named "The Prairie Queen."

The real society went in for matched bays, specially built carriages, high-stepping chestnut trotters, Morgan reds that hinted at having Arab bloodlines, all in silver mounted harness. An English coachman was a must; anybody could have "a darkie in livery or a mick," wrote one society matron, "but to be accepted as the ton, by one's Cockney coachman, was a sign of approval almost as great as kissing a Cardinal's ring." Many a "Ruggles of Red Gap" coachman, groom, or butler had an affair with the lady of the house, to hear the gossips tell it.

As the sports of a later age graduated to Stutz Black Hawks, Pierce-Arrows, Cadillacs, to Duesenbergs, to Porsches, so the knowing Chicagoan of the century's turn got flashier horses, more expensive rigs, tallyhos, drags, gigs, with the best of the Boston Club or Calumet Club families on deck. Or there were victorias, phaetons, hansoms to carry off an actress, a dancer, a mistress. One of the McCormicks caused a sensation with a pair of splendid roans and a London-built drag. Potter Palmer carried off the real honors in horseflesh and wheels with his French char-a-banc and its leopard-skin upholstered seats.

Potter Palmer, fastidious, pernickety, always a social presence, was amazing Chicago's elite. He had retired as a millionaire when he sold out Palmer's Dry Goods to Marshall Field and his friends. Sensibilities alerted to the city's needs, he had built the first Palmer House, the one before the Great Fire, and in 1871 he decided to marry, and so had reserved the bridal suite at his own grand hotel. He was forty-four and an audacious businessman. He had bought a million dollars' worth of lots on State Street to build his hotel in the center of it. He had had a career of sporting life as playboy and spender, private dinners, champagne, gay ladies in feathered hats, and morals as loose as their lacy garters.

Palmer was Quaker born, but he had tasted of life beyond the gray goodness of his forefathers. He was seen driving down respectable streets in his gig, tall hat akimbo, boisterous, *and* beside him a public wench!

The bride he picked was a "peacherino," as the sporting crowd's limited vocabulary admitted. Bertha Honore was twenty-one, "Kentucky bred out of an aristocratic family," which term fitted almost any white girl in the South who didn't have to do the family dishes. But the Honores showed Chicago they were tediously society. The July wedding saw the bride in a fabulous Paris gown, rose point lace and white satin, orange blossoms as decoration.

Seven hundred guests were present for the reception of the couple, with the usual splendid Kinsley catering. ("Who could forget his woodcock flambée à la riche?") No cut glass, but *everything* of sterling silver.

The groom gave his bride his biggest asset, the Palmer House. It burned down a little later in the Great Fire. Mr. Palmer lost nearly a hundred buildings in the blaze and $220,000 in rents. He was so strapped, he couldn't even pay $15,000 in land taxes for the burned-out lots. However, neither exhausted nor decrepit, Potter moved quickly; with no true collateral, an insurance company lent him $1,700,000. Soon after the Great Fire the new Palmer House was there, built in 1875, even grander than the first. Costs ran so high that Palmer refused to let his bookkeeper show him the accounts. He ordered the magnums and jeroboams of wine for the opening. He, himself, liked a Krug's Private Curee.

Mrs. Potter Palmer, of limpid sweetness and wise eyes, firmly held the reins handed her as a driver of the city's society. The new hotel finished, she arranged a marriage for her sister Ida to the son of President Grant, Frederick Dent Grant, a dullard and a man whose entire life consisted of being the general's son. But he was the catch of the season—a David Eisenhower—and the general was there with his wife. The President was spruced up, fairly sober, and turning from the truffled foie gras to greet the wine. Mr. Palmer was in a gray topper, gray gloves, one huge pearl in a gray cravat. Mrs. Palmer wore an anthology of jewels. Diamonds and pearls mostly. Pink tea roses were in her hair, her gray flared gown set off with a trimming of Chinese red. It was an age not yet hostile to the individual—one could dress up.

The Palmers had brought along to the wedding their firstborn, the heir, little Honore, going on eight months, to watch the event lying on a satin pillow, wetting a little dress with a three-yard train. The bride's costume—sister Ida's—was white satin d'orange and had underneath, as one newspaper reported it, "a corset of the same satin made to order with one hundred whalebones in it." Of her trousseau, mention was made of lavender foulard matching underwear and stockings catalogued as for *opera, carriage, reception, morning, evening*. "Nothing for *bed* or cleaning the house . . . ," one catty guest wrote.

The groom, Lieutenant Grant, came driving four army mules

in special harness, silver snaffle reins, blackened hooves, attached to an open wagon. Everybody said it was a jolly joke; his father took a drink, not being susceptible to sophisticated jests.

Mrs. Palmer was for women's rights, given to some doctrinaire idealism, but added, "One hears so much about the new woman, that one is in danger of being bored by her unless she arrives quickly." Mr. Palmer bored easily. She wrote, "The fact of sex in women, instead of being fixed and unalterable, seems to have been a variable condition." In the matter of dress she was ahead of her era—she said to women, "The more you put on, sometimes, the worse you look, and the more you take off, the better you look."

The burlesque queens downtown, when they heard this, agreed.

It is too bad she didn't follow this philosophy when Mr. Palmer planned a house for them in 1882. It turned into a garish Rhine River *schloss* of brownstone—overripe with minarets, towers, and turrets, strung with balconies. It had some grotesque features. There were *no* outside locks or doorknobs. An always-present servant from inside could let an expected visitor in. Visitors to the Palmers were rigidly by appointment only, in writing. And if one can believe a newspaper story, one's card had to pass through the gloved hands of twenty-seven servants, butlers to maids, to social secretaries, to reach the heads of the house. It reads more like a charade masque than life itself.

There were two private elevators and rooms "done" in French, Spanish, Japanese, Greek (ancient). Mention is made that Mrs. Palmer slept in "a Louis XVI bed ten feet high." As no mention is made of Mr. Potter, one clubman wondered if (states a private letter) "poor Potter had to send in his card through the twenty-seven hired hands, to get laid."

At her parties, Mrs. Palmer was ravishing, of "stunning carriage, the smooth pink and white skin, the perfect teeth, wonderful hair . . . and the sumptuous way in which she conducts her menage" (newspaper report). Her formal dinners of fifty saw her wearing her thirty-thousand-dollar dog collar of seven huge diamonds and 2,268 pearls. She received her guests standing—as if for a posthumous portrait (by Sargent)—before her collection of Corots, Degas, Monets, and some painters now better forgotten. She was an early buyer of French Impressionism and had enough Monets to panel her ballroom nearly solid. Mr. Potter, besides not sharing the great bed—and with an immunity of the *outré* art world—hardly ever was at the parties, locking himself away in one of the towers with a racing form—his idea of fun was fast horses to bet on, and making money.

Mrs. Palmer put their son Honore—when grown—up for the post of alderman for the Twenty-first Ward. She had him photographed at the Palmer House in a waiter's uniform, carrying a tray. Every saloon and restaurant worker in his district cheered their fellow worker. The same crowd of barflies and packinghouse hands, four hundred, were invited to the Palmer castle for music, drink, and food. Mrs. Palmer shook every rough red hand from skid row, flophouse, barroom, gambling house, laborers' cold-water flat.

Honore was elected twice, caused no scandals, ruffled no ponds, offended no one, and sponsored no great reforms.

His mother once gave a reception for Honore and his wife, in Paris, hiring the Russian ballet for the event. She gave charity balls in Chicago, and the *Tribune* reporter with an attack of grandeur wrote, "what rich city of the antique world . . . could have shown an assemblage of burghers rivaling in gold power and gold necromancy, the achievements of these decorous merchants?" Some of those merchants were not so decorous when later that night they carried their surplus energies to the luxury brothels and private intimate dining rooms around town. For during the 1880s when Mrs. Palmer was giving elegant balls, so were the ward heelers Bathhouse John Coughlin and Hinky Dink Michael Kenna.

Of the First Ward Ball, the *Tribune* wrote that "if a great disaster had fallen on the Coliseum Ballroom there would not have been a second story worker, a dip or pug ugly, porch climber, dope fiend, or scarlet woman remaining in Chicago." There were two bands, two hundred waiters, one hundred police, seventy-eight kegs of beer—besides thirty-five thousand quarts of beer and ten thousand quarts of champagne. One hundred pug uglies kept order or broke noses. Hinky Dink surveyed it all proudly. "It's far ahead of anything I ever saw in Paris . . . nothing like it in the world."

When some bluenoses complained the First Ward Balls were

orgies, Bathhouse John announced, "All right, so we'll compromise. We won't let the parents bring their kids."

He also wrote a verse, suggesting some rules of order no one obeyed:

> *On with the dance*
> *Let the orgy be perfectly proper*
> *Don't drink, smoke or spit on the floor*
> *And keep yer eye on the copper.*

There never was again a social queen in Chicago like Mrs. Potter Palmer. Bertha Honore Palmer, well into the 1890s, firmly watched over her demesne, her famous pearl dog collar holding her head up proudly. Her most successful coup was at the Palmer Wyoming ranch, playing hostess to the visiting hedonist, the Prince of Wales (the sinful, portly Edward VII to be).

Later, there was the social disaster at the Palmers' when a famous railroad king, invited for a stay, showed up escorting the notorious Mattie Silk, the most beautiful madam of Denver's fancy brothel. Mattie and Mrs. Palmer did not strike up an enduring friendship. Mattie Silk was quoted later (by Ben Hecht) about the love journey into society with the railroad man. "I showed those . . . society dames I was as good as any of 'em. But not one of 'em could of made the grade as a boarder [whore] in *my* parlor house."

The shock of Mrs. Palmer's life was discovering a brewery using her regal photograph on their popular saloon calendars advertising their brew. She protested violently, but found there was no statute in the state against this invasion and use of her name and features. The *Western Brewer*, bible of the beer set, commenting on her protests, wrote that Mrs. Palmer was no private citizen, and her face and name were a national public resource. "Greatness," it concluded, "is a death to privacy." (Mrs. Palmer did not live to see in print and pictures the wife of her great-great-grandson posing with a cigarette to endorse a brand called Camels.)

The Prince of Wales, besides meeting Mrs. Palmer, also shook the mighty hand of John L. Sullivan, champion heavyweight boxer of the world.

21

THE AFFAIRS OF MRS. CARTER

O sigh not so! O sigh not so!
For it sounds of Eve's sweet pippin,
But these loosen'd lips you have tasted the pips
And fought in an amorous nipping.
ANON.

One exists with one's husband
One lives with one's lover.
HONORÉ DE BALZAC, THE PSYCHOLOGY OF MARRIAGE

Certainly if any woman seemed to take the advice of Balzac, it was
Mrs. Leslie Carter, whose later life as an actress also had its bizarre
moments. She made one of Chicago's "best" marriages and also created one of the city's most amazing and shocking courtroom trials
in 1889, when Mr. Carter, after much forbearance, compassion, humility, named five men as corespondents in his countersuit for divorce.

She was born Caroline Louise Dudley in Kentucky; she insisted her mama "was a daughter of Southern aristocracy" (which
could have meant anyone with an outlaw mountain distillery, or
owner of his own horse). Daddy was a British businessman, who, it
was suspected, was a remittance man, paid to stay away from England. But this may have been gossip and her background truly
proper and highborn, for Caroline's father ended his life "with a position with the Standard Oil Company." Just what the position was
is a bit foggy. But when they had money, the family hired tutors

and maids; when Mr. Dudley died, there was nothing left, so Mama and Caroline went to Chicago to find rich husbands.

Caroline was a beautiful girl, and a reporter later wrote of her as having "hair . . . the color of an August stubble field and her lips red and inviting." Another journalist admitted she was "a decidedly attractive woman of the blonde type . . . her poses have a languorous sentimental air and her face suggests an ardent temperament rather than a weak will."

As George Ade at the bar of the Press Club was later to speak of the reporting, "They certainly weren't describing just a pound of round steak."

The willing victim, as described in a letter, was "as innocent as an atheist Bishop," was Leslie Carter, one of the great marital catches of the 1880s, a man set with congruity and money in the best of Chicago's society, president of the Chicago Dock Company, and having served as president of both the highly esteemed St. Luke's Hospital and the Chamber of Commerce. Some said he already showed signs of the wearisome burden of mortality.

Mr. Carter met Caroline at a party and became emotionally unhinged—a wedding followed in the proper time. The Carters didn't live together very much. It was soon clear to the town that Mrs. Carter loved traveling in Europe, and, when back in this country, preferred the more socially prominent East with its subtlety and complexity beyond Chicago's efforts. However, she continued spending as if Mr. Carter had an orchard of money trees. He was obviously a man of bland benevolence who was willing to ruin himself for his beautiful, headstrong wife. He proceeded to mortgage his holdings to meet the bills Mrs. Carter ran up among the folk of the *Almanach de Gotha* and Newport dudes. Philistine interest became keen when Chicago saw it announced that Mrs. Leslie Carter was suing Mr. Carter for divorce with charges "too sensational to be printed."

Mr. Carter came awake, and aware he had been living a shocking dream. He filed a countersuit for divorce, charging adultery. The first day in court was mainly devoted by the press to describing the color of Mrs. Carter's hair and the details of her costume. The hair fetishists had a field day. "Pale auburn, a breath of autumn sunset, neither yellow nor red . . ." Another found her hair, "golden as the dandelions which dot the meadows . . . not blonde . . . it was yellow as a sunflower, yellow as a buttercup, yellow as yellow." One reporter wrote that "a silver scent bottle hung from her swelling bosom . . . in case she was to faint."

The *Tribune* reporter (it may have been a woman) went into chic costume details, saying Mrs. Carter wore "a rich, tight walking suit of black that showed her mature figure to excellent advantage. . . . One feature alone detracted from the beauty of the fair com-

plainant—the mouth with its red, strawberry-like lips looked too coarse for the fairer emotions."

Emotions, exotic and erotic, certainly had animated that mouth, for as the jury took its seats, the lawyers for Mr. Carter informed the court they would name the five male corespondents with whom this wife had been sexually intimate in many beds in many places. The lawyers made clear they only had to prove *one* little case of infidelity, even if they had a half-dozen fornications in reserve—and could have had more by taking "depositions of a number of gentlemen in Europe." But the injured husband had decided merely to "avail himself of her infidelity on *this* side of the ocean, which was ample." Wrote one Chicago lady to an aunt in Newport, "Mr. Carter seemed to have decided to keep her copulating American."

The lawyers for Mr. Carter carefully named the gentlemen (no low-class sexual intercourse was listed) and also the times of the adulterous games. 1. *D. S. Gregory* was witnessed kissing Mrs. Carter in a rose garden at a Cooperstown, New York, hotel, and being doused by a chambermaid with a pitcher of cold water, the way one separates amorous dogs. The hotel was named as the trysting place. 2. *Senator James F. Pierce* of New York, who wrote poems of sensibility and love to Mrs. Carter, and at three o'clock one morning had been observed going to her room, shoes in hand, at Cooper House. 3. *Dr. J. B. Gilbert,* who made *very* late night calls on Mrs. Carter in her rooms, and witnesses were able to swear as to the exotic dialogue and pleasantries, and lovemaking audible to listeners. Mrs. Carter, with calm dignity, maintained that "the doctor acted like a gentleman." 4. *Kyrle Bellew,* actor, who gave her dramatic lessons, twenty-five dollars each, had a room adjoining hers at the Colonnade Hotel, New York. They had also been observed often—in the exaltation of mutual admiration—at Delmonico's, purring like lovers over the entrées and the wine. 5. *William K. Constable,* who provided Mrs. Carter with forty-five thousand dollars for a trip to Europe, an amazing sum at a time when a splendid meal cost a dollar and the best hotels, with sturgeon and truffles and cockscombs added, charged rates comparable to a second-rate motel of today.

Theater agents were present in court to offer Mrs. Carter a contract. She took the stand in her own defense, as if to audition.

Naturally, she denied any indiscretions at all, and a *Tribune* headline asked, "Was the woman lying?" The drama set in when Mr. Carter's lawyers came to the charges she had made against him, that disreputable item "too sensational to be printed." America in 1889, the year of the trial, was not yet ready for freedom of language. The Anglo-Saxon four-letter word, or even its equivalent in *Latin*, certainly had not appeared in public print. A poor baffled reporter could only retreat into fancy prose, saying, "Mr. Carter's lawyer working over the witness, hovering awhile around the edges of the cesspool which furnished Mrs. Carter's cause of complaint. Mr. Carter's lawyer made a dive into it, dragging the witness with him, and for a while there was in the room the oppressive atmosphere of Phallic rites and other bestialities."

In the private notebook of one old Chicago lawyer—permission to quote refused—there are lines that indicate what caused all the horror: Mr. Carter, perhaps in failure of potency, indulged in oral-genital acts, and induced, or, as she claimed, forced her to perform the same on his *penis erectus*.

Why this shocked our grandparents enough to avoid seeing it plainly put down in print is hard to understand in this more permissive but ambiguous age. What the press called "unnatural acts" were easily available only a few blocks from the Chicago courtroom at prices ranging from ten cents to a dollar. (A family doctor, whose practice was among the upper middle class of Chicago, wrote in his day book [now in a private erotic collection], "It's hard to believe the well-dressed smiling people I met at fetes and gatherings, do in private confess to me some of the most outrageous bed habits that only match some of the saturnalia of certain Greek and Roman writers like Petronius." Also in this private day book are the lines: *Cunnilingus, one who licks the vulva . . . Fellatio, from Latin fellatus, to suck.*)

However, Mrs. Carter on the stand could not be so frank. The lawyers for her husband wanted a direct answer, *yes* or *no*. Had there been what she claimed in her charges, had such things taken place, *yes* or *no?* She could not make a positive statement in court—for if she said *yes*, she would appear a sinful woman for not crying out when the unnatural acts first took place, for waiting perhaps years to bring them to court. If she fully denied such acts, her whole case of divorce would fall in ignominious defeat.

Mrs. Carter managed to avoid any direct *yes* or *no* answer, and the cross-examining got no place. The trial moved into its first weeks, attracting crowds, being the best show in town. Bailiffs barred the doors to the mob, but took folded bills from some, to permit entrance to a few saved seats. The press reported on flashy young men known in common parlance as dudes, hinting such were Mrs. Carter's habitually depraved partners.

Victorian morality caused Judge Egbert Jamieson to limit the audience to a hand-picked thirty-five and, cried the *Tribune*, "excluding most of the ladies . . . for press and witnesses and clerks took up most of the available seats." The judge also took notice vocally of the number of "graybeards and baldheads among the spectators. . . . We have no desire to take the place of the departed Gaiety Burlesque Company. An old curiosity monger is quite as reprehensible as a young curiosity monger." The chief bailiff, a notorious bribe taker and tip grabber, added, "We must check the spread of immorality among the old and decrepit." Which statement seems cruelly to deprive these male relics of sensuality of their last raunchy kicks.

The trial went on for five weeks, while the travels and games of Mrs. Carter were traced in great detail. All the men named as in active adultery with her came as witnesses—all but Mr. Constable, who had given her the forty-five thousand dollars. It was announced by *Mrs.* Constable that her husband was just "too ill to travel."

The actor, Kyrle Bellew, was appearing as Mark Antony in Shakespeare's *Antony and Cleopatra* at the McVicker's Theatre in town. On the witness stand, his most forward testimony consisted of the information, "Mrs. Carter has some talent for a comedienne . . . with some development she should . . . show talent for high comedy." His attentions to Mrs. Carter, he said, were pure; merely professional. Dr. Gilbert, too, used the word professional for his loud, late-hour visits to Mrs. Carter's rooms. It was blasphemous to think that he, a medical man on a late call, would—

The jury of this *cause célèbre* took twelve hours to deliberate. As with the habit of most juries, free hotel meals may have prolonged the proceedings as to a verdict. They found Mrs. Carter and Kyrle Bellew guilty. (In the theater, Bellew had been hissed for a whole week.) Mr. Carter was acquitted of "Phallic rites and bestialities" and granted his divorce. Mrs. Carter was not in the courtroom when the verdict came in. She was found by the press, weeping in her hotel room, looking divine, every lock of hair (red or yellow) in place.

There was nothing now for her but fame. She went to New York and got an introduction to the great fraud and ham, David Belasco. He asked her if she would like to "appear in comedy or tragedy"?

Mrs. Carter gave him the smile of those crimson lips. "I am a horsewoman and wish to make my first entrance on a horse, leaping a fence." She failed to impress him, or he to find a saddle part like that, but later he admitted he fell for her "bizarre and alluring appearance . . . copious and resplendent hair." And as she told her story, he felt there might be "possibilities in her—if she could only act on the stage with the same force and pathos she used in telling her story." All this took time; meanwhile it wasn't easy for her—she was down to twenty-five-cent "table d'hote on Fourth Avenue," and Charles Frohman, another producer, fearing horrible indignities, made it clear: "Stockholders request me *not* to have Mrs. Carter use our stage." The manager of Hooley's Theatre in her hometown of Chicago came out in the open: "This is the most famous fashionable theatre in Chicago. Mrs. Carter is not wanted here . . . we cannot afford to make enemies." ("Chorus boys and rich homosexual Chicago businessmen kissed backstage at Hooley's." Ben Hecht to the author.)

Belasco, whatever his faults as an artist, was a showman, and he soon saw Mrs. Carter's merits—her charisma. He made her a star, so, he said, the name "Mrs. Leslie Carter was on every billboard and fence post in the country." Belasco had written a melodrama, *The Heart of Maryland*, for her, and stardom came to Mrs. Carter with that exciting bit of Civil War hokum. Glory followed as she appeared in *Zaza* and *Du Barry*. A critic in Chicago said that on the stage there was nothing artificial about her acting which might be suggestive "to those who were familiar with her more uncouth endeavours."

Of her success across the country—very couth—she said she was delighted, "especially when the tour takes me to Chicago." She was rubbing the town's nose in the lobbies of her packed theaters. She filled the need of the American middle class to sin secondhand.

What of Mr. Carter, whose last name was on the billboards, whose obsessive desire had, if true, delighted and shocked the nation for five weeks in a courtroom? His ending is out of the novel *Sister Carrie*, the defeated male who goes down, down. Mr. Carter lost the rest of his fortune; his lawyers saw to part of that by their huge fees. His mind began to wander, and like the character Hurstwood in Dreiser's novel, he turned on the gas in a kitchen stove, put his head in, and so ended a mixed-up life, the truth hidden too long until it could not be endured.

Dreiser knew Chicago history and scandal, and his Sister Carrie, like Mrs. Carter, became an actress, pursuing her amoral life "with as much success as attended any other human proceedings."

22

VISITORS

Chicago has the best bifstiks.
SARAH BERNHARDT, IN NEWSPAPER ITEM

Better actresses than Mrs. Carter came to Chicago. Sarah Bernhardt, near the turn of the century, took the city with her vitality
and genius. She had a suite at the Palmer House and used a five-
glass landau to drive her in regal style to the theater. Her problem
was that she was being used for publicity purposes by a smart Yankee named Henry Smith who had a dead pickled whale on tour.
Sarah had foolishly accepted a whalebone from the creature "for
her corset." Yankee Smith at once put his whale on tour in every
city the Divine Sarah played—meeting her in the Chicago railroad
station—advertising the whale in spite of her rapid and foul French
curses at him in public. His Chicago posters read:

COME AND SEE
THE ENORMOUS CRETACEAN
WHICH SARAH BERNHARDT KILLED
BY TEARING OUT ITS WHALEBONE FOR HER CORSETS.

She also had her own opinion of the Chicago female. "Women here, as everywhere else in America, do not work, but they do stroll about in the streets . . . they walk quickly; they are also in a hurry to seek amusement." Of their partners, she wrote, "The men pass each other without stopping, with knitted brows . . . the desire of success awaits them."

Early frontier habits died hard in Chicago. Like the rest of the nation, it was unaware how primitive it looked to visitors from Europe. Chewing tobacco was a male delight, wrote Charles Dickens in *American Notes* (1842). "I was surprised to observe that even steady old chewers of great experience, are not always good marksmen, which has rather inclined me to doubt that general proficiency with the rifle, of which we have heard so much in England. Several gentlemen called on me who, in the course of conversation, frequently missed the spittoon at five paces; and one (but he was certainly short-sighted) mistook the closed sash for the open window at three."

Another mid-nineteenth-century English visitor remarked that "The manners of the first-rate merchants . . . are not at all inferior to those of Liverpool or any other of our great commercial cities. First-rate merchants and lawyers compose a very small part of the population. Beyond that there is a sad change for the worse."

Mrs. Trollope described the men at table with her: "The frightful manner of feeding with their knives, till the whole blade seemed to enter the mouth, and still more frightful manner of cleaning the teeth afterwards with a pocket knife."

Thomas Hamilton, another Englishman on the scene at meal-time: "It would be difficult to find a parallel beyond the limits of the Zoological Gardens. Men didn't eat—they devoured, under the uncontrollable impulse of some sudden hurricane of appetite."

As soon as Chicago began to grow, there was advice on how to raise the new generation that would inherit a great city someday. And how to improve the fathers' and husbands' general appearance. The *American Gentleman's Guide* (1867) was against "long hair straggling in uncombed and unkempt masses over the coat collar. A miserable imitation . . . of the flowing hair that in days of yore fell naturally and gracefully upon the broad lace collar . . . of the cavaliers. . . . The close cropped hair of the thorough Englishman was just preparation for a strait-jacket."

The Gentleman's Guide to Politeness and Fashion (1857) vetoed "beard and moustache arrangements, Ram's horns or roped curls." *Illustrated Manners* was for beards. "Who would think of a close shaven Jupiter or Hercules? The gods and heroes wear beards." Said *Social Customs*, "Parents who bring up their children well and carefully . . . deserve the gratitude of the State, as well as that of their offspring."

Picked at random, here are some items: "What has caused such a terrible epidemic of crime in our midst? . . . Parents concentrating on riches and the pursuits of fashion, while their children are left to hirelings.

"Defaulting bank cashiers . . . and an army of embezzlers had proved to be young people, astray for want of proper training. . . . Many a boy has been ruined . . . from being allowed to associate with vulgar, unrefined and vicious men employed about his father's premises and warehouses."

America's little girls were spoiled darlings, "A rosebud set with little wilful thorns. . . . If a mother allows her children to associate chiefly with those of low origin and manners, she cannot think that they will not be influenced by them."

Yet for all its claims to social graces, Chicago, in his hurried visit, irked mandarin Henry James, nor did the nation please him as he jotted down some notes: "Oh, yes, the United States—a country without a sovereign, without a court, without a nobility, without an army, without a church or a clergy, without a diplomatic service, without a picturesque peasantry, without palaces and castles . . . no museums, no pictures, country seats, or ruins, without a literature, without novels, without an Oxford or a Cambridge, without cathedrals or ivied churches, without latticed cottages or village ale houses, without polite society, without sport, without fox hunting or country gentlemen, without an Epsom or an Ascot, an Eton or a Rugby." One can almost see him, in ominous irrationality, writing furiously among his teacups and walking canes.

Yet it was all there in Chicago to see, if James had looked for it or had been more observant: kings like Mark Hanna and Marshall Field, soldiers who had fought a fearful and long civil war. As for a picturesque "peasantry," had he gone to see them—the European peasants in Swift's and Armour's slaughtering plants—hacking for

the roast beef and the grilled chops that Henry James himself favored? The Great Fire had left grand ruins, for a time, and as for
palaces and castles, there were scores of them around the best lakefront Chicago streets, and with plumbing and steam heat, too. No
museums, no paintings? Yerkes, the Potters, the Fields took great
pride in the private museums and their old masters, preserved behind dark varnish, some not yet dry. They hunted foxes near Lake
Forest, and sometimes ran to earth a raccoon. As for dignitaries and
protocol, the Chicago Club, the opera, the horse show were class,
"not just classy."

And had not some Chicago boys been on the football team at
Rutgers that beat Princeton in the first of all intercollege games of
that sport? Chauncey Depew, visiting Chicago, said privately of
James's remarks—at the Chicago Club: "The poor deballed sonofabitch wears lace on his drawers" (Elliot Paul).

What Henry James, and so many other visitors missed in visiting Chicago, was the fact that while all the trappings and artifacts
of the ingenuous expensive European culture were there *someplace,* if
you hunted them out, the city plausibly took more pride in its rail
lines, gross poundage of beef, iced and shipped, the number of pigs
killed, the amount of ore shipped down from the iron ranges.

23

THE IRON HORSE

The railroads are not run for the benefit of the dear public. They are built for men who invest their money and expect to get a fair percentage of the same.

W. H. VANDERBILT, CHICAGO DAILY NEWS, OCTOBER 8, 1882

A generation or so ago one could still talk to old grade-crossing guards in the Middle West, some with a missing arm or leg, who would recall the great days of railroading, the steam Baldwin locomotives highballing along the right-of-way past green signal blocks into the Chicago stockyards. Then there was still the plush grandeur of the 20th Century Limited or The General, rounding the last sand dune and making for the lakeshore, carrying gourmet dining cars, waxed Pullmans, and fine folk intended for the Palmer House, or the guest rooms of an Armour, a Field, Patterson, or McCormick.

At these country crossings there was talk of there having been two great, tough, fun-loving railroad towns: "Caycee" (Kansas City) and "Chi." In my interviews, the vote usually came around to Chicago as number one, with its fantastic networks of rail lines merging and crossing the city, freight yards covering acres of grimy areas, sorting, busy cutting out distant C & O, Pennsy, Santa Fe strays. The transport of hogs went on—pigs alive, and hogs already hams and bacon. Also fowl, steers, sheep, which when processed

159

hung in reefer cars (invented in 1869), brakemen in the caboose with red lanterns, going out to feed the Eastern cities. Incoming were the fruits of California, Florida, Arizona, and the wheat and corn of thousands of growers and farmers being brought to Chicago commodities speculators.

"Land O Goshen," wrote one country editor visiting the yards in 1897, "it's a Horn of Plenty. How would the nation clothe itself, feed itself, keep warm if it were not for the railroads of Chicago?" Chicago brokers gambled in futures in trainloads of hog belly, steer carcass, corn, wheat, rye.

Yet back in 1848 there was not a single mile of track in the city. However, somehow, in only six years Chicago was the railroad hub of the West. In October of 1848 a used, wood-burning, ten-ton locomotive renamed *Pioneer* did a test run from Oak Park to Chicago *and* back. A month later the *Pioneer* steamed into the city with a load of Des Plaines River wheat. The first terminal (usually called a depot—pronounced *dee-poe*) of the new Galena & Chicago Union R.R. was set up at Canal and Kinzie streets.

Two years later four lines sent their rails into Chicago. By 1858 ten trunk lines were in the city, lines that had put down three thousand miles of rail. Fifty-eight passenger trains, thirty-eight freights came in or left the city every twenty-four hours. The first pickpockets went to work, and "friendly little card games" found victims.

Stephen A. Douglas supported the planned Illinois Central, as did former mayor, Long John Wentworth, both active in the U.S. Congress. Pressure was needed to get the city to give away a belt three hundred feet wide for a right-of-way all along the lakefront. Later the city tried and failed to regain this gift of very valuable public lakeshore property. The Illinois Central also got part of old Fort Dearborn for its northern terminal. Senator Douglas sold the line some of his holdings at a good price: that's how railroads were born.

Land speculation was active as to *where* the railroads would need track space, and where terminals would rise up. It became a cagey game, and often a dishonest one. Mark Twain wrote of the skulduggery in *The Gilded Age*. The most imposing of the Chicago railroad structures of the time was the LaSalle Street Station, at La-

Salle and Van Buren Streets. It was built by the Rock Island & Michigan R.R. in 1867, at the then fantastic cost of $225,000.

The names on old railroad timetables and records, on lithographs of famous Chicago-run trains, yellowing photographs of walrus-mustached train crews, bring back images of fancy lettered signs, names of those adventuring in railroading, with Chicago as the hub of a great wheel, and the rail lines and their destinations its spokes. Chicago & Northwestern; Rock Island and Pacific; Chicago, Burlington & Quincy; Chicago and Alton; Michigan Central; Lake Shore & Michigan Southern; Erie; Pittsburg, Fort Wayne and Chicago; Chicago, Danville & Vincennes; the Indiana Central.

Nine rail lines had put up the money to consolidate the Chicago stockyards into a place where their long lines of cars could unload the live hogs and cattle directly into the corrals for the last mile to the killing ramps. By the 1870s the new refrigerator cars opened up vast markets, reached by ever-increasing rail lines.

Dearborn Railroad Station, at Polk and Dearborn, went up in 1885 with a proud tower, huge clocks on its four faces. And only a fire brought the landmark tower down in 1922. The entire Dearborn Station, the oldest of the six busy downtown stations, its need diminished by air travel, was replaced within recent times. One surviving station, the Central, on Park Row and Eleventh Place, once housed at least six great rail lines in its time, including the "Big Four" of the New York Central. For railroad travel was safer since twenty-three-year-old George Westinghouse, in 1868, perfected his compressed-air train brakes.

Chicago was the midcontinental transportation center. Even against trucks and early manned flight, it held its own. The steam train would outcarry and outlast the newfangled modes of the moment, so the old railroad men told their passengers as they took from leather-piped pockets their old Elgin or Waltham railroad watches ("Never more than four seconds off a week").

In the six downtown stations on cold, windy nights, scores of sticky children slept, some with hand-printed tags on their coats telling their destination, in the Dakotas, Montana, the logging country, the ore ranges. Immigrants—since the Civil War, until Ellis Island closed—sat with worried, staring eyes, holding onto their rope-tied bundles, peasant women with shawls on their heads huddled in awe of the hissing and roaring of departing trains, the *jong-jong* of iron on iron which was taking their kind out to homestead in sod huts, to raise up big broods of "svenskies, bohunks, polacks."

Those escaping the city by train met arriving folk on holiday, or in for a selling trip. Country girls like those in the fiction of Dreiser or Cather were setting out to win a place in the city, and Sinclair Lewis' best seller, *Main Street* (1919), set to dreaming the prewar doctor and his wife about a trip to Chicago by train, with the city as a source of all culture: theater, music, literature, and the arts.

In summer the railroad stations saw the wandering actor in his straw boater with a color band, an actress in white high-button shoes, managers collecting their stock companies to move on by rail to one-night stands for either the simple folks' *Uncle Tom's Cabin* ("with real bloodhounds") or the various popular melodramas of the period, *Bertha, the Sewing Machine Girl, Monte Cristo*.

After the traveling burnt-cork minstrel shows came vaudeville, moving its acts in and out of Chicago by rail; burlesque troupes of hefty girls called "beef trusts" (not yet "strippers") and red-nosed comics, booked out of the hub city for Sun Time or Columbia Wheels (playing routes). Some burlesque groups claimed high moral principles. Charles MacArthur (coauthor of the later play about Chicago newsmen, *The Front Page*) remembered hearing a story of a burlesque-group manager addressing his show folk in Dearborn Station:

"This is a moral group and there's to be no unmoral playin' around—you hear? Whoever you start this tour sleepin' with, that's who you end the tour with."

Trains had names, prestige—the proud high iron of the best runs into the city or the yard "hog" that pushed or made up mixed freights. Crews were loyal to the polished extra-fare trains that made record runs to and from New York, Philadelphia, Washington. These seemed eternal, like the lake, the silver dollar. But already by the time of the Great War (1914–1918), electric power lines were marching across the Middle West, and the diesel was being tried out. "But steam would remain king in the smoky freight yards, the great terminals of Chicago" (*Railroad Magazine*, 1912). Look at the activity at the Classification Hump of the Proviso

Yards, which uncoupled and coupled up as many cars as ever. Or the private railroad cars of Bet-a-Million Gates, the McCormicks, Astors, Huntingtons, Hearsts passing through.

The Santa Fe's Corwith Freight Yards in Chicago were soon to begin to carry autos in piggyback fashion; already the tin lizzie, the flivver were in vogue. Steam and railroads continued their progress through the period covered by the history in this book. Ahead and beyond the boundaries of this text lay Chicago's Century of Progress Exposition, and there in the "Pageant of Travel" arriving was the *Zephyr Pioneer*, the first diesel-powered, stainless-steel train. Even the airports, still mostly cow pastures, were creeping closer.

The freight trains were to continue to come and go in Chicago over twenty trunk lines, carrying longer strings of cars. But the great nineteenth-century passenger terminals, with time, were to become empty, echoing caverns of cracked marble walls, drippy plumbing, dead, unreplaced light bulbs in odd corners.

Collecting material for this book for twenty years, I saw the red caps grow older and fewer, the smell of cooking grease and rancid, buttered popcorn in Chicago stations drift away. Only unswept floors littered with empty cigarette packs, torn newspapers, bits of string remained. The grand terminals were doomed by the wreckers' ball. They no longer paid their way.

24

SUPER BLUEBEARD

Blood, though it sleep a time, yet never dies.
The gods on murderers fix revengeful eyes.
GEORGE CHAPMAN, THE WIDOW'S TEARS, 1612

The alchemy of personality works its plausible exaggerations on criminals, as on politicians, athletes, actors. Some in their naked megalomania and popularity reach the status of folk hero or even monster. They are accepted by historians of society with a stunning solemnity. Yet others whose notoriety, crimes, sadomasochistic habits or madnesses are even more striking somehow often seem to sink into the quicksands of neglect. Only an overconfident psychiatrist could claim to be sure why.

Mention Bluebeard and Paris and most peaceful citizens will think of Landrau, the French charmer and killer of a dozen or so ladies. For all the horror of his crimes, Landrau had some piquant purposeful grace that has made him as enduring as a Captain Kidd or a Kennedy as a historic waxwork. Yet, compared to H. H. Holmes, Bluebeard Landrau, as predatory lover, as a promiscuous killer, as a strange criminological freak, and odd member of the human race, was minor league. Death without bereavement or remorse was the major work of both men's lives. Both lived by women's reckless abandonment of reason and logic when overcome by hopes of sexual ecstasies. Holmes was the more amazing man, the greater killer, the more involved in the enigma of *psychopathia sexualis*. Yet, today, only the specialist in some diabolical genre of crime can identify H. H. Holmes of Chicago.

It was not so when Holmes was exposed and some of his hundred or so victims catalogued. His was then the honor of having the most depraved of criminal names attached to Chicago or any other city of any time—an accolade not to be taken lightly. Much debating is held by rival claims to the title—the Boston Strangler, the Axe Man of New Orleans, the Manson family of splendid domesticity, the Church Belfry killing of a virgin in San Francisco. But when the claims of Herman W. Mudgett, better known once as Henry H. Holmes, are ticked off, Chicago, near the turn of the century, easily wins the horror sweepstakes of mass murder.

Holmes had his own castle of crime; Count Dracula's Transylvanian vampire-inhabited manse had nothing on him. "Holmes Castle," on the southwest corner of Wallace and Sixty-third streets in Chicago, was impressive: three stories high, of Walter Scott towers and battlements, clapboard and brick, a Gothic horror of bay windows blinded by sheet-iron coverings, and a basement mysterious and sinister, redolent of sadism, diabolical pain, flagellation, mad surgery. The house contained about ninety rooms, the entire building designed by Holmes himself, combining in itself much of the worst of Victor Hugo's bell ringer's saga, the sprawl of Victorian detail as if designed by an Aubrey Beardsley. Here the curious, and the police, talked later of "thirty victims," or "several hundred." (No actual score was ever fully compiled, and the city wrote it all off at last as psychopathic monstrosity.)

Henry H. Holmes was in appearance a handsome-looking chap, rather on the calm side, five feet seven, 147 pounds, noble forehead, proud, firm chin, a bushy, long moustache—and what was called a melodious voice. Baby-blue eyes over the proud upturned moustache with twirled ends signaled a lady's man. The moustache style was to go out of fashion by World War I but make a splendid comeback in the radical chic and yippie protest dropout set by the 1970s. Holmes, with his charismatic charm, preyed in sartorial grace on women, literally until their death. He was a biga-

mist, besides possessing talents as a forger, embezzler, confidence man, a hunted horse thief in an age of animal-drawn transportation, and, of course, a killer beyond the dreams of the ordinary criminal who murders once or twice.

The castle had its torture chambers (soundproofed), an efficient crematory, vats supplied with acids and quicklime to dissolve flesh, and a full laboratory that Boris Karloff in his best bestial roles would have been proud of. Here Holmes often assembled and articulated some of the better bones of his victims, as skeletons, for sale. The Marquis de Sade would have felt at home with Holmes as one of us. The fellow himself, in a modest moment, merely claimed to be an "honest dealer in human remains."

Herman W. Mudgett was born in 1860, in Gilmanton, New Hampshire, to a well-to-do family. His father was a U.S. postmaster for many years. There was in Herman's wholesome background none of the environment, deprived life, lack of love, so much favored by Freudians. From somewhere, to Herman, had come the criminal genes. One biologist expressed to this writer the thought that Holmes was most likely born bad and acted on this impulse almost as soon as he could pinch, hit, and bite. He skillfully, and with infinite patience, tortured small animals and children. He was a natural-born monster before he was out of his teens. Nor was he a cretin or moron, not aware of what he was doing. Herman was, town folk said, one of the town's bright lads, "smartest boy in the local schools." Mean, and a bad one was the added comment, "but he has a head on him." And it was an attractive head, clear-eyed, a solid New England head of fine Anglo-Saxon heritage. He had read *King Lear*. "Humanity must perforce prey upon itself, like monsters of the deep."

In 1878, Herman was eighteen, the town too small for his hopes, and perhaps it was time to leave. He did, eloping with Clara Lovering, a rich farmer's daughter, an heiress with a small legacy. He was eager to study medicine. Later, she could explain only part of his attraction. "I don't really know. It was his eyes, I guess; they fascinated me. When he looked at me, I felt weak and helpless and unable to do other than what he told me. Herman always had a great interest in mesmerism. Looking back, I'm fairly certain he mesmerized me, but I didn't realize it at the time."

At a Burlington, Vermont, college the couple settled in, on his wife's money. Herman examined bones and bodies, loved dissecting cadavers, studied Gray's *Anatomy*, expressed an interest in living organisms that never left him. The next year he was at the Ann Arbor Medical School of the University of Michigan, already wondering if his gifts of sadism could not be turned into cash. Weekends he'd take home a dead baby for dissecting.

He plotted with a schoolmate to insure himself for twelve thousand dollars—a huge sum in those days—and then to disappear. Holmes stole a body from the school's dissecting room, claiming it was his classmate. Somehow the switch worked and Holmes collected the insurance.

His wife presented him with a son, and Holmes graduated from medical school. With the insurance loot he deserted wife and child. The insured schoolmate never got a cent of the swindle, but later became a very prominent New York society physician with a comforting bedside manner and a very large income.

The wife and child went back home to New Hampshire, and out of the life saga of Dr. Herman W. Mudgett. He never interned or opened a doctor's office, practiced medicine in public.

The next decade saw him as a confidence man, never in medical practice, at least not for the public good. In St. Paul, he was named the receiver of a bankrupt store, his charm getting him the appointment. He loaded the place with extra stocks obtained on credit, sold out cheaply, and moved on to New York as agent for a landscape nursery; later he taught school in Clinton County. There was a turn as assistant administrator of a Norristown, Pennsylvania, insane asylum. He asked five thousand dollars to free one rich inmate who was later found drowned, his wallet gone. Herman's first murder?

He seduced the wife of a Moore Forks farmer who gave him board and room. When he left, she was pregnant, his bill unpaid.

Chicago first saw Herman in 1885, in the North Shore Chicago suburb of Wilmette, where he became H. H. Holmes and had an office as an "inventor." His inventions there are not on record. He committed bigamy by marrying a rich man's daughter, Myrtle Z. Belknap (the name suggests a character in a Dreiser novel). She also produced a child. Holmes forged some deeds to the wife's father's property, and twice tried to poison the father and failed; as a medical man he had not studied his drug courses very well. Mr. Belknap, producing a shotgun, told Holmes, "Get out of here! If ever I lay eyes on you again, I'll let you have it—both barrels!" The wife left Holmes in horror and father Belknap went to the police. Holmes had left town and was unlucky enough to have a minor land scheme and swindle blow up, and that put him in jail for three months.

But jail served some purpose. It decided his fate, for he made connections with Marion Hedgespeth, a notorious train robber, on his way to the penitentiary, and Benjamin F. Pietzel, an alcoholic confidence man, and a poor one, trying to support a wife and five hungry kids. Holmes decided not to make the mistakes of these professional criminals, but, as will be shown later in these pages, the two men brought Holmes's destiny to its final drama.

He appeared in 1889, ready to dazzle Chicago with the A.B.C. Copier, his office in the Monon Block on South Dearborn Street, as one of those men who, like the inventors of the mazda light and the typewriter, was offering to help Chicago business grow with better tools. He fled his office a few months later, leaving notes and debts uncollectable, for nine thousand dollars. Life for an *homme moyen sensuel* needed a lift with some bolder scheme.

Holmes was set in Chicago, and what he needed was room to operate in a better background of his own designing. He found it in the South Side in the Englewood section, and with it the widow Holden, in whose drugstore at Wallace and Sixty-third streets, he was first clerk, then bookkeeper, then lover to the owner, then murderer. Mrs. Holden made the mistake of calling in an accountant to go over Holmes's odd bookkeeping. Holmes's explanation, in 1890, when asked *where* Mrs. Holden was, neighbors not seeing her about or in the apothecary business, was that the widow had sold him the store and moved away "to California." No one asked him to present any papers or deed of any sale. None was ever recorded. But he managed to mortgage the business and building.

Opposite the drugstore was a plot of land on the southwest corner of Sixty-third and Wallace streets he wanted to buy, and did. Here Holmes erected his extraordinary palace, soon to become known as Holmes Castle. Three stories high, containing secret hallways and cellars. It suggests Kafka's castle and the strange prison prints of Piranesi. Holmes himself supervised the building of his dream *schloss,* and claims were made he managed to avoid paying for most of the material and furnishings that put together the place. He mortgaged, signed notes, repudiated debts, payments. He was a demon foreman of the project, changing bricklayers, plasterers, carpenters after short periods of work, and managing in most cases to avoid fully paying them off. The scheme seemed to be, by means of this large labor turnover, to avoid having anyone but himself know the secrets of Holmes Castle, certainly Chicago's most bizarre building.

Years later, the police and press gained entrance to the place, when the doctor's crimes were causing public horror. Floor plans had to be made like road maps. The first- and third-floor rooms seemed never to have been occupied. The control center of the place was the second. Certainly it would have confused any invader hunting down the doctor. It offered numerous escape hatches for anyone fleeing intruders. Facing Sixty-third Street on the second floor was the doctor's own apartment, just two small offices, a bedroom, and primitive bathroom whose thick dusty rug hid a trapdoor that led to a secret, eight-foot-square, windowless chamber, escape from which could be made by a chute to the cellar and by a door to a staircase to the street. There were several such chutes. There were at least thirty-five other rooms on the floor, and some six seemed to have been orgy bedrooms stocked with various women being made love to before being gassed, going to the chopping block, or to the vats of acid baths. Some rooms were windowless, and seemingly could be made airtight.

One contained a huge, almost-room-filling steel bank safe fitted with a pipe that could pour Chicago's city gas into it, and kill anyone placed there on deposit. There were also more soundproofed rooms, paneled in sheet iron and asbestos, and some scarred by fire, suggesting roasting sessions, slow torture in the manner of the Church's Inquisition. Most rooms had trapdoors and ladders below. More gas pipes led to many, and the master himself could turn on valves controlled from his private sleeping chamber, where he used science for his own delight.

The police suggested that these valves were used to kill with fire in heatproof, soundproof rooms by some form of remote control. The entire second floor had elaborate bells and alarms that rang when any door was opened by a stranger, or by some escaping female whose dimensions of suffering and anguish had reached a panic level.

It was the cellar that caused goose bumps, as reported to the newspaper readers; the details of that basement called for colorful horror reporting. Seven feet high, it ran under the entire place. It even ran beyond the building and out under the Sixty-third Street sidewalk.

Under one chute from the second floor stood a surgeon's table and a large dissecting surface; also present were cases of surgical lancets, knives, and other mean-looking steel tools, some worn and resharpened, obviously not for mere display. Here on the table the bodies of Holmes's victims or loves lost their human shape, were disposed of.

Under the dissecting table there usually reposed several collections, in loose bone form, of female skeletons. There was also in the basement a crematory that could have served as an efficient model for the Germans in World War II. Rollers, as at the Buchenwald and Auschwitz concentration murder camps, slid the body over the grate for burning. The Germans never improved on the simplicity of Holmes's original design. Like the Himmlers, Holmes never felt the anguish and agony of despair over mass murder.

Buried in the floor of the castle's cellar were a huge vat of corrosive acids, two vats of quicklime, and a stall where loose quicklime was kept. Here, the sinister discovery was made of the naked footprint of some woman, just one clear, laconic print, and no answer to her desperate fate.

There was also something the ghoulish press labeled the "Elasticity Determinator." This machine seemed to function in the manner of the medieval rack beloved by ancient Grand Inquisitors of the Church, and various local dukes of the Renaissance. The doctor did claim his machine could "stretch a human body to twice its normal length," with him at the controls. He modestly explained he was interested "in producing a race of giants." One can almost hear the maniacal screaming of the benefactors of his machine.

None of the special fittings, machines, vats, and furnaces were, of course, known to the neighbors of the handsome Dr. Holmes. His explanation for the castle's huge size was that the Columbian Exposition was due in 1893, when his building would be ready for housing visitors come to see the great fair. Some reporters claimed fifty to one hundred transient young girls vanished into the castle never to come out again.

He advertised the castle as a proper and well-furnished boardinghouse, and many came to partake of the charming Dr. Holmes's hospitality. Most were sooner or later reported as missing persons. But no evidence could be produced showing that Dr. Holmes's boardinghouse was their last stop—and no one suspected he had done away with them. He operated a total human assimilation after sex and torture.

25

CASTLE HORROR

Everybody is a potential murderer. . . . I frequently get satisfaction reading the obituary notices.
CLARENCE DARROW, NEWSPAPER INTERVIEW, 1937

Before we proceed with H. H. Holmes's story, let us wonder why the fame of the master in the field of murderous rapacity has not lasted. Perhaps because the world soon rushed into greater slaughter in the Great War, into new tyrannies, stupidities, greeds, and today into acceptable mass murder of men, women, and children as national war policy. With our Doomsday Bomb ticking away, Holmes belonged to a more innocent age, free of the innocuous cant that tries to point the difference between murder on a vast scale and the still illegal crime of murder by one.

He had a mind that with laconic candor fell down before his concupiscent images; those he dared to attempt to fulfill. But always for him there had to be the material reward: money, that pathetic tenacity he had with J. P. Morgan, Hetty Green, P. T. Barnum, a coarse delight in the dollar. William James's "Bitch Goddess Success" hypnotized Holmes as deeply as she did any robber baron of the nineteenth century. He merged horrible sex with hopes of a fat bank balance.

The evidence seems to indicate the first victims at the castle, in some sort of trial run, were the very beautiful brunette Mrs. Julie Connors and her eight-year-old daughter, Pearl. There was also a Mr. Connors with his family of three who came to Chicago in 1890. The husband and wife were put to work by Holmes in the drugstore. When Mr. Connors was told by Holmes that his wife was also his mistress, he may have left town in a huff, or was murdered. Mrs. Connors was left to run the drugstore while Holmes went down to Texas, where he took his vacation by organizing a gang of confidence men, horse rustlers, and outlaw gunmen. The Texas Rangers took care of the gang, and got out a warrant for the arrest of Holmes for stealing a horse. He escaped its serving. The doctor had met and charmed two young Texas girls, sisters, Minnie and Nannie Williams of Fort Worth, and he was delighted to discover they were heiresses to property valued at fifty thousand dollars.

It was a combination Holmes could hardly pass up—beauty and loot. So, escaping from a Texas warrant for arrest, back in Chicago he soon sent for pretty Minnie, whom he introduced to neighbors as his secretary. It was soon clear by the simple girl's actions that she was mad about the man and resented Mrs. Connors and her more well-curved charms. Querulous complaints, battles between the women took over. Soon, Mrs. Connors and daughter Pearl were no longer in sight.

"She's gone to join her husband," the doctor explained to the friends she had made. *"Do I think she'll return? No, I'm afraid she never will."*

Later, when accused of the double murder, he said Mrs. Connors had died while he was performing an abortion on her and that Pearl had just "wandered off someplace." Later still—epicurean even in defeat—he confessed Minnie Williams had been so jealous he had murdered the mother and daughter, but explained of Mrs. Connors, "I would have got rid of her anyway. I was tired of her." Holmes's other interests were selling a cure for alcohol, an elixir of youth, and pills to perform wonders made of sugar and bismuth.

There seems some truth to the image of Minnie Williams as a sort of Bride of Frankenstein monster for a while. Minnie certainly knew of the fate of Emily Van Tassel who lasted a month on the job at the castle in 1893, and of Emeline Cigrand, nineteen, and said to be the prettiest of all the girls who passed under Holmes's ardent charm. Holmes in his prime, in his early thirties, found Emeline an incandescent delight.

Emeline's beauty was her downfall. She had been a typist at the Keeley Institute in Dwight, Illinois, that place being, before the rise of A.A., one of the last hopes of the alcoholic on the road to ruin, delirium tremens, and death. The "gold cure" there (a worthless method except for its suggestion of hope) attracted the attention of Ben Pietzel, the confidence man and alcoholic friend of Holmes, whom we have mentioned earlier as being in jail with him. Pietzel,

who seems to have pimped for the doctor, brought back from Keeley's, to Chicago, news of this beauty Emeline, and Holmes went to see her, charmed her to come to work for him in the castle. He later confessed she was held prisoner in one of his soundproof rooms and he, in the popular term of the day, "forced his attentions on to her." Minnie objected to the doctor's attention to his prisoner, and so much did Minnie threaten that Emeline Cigrand vanished into the basement of the *monstre sacré*.

But there were problems. Emeline had been the love object, platonically, of a Mr. Phelps, a man much older than she, and they were engaged. Robert E. Phelps was a man of wealth and social position. He went to Holmes Castle to visit his fiancée, and that was the last ever heard of him. Holmes later admitted Mr. Phelps had died for science, having passed on during one of Dr. Holmes's cellar "experiments." Certainly not a pleasant one. The unabashed audacity of it all, and no investigations, amazes one.

Minnie's sister Nannie came north to Chicago to visit in the summer of '93. She fell at once for the doctor's charm and bed. "Dr. Holmes is a wonderful man. He's taking Minnie and me to Germany, where I shall probably study art. He says I'll never want for anything for the rest of my life and the folks back home need never worry about me." Result: she signed over her half of the Fort Worth property to him. After which Nannie vanished and Holmes said she had "gone to Texas," a popular expression of the period.

Ben Pietzel, an unreliable drunk, seemed to have been Holmes's one charity for a time. He was appointed manager of the castle while Holmes and Minnie took the steam train west to Denver, where Holmes had some unfinished business with Georgianna Yoke from Indiana who, in passing, he had courted some years before. Under the name of Henry Howard, with Minnie as one of the cold-eyed witnesses, he married Miss Yoke. Miss Yoke never knew the few weeks they all lived in Denver that Minnie was Mr. Howard's paramour. If the strange man could love at all, the bigamist seems to have loved Georgianna Yoke, for he sent her safely back to her folks in Indiana, promising he'd join her soon. And he did from time to time, for several flying visits, even traveled with her occasionally, but not for long. Precariously he spared her life, and she survived to testify at his trial of his virile kindness. There is no hint that at any time he had any designs on her life. These lyric and serene interludes are odd in this paranoid man's life, and can only be explained that even a monster has his weaknesses, or some Rorschach pattern we cannot interpret.

At the end of the year, Minnie Williams also signed over her share of her property, and she, too, was never heard of again. When the law caught up with Holmes, he insisted to detectives that Minnie had murdered her sister Nannie in a fit of jealousy over him, claiming full stud rights for herself, and had then run off to Europe with a younger man. Later, always loquacious, he sighed and admitted that the bones of the Williams sisters rested with those of Emily Van Tassel and Emeline Cigrand in the box under his dissecting table. Something, perhaps some shred of sentiment, a last surrender to romance, had kept him from selling or destroying their remains.

If he mined women for their assets and their bodies, he was not above the petty swindles of greedy storekeepers. He sold Lake Michigan water in his drugstore at five cents a glass, as the "finest mineral water." He made pills of powdered chalk when filling some prescriptions for a deathly ill person. In a jewelry store, he ran a sideline, palming off glass as precious stones, and brass as gold.

He felt he was made for bigger things and aspired to some really great swindle against the city of Chicago—the sort that Charles Yerkes and the Traction thieves, the gas and water rights manipulators were practicing on the citizens of Chicago. It seemed to Holmes he had a good sales item in lake water; why not turn the water into gas and sell the gas to some political set of City Hall thieves who would somehow get it into the city's gas mains? Holmes built a fantastic Rube Goldberg machine in his lab cellar with tanks and intricate piping, and informed the gas company it should send one of its experts to come and see how cheaply plain water could be turned into gas.

The *Chicago Tribune* reported that the expert saw a "contrivance such as he had never seen before, with a stream of water running in at one end and a strong flow of gas at the other. Holmes assured that the cost of manufacture was next to nothing, and the result was that the gas company gave the invention such a strong recommendation that Holmes was enabled to sell it to a Canadian for $2,000. When the machine was taken out, it was discovered that Holmes had tapped the gas company's mains."

Holmes's first success at medical school had come from defrauding an insurance company. And as insurance companies had caused several scandals and created investigations of their dishonest methods, the doctor felt, as did many, that taking an insurance company was just plain justice. He took a body with a disfigured face (who? how procured?) to a Rhode Island hotel, where he himself registered as H. H. Holmes. He placed the body on a deserted stretch of beach. Then Holmes shaved off his moustache and the beard he also wore at the time. So changed, he appeared at the hotel and asked for his friend Holmes. Soon the body was discovered on the shore, and the doctor identified it as his late, lamented friend, H. H. Holmes. The insurance company was not in any mood to pay a claim without some legal razzle-dazzle of its own, and held up payment. Holmes decided not to press any claim against the rascals of the wily insurance company. He sensed a certain disquietude there, a mistrust.

Besides Ben Pietzel, Holmes had met the train robber, Marion Hedgespeth, early in his career while jailed for some mortgage swindle. From the robber, Holmes got the name of a St. Louis lawyer, Colonel Jeptha D. Howe. (The names given here to most of our actors are actual—a strange strain of Dickens at his worst seems to identify the American people at this period. As for the title "Colonel," Mark Twain, in conversation, said, "It's as common as whale shit.")

Colonel Howe seemed to bear out Abraham Lincoln's jest when he saw a gravestone marked HERE LIES A LAWYER AND HONEST MAN: "Since when are they burying two men in one grave?" Howe and Holmes went to work on simple, boozy Ben Pietzel. They got him to take out a big insurance policy favoring his wife and brood of children. He was then to hide out and Holmes would produce a handy cadaver, claim it was Pietzel, and collect. Pietzel, most likely in his usual rummy condition, got insured by the Fidelity Mutual Life Association for ten thousand dollars. Holmes explained to Ben that friendship is an affair of infinite delicacy *and* trust; he would, he said, see that Ben got his share of the insurance money. A few weeks later, in Philadelphia, Ben Pietzel's actual body was found in an office he had rented, passing for a patent attorney as "B. F. Perry—Patents Bought and Sold." He was killed and singed by a benzine fire, it was claimed, in an accident. However, the autopsy showed death was by chloroform. No matter, lawyer Colonel Jeptha D. Howe came to Philadelphia with flamboyant plausibility as representing Mrs. Pietzel, to collect the insurance. Payment was made and Holmes pocketed it, all but twenty-five hundred dollars that went to the lawyer. Mrs. Pietzel claimed she was entitled to *something,* and Holmes let her hold five hundred dollars for a few days, then took it back to be sure she "invested it properly." He promised they'd join Ben—in hiding—soon.

The real problem for Holmes was that the colonel and the wife both thought Pietzel was not really the body found and paid for. Pietzel, they were told, was alive and well, someplace, and would turn up when the coast seemed clear, to collect from Holmes. Ironically, no fraud had actually been done to the insurance company. Pietzel was truly, fully dead. Somebody was entitled to the insurance. And Dr. Holmes seemed to have such an appetite for responsibility.

Holmes was delighted at the scheme's success—and feeling he had to tell somebody of how splendidly the swindle had worked, he told the train robber, Marion Hedgespeth, still in jail, the details, while visiting. Holmes was a man swollen with secrets—he *had* to talk to someone. Hedgespeth had expected five hundred dollars for finding the lawyer, Colonel Howe, for him. Holmes felt a man in prison didn't need money and he paid nothing. The train robber, a simple man of middle-class parochialism, overlooking the fact that if he snitched on Holmes, his five hundred dollars was gone for good, told the whole story to the prison warden. Everyone was talking too much. The warden told the insurance company his prisoner's tale, and they called in their best bloodhounds, the Pinkerton Detective Agency, who between strikebreaking (and blowing off the arm of Jesse James's mother with a homemade bomb) did insurance investigating. They soon proved the body in Philadelphia was the real Pietzel, and that he had been murdered about three days before the charred body was found.

Detective Frank Geyer of the Pinkerton Agency had little trouble settling on Dr. H. H. Holmes as the mastermind. First of all, his record was bad. He had also identified the body, and he had been seen with the insured man, Pietzel, alive in Philadelphia several times. There were also insurance records that "H. H. Holmes" had been found dead on the beach and no claims had been pushed for *that* money. The strategies of fraud were too similar.

Police were alerted to arrest Holmes on sight, and Texas was pushed to serve its warrant for his crime down there, which was not murder but horse stealing, a much more serious crime, in those tall-in-the-saddle days, than a casual killing. Holmes to himself was like some Greek tragic hero now—a true hero because of his conscious acceptance of his fate. But not just yet—first some games of fox and hounds.

Holmes, on the move, acted quickly. He activated Mrs. Pietzel to take two of the five children and hide out with her parents, and he would take the other three and meet her in Detroit in two weeks, where the long-lost husband, Ben, would be with them at last. On the run, he again took on his love, Georgianna Yoke, the three children, *and* Mrs. Pietzel with the others, all in separate sections on the same train. The three parties were separate but together.

One reporter said, "During these travels, Holmes carried with him three separate detachments—Mrs. Pietzel, Miss Yoke, and the children—all within four blocks of each other in all the different cities, almost traveling together, under Holmes' leading strings, and yet each detachment ignorant of the presence of the other two."

The man would have made an amazing field general. He had the admonitory eye.

The chase of Holmes continued, and his rushing about was hopeless. It was two months before he was run to ground in Boston, on November 17, 1894. From there he was moved to Philadelphia to stand trial for the insurance murder. He stayed shut mouth at first when asked about the three children he had traveled with. Then he said, "South America . . . Ben took the kids and flew." Mrs. Pietzel, arrested and released, also wondered where her three missing children were. After many leads, in a cellar of a house in Toronto, Canada, the bodies of Nellie and Alice Pietzel were found, and also a trunk with a gas pipe leading to an outlet. It was clear they had been gassed and then buried. Little Howard was still missing, then his charred body was found in Irvington, Indiana, in a house Holmes had rented for a week.

Holmes told a new story—the three children had been done in by the young man who was supposed to have run off to Europe with Minnie Williams. "They're in England. I had them in Niagara

Falls, but a girl named Minnie Williams kidnapped them from me —out of spite, I think, to get me in trouble. Minnie was jealous. Some time ago, she murdered her sister, Anna, just because she thought Anna was making eyes at me. I disposed of Anna's body for her, in a lake, but she was never one to recognize a favor. Minnie ran off to England with the kids and a chap named Ed Hatch. Maybe she's calling herself Mrs. Hatch by now, I don't know for sure, but I have an idea she's running a massage parlor in London. I daresay if I inserted an advertisement, addressed to her in cipher, in the London papers, she would answer."

In his last confession, Holmes suggested Alice and Nellie had come to him after their death, ". . . the little faces as they looked when I hurriedly left them—felt the innocent child's kiss so timidly given—and heard again their earnest words of farewell." Words almost worse than his crimes in a world that cried over Mr. Dickens' fiction; feelings perhaps were greater than ours can ever be.

The man Holmes remains a mystery, tawdry, callow, an isolated phenomenon in mass killing, some sinister compulsion to rape, torture, dismembering to be gratified, killing with pleasure. And with a studied care.

In October of 1895, Holmes stood trial for the murder of Ben Pietzel. By that time, his castle's remaining secrets had been discovered, sifted through, and the full shocking details of its contents and design brought to the light of day.

The *New York World* reported on some of what was found in the basement when a hollow-sounding wall was broken down: "As soon as this wall was broken through a horrible smell was encountered and fumes like those of a charnel house rushed forth. A plumber was sent for, and the workmen gathered about while he proceeded to investigate. The first thing the plumber did was to light a match. Then there was a terrific explosion that shook the building, while flames poured forth into the cellar. The plumber was the only man who escaped uninjured, and an ambulance took the other workmen to the hospital. Then a thorough search of this mysterious chamber was made by the police. They found that the brick wall had concealed a tank curiously constructed. This tank had contained an oil whose fumes, the chemists say, would destroy human life within less than a minute. There were evidences about the cellar of this mysterious and deadly oil having been used . . . A small box was found in the center of the tank. When this was opened by Fire Marshal James Kenyon an evil smelling vapor rushed out. All ran except Kenyon, who was overpowered by the stench. He was dragged out and carried upstairs.

"In a hole in the middle of the floor, more bones were found. These have been examined by physicians, who declare that they include, among others, the bones of a child between six and eight years of age. There were seventeen ribs in all, part of a spinal column, a collarbone, and a hipbone. In spite of the retort, the deadly oil tank and two vaults of quicklime, all working at the same time, is it possible, it was asked, that Holmes was murdering people so fast that he had to bury some of them?

"There are hundreds of people who went to Chicago to see the Fair and were never heard of again. The list of the 'missing' when the Fair closed was a long one, and in the greater number foul play suspected. Did these visitors to the Fair, strangers to Chicago, find their way to Holmes' Castle in answer to delusive advertisements sent out by him, never to return again? Did he erect his Castle close to the Fair grounds so as to gather in these victims by the wholesale, and, after robbing them, did he dispose of their bodies in his quicklime vats, in his mysterious oil tank with its death dealing liquids, or did he burn them in the elaborate retorts?"

The newspaper then awarded him a special accolade: the honor of being "the first criminal of the century."

Holmes made an exciting spectacle of himself at his Philadelphia trial for murder. Georgianna Yoke, who had thought herself married to him, was called to testify in court for the state, and Holmes moaned and wept and wrung his hands and cried out loudly. Then in the gambit so often tried by master criminals, reading Stephen's *Digest of the Laws of Evidence*, he fired his lawyers and decided to conduct his defense himself. He made a fairly good lawyer. He attacked witnesses with gusto, he cross-examined, he brought up hair-splitting points of law. It certainly did not help him for a conscientious and grim jury to observe the cunning of the man. Yet some narcissistic drive held him to the end. In those days, a trial for murder rarely lasted for long. Only in the later California court circuses of the twentieth century would such a trial have dragged on for month after month, taking nearly a year. In Philadelphia, 1895, on the sixth day of Holmes's trial, the jury brought in the expected verdict, "Guilty of murder in the first degree." The jurors confessed later they had agreed in a little over a minute, but as proper Philadelphians, "stayed out two and a half hours just for the sake of appearances."

Nor were there the legal delays of years so popular today, of appeal on appeal, and the razzle-dazzle of hot-mouthed lawyers weakening justice. Holmes's one appeal was to the Pennsylvania Supreme Court, which let the verdict stand on April 30, 1896. The governor said he would not intervene. Seven days later, just before his thirty-sixth birthday, H. H. Holmes prepared to die on the Moyamensing prison yard gallows. Justice would be clear and swift.

The *Chicago Journal* wrote of the condemned man: "Murder was his natural bent. Sometimes he killed from sheer greed of gain; oftener, as he has himself confessed, to gratify an inhuman thirst for blood. Not one of his crimes was the outcome of a sudden burst of fury—'Hot blood'—as the codes say. All were deliberate; planned."

At the end, the drop gave under his feet, his body fell, his neck snapping. The *Chicago Journal* suggested that "a sigh of relief will go up from the whole community with the knowledge that Herman Mudgett, or Henry H. Holmes, man or monster, has been exterminated—much the same as a plague to humanity would be stamped out."

Wrote one reporter: "The good doctor was always a modest man—not to mention something of a liar. Authoritative sources place the number of his victims . . . as to four times twenty-seven. However, from the standpoint of justice, it no longer matters how many he killed. A man can only hang once, and I had the pleasure of seeing Dr. Holmes do that very thing this morning."

Whatever malformation of the mind and passions Holmes had, we can only dimly visualize the charm he used on his women victims. If he had any philosophy, it was the one a morbid philosopher pointed out: that nature is never economical, it is always feeding hummingbirds to the cats.

BOOK THREE

ROGUES AND CITIZENS

26

OFF STAGE AND ON

It is given to some cities and to some lands to suggest romance and to me Chicago did that hourly. It sang, I thought, and in spite of what I deemed my various troubles, I was singing with it. . . . Chicago was so young, so blithe, so new.

THEODORE DREISER, NEWSPAPER DAYS

Chicago, as the nineteenth century came near its end, continued in some of its old ways, but with a clairvoyant knack also braced itself for the coming century. Prices were going up a bit, but at no galloping rate, as in our own times. "Ten Dollar" Tom Murphy, apparel merchant, still maintained his price for *any* suit at ten dollars —"a sawbuck"—true to his motto, "Good enough for me to wear, good enough for you to wear." The derby, known as "the iron hat," seemed to cover most male heads—to go bareheaded, rumor was, would bring a seizure of vertigo—and the high silk hat, the Lincoln stovepipe, were following the beaver topper to the mothballs—except for official events and for the opera. The most dangerous male attire was the celluloid collar, worn high; a fire hazard, for it could burst into a blaze impossible to put out if it came near a flame. All gamblers, pimps, gentlemen bike riders, politicians, all faced the dangers of incineration by celluloid collar. The last known person almost cremated by his collar was admitted to the Chicago County Hospital in 1903. As the victim, Howard Elling, of North Marshfield Avenue, explained it, "It just happened all at once. . . . I was at the corner cigar store, and I leaned over to light my cigar at the gas jet."

The one advantage of the celluloid collar—besides its enduring forever—was that it could be cleaned with the eraser at the end of a pencil. For the criminal of Chicago, its edge was also the tool to open doors guarded by spring locks. Taking off the collar, one inserted it between the door and the jamb with simple muscular coordination—to push back the bolt of certain locks.

Female style was set for most—hardly Parisian—at Marshall Field's, Mandel Brothers, Siegal and Cooper, Schlesinger and Mayer, A. M. Rothschild, Carson, Pirie, Scott. Streets were swept by the long trailing skirts of the ladies, both patrician women and their painted sisters at the foot of the lamppost.

Costs were not high for a good shopper. A splendid straw hat cost $1.25 but could, at sales, go for 50 cents. A man's shirt was 75 cents, shoes $2.50, neckties 25 cents. Tailor-made items cost somewhat more for those who had susceptibilities for proper fitting.

If you rode the streetcars, a nickel was enough—a "jit" which was also the cost of a sandwich, a bag of peanuts, a fairly good cigar, a fine glass of draft beer (with *all* the free lunch you could eat).

Newspapers cost a cent; so did a huge dill pickle. You could visit Sharpshooters' Park, Sans Souci, or Chutes Park. If lucky, you might hear a policeman's daughter, May de Sousa, sing a popular song by the ward heeler politician and alderman Bathhouse John Coughlin. "Dear Midnight of Love" was the number one hit of 1898.

> *Dear Midnight of Love,*
> *Why did we meet?*
> *Dear Midnight of Love*
> *Your face is so sweet.*
> *Pure as the angels above,*
> *Surely again we shall speak,*
> *Loving only as doves,*
> *Dear Midnight of Love.*

The music critic of the *Chicago Journal* noted "the piece is written in dactylic tetrameter and hypercatalectic meter." Bathhouse

John didn't know if he should sock the critic or buy him a drink.

Musically, the city was still a long way from the jazzmen's invasion when the riverboats began to bring to Chicago such sound makers as King Oliver, Louis Armstrong, and others driven out of Storyville in 1917 by the navy closing the sporting houses of New Orleans. As Nell Kimball, one of the madams there, put it: "It was all right for the boys to die for their country, but not to get laid."

There was a fearful outcry when the suggestion was made to turn from gaslight in the streets to the electric carbon arc. It was a ritual, that gas-time hour—as dusk fell like soot onto Chicago—for the streetlighter to appear with his little ladder, flick his torch through a hole in the bottom of the streetlamp, turn the flow of gas on, and light the Welsbach burner . . . for every gas streetlight in the city was turned on by hand. Said one old lamplighter to a reporter in 1912: "Looks like an easy job, eh? But we got to git up at half past four or five in the mornin' and go round turnin' all the lights out agin." The electric arcs soon came to State Street, Jackson Boulevard, Hyde Park, and from there were soon everywhere.

At first, the criminals felt the new electric lights would make street robbery more difficult, overemphasizing everything too clearly—but there were plenty of dark spots to keep the heist artists or sandbaggers in business. It had to be a major crime to cause a stir in town, as when some secret Irish societies in 1889 dedicated to the overthrow of English rule in Ireland executed a Dr. Cronin as betrayer of the Clan-na-Gael Society in Chicago. Or so it was claimed. Certainly he was foully murdered on a well-lit street, and his body found in a catch basin on the corner of Argyle Street and Evanston Avenue. Two Irish members of the Clan-na-Gael served three years each in Joliet for the murder after indictment and a trial. Said one of the released men in 1898: "I don't like indictments. I don't like trials. You never know how they are going to come out." The sentiment sounded like a Sean O'Casey line but also was to be expressed by one Al Capone a long time later.

Food and drink interested Chicagoans as much as gambling or the gay ladies, or a winning horse at Washington Park. For some, satisfaction came with a frankfurter costing two cents, a cup of coffee, one cent, watermelon, a penny a slice. But for people with a little loose silver in their peg-top pants, there was Billy Boyle's Chop House, where besides reporters, the City Hall boys gathered to eat a thick sirloin steak at fifty cents, lamb chops at thirty-five. There would be aldermen Bathhouse John and Hinky Dink; con men like "Yellow Kid" Weil, gambling men, city contractors, and often a popular actor would come in, a shaggy fedora worn to one side, a fairly good fur collar on his toe-touching chesterfield.

A reporter, enjoying a cut of roast beef, quoted Dryden, "Here is God's plenty."

For the Old World feeling, over on Randolph Street, was the Union Restaurant, a Munich-type rathskeller with a fattening Teutonic cuisine. Strauss waltzes with *Schlamperei* Wiener Schnitzel Union was cooked in Madeira, and for the drinker of the steins of Chicago Pilsener, there were spicy, salty cold cuts on a three-foot tray, the *Kalter Aufschnitt*. A brewery owned the building, and only its beer, naturally, was available. A digestive system had to function at the full of its potential at the Union.

Beer in Randall Street also cost a nickel and cold cuts also were offered as free lunch.

An official guide to the city truly claimed "there are 624 restaurants located at convenient points along the principal thoroughfares."

Letters from travelers mention the fine food of "Cardinal" Bemis and his Richelieu, also Rector's, Kinsley's, Chapin & Gore's, De Jonghe's, King's, and the Saratoga.

But decline was already in sight. John R. Thompson invented the one-arm lunchroom where your chair also served as a small table. It was only one stomach-destroying leap from there to the steam table of 1920, the cafeteria, precooked food, instant garbage.

Sex, like food, was taken with leisure and infinite detail in some of the best Chicago eating places that were also used for the act of love. The private dining room with the key on the inside was boldly advertised. "The Saratoga Restaurant and Oyster House at 155 Dearborn Street, opposite the National Bank . . . sixteen supper room boxes, opera box style . . . carriage entrance at the rear."

No need for a hedonist, or sportsman, or visiting banker to parade through the entire place to reach his private dining room with a veiled lady or two on his arm, soon to be in his hands. The habit of late dining after the theater was more civilized than rushing the food into a growling stomach in order to make the first-act curtain.

A late hour, too, gave one grace to attend to the leisurely detailed pace of a proper sexual evening with whatever subtle variations one desired. A student who wrote a letter about the buggy as preferred to the bicycle for achieving one's desire with a female partner, also noted the problems of a nineteenth-century undressing of one's love object. "It's even-stephen the little darling will repel you if you don't understand all about the significant secrets of costume, the hooks-and-eyes, the jet buttons, the whalebone stays, the petticoat or petticoats! the intricate Rainy Daisy skirt, storm ruffles, 'rats' in the hair, and oh golly, those switches. I tell you, Scudder, it's like peeling an onion, unlacing, unhooking, beginning with the button shoes, the freeing of the stockings, until one gets, at last, hardly at a fast pace, to the center of the whole drama, the jewel—as one would say—in its bosky dell. . . .

> "Oh since the thing we beg 's a toy
> That's prized by love alone,
> Why cannot women grant the joy
> Before our love is gone?"

(I have been unable to identify the poem, or the poet, quoted in the letter.)

The Chicago theater flourished, and still does in the city, but not as it once did when scores of touring companies crisscrossed the nation. The turn of the century was not all *East Lynne,* and *Uncle Tom* shows, nor such melodrama as *Nellie the Beautiful Cloak Model*, *Ace Diamond in Mississippi*, *With the Rough Riders in Cuba*, *The Midnight Express* (Lillian Russell at the controls of the speeding train).

Writing in 1891, the historian John Flinn recorded, "Chicago in recent years has become a dramatic center of the first rank." Madame Adelina Patti had loudly opened the new Auditorium built by Louis Sullivan. Hooley's Parlor House of Comedy ran plays by William Gillette, Clyde Fitch. Also here one wept with Maude Adams in *The Little Minister*, and cheered her in *Peter Pan*, clapped hands so Tinker Bell might live; Mrs. Leslie Carter, Chicago's own scandalous lady, swung out over the audience on the clapper of a church tower bell to save her lover in *The Heart of Maryland*. One night, Ben Hecht told me, she swung out wildly without a certain undergarment and some wit yelled, "Mrs. Carter, you weren't always a redhead!" Ethel Barrymore appeared in a calmer play, *Trelawny of the Wells*.

Clean and bland as a Disney film were the shows at Havelin's on Wabash Avenue: *Sherlock Holmes*, *Rip Van Winkle*, also dramas of unreciprocated but noble love, comedies of effusive amiability. May de Sousa, who had introduced Bathhouse John's "Dear Midnight of Love," appeared at the Chicago Opera House, and also offered "After the Ball," "Go Fly a Kite," and by popular demand, "Ireland Is the Spot That I Call Heaven."

Much later, by 1902, change in its fecundity reached the Opera House. It was showing *The Kinedrome—Greatest of All Moving Picture Machines*, exposing the first Western film feature, historians claim—fifteen full minutes of *The Great Train Robbery*, made in New Jersey, and starring Bronco Billy Anderson, who couldn't ride a horse.

Fashions, certain years, called for huge hats on ladies and led to signs in the theaters: "Ladies, the prettiest, wisest, most charming women take off their hats in a theatre." Some managers ignored the soft sell and were tougher. "Comply with an ordinance passed by City Council. Those failing to comply [removing the hat] will be requested to do so by an usher" *(Chicago Tribune)*.

The more depraved shows were in the sporting-house districts, in the saloons and cafés. Wrote an explorer: "Nothing seen in the worst dives of Port Said, and French seaports, could not be found in the city." Some visitor claimed "Chicago is the wickedest city in the world" (Bronson Scrapbook).

As this last remark was often printed in the local press, it would appear many citizens were proud of the title. There was a curious pattern to the city—some seeing it as an abomination of vice and desolation, others as a growing, proud city—while one visitor on a postal card insisted it would never lose a "certain provincialism natural to the mid-west."

27

THE IMMIGRANT

Chicago . . . another Pompeii in luxury if not in licentiousness.
ELIAS COLBERT, HISTORIAN, CHICAGO TRIBUNE

Chicago . . . a city of everlasting pine, shingles, shams, veneers, stucco and putty.
CHICAGO TRIBUNE, 1875

Chicago had always been a town for the immigrant, the drifter, the pogromed refugee, the exile, the hungry—all those courageous enough to make a leap across the seas. Government reports in 1870 saw the tide rise and by 1900, the flood was at a high-water mark. They came in odd clothes, in earrings, gypsy shawls, in green felt hats, carrying rope-tied bundles, bursting trunks, suitcases strapped and patched, men, women, and children burdened by odd assort-ments of carryalls. They flowed into Chicago. Immigrant Society files show some went on to homestead the West, to farm, to burrow in sod huts. The records were often slipshod for those who stayed on in Chicago.

When in doubt it was the custom to list them as "Austrians" even if they were Poles, Dalmatians, Croats, Slavs, Herzegovians. There were 120,000 Russians who settled in, many being the tsar's bruised Jews driven out by royal order, by Cossack whippers, rap-ists, looters. In the first decade of the new century, thirty thousand Italians came, mostly hardworking, frugal peasants loyal to pasta

and their bambinos; but some were criminals from the Sicilian murder cults, known later as the Black Hand, the Mafia.

The blacks, too, were on the move, lynch posses of peckerwoods and rednecks at their heels, coming from starvation on sharecroppers' hard-scrabble acres, coming north, fifteen thousand of them—to become laundresses, spittoon cleaners, shoe shiners, the salty ones whores, razor bucks, gamblers.

The slums expanded—rows of shacks punctuated by lampposts—streets took on primitive colors. The Anglo-Saxon Juke types, also the Protestant old Yankee stock down on its luck, had to share Halsted Street, Milwaukee Avenue, other run-down rows with the new immigrants. Soon synagogues, Greek cafés, Italian theaters, German and Magyar coffeehouses that aped Vienna or Budapest crowded in. Figures of foreign-language priests in cassocks appeared. Also wonderful new brews, strange sauces, smoked fish, black olives, spices unheard of before, all scented the air already polluted by yard privies and the stockyards and packingplants.

The Latins continued Old World Byzantine vendettas, the Balkan secret societies killed or maimed for reasons going back to the hundred years' wars among the goatherds and cheese makers. Bigotry, intolerances seeped down to make trouble among the younger generation—many grew up wise guys, knowing ginks who saw the power of the ward heelers, and knew what fence would buy lead pipe, copper wire, stolen luggage, a hijacked pushcart full of sweatshop pants. The fathers of future Studs Lonigans could be Italian, Jewish, Bohemian (or a kid off an Alabama farm).

By the turn of the century, the amazing thing was to discover how many of this younger generation educated itself, took full opportunities for higher learning, and in time, often ashamed of their parents' accents, the native garlic-flavored stews, smoked herring, or cabbage soups, melted away silently into the American mass. Many anglicized their names, so that by the third generation, many had no ethnic memory of the Mustache Petes with their enormous hair growths, or a pious grandfather who read the Talmud.

(What were blandly listed as "Native Whites" increased in ten years from 1900 only by 90,760, compared to the foreign-born score of 195,797.) The foreign immigrants were harassed. The German beer gardens were closed on Sundays at one time. The native whites organized the Law and Order League, a kind of forerunner of the later Birchers. Sunday closings of everything but churches was their gambit, which was a hardship on the workers who only had that day free to see the city, its exhibit halls, time to enjoy their glass of beer and wine.

There were protests. "We are against the dictation of men who go to church on Sundays with long faces and then go to the Board of Trade on Monday to swindle their colleagues out of many bushels of grain." German newspaper editors banged away. "They give you no cheap concerts and lectures to educate you. . . . I ask them, what harm there is, after you have been working hard in a dirty, dusty shop all week, to go to Lincoln Park on Sunday with your wife and babies to breathe a little fresh air." (Bronson Scrapbook.)

The trouble with what were to be called anarchists was not long in coming, as the ethnic groups found they would only be heard by the Establishment by making noise to show their aggravated sensibilities.

When bad times came and stock market losses grew, the homeless workers were arrested if they dared protest, gather, try to form into groups: twenty-five thousand in the bad times of 1874, mostly laborers and tradesmen. Wages, wretched to start with, were down to seventy-five cents a day.

The native whites sipped the free soup put out by some aldermen, gambling houses, and Christian missions; these whites began to join the protests of the "Polacks" and "hunkies" under banners of BREAD OR BLOOD. In 1876, the socialists formed in Chicago the Workingman's Party of the United States, and while there was talk of Marx and Engel, few could read them.

Many of the newcomers were natives of the land. The blacks had been coming north since the Underground Railroad slavery days of before the Civil War, but as the nation turned more and more to expansion and to industry, and the South to bigotry, lynchings, and burnings, the blacks began to crowd into Chicago. Life was hard and some turned to vice, and some to their sawed-plank churches, church groups finding relief in the Old Testament. Their version of it in old hymn books of the nineties:

Old ark she land-ed on a moun-tain top,
Ham, Shem and Japheth was settin' one day
Talkin' on the upper deck and lookin' at the bay
While they was disputin' 'bout this and that,
The Ark done bump on Ararat.

The poor whites who came—often adrift in a sea of mindlessness—were the dispossessed sharecropper, shantyboater, mudsill, redneck, peckerwood, clodhopper; Chicago had many degrading names for them and their broods. They, too, found the city "tough tittie," and used drink and rioting for their outlet after the long hours of stink in the stockyards, the reek of the slaughter rooms, the low wages of Mr. Pullman, Mr. Field, Mr. Armour, Mr. Yerkes' horse and cable cars.

When I die, don't bury me at all,
Just pickle my bones in alcohol;
Put a bottle o' booze at my head and feet,
And then I know that I will keep!

The rose is red, my nose is too,
The violet's blue, and so are you.
And I guess, before I stop.
I'd better take another drop!
CHICAGO RAILROAD HOBO SONG

Each ethnic group as it made its way had to overcome bigoted native American Know-Nothing philosophy (an early form of Birchism).

In time by 1900 the Irish spoke badly of the "coons," the "hunkies," and the "dagos." Even a respectable weekly like the *Illustrated American* wrote (in 1893) that the Italian immigrant from "Naples and Genoa and Palermo in particular . . . seems to choose by preference—as do the general run of immigrants—the most wretched abode he can find.

"In the few schools that have been set up for the instruction of Italian children—and a considerable percentage of immigrants arriving here from the Mediterranean ports are under fifteen years of age—only the faintest pretense is made at teaching the English language . . . the immigrant has little interest in acquiring the language beyond a desire to familiarize himself with words and phrases that have to do with the noxious features of his new conditions. As a result, there has gradually grown up 'un gergo italo-americano,' the bastard product of the native and adopted tongues of the people. It is interesting to observe the monstrosities that have come from this uncongenial union. From a conversation reported literally I take these convincing examples: *friloncio*, free lunch; *panblocco*, pawn-broker; *vischio*, whiskey; *coccotella*, cocktail; *cippe*, cheap; *picci di laga*, pitchers of beer; *loferi*, loafers; *aisboxa*, icebox; *stimbotto*, steamboat; *Morbida stretta*, Mulberry street; *Giacomo squea*, Chatham Square; *doc-cio*, Dutch; *nipo*, depot; *jessa*, yes, sir; *ovacutto*, overcoat; *l'oliveto*, the elevated railroad; *pinozze*, peanuts . . . while a good looking donna is one *che guarda bene!*

"It would be unfair to judge the entire body of Italian immigrants wholly by the measly lot that settles in the . . . slums. As a rule, it is the worst element of the invaders that is content to take up the career that is offered them. . . . For most of them, of course, nothing else is possible. The average possession in money of the Italian immigrant is about seventeen dollars! Plainly, the poorest of the herd must have next to nothing to bring the mean down to that impressive figure.

"Those who arrive here with any sort of equipment for life in a new country prefer to make their way to the far West and South. In Florida many of them find congenial and familiar occupation in the orange groves; in the vineyards of California there is also work to their fancy. Those who forsake as quickly as practicable the crowded cities of the East, come in the main from the nothern provinces of Italy. But the riffraff and ragtag from Calabria, Naples, and Sicily, often men exiled by their government because of crimes of rapine and murder, prefer to take their chances in . . . the large cities. . . .

"The most obvious evil of Italian immigration—one that has already been intimated—is the stubborn persistence of the new comers in maintaining their own national characteristics and prejudices. In no degree do they seem willing to become an integral part of the community in which they take up their lives anew."

The Italian immigrants, locked in with their own kind in a dismal Chicago slum—Little Italy—could often admire the gangster who made it big in the outer world. They could hardly understand why these men should be condemned.

Of the Italian gangsters as they moved toward the twenties—wrote the chief investigator of the Illinois Association for Criminal Justice, "Why should they be outcasts in the opinions of the ignorant, humble, needy, hard working people around them? They are the successes of the neighbourhood. The struggling, foreign born peasant woman sees them in their expensive cars and their fur trimmed overcoats. She hears they are sending their children to private schools. . . . She hears them called 'beer barons' and if she can read the headlines in the English language newspapers, she sees them described as 'beer barons' and 'booze kings' in print . . . the words 'king' and 'baron' have a most lofty significance. About all she knows is that these richly dressed young men are making or selling something that the Americans want to buy.

"Incidentally, she hears in gossip with another toilworn neighbour that Johnny Torrio, 'king' of them all, gave his mother back home in *Italia* a villa with 15 servants to run it.

"If the robber, labor thug and racketeer . . . Tim Murphy, who was the co-criminal of the gangsters . . . spoke at a 13th Ward meeting in behalf of one of gangdom's political henchmen, that did the candidate no harm. For was not a priest sitting next to Murphy on the platform? If some tactless soul asked, 'Is he the Tim Murphy that they said robbed the mails?' the response was deeply resentful. The attitude of the ignorant foreign born who judged gangdom in the terms of its success would be, first, that it was doubtful whether Murphy did rob the mails and, second, 'What harm did that do us?'

"Thus, and in a hundred other ways, the whole issue between good and bad government and good and bad men is befuddled and the sole conviction of the ignorant is that these 'successes of the neighbourhood' seem to take vastly more interest in neighbourhood matters than men not in the . . . racket do."

The impression was that the German immigrants worked the hardest—but that may be only because they often spoke smugly of their virtue, their dedication, their stern disciplines. Dreiser said, "They beat their children more often, and treat their wives like a milk cow—for use rather than affection. They cry at sloppy music—Schlamperei—and overeat." Dreiser, whose father was German, a mean, hard-driving failure, perhaps colored Dreiser's picture of the

Chicago Germans—many of whom were intellectuals and radicals, gathering with other Germans in Chicago's beer gardens to sing and drink.

> *Was ist das, mein Sohn,*
> *Was ist das, was ist das?*
> *Das ist ein Schweat-maker.*
> *Das was es ist.*
> *Schweat-maker.*
> *Kap-bearer,*
> *Oo-la-la-loo,*
> *Das was wir learn in der schule.*
> GERMAN SONG FEAST, N.D.

True, they were great eaters of Heringskartoffelen Bratwurst, Sauerbraten, Kasseler Rippenspeer, and *Gross Gott!* all that *Schmierkäse* and hog's head cheese. Still, the hard-working German liked his Sunday beer and his endless rounds of

> SCHNITZELBANK
> *Ist das nicht ein schnit-zel-bank?*
> *Ja, das ist ein Schnit-zel-bank.*
>
> *Ist das nicht ein Hin und Her?*
> *Ja, das ist ein Hin und Her.*
> *Ist das nicht ein Lichtputzscher?*
> *Ja, das ist ein Lichtputzscher.*
> *Lichtputzscher, Hin und Her, Kurz un Lang,*
> *und Schnitzelbank.*
> GERMAN SONG FEAST, N.D.

Long before the social scientists were aware of it, the Chicago immigrant was preparing to take over his share of the city.

28

FOR THE LOVE OF MIKE

It's not true we have a typed-up list of the rate for bribes; we do it all by telephone.

ATTRIBUTED TO A CHICAGO OFFICIAL, *c.* 1912

The name Michael Cassius McDonald, born 1839 near Chicago, belonged not to a ranting actor of badly done Shakespeare, but to a gambling-house keeper, once a bounty broker during the Civil War, and one who was such a powerhouse of a politician in Chicago that he, for money, allotted the gambling rights to those wanting card and dice setups and sites for gambling houses.

"See Mike" was the rule any three card monte sharper, confidence man followed, and Mike would collect and see that the proper police and city officials got their cut. Mike was the leader of the Cook County Democratic party for many years, an adviser to such mighty men as Mayors Carter Harrison, Sr., and Harvey Colvin. Some insist Mike was the one and only true boss of the town, its ruler, ready to go for the jugular of any who opposed him. A friend once explained his way of doing things: "A crook has to be decent to work with Mike."

As Clarence Darrow was to say in conversation, "The American problem has always been that in politics we think there is an

199

honest thief and a dishonest thief, and that there is a difference between them."

The true power of Mike McDonald—usually free of rancor—was based on the fact he'd do dishonest business with anyone who'd do *what* Mike wanted done. The *Chicago Herald* figured him as a boss who "never held office, but he ruled the city with an iron hand. He named the men who were to be candidates for election, he elected them, and after they were in office they were merely his puppets. He ran saloons and gambling houses, protected bunko steerers and confidence men and brace games of all kinds without hindrance."

He was only a youth of fifteen when he began a career as a train butcher (salesman of papers, fruit, and candy en route), cheating the passengers, bracing suckers for card games on the train, and offering packages with "valuable prizes" which turned out to be trash. He worked the trains between Niagara Falls and Detroit, and those between New Orleans and Chicago. When war came, he signed a manifesto urging the Chicago Irish to go fight for the Union. But he himself had better things to do than to carry a rifle. With messianic zeal he organized bounty jumpers, those who enlisted and deserted many times to get the cash bounty for each enlistment. Mike made a wartime fortune as their agent. Said Mike to one who knew him, "Anybody who couldn't get rich in a war, couldn't eat soup with a spoon."

Mike helped run a faro bank, and by 1867 he and con man Dan Oaks had their own gambling hall at 89 Dearborn Street. They ran rigged games, and embezzlers on their way to complete ruin were their meat. In 1869, the assistant cashier of the Chicago Dock Company dropped thirty thousand dollars of that firm's money to Mike's cards. With a queasy turn of fate, Mike spent three months in jail for this—no one wanting to risk sixty thousand dollars in bail on him. The trial was a joke of fervid misjustice. Mike had witnesses to swear he *always* ran an honest game, and, anyway, the debauched cashier had "begged earnestly" to be permitted into the game; he had not been lured or enticed. Acquitted, Mike, after paying his legal sharks, found he had nothing to pay off the police to permit him to run his gambling house. He got used to being raided two or three times a week for months, paying his fines;

but it cemented his lifelong hatred of the police, who let you alone if you paid graft, but harassed you if you didn't.

When he was the boss, he made mockery of the police and humiliated them whenever he could. He learned from Machiavelli, "Bitter foes today, sugared darlings tomorrow, kissing and scratching in a breath."

He originated the story of somebody coming to him to raise funds to bury someone. "Mike, can we put you down for two dollars?"

"Who's it for?"

"We're burying a policeman."

"Grand! Here's my ten dollars, bury five of them!"

After the Great Fire, Mike's luck turned for the better, and he took on partners in one place, making a hundred thousand dollars a year. Mike was an organizer, and he brought together all the saloonkeepers fighting the Sunday Closing Law, formed them into a pressure group called, with ironic callowness, the People's Party. They backed for mayor a fancy womanizer and big-time bettor—general agent for the U.S. Express Company—Harvey D. Colvin, and elected him. It was said of Colvin as mayor, "He wore his rank of office around his balls."

With Mike McDonald having the new mayor on a Yo-Yo string, gambling houses flourished. Harry Varnell and the Hankins brothers, big gambling-house people, joined with Mike in 1885 to form a strong syndicate of bookmakers who controlled the betting at Chicago and Indiana horse tracks. In one year, the group made nearly a million dollars. (As one barroom bettor put it, "Some of them races was so fixed you could smell the brakes smokin' when the jocks pulled a hoss on the turn fer home.")

Under a captive mayor, Mike formed many partnerships—there was no *terra incognita* in Chicago gambling territory—one merger was with two sharpers to run a braced game on State Street in a big house called The Store. The saloon took over the first floor. The biggest gambling house in town was on the second. There were rooms to rent on the third and fourth floors for private games, orgies, or discreet couples, and cruising whores. Mary Noonan McDonald, wife of Mike, was in charge here, and often Mike watched her, like Lot scowling at Sodom. Mike was warned about Mary's eye for young men.

Roulette and faro wheels filled the gambling floor, and card sharks working for the house dealt seconds from packed decks or put in a cold deck. These men—experts at cheating—dominated nearly every table of play for the house. When in 1873, The Store first opened for gambling, one of Mike's partners with furrowed pensive face showed panic at the size and cost of the operation.

"Mike, we'll never get enough players to fill up the games."

"Don't you go worrying about that." He quoted P. T. Barnum, *"There's a sucker born every minute."* That statement joined American folk wisdom right then and there as it was repeated around the city. Mike's dice expert, Nick Hogan, had only one arm. The talk was, "If Nick had *two* arms, he'd have all the money in the world."

Mike soon dropped his partners; they lacked his drive and sense of timing. The Store was the meeting place, the club, of the city officials, ward bosses, and the more prominent criminals, those who had a sense of class. In fact, the saying was, "Don't bother goin' to City Hall for anything—go to The Store to Mike's office, second floor, that's the *real* City Hall."

Mike had a sense of humor of irresistible simplicity. Twice a year reporters were invited to see the police make a traditional raid on The Store, break up some old tables and wheels, then arrest six or eight croupiers and dealers taking a rap—all freed after a few small fines. It was "all clear" now for six months more. The press got a headline story and some innocent people nodded and said, "We're cleaning them out."

There were, of course, honest police; not with the unique madness of saints, but honest. A very few, and Mike McDonald made their lives hell when he could with his political power. Mayor Carter Harrison, Sr., in 1879, had appointed by chance an honest superintendent of police, Simon O'Donnell, who, looking over the complaints of robbings and cheatings at The Store, felt McDonald was not above the law. In 1880 the chief set off a real raid at The Store, not for show. He was busted to captain for this and given the worthless jobs handed out only for punishment; he was never again to be in any position of power.

Mike had his own man appointed chief of police, William J. McGarigle (it is interesting to note that the Irish, as ward politicians controlling votes, pretty much got most of the big-city plums).

McGarigle pulled some fancy swindles against the city for Mike, selling them chalk and water as a new kind of paint preservative for the Court House. Mike nearly collected $128,000 for this scheme before the swindle was discovered. McGarigle had to run for it to Canada; but Mike wasn't ever prosecuted, the boys at City Hall shaking their heads at the paint caper: "*That* Mike . . ."

Mike, as we've noted, had a wife, Mary Noonan McDonald, and while most police raids never went above the second story of The Store, once when they did, getting into the rooming-house section, Mary took up a pistol and wounded an invading policeman. She was defended by Mike's legal eagle, A. S. Truede, as American womanhood defending her domain from invasion. Mrs. McDonald's boarders were a strange lot, many of them card handlers and wheel spinners from below. Also bunco artists and confidence men who bilked the marks, but they in turn were protected by Mike who had a simple formula: twenty percent of their loot to go to the police, forty percent to Mike, and the thieves could keep the other forty percent, if they said, "Thank you, Mr. McDonald." Mike felt he earned his share. He had expert "witnesses" on call, shyster lawyers of cunning skill in confusing the courts, and city officials or ward bosses who could always feel that money from Mike was just taking on a nonrepayable "loan." It was unctuous, smooth, and effective.

No one could run any kind of gambling layout without the approval of Mike McDonald; his own protected gamblers had a full city to work over, and *all* its visitors. The visitors, some very impressive, seemed easy marks. "Hungry Joe" Lewis cheated Oscar Wilde out of several thousand dollars when Wilde lectured in the city; Charles Francis Adams, Bostonian and Washington diplomat, fell to Red Jimmy FitzGerald for seven thousand dollars. Both visitors had read Goethe: "All possessions are threatening." Small condolence.

Tom O'Brien, "King of the Bunco Artists," invented the gold brick sales idea (each brick had one small plug of gold for testing, set in a solid brass brick).

Carter Harrison, Sr., couldn't be mayor forever; after his fourth term, a reform mayor came in, John A. Roche. (The term reform is relevant; said Edgar Lee Masters, "A reform regime took a little longer to learn how to steal, how to collect the boodle.")

Mike had to tone down his activities. He took two million dollars of his fortune and, like the later Mafia and Cosa Nostra, went into legit businesses and also retained his position as the Democratic party's chief. He owned a newspaper, *The Chicago Globe*, for two years (Dreiser worked there as a young reporter), was treasurer of the company that built the first elevated railroad line in the city, the Lake Street mileage. Also since the city was a big buyer of sand, stone, and gravel, he bought a Lemont quarry. The honest graft, in selling to the city at high prices, with its kickbacks and markups, showed him gambling with rigged gear wasn't the only way to make easy money.

Moving from The Store, the McDonalds, Mike, Mary, and their two children, built a huge fancy mansion on Ashbury Avenue within shouting distance of old pal Carter Harrison, "in case they needed to borrow a cup of sugar."

We come now to Mrs. McDonald's story, and it is well worth retelling in all its strange manifestations. A few months after the family moved into the new house, Mary was gone from it. Mike McDonald confessed to friends his wife had run off with a minstrel singer, Billy Arlington, who had come to play in blackface in Chicago, with Emerson's Minstrels. Mike traced his wife and her paramour to the Palace Hotel in San Francisco. He hurried to the coast and Mary greeted him with, "Don't shoot for God's sake, it's *all* my fault. Take me back for the love of God." They became reconciled and Mike brought her back home. However, in 1889, she was gone again, this time with a young priest with whom she had knelt in worship—at private Mass—in the chapel in the McDonald mansion—the Reverend Joseph Moysant, assistant rector of the Catholic Church of Notre Dame. "And with her the stalwart young priest celebrating an even more ancient mystery than the Mass" (newspaper report).

They ran away to Paris, where they lived together for six years. Then the full burden of his fall from grace into carnal sin came to Father Moysant, and he went into a monastery.

Mary McDonald came back to Chicago, again to run a boardinghouse: like a suburban housewife returning from a shopping trip.

Mike, feeling betrayed by the Church, had smashed the family altar and renounced Catholicism and gotten a divorce from Mary. In 1898, he was sixty-six years of age, but still raunchy, and he married a Jewish girl of twenty-three he saw in the chorus line of a show. Dora Feldman was the ex-wife of a baseball player named Sam Barclay. Mike, infatuated, became a Jewish convert and married Dora with Hebrew rites.

Mike had no luck with wives. He built Dora a splendid house on Drexel Boulevard, but Dora was also unfaithful to him; not with her rabbi, but with a commercial artist named Webster Guerin. She was madly infatuated with him, but for reasons never fully explained, in February of 1907, she shot and killed him. Said Dora, "I told him I knew where his heart was and I didn't miss it an inch." (The artist's mother, some said, didn't want to lose her baby boy.) This was too much for Mike. He said to his lawyer, "I don't want to see the goddamn bitch again, but save her if it costs every dollar I've got." He took to his bed, called in a priest, and was again received into the faith, and he announced that Mary McDonald was his "only true wife" in the sight of God and the pope, and he died anointed, Mary at his side. However, Mary got none of his estate. Dora Feldman McDonald got one-third of his fortune and forty thousand dollars for lawyers' fees in her coming trial for murder. She was acquitted in 1908. The rest of her career and Mary's weren't of much news value and do not appear to have interested reporters.

Mike's fortune was never fully estimated, but in 1891 he had helped elect Carter Harrison, Sr., for his fifth term of office. (Fifth terms are a habit of political bosses of Chicago. Both Harrisons, father and son, were mayor five times. And last of the old-time bosses is Richard Daley who, in 1971, was also elected to his fifth term as mayor of Chicago by a machine old fashioned, but delivering the goods.)

Mike had collected a huge campaign fund from the town's gamblers. After the election, Mike had laid a charge of forty to sixty-five percent of every gambler's income for a special fund to pay off the police through the mayor's office. The knowing William Stead reported in *If Christ came to Chicago* that the money "which amounted during the World's Fair, in some districts, to a colossal fortune, was divided. Many people had a finger in the pie before the residue reached Mr. Harrison. But however many there were who fingered the profit en route, there was enough left to make it well worth the Mayor's while to allow the houses to run. Everyone in Chicago knew perfectly well that they were running. . . . They were all in existence and prospered under the protection of the administration."

It should be pointed out that not all murder cases had as happy an ending as Dora's. Hunting in the files of the *Chicago Times* in the 1870–1880 period, one finds the ending to some other sensational murders—also samples of nineteenth-century newspaper headline writing, as when Christopher Rafferty, a hoodlum, was guilty of the murder of Patrolman Patrick O'Meara.

SHUT OFF HIS WIND

A SATISFACTORY JOB FOR JACK KETCH AT LAST

THE HANGMAN'S ROPE AWARDED TO
CHRISTOPHER RAFFERTY

NOW, DO NOT REPRIEVE NOR PARDON HIM,
NOR GIVE HIM A NEW TRIAL

THE JURY CONCLUDES, IN JUST TWENTY MINUTES,
TO STRING THE RUFFIAN UP

29

THE SURE WINNERS

What if we steal this city blind?
If they want anything, let 'em nail it down.
CARL SANDBURG

While the public might connect "Big Jim" O'Leary with the famous cow owned by his mother, which was wrongly accused of burning down Chicago, Big Jim was to die a millionaire as an old man, after a fantastic career as a top gambler. He first surfaced as a youngster, a handyman for Mike McDonald and his friends. Then he went on to serve "Silver Bill" Riley whose establishment, a poolroom, was the first to take horse bets exclusively. Silver Bill was a puritan about most things except for wagering on horse races. With a sense of individual isolation, he was against alcohol and cardplaying; wrong by God's moral order, as was smoking and cursing. He did not permit minors to gamble on the premises. He lived in the pessimistic world of blind force.

As he grew up, Big Jim left Silver Bill and switched to more normal settings. In the 1890s he had a share of John Condon's gambling house, and when John went blind, it didn't stop the partnership. They went together into a gambling syndicate set up twenty-three miles from Chicago at Long Beach, Indiana, a Hoosier Monte

209

Carlo that failed to attract attention among the country jaspers. The two city slickers lost their investment.

Big Jim was soon back in Chicago, on South Halsted Street, near the stockyards, and began to operate in a big way, forming a better, bigger syndicate of bookies, poolrooms and handbooks with other gamblers. In the end Big Jim, by force of character and what we today call clout, pretty much controlled all the gambling and betting on the South Side.

Big Jim was the tough boss-man of six hundred bookies and poolrooms. He even went on water—not to walk, but to gamble. From 1904 to 1907, there was a floating poolroom aboard the steamer *City of Traverse*. How the few who only wanted to play pool were able to control the rolling billiard balls in the dipping lake tide was a wonder. Whatever else the steamer was, it was the first gambling ship on record in America. The ritual was for it to make an afternoon sailing from the South Chicago docks of the Illinois Central, carrying at least a thousand sportsmen and horse handicappers for a cooling sail around the lake, at least to stay afloat until the day's horse racing results were in. Wireless, a novelty in private hands in those days, sent the betting odds and winners out to the waiting seaborne players. In this askew game ship, the gamblers seemed safe.

But the police began to arrest the passengers when the boat docked, and also, using the device of a later age, began to scramble the wireless messages. The last lake trip of the *City of Traverse* was made in May of 1907, and was infiltrated by eighteen Chicago detectives, seven journalists, for only forty-two authentic bettors present.

Big Jim O'Leary's unique quality of leadership remained on land. His gambling-house headquarters was on South Halsted, which was a fancy structure even in a day of lavishly equipped places. There was a Turkish bath for steaming out the pores of winners or losers, or well-heeled drunks, a fine restaurant in a day when Americans knew how to eat better and had never heard of calories; a bowling alley, billiard room for tables with good cushions and straight cues that had never vulgarly bashed a head, in a world where a pool cue made a dandy weapon.

The billiard room was the pride of the place, with the softest deep chairs and silver-plated gaboons, potent drinks served by polite servants. And all the while, constantly changing blackboards were under observation, boards that listed the betting odds and results of every major horse race in Canada and the United States.

One could not only bet horse races with Big Jim; he'd give or take odds on wrestling (before playacting took over the sport), boxing, football, baseball, and political elections. If someone wanted to get on the weather, or harvest figures, Big Jim was game for that, too. "No one ever tried to bet on the end of the world by morning— but Big Jim woulda taken it—at his odds." He won ten thousand dollars betting on eighteen days of continual rain during a month of May.

He took no chances of the premises being molested, for the place was, he said, police-proof, fireproof and bombproof, with its iron-reinforced heavy oak doors, steel plates set in the walls, and rooms lined with zinc-covered timbers. When the Gamblers' War of 1907 broke out, a civil war for control of Chicago territory among the various gamblers, attempts were made to plant bombs at Big Jim's place. The police in their attacks on the place used axes and sledgehammers to break in when it was politic to have a spectacular raid for the press. But Big Jim usually had warning of these raids, and once he filled his hollow walls with red pepper. When the police axes cut through the zinc sheeting, the choppers were blinded by the pepper, and most had to have hospital attention. Defense to Big Jim was more than just the usual facile optimism of gamblers.

By 1911, Big Jim O'Leary was ready to retire. He made one of those warm, ungrammatical statements that should be taken with a pound of salt: "I never paid a dollar for protection. I could have had all kinds of it, but let me tell you something. Protection that you purchase ain't worth nothing to you. A man who will sell himself ain't worth an honest man's dime. The police is for sale, but I don't want none of them."

This is nonsense. There were times when he paid like everyone else for protection, and things ran smoothly; times when reform for a while made things tough, and periods when he, the city officials, and police didn't agree as to the cost of the fix. So, a raid.

On the West Side, while Big Jim was rising to his prime, other combinations were taking over gambling: Alderman Johnny Rodgers, Patsy King, and the first mention of a major Italian personality named Johnny Gazzola. Almost up to the end of the nineteenth century, the floozies, brothels, gambling houses, the Irish shebeens (home stills) were in the hands of native-born Protestant stock, Irish Catholics, Jews, and blacks. Italians, who were in a generation or so to show how a nationwide loose association of Latin crime masters worked, were as yet still involved within their own ethnic group, preying on them through an organization called the Black Hand. But with Gazzola in the early 1900s among the pioneers, the Italians were to move into the mainstream of the Chicago underworld. In crime there was no permanence; Einstein was beginning to formulate that "the speed of light is the *only* absolute in the universe."

The Loop vice was still held by the Celts: Tom Mcginnis, John and Pat O'Malley, Alderman Hinky Dink Kenna, and Bathhouse John Coughlin; gamblers paid off, as did whores in soiled peignoirs, polished confidence men.

The North Side was Mont Tennes' territory, aided by "Hot Stove" Jimmy Quinn, victim of the popular jest, "Jim Quinn, he'd steal a red hot stove." Hot Stove mostly devoted himself, by 1910, to selling protection only—for card games, and his own "permits" at a hundred dollars for a whorehouse to sell whiskey. His political muscle for his deeds was Barney Gorgan, a West Side Democratic boss.

Mont ran gambling on the North Side where he controlled several hundred bookie joints, and was the kingpin in Chicago racetrack bookmaking. The Illinois Crime Survey gave him a detailed study in one of its published reports: "He was avowedly a real estate man, for a period the owner of a cash register company, and for more than a score of years the proprietor of the General News Bureau, controlling the wires for the gathering and dispensing of race track news in Chicago and principal parts of the United States. Repeated exposés have always found him in control of strings of handbooks and gambling houses in Chicago . . . other urban centers."

Mont bought the Payne Telegraph Service of Cincinnati. It cost three hundred dollars a day to run wires to poolrooms and bookmakers, who paid from fifty to one hundred dollars each for the service. Also he got one-half of their total receipts, out of which Tennes paid one-half of the losses. Tennes was boss of every gambling joint in Chicago, since they could not operate without the telegraph service only he could furnish. The Loop and South Side syndicates declared war.

In June of 1907, when Mont was promenading peacefully with his wife, he was set upon by sluggers and beaten. Bombs were planted and exploded in places owned by Mont, and five bombs were set off among his biggest rivals, Jim O'Leary among them. Oddly, some officials were deaf, stone deaf. With bombs within hearing range, Chief of Police George M. Shippy firmly stated that "there is no gambling worthy of the name in existence here at the present time." (Someone on a bookie tote board, in chalk, nominated the chief for "The see-hear-know nothing Three Monkeys Award.")

If you can't beat 'em, join 'em, Mont Tennes figured out. "*Then* take 'em from the inside by boring from within," as the Marxist intellectuals were beginning to work it. Mont went to make peace with the other gamblers. The combine worked fine with Mont; by 1909, he was the ruler of the racetrack business. He extended his special friendship deeper into the Police Department and got their happy nod, as they counted their payoffs and stood by as he took over the city's biggest dice games, busiest roulette wheels, and poker setups. Carter Harrison, Jr., equaling his father's record, had just been reelected mayor for the fifth time in 1911, helped by the vice districts, and the lid was off the city. Hotels ran big dice and card games openly; fifty gambling joints were active in the Loop, "taking the marks for their rolls."

Mont Tennes' Syndicate had a fair set of rules for payment for every kind of protection fees. "Steep, yes—but *no* police troubles."

> Pool rooms—*forty to fifty percent of win.*
> Roulette—*forty percent of win.*
> Faro—*fifty percent of win.*
> Craps—*sixty percent of win.*
> Poker and other games—*fifty percent house share.*
> BRONSON SCRAPBOOK

Mont was most likely the first sanguine big crime boss that took nationwide control of many criminal interests. Mont Tennes was the Daniel Boone of big crime, a forgotten pioneer of the methods the Capone mob and their rivals and today's Mafia groups were to use with such success from Vegas to narc peddling. Like so many beginners of movements, Mont has not gotten his deserved credit by genre historians and a *bien pensant* press.

In 1910, Mont had set up his own General News Bureau for getting results on horse races and betting odds, sending the old Payne Service into outer darkness. Ninety pool joints in Chicago alone paid him three thousand dollars a week. He controlled race betting in much of the United States and Canada, and bought so many police departments across the country that his gangs could use shotguns and dynamite bombs on all who opposed or tried to muscle in on Mont's organizations. His income was said to be several million a year, and no Internal Revenue to plague him—our modern income tax "didn't begin to chisel the nation until 1913—and then for peanuts until the Welfare State came" (letter to *Chicago Tribune*).

Mont was investigated right into the 1920s, but was only once indicted and he beat that. When he retired (The Goo Goos, a Good Government reform movement, had closed two hundred of his bookie joints that paid him a yearly profit of $364,000), he sold most of his interests in his horse wire service to the Annenbergs, the circulation pushers for the *Tribune*, who organized squads and tough crews to pressure newsstand owners who didn't see the *Tribune* as a great newspaper. The Annenbergs also owned the publication *The Daily Racing Form*.

"The Annenbergs tried, later on, for respectability, and so never made their full impact felt on the gambling scene the way a bolder Mont Tennes did. All the Annenbergs got from their efforts were millions, a scurrilous press" (Ben Hecht). And an odd ambassador to the Court of St. James.

Chicago was already a very large black city, and the black had been an ever-growing personality there since the first days of the Underground Railroad that smuggled slaves into Canada before the Civil War. The black man, in certain sections of that pressed-down ethnic group, enjoyed gambling, whoring, violence as much as his white equal in those fields. Few paid any attention to the black street preacher: "What makes men evil and cruel is the idea they have souls—and so they want their souls saved."

Starting in the 1890s, John V. Johnson, full of self-esteem, better known as "Mushmouth" Johnson, was the black king of gambling, the political boss controlling *and* voting huge blocks of black votes. He was the kingfish of the policy and numbers, gambling, dice games, poker, and faro as played in the Bad Lands and Little Cheyenne districts. The Chinese feared him and paid three dollars a week a gambling table to be left alone by Mushmouth's sluggers and razor bucks.

Mushmouth had hit Chicago in 1875, coming from St. Louis where he had been a waiter. He took up the same trade for a few years at the splendid Palmer House. "Yes sir-ring in a fine baritone. Yak-Yaking the ofays." By 1882, he was branching out into gambling, with various partners, and soon had control of 311 South Clark Street which became known as the place for action, cheap action, or as high as you wanted to make it. It was a black-and-white joint. You could play in nickels at the wheels or at poker. In 1890, Mushmouth sold out and opened a more exclusive place on State Street, with a fine saloon and a gambling setup. In 1906, with two partners, he opened the Frontenac on Twenty-third Street. Here only whites could command action, and even so had to show a ten-spot at the door to be admitted—no tinhorns here. The three partners would always divide the take after a hard night's play, at six o'clock in the morning. Mushmouth Johnson didn't play cards or roll dice for money, and he didn't bet on the horses. "That kind of thing was for suckers."

Mushmouth ran dives that never had the class of some of those of the white gamblers. He also seriously claimed he lost money running gambling hangouts. But his remarks may have been as honest as his wheels and dice. "I spent more than a hundred thousand dollars for fines and a big sum for police protection. I had to pay out four dollars for every one I took in at the game."

This statement belongs with Big Jim O'Leary's about "never paying a penny for police protection." It was, some claimed, their alibis in the event of their being taken by the officials.

Among the best-known gamblers of the turn of the century was Johnny Rafferty who came to Whisky Row in 1893, and never saw an honest day come to night. "I love a thief," he told anyone who would listen. But he drew the line on some things. He told the *Chicago Journal* in 1903, "I never gouged out an eye, cut off a goat's tail, beaten a policeman, held up a train or bitten off a bulldog's nose."

Lucky, or unlucky, gamblers had the reputation of feline grace as seducers, a way with women. The men whose women went off with a gambler had their own lament:

> *Bow down your head and cry, poor boy,*
> *Bow down your head and cry;*
> *Stop thinking about that woman you love,*
> *Bow down your head and cry.*
>
> *I followed her for months and months,*
> *She offered me her hand;*
> *We were about to be married, when*
> *She ran off with a gamblin' man.*

The most popular story in song was of a gambler and pimp named Johnny and his whore, Frankie. The Chicago version is a classic (as Dreiser gave it to me). The verses build until Frankie discovers Johnny has not been true to their love—for Frankie, like so many prostitutes, is oversentimental.

> *Frankie looked over the transom,*
> *And found, to her great surprise,*
> *That there on the bed was Johnny*
> *A-lovin' up Elly Bly.*
> *He was her man, but he done her wrong.*
>
> *Frankie drew back her kimono;*
> *She took out her little forty-four*
> *Root-a-toot-toot, that girl did shoot*
> *Right through that hardwood floor*
> *She shot her man, 'cause he done her wrong.*

Then Johnny makes his exit with a splendid death speech, in the proper Chicago style, with a sense of drama suggesting every love is a lost love. His words have the element of fluidity of literature—the Hemingway instinct of grace under pressure.

> *Roll me over easy,*
> *Roll me over slow,*
> *Roll me on my right side,*
> *'Cause the bullet hurts me so,*
> *I was her man, but I done her wrong.*

The prime hangouts in Chicago for busted gamblers and hoboes off the road, and for pickpockets, were two places run by Bob Duncan, also known as "King of the Pickpockets." His Whisky Row place had everything: whores, rooms for carnal pleasure, whiskey, faro, poker, and dice. Wyoming Silvers, a noted tramp, always made Duncan's his home ground when off the rods in Chicago. In 1896, Wyoming—on an arduous pilgrimage—married a Minnesota widow, who, when she died, left him richer by ten thousand dollars. Wyoming and some bindle stiffs, road buddies, went on a six-month bender, consisting mostly of booze, more booze, and boozy fights. Ten of the buddies died in delirium tremens, and Wyoming, who seems to have been a poor barroom battler, lost three fingers and one ear in saloon fights, ending with a nose like a frayed rose.

One of the decorations at Duncan's was a pickpocket named Eddie Jackson, who began lifting leather at the age of fourteen, in 1887. In forty years of his art, he was arrested two thousand times, got off mostly by paying fines, or returning the loot. He would often also pay off a policeman to confuse some victims with threats—and he had a lawyer on standby terms; orders were if Eddie didn't report once every hour, the lawyer was to hotfoot it to the station house with a habeas corpus and a valid bail bond. At picking pockets, Eddie's average score was fifteen hundred dollars a week. He died, like so many more honest men, in the paupers' ward of Cook County Hospital. As with Mushmouth Johnson, Eddie complained at the cost of bribing officials and police, the heavy expense of crooked lawyers. A shover who worked with Eddie (a shover distracts the victim while the pickpocket reaches for the wallet) said, "The only people who really pile up the tainted mazuma, big money, are the law, them stinkin' shysters, fences and most politicians."

30

THE TIME OF THE TROTTER

Good horses make short miles.
GEORGE HERBERT

There are still some who remember the grand days when owning a trotter in Chicago was fun and a sign of social status. Alice C.—once courted by this author's grandfather—wrote to us in exaltation of the family trotter: "I remember those wonderful golden Sunday mornings when Papa—his mind free of La Salle Street wheat and pork prices, would have Jack the stable boy get our trotter, Georgie Boy, harnessed to the light four-wheeled rig—the horse, after a week's light runs, knowing today was special. Papa in his driving jacket would come out of the house with his light whip, which he never used but would flick over Georgie Boy's twitching ears. I'd be in my little jacket with its violet collar, on the seat by Papa's side, and had to promise I would hold on to the thin iron hand grip and not stand up and not yell out. Then Papa would crack the whip and cry 'Go, Georgie,' and Georgie Boy would start his trot down our blue stone drive. Papa would sit very straight and hold the reins in his gloved hands and make clucking mouth sounds, sort of like kissing, and the trotter would extend himself. By the time we were on the street under the elms, the sun through the branches flecking and spotting us like brook trout, we'd be rolling along and there would be two or three more drivers out with their trotters, all heading out of town for a country road. Papa would raise his gray derby to them, holding the reins in one hand, and soon all the trotters would be out on the pike, rolling along, wheels spinning, and the best sound I know was the *kop kop* of the hoofs on the well-packed pike.

"When I was twelve, Papa let me handle the reins on a straight stretch of road, and I was as proud as if I had reached the North Pole. Those Sundays were always the best part I remember of the summers we stayed home. All of the city owners of trotters would go out about four miles along the pike and wheel and turn into the empty fairgrounds where we'd use the track, and Papa and the other men as they rubbed on liniment, would talk of sulkies and horse lines. About trotters like Volunteer, son of the great Hambletonian, and of the ale at Farmer's Hotel on the River Road on the run home from the races at the Park. After a while, Papa would join the trotting *crack*, as the drive to the Red Lion was called; and while the trotters were cooling off, everybody went in for a cider or a whisky, and I'd have a cup of tea and rock cake and look at the prints of Goldsmith Maid and Judge Fullerton and others on the walls.

"Coming back in the afternoon, Papa would recite:

> *On top of the Crumpetty Tree*
> *The Quangle Wangle sat,*
> *But his face you could not see,*
> *On account of his Beaver Hat.*

"On the run home, just before we came to the first brick-paved streets, Georgie Boy was encouraged to run, and Papa would say we'd break the two minute mile for sure—only we never did. Jack the stable darkie would be waiting for us to unharness Georgie Boy and rub him down and wash out his nose and mouth and walk him about—'cool walking,' he called it. Papa would promise to take us to the harness races at Washington Park, and I said when I got married some day, I'd want a trotter of my very own. But, of course, by that time the fashion of private families as owners of trotters was gone . . . and nobody could keep horses in Chicago for trotting."

A substantial part of the Chicago population that could afford a good horse desired a trotter more than cotillions or *fêtes champêtres*. At business meetings in saloons and barbershops, trotter talk went on. By the time the nineteenth century was feeling its stride, a sportsman knew that the item to own was a trotter, a horse that had been trained to trot consistently along the lakefront, to move a foreleg on one side and the hind leg on the other all at the same time. Horse impresarios claimed it gave a smooth gait and made for endurance. It also gave one style to be driving something that beautiful and alert. Way back in the sixteenth century, the horse historians said, the French used a word meaning *to tread*, and from that came the English term *trotter*.

Just as today a sporting coterie might brag of its XKE Series Jag, or dune buggy, or drag racing, in those days a Chicago sportsman spoke of his bay, chestnut, or tobacco-brown trotter. The fashion was against a trotter being a spotted paint pony or all white or sorrel. At first, some rode trotters, but in the end they were properly hitched to a four-wheeled surrey or a two-wheeled sulky. In time, the bicycle-wheeled sulky was the official racer; the trotter pulled,

the driver sat legs apart and leaned way over trying to lift the sulky by the seat of his pants.

In winter, along the sand dunes and lake streets, one got out the fast cutter, the varnished sleigh, and gave the trotter exercise by steel runners on the crisp, crunchy, fresh-packed snow, "Bells tinkling, cheeks burning in the frost, the ladies in their furs smelling of frangipani and violets, and over us the cold blue sky."

When the season came for the fairs, the showing off of prize hog, corn, or the biggest harvester, the main interest of the sporting crowd and the horsey set were the trotting races. Every Chicago home or inn or club that cared for sporting scenes had a few trotter prints of the best of the breeds on their walls—the grand champions coming around the track, pulling their two thin wheels, and the cap-topped driver holding on for dear life. Firms such as Haskell & Allen, Meyer & Merkel, H. Pharazyn, Currier & Ives, others, sold millions of hand-colored prints of Smuggler, Columbus, Fanny Allen, Lancet, Fearnaught Boy.

Raising trotters and racing them became a sport for much of the population, and someone wrote that trotter races were "the people's sport, the people's pastime." To keep a fast and famous horse and a shiny buggy was almost the equal of keeping a fast woman. Lovers took their sweethearts to ride at their side in the surrey, while they flourished the whip over a horse training to do, perhaps, that two-minute mile. A chaise that raised the dust ahead of other spanking rigs showing off their horses was the town talk, with a girl in striped poplin and tightly scarfed hat by the driver's side.

On a clear day all over the nation the places to see the best trotters being given a run were at Washington Park, Chicago; Brighton Road, Boston; Harlem Lane, New York; Rope Ferry Road and Point Breeze Park in Philadelphia, with sportsmen at the taut reins. The season for trotting races ran from April till November, and at times overlapped at both ends. The smooth-haired, polished horses began to run faster, working toward that two-minute mile. Chicago trotter drivers would talk of 1806, early and ancient history for trotters, when Yankee had run a race of a mile in 2:59. In 1845, Lady Suffolk came in at 2:29¼. By the sixties, Dexter was flashing across the line at 2:17¼. And there in irritable defiance of heart and hope, it seemed it would stay. That same year, Rarus, try as he would, took only a fraction of a second off that. But in 1880, St. Julian made it in 2:11½, and Maude S managed 2:10. Again, the Lake Shore experts said with pugnacity, well there it is and there it will stay. No horse on the Grand Circuit, the big show and league for trotters racing in harness, would ever show anything better.

> How big was Alexander, Pa,
> That people called him great?
> MC GUFFEY'S READER

Trotters who raced in Chicago were famous like later film stars, baseball and football heroes. The horses were painted, drawn, adored, cheered, and remembered as bringers of fortunes. Chicago was a betting town. Meets became massive sporting events that drew everyone in the city prone to gambling, drink, and food. Wild times were common on the tracks, and the moralists sniffed, "We told you so."

By the turn of the century, trotter harness racing in Chicago was more popular than ever, and a season could no more exist without a series of meets than the ladies at the track without a drop of bergamot on their handkerchiefs.

And in 1912 it happened. Chicago papers printed extras. *A gelding named Uhlan ran the mile, pulling his wire-wheeled sulky at 1:58.* Hats were in the air, and in the Levee saloons there was talk the ultimate had been reached in a trotter's speed. But a decade later, as the band played "Hindustan" and "Wait Till the Cows Come Home," the horse Peter Manning was clocked doing the mile in 1:56¾.

It was at a Chicago trotter track years ago that an old joke was created: that of a gambler, his coat collar way up to his ears, who said to a companion, "What would you do if you had a bad day betting, lost everything as I did?" Said his friend casually, "I'd cut my throat." Said the bettor, lowering his collar to show his neck, "See, I did."

The jest has survived as a traditional racing story.

31

THE REVOLUTION ON TWO WHEELS

Th' past always looks better than it was.
'Tis only pleasant because it isn't here.
MR. DOOLEY

The bicycle craze first hit Chicago like a giant blizzard in the 1870s. By 1893 when some sort of records were kept, there were 50,000 bikes for a population of a little over 1,200,000 people. The big six footer of the early 1880s, with pedals attached to the axle, was gone, the "safety" was soon in with both wheels of equal size. The Chicago Cycling Club, the demigods of the handlebars, began to issue guides; also popular were groups like the Kenwood Cycle Club, Sheridan Road Wheelmen, Northside Touring Club, and nearly a thousand others.

Three hundred scorchers, as wild riders were called, en masse, bells jangling, could frighten horses. The national organization was called The League of American Wheelmen. It wasn't all just fun and sport, or the horse sent to obsolescence. The clubs felt their political power. The Viking Bicycle Club put their organization on record with the ward heelers with no delicacy of language.

"This club and associates controlled 1500 political votes and would support those candidates favorable to wheelmen and wheeling."

It was soon clear to politicians these clubs could serve for more than just promoting good wheeling laws; they could deliver votes.

The most glamorous bicycle rider was Lillian Russell, once barred from a Chicago racetrack by some who felt she wasn't really respectable, but an actress full of lust and enticement. Lillian rode on a gold-plated bicycle in *haute noblesse* style—a gift of her good friend, Diamond Jim Brady. He not only had a gold-plated scorcher himself, but had a miniature bicycle set of jewelry made of diamonds and held in gold, which he wore at times on his waistcoat.

Some bike clubs, like the Calumet Swamp and the West Wheeling Wheels, had special costumes, athletic *and* exposing, while lady groups favored flounces and gewgaws. Of course the criminals were busy stealing bikes, as later generations were to become auto thieves. Well-organized wheel-snatching rings sprang up in Chicago, and a black market and stealing to order began of Columbia, Iver Johnson, English imports, French jobs with handlebars like bull horns—soon a trade in itself. Like the later TV repairmen, pirates took over accessory shops, repair, paint, and tire organizations.

Besides the overdone song of "You'll look sweet upon the seat of a bicycle built for two," a real rouser, but now forgotten, was a sad dirge that contained such a lyric as:

> For I ride alone to the distant blue,
> My bicycle gliding away
> To the fields of green where my loved one lies
> Awaiting the judgement day.
> MUSIC SHEET, C. 1900

Hardly the stuff to inspire a love of joys of wheeling through life together. But Chicagoans of those days seemed to have had the Elizabethan love of "the skull beneath the skin."

The medical profession, like later doctors at ski resorts, soon found a lucrative trade in serving Chicago bike riders, and they, too, issued warnings of the danger of such new plagues as cyclist's crouch, handlebar cramp, headlight eyestrain. The worst of these fearful ailments was cyclist's crouch, caused by bending one's spine too far over the handlebars, causing the cramping of important interior organs and entrails. Medical men cried in horror at the crouch and insisted, as noted in one newspaper, on a "genteel up-right posture." "If their warnings were not heeded, the rider would help produce a nation of people having trouble breathing, swallow-ing their food, or standing upright only with a crutch."

For women wheelers the disease was called scorcher's flush, which dermatologists claimed was destroying the Gibson Girl's complexion. The makers of creams, soaps, and lotions, with Hercu-lean effort, rushed in to keep the American girl "as beautiful as she was before the coming of the bicycle." Not only was the sun destruc-tive, but the Chicago lady rider needed a sure protection "against flying particles of sand, cinders, grit and other abrasives," of which, it must be admitted, the city had plenty.

In 1896, an anatomist, Dr. Marcus Edwards, warned that so much leg exercising as bicycling would "produce a race with legs all out of proportion and the human race would walk around on stilts of their own making."

The most severely hurt, it turned out, were the livery stables and the inns, for bike riders just shot past. But in one private letter by a University of Chicago student comes the line, "Wheels are jim dandy for getting a girl into the country, but if she is afeared of wet grass, believe me the best place to undress her is still a hired, cur-tained buggy."

> Though flowed no tear to tell of woe
> Nor breathed those pale lips love's despair.

32

THE MISTRESS

A mistress should be like a little country retreat, near the town—not to dwell in constantly, but only for a night and away.
WILLIAM WYCHERLEY, SEVENTEENTH CENTURY

There is one aspect of Chicago upper-class life for which almost no documents exist, and no social historian has attempted to find enough of the surviving fragments to make an entire book. Rue Carpenter, the Chicago decorator, wife of John Alden Carpenter, the composer, in a letter passes it by with a few lines. "Many of Chicago's well-off citizens kept mistresses. . . . Establishments of fine houses on polite, discreet streets, some place between Prairie Avenue and La Salle, with a cook, a maid, coachman, a good pair of horses and a carriage . . . Pier glasses, black-leaded Balmoral grates, and hedges for hiding ingoing and outgoing."

Charles Yerkes, the Traction Trust king, kept many women, was notorious for his seductions, affairs, womanizing. One woman, Maude (her descendants are still prominent in the city and kindly permitted me to see some of her papers), was, for several years in the late nineteenth century, Yerkes' mistress. She kept a household book—regretfully undated by the years—of costs, expenses, which Yerkes looked over and added up, and of course had the bills paid.

227

The household book—in a hurried Spencerian handwriting—lists not only menus for the cook, but also women friends who came to tea, and the few times, very few times, Yerkes brought two or three male guests to dine with Maude, listed only as F., J., and N. Some pages detail where they were going out to eat, what places would be an evening on the town. The setting is in no unstable transitory phase, but a lasting affair.

From jottings in the house book, one can catch a glimpse of an upper-class mistress of a rich Chicagoan, as if we were passing a partly open door at a walk and taking a quick look.

Like Maude, most of the mistresses appear not to have been common whores from Levee houses, and not many were from the stage, the chorus line. One could call them courtesans, the demi-monde, but almost never hookers, hustlers, parlor house girls, even if several did at one time work the better bordellos like the Everleigh sisters' club. The Marguerite Gauthier image of *La Dame aux Camélias* was not Maude's—she was not much given to too many clients.

Maude came from a small town in Indiana, her father the village druggist. She had sung in the town's church choir, and went on to New York to study for opera. After a year in New York, she went on to Paris and for two years studied singing there. Most likely some rich man paid for her training, certainly not an Indiana village drugstore. Perhaps she had no plans to become a careerist of the flesh. However, her voice did not prove good enough for professional singing. Several items about arrangements to go to the opera, in the house book, hint at this. "*If I had her high notes,*" or "*could I have had better teachers,*" point to the fact there was no future for her as a singer. We do not know how or when she met Charles Yerkes, but there is mention of "*Charles presenting two splendid matched chestnut carriage horses.*" "*Charles says must dress in the beaded Zouave jacket . . . Char. [Charles] dislikes plum velvet portieres . . . Ordered Chablis (oysters) Sherry (soup) . . . Char. angry broke three Crown China cups . . . Charles sent Jacqueminot roses . . . In bed . . . influenza—steam kettle . . .*"

We begin to form a picture, very unlike Baudelaire's Madame Sabatier—or his *Venus noire*, Jeanne Duval—but rather of a mistress of a very rich man in Chicago. The portieres he didn't like, the china he broke (in anger?), and the wine he wanted for the oysters, perhaps for some night he brought some friends to dinner. The cook is German, Mala; the maid "Swenski" (Swede) not named. The

coachman Bob is a Scot. "*Bob drowned six kittens in coach house, poor Mocha.*" (The cat?)

There is a certain domestic felicity in the horse talk, "*Char. says to look at the withers . . . good hock action . . .*"

Food, wine are important: pâté de foie gras, chilled lobster, chocolate éclairs, Moselle, claret, port, crab ravigotte.

The macadam paved road by Pine Street, where Maude appears to have been set up in style, was well-known to the grocery boys, wine merchants. There is mention of teas with women friends listed as Alice, Nancy, Drucilla, Pooky, Mrs. Latina. Most likely they too were kept women. One owned a Victorian pug dog called Mr. Billy. Notes in the household book list fashions, the mode, a great deal. *Violet* brocade, white bengaline silk with seed pearl embroidery, "*a set of chinchillas,*" frise-caniche jacket, long-trained peignoir—events like a *bal poudre*, a note to see, hear, Minni Hand singing *Carmen*. Some pasted-in program notes of *Tannhäuser, Lohengrin, Pygmalion and Galatea*. "The Valse de la Kermesse" from *Faust* . . . Organ-grinders. *Le Parlate d'Amor*. There is even some mention of art, literature. *Char. likes Barbizon painters, Millet, Corot . . . Carlus-Duran portrait, glass cracked*. (Of her? No known portrait painting of Maude exists.) Ruskin's *Stones of Venice. Trilby. Barriers Burned Away* (a novel of the Chicago Fire, by E. P. Roe?). Card games. Bezique, poker, Red Dog. How one wishes for details, scenes. There is pasted on the back of the marble-patterned cover of the household book two verses of the song "Greensleeves."

> *I have been ready at your hand*
> *To grant whatever you would crave;*
> *I have both waged life and land,*
> *Your love and good-will for to have.*
>
> *If you intend thus to disdain,*
> *It does the more enrapture me,*
> *And even so, I still remain*
> *A lover in captivity.*

Maude left for Europe before 1900, never returned to America. There are few later facts. She died sometime during the First World War, so some relative assumed. Venice? Vienna? No one is sure. In

Chicago was found a trunk; contents: some lavender-scented clothes, dried-out bottles of eau de cologne, a French toque with egret feathers, a volume, *Sesame and Lilies*, and the household book; a trunk stored, forgotten for a time in the cellar of the Palmer House. Still suggesting a fastidiousness, a sensibility.

In a letter from Elliot Paul to me there is mention of another of Chicago's rich man's mistresses. "In the mid-twenties in Paris, there was an ancient, very ancient, fat, jolly, painted horror known as Miss Brown, often after dark in the Pigalle bars, seen spending money at Lipp's, The Flora, the Deux Magots. She claimed to have been long ago a musical comedy star in Chicago, and the mistress of a newspaper publisher. So she existed past her era—wigged, painted, overweight, lurching on tiny feet. The French said she had *folie de grandeur*. She also had some sort of fixed income—not too much, I gathered—paid her monthly by the branch of an American bank in Paris. There was a joyous, ubiquitous vulgarity about Miss Brown, like a carnivorous flower gone to seed. She lived off alcohol, souffles and brioches—and her hotel room was shabby, but for a fine Bechstein concert grand. She couldn't play it. As I had been to Chicago, she would talk to me, drinking what was called a *Mardarin-curaçaos*. 'Hell, we used to come to Paree in style, me and my bien aimé—the old cocksman, threw twenty dollar gold eagles around like they were pebbles—yes—how do you like that? we'd eat high with marquises habilleuses on the terrace of the sporting club on Champs Élysées . . . go down to the Côte d'Azur in real ass-shaking style . . . had his yacht waiting . . . guests . . . Lily, Bertie . . . Toscana cigars . . . Darjeeling tea, wine, wine . . . I was something to look at in those days, believe me . . . up to my navel in couturiers . . . Russian wolfhound big as a calf . . . Don't look at me . . . wasn't always like . . .'"

33

"WHAT PAPER DO YA READ?"

It is a newspaper's duty to print news, and raise hell.
WILBUR F. STOREY, CHICAGO TIMES

Back in 1860, the *Chicago Tribune* was on its way. "Whatever way that was." As Ambrose Bierce once remarked in a bar, "A newspaper can be more dangerous than a Gatling gun."

For five years the *Tribune* had been published by two Republican hopefuls whose aim it was to get a Republican into the White House. Dr. Clares H. Ray had owned the *Galena Jeffersonian*, and Joseph Medill had edited the *Cleveland Leader*. Now Chicago was to feel their combined muscle as they severed their umbilical cords with other cities and sent up their cries.

Medill was the power in the combination, having character, "much of it bad and an unsalvable soul." He was the big supporter of the Know-Nothing movement and its doctrine that native-born Anglo-Saxons owned America forever, and that the workingman, in Medill's view, didn't need to organize for his betterment; like the New York employer who announced God had put the rich on earth to take care of the poor, *not* unions or any organizations talking of a need for better wages or life. All workers' organizations were to Medill a plot by the foreigners against our way of life, pointed to a sustained disintegration of the nation and an ominous danger to real Americans.

Oddly enough, Joseph Medill was not born an American, but a Canadian, in St. John's, New Brunswick, in 1823. At twenty-six, he owned a small newspaper in Coshocton, Ohio, and admitted he had "tasted the delights of Franklin's nectar" (printer's ink). Tall, redheaded, feeling the dignity of his profession, he dressed most of his life in rather outworn styling: Congressional gaiters, black tie and black claw-hammer coat, a starched, "boiled" shirt. He didn't drink, sometimes chewed, but *never* lit a cigar. In time, he became "deaf as an earless snake" and used an ear trumpet. He also swallowed a daily dose of digitalis to flog his heart action, which was extremely eccentric and hinted at coronary thrombosis.

The Civil War helped the *Tribune*. In 1861 it was incorporated with a capital of two hundred thousand dollars, no mean sum in those uninflated days. Medill continued to be a psychological oddball; a fire-eater, but at safe distance from a battlefield. "We shall permit no nation to abuse Mexico but ourselves. We claim the right to turn her up on Uncle Sam's knee and spank her bottom for not behaving herself. . . ." A Freudian might make something of a bare-assed Mexico, seen as a female across his knees being spanked enjoyably by Uncle Sam. Medill graded people by color, as to their worth. "In future wars black and yellow men will be used freely to fight. We will not be so careful about spilling the blood of niggers."

By 1863 he had bought out his partner and was editor in chief of the *Tribune*. The war over, with the potentialities of his strange mind, he mulled over the problem of *what* to do with Robert E. Lee. He suggested "some penitentiary where his work in hammering stones will be small compensation for the bread he eats . . . if he prefers liberty, we will hire him to tote paper for the *Tribune* press rooms." Someone suggested that Lee was too old for the job.

The textures of the different levels of Medill's consciousness led him to politics. In 1871, he was elected mayor of Chicago after the Great Fire. (Unlike Nero facing a charred Rome, Medill did not himself set the torch to his city.)

Chicago was the fourth largest city in the nation, topped only by New York, Philadelphia, and Brooklyn. His major civic duties,

Medill felt, consisted of building a bell tower to warn the city of future fires, and asking for a bigger police force; he was a firm law-and-order man by today's standards. He bragged that the "public affairs of the city are conducted with as much care, fidelity and economy as by officers of well-managed private corporations." This *just* before the treasurer of his administration was exposed as a major embezzler.

As police chief, he appointed Elmer Washburn, who was a humorless, tactless driver of his men. He began by ordering the police

to a full twelve-hour daily duty. Medill, a nondrinker, had the chief enforce the Sunday Closing Law, which enraged patrons of beer gardens, saloons, and cafés. Most of them had voted him in as mayor.

The immigrant voters were outraged and helped form the People's Party to drive Medill from office and bring back Sunday beer and whiskey. Medill couldn't face firm opposition, nagging intonations he was not perfect. He resigned and fled to Europe after a few months in the mayor's chair.

To explain himself, he again needed the *Tribune*. On returning from his Grand Tour, he talked Marshall Field into putting up the money to buy control of the *Tribune*. He paid ten-percent interest on the money to Field, an honest but wary lender—and soon editor and lender were enemies, as Field found Medill full of deceits and overheated patriotism. Field gave Medill too much good parochial advice "on almost everything under the sun, especially on how to run a newspaper," it was reported.

Medill, acidulously prejudiced, saw no sense in juries, long court trials, and civil rights. He printed his provocative ideas clearly. "Judge Lynch is an American by birth and character. . . . The Vigilance Committee is a peculiarly American institution. . . . Every lamp post in Chicago will be decorated with a communistic carcass if necessary." As with latter-day leaders with contemptible resentments of rights, a "communist" was anyone who disagreed with him. At times, Marshall Field had such a red rating with Medill. (As for the unemployed, the drifting migrants, vagrants, the solution Medill saw: "the simplest plan . . . is to put a little strychnine or arsenic in the meat and other supplies furnished tramps.")

He was one of the discoverers of facts that careless scientists had overlooked. Sunspots he saw clearly as spots that caused *all* the misery and trouble in the world. He then came out for microbes as the catastrophe maker and also advocated the eccentricities of simplified spelling.

Wilbur F. Storey of the *Chicago Times* was also an expert—he specialized once in the signs of virginity, or the lack of virginity, in women on the Chicago stage. He questioned, in print, the chastity of Miss Lydia Thompson and her British Blondes, appearing buxom in flesh-colored tights at the Opera House. This led to an attack on him by the lady herself—in public, carrying a whip. She was cheered and aided by some admirers in the street. As Storey told of the incident in court, pointing to the outraged Miss Thompson, "*That* creature there undertook to strike me with a whip. I caught her by the throat and would have choked out her life, when *that* little chap jumped on my back and *that* ruffian there attacked me from the front."

The judge politely asked the powerful publisher, "Why did you not use your pistol?"

"Because I did not need it, sir." Actually, he took a bit of flogging.

The *Tribune* did not approve of the *Times*, a paper that specialized in scandals "in private life, revolting details from evidence taken in police court trials, imaginary liaisons of a filthy character, reeked, seethed like hell's broth in the *Times* cauldrons."

Medill preferred to get his kicks on the editorial page rather than in the news columns. Adultery to him was not very interesting as a spectator sport.

Storey of the *Times*, given to strange audacities, was as odd a man as Medill. He told his reporters to hunt up scandal and "we must go for gut-fat." He, himself, sank into madness and paralytic strokes, catatonic states, and began to meet, he claimed, in the spirit world the ghost of an Indian girl called Little Squaw. She insisted Storey take an ice-cold bath every morning in his huge Gothic castle on the South Side's Grand Boulevard. Blind, mind gone, Storey lingered on until 1884, one of the pioneer founders of a debased Chicago journalism.

The most popular newspaper of the city was the *Chicago Daily News*, with three times the readers of the *Tribune*. It first appeared on Christmas Eve, 1875, and in a trial issue tried a special headline:

FOR PRESIDENT
OF THE UNITED STATES, ALASKA, THE WESTERN ISLAND,
AND PERHAPS CUBA.
HON. JOSEPH MEDILL
OF ILLINOIS.

"A great man in idleness is at once a dangerous and pitiable object."

The *News* ended up the property of Victor Freemont Lawson, impressive in flat crown derby and full beard—who had made millions in real estate. One of his problems was columnist Eugene Field (no relation of the Marshall Field family) who was usually drunk and always broke. Eugene also annoyed the Eastern press. Wrote the *Illustrated American* of one of his columns:

"That vastly overrated literary humbug, Eugene Field, who was never anything but a vulgar, ill-bred rhymester, largely given, we believe, to the writing of verses of a pornographic quality, and the character of whose mind is distinctly reflected in the witticisms with which he is wont to enliven the society of Chicago brothels and barrooms, has lately been expressing his opinion of Eastern men of letters. From the Chicago paper in which Field is allowed to make a display of his baseness, we cull this paragraph: 'The way to the founding of a great magazine in the West must be made clear by and with a weekly publication that shall faithfully represent the West and honestly reflect Western sentiment; that shall wage a merciless war upon the intellectual hermaphrodites and dawdling perverts and petticoated clay-eaters who, on little tinsel thrones along the Eastern coast, presume to set themselves up as dictators in the great realm of American literature. We are not for any skirmish with those humbugs; we are for a war of extermination. That war is bound to come sooner or later; it must not be begun, however, on the part of the West until the West is fully prepared to sail into and disembowel every last mother's son of those twiddling-twaddling squirts and their queer little parasites.' "

Journalism was once a more colorful user of language.

Perhaps because of the heavy drinking of Lawson's editors and reporters, the *News* accepted no liquor advertising, but plenty of tonics for "womanly weakness," usually fifty-percent alcohol.

Near the turn of the century, Joseph Medill, stone-deaf, with his heart giving him trouble, was still a vocal firebrand on the editorial page. In 1898 he cried out, "The people . . . demand war! The merchant princes thinking erroneously that war hurts business, are for peace. . . . Spain is the yellow dog of nations . . . entitled to the same treatment that all snapping, biting curs receive." He couldn't suggest poisoning Spaniards like tramps. But he did feature an article:

WAR MAKES MILLIONS FOR CHICAGO BUSINESS MEN

The only unhappy people really damaged were the Spaniards, in decline as colonists, who were not at all the monsters in Cuba the Chicago and American press called them. In fact, most of the so-called "news" from that island was pure fiction. But Hearst and Pulitzer wanted a war, and so did Medill, and thousands of young Americans in the irresistible momentum of a desire for change went to war—many of them to die, poisoned by Chicago canned beef.

The war didn't help the *Tribune* raise its circulation of 78,000 to anywhere near the *News*'s 260,000. Medill did get new blood into the family when his daughter Katherine married Robert Sanderson McCormick, a son of the brother of the great Cyrus. Robert, as first secretary of the American Legation in London, began his marriage by borrowing ninety thousand dollars from his father-in-law. Medill's younger daughter Elinor married Robert Wilson Patterson, Jr., son of a Presbyterian minister. Patterson became a reporter on the *Tribune* at twenty-three, and married the boss's daughter at twenty-eight. Three years later he was managing editor. Medill had four grandchildren and spent a great deal of time warning them against the dreadful menace that nation faced from immigrants not of Anglo-Saxon origin, or having no white skin. Medill died at sixty-seven in some uncharted fulfillment—and his last words were supposed to be, "*What* is the news?"

Ben Hecht always doubted this. He told me, "The old buzzard didn't give a good goddamn about real news. He was always trying to project some crack-brained, spurious scheme and attacking first- and second-generation Americans who didn't belong to his clubs or had the wrong shaped nose. To most Chicago newspapermen he was a cantankerous sonofabitch."

What was left to the heirs was a sort of Medill Trust, which gave the related McCormicks and Pattersons control of the paper. Ambassador McCormick remained with the State Department until President Roosevelt ended his career, even if the *Tribune* often supported Teddy. The ambassador was placed in a sanitarium, as incompetent, by his widow. The other son-in-law, Robert Wilson Patterson, died, some said of apoplexy, in a Philadelphia hotel room.

The grandchildren of Joseph Medill were high-strung fire-crackers, fully inheriting eccentric genes. Joseph Medill Patterson was the most sensitive, educated at Groton. To escape his own disenchantment, he began to dislike Mama and Papa for such an expensive education. He had a guilt complex about being rich, recording he was "supported through fashionable day school, fashionable boarding school, fashionable summer resorts, fashionable dancing classes, etc., etc. . . . taught to be a perfect gentleman." Like a modern protesting hippie, he appeared at the family box at the opera in muddy shoes, tieless, open flannel shirt. He never achieved emotional equilibrium.

His favorite masochist sport was to go down to the low Chicago dives, the tough saloons of the Near North Side, and pick fights with the barflies and tough factory workers and wagon drivers. They would rough-and-tumble him up and toss him out onto the sidewalk, bloody, but satisfied by group therapy. Perhaps it was not as dangerous or daring as it sounded. The police on the beat were aware who Patterson was, and saw he got home battered but proud of his roughhousing and working-over. He dressed like a riverboat roustabout, or a saloon bouncer. His playacting was part of his odd defense of his family wealth, and also something sick inside him that had to be acted out in a personal psychodrama. Taking one of his daughters to school one day in his usual dogcatcher's outfit, he kissed her good-bye at the school door. A few minutes later the school phoned the Patterson house. It was the headmistress talking to Mrs. Patterson (a daughter of Marshall Field's partner, Harlow N. Higgenbotham). "I thought I ought to tell you, Mrs. Patterson, that I saw your houseman kiss your little girl this morning."

Patterson served a term in the State Assembly and then was appointed commissioner of public works, where his major project seemed to be getting to the newspaper newsboys and keeping them from fighting each other; it hurt the sale of newspapers. He also, in a pseudoscientific spasm, felt that Chicago capitalists were almost all anarchists. "I believe men are anarchists, no matter how big their bank accounts, who take the attitude that the law does not exist for them."

This was hardly news to the local rich men who ran Chicago, but they expected the law should be used to protect their interests.

Unlike Patterson, they had no self-loathing because of their wealth.

Joe Patterson resigned, and announced he was now a socialist. He was twenty-seven years old and came to the horror of discovering that "What a man wants most is money." This was a precarious shock, but he was not as much of a fool as people thought. "Whenever socialism comes in, I shall abide by its rules, but at present I do not intend to give any money I have to less fortunate individuals." As for New York and its foreigners: "New York is the last place I'd settle in."

Addressing a Socialist party meeting of have-nots, Joseph Medill Patterson put it strongly: "You will *never* get anything from us capitalists by asking for it. The only way you can get it is to fetch us down. . . . Lie to your employers . . . brazenly . . . without an iota of . . . regret or remorse."

The naïveté soon seemed less virile, and the Medill genetic factors took over, for in time Patterson calmed down and went back to, as Ben Hecht told me in a conversation, "the *Tribune*, the family milk teat," being elected secretary of the newspaper. But for safety, his cousin, Robert Rutherford McCormick, out of Groton *and* Yale, very antisocialist, in 1904, had read law and decided to run for city alderman of the Twenty-first Ward, as a Republican, of course. He won, and a year later won the job as president of the Sanitary District, in charge of the vast, improperly functioning sewage system of Chicago.

A rambunctious fellow, he didn't like the local democratic way of getting elected. "I have felt obliged to spend ninety percent of my time in saloons, and the remaining ten percent in barrooms. . . . I would advise no one to take to politics as a profession." It was true —dishonest, saloon-run, corrupt wards served the political parties, controlled the voting, often fraudulent.

Robert McCormick lost the next election—boozy potency in saloons perhaps failing—and in 1911 he became president, and soon editor, of the *Tribune*. The newspaper circulation wars of sluggers and killers increased out on the Chicago streets, crippling, beating, and even killing newsboys. Robert McCormick made it a good paper, and Max Annenberg was to be in charge of the *Tribune* wrecking crews. Soon the *Tribune* went on record in its masthead as

THE WORLD'S GREATEST NEWSPAPER

34

CHICAGO'S SHERLOCK HOLMES

A crowded police docket is the surest of all signs that trade is brisk and money plenty.
MARK TWAIN, 1872

He was known as the "damned little fly cop," and was as odd a character as some of the people he arrested in the 1890s.

Detective Clifton W. Woolridge played at Sherlock Holmes, in an involvement of fastidious detail, with at least seventy-five disguises, but was still a very good plainclothes man. He modestly called himself THE WORLD'S GREATEST DETECTIVE, "the incorruptible Sherlock Holmes of America," and meant it. As he set down with jaunty self-assurance in one of his books about himself, *The Devil and the Grafter*, "No braver, more honest or efficient police officer ever wore a star or carried a club."

From 1888 to 1910, with unrestrained energy, he gave the madams and the girls a hard time. He would even arrest a girl just for smoking a cigarette in the streets, and, if he brought in a large healthy thief, would often ride him piggyback to the station house. Woolridge made about twenty thousand arrests during his demonic career, got two hundred convictions that ended in penitentiary terms, filled the House of Correction with three thousand added inmates. He specialized in rescuing girls from brothels and white slavers, was an enemy who closed scores of panel houses, and recovered over a half-million dollars' worth of stolen property. Another enemy he fought was the fake matrimonial offices that fleeced lonely fools. He also claimed to have refused five hundred bribes, sums running up to five thousand dollars each. No wonder he was wounded twenty-two times, and shot at twice that many times, slugs debouching to the left and right of him, ricocheting from all directions.

Yet for all his existing and survival of Chicago's Walpurgis Nights, he was a little fellow of only five feet six, all of him 155 pounds. He could outfight anything up to two hundred pounds and over. He always carried two "hoglegs" (revolvers), and his record shows that for all his skill in wounding criminals in legs, arms, and behinds, he never killed anyone in the line of duty.

As an old campaigner against crime, he often found the female of the race more deadly than the male. He helped in the 1890s to destroy a deadly gang of black women of demoniacal ferocity who banded together as street robbers and, working in pairs with razors, brass knuckles, shivs (knives), revolvers, and short baseball bats, committed hundreds of street holdups. They all had an alienated antagonism toward decent people. To get a victim to raise his hands on command, they would slash him across the knuckles with an open long razor. Some of the more notorious of these black carnivorous Amazons, who loved to see blood flow, were Laura Johnson, Hattie Washington, Flossie Moore, and a sister act of Pearl Smith and Emma Ford. The Stranger (Mary White) in three years got together loot worth fifty thousand dollars. Ella Sherwood was an opium smoker of diverse dreams and actions. She stashed some $375 from a holdup with a saloonkeeper to hold until the police hunt for her cooled off. When later he refused to admit Ella had ever given him such a sum, she smashed all his windows with a baseball bat, shot off the contents of two pistols into his mirrors and bar bottles, "just to keep him honest." In action, unlike most opium smokers, she knew the discrepancies between reality and fantasy.

The Amazon hangout of these black Calamity Janes was at 202 Custom House Place, run by Lizzie Davenport, "Queen of the

Panel Houses." In eight years Lizzie made a half-million dollars at that game.

In one way, these harpies agreed with Henry James's remark, "Money is the great American sedative." The girls in the money found Lizzie's place a good one in which to talk of one's take.

To keep the police from arresting some of the street robbers, Lizzie built a hideaway closet for her friends—solid, of three-inch oak boards—where they could hide during a police raid. Detective Woolridge bored holes through the oak door of the closet and blew black pepper through them until the Amazons came out gasping to give up.

Emma Ford, the strongest and most dangerous of these women, was not so easy to capture. Emma, truculent and trigger-tempered, was over six feet, hit the scales at two hundred pounds. No molasses-colored Venus, she was built like a man with very long arms. To stop her, nothing less than a pistol pointed directly between her eyes would make her reasonable enough to submit to an arrest. In prison she was a holy terror; once in Cook County Jail, she tried to drown a turnkey by holding him down under water in a horse-drinking trough. Locked away in the laundry of the House of Correction, she went berserk with a red-hot flat iron and badly burned and scarred a half dozen of her screaming fellow inmates. She once grabbed a prison guard who displeased her off the floor by his beard, plucked it out by the fistful, and tossed the loose hair in his howling face. She remained a terror of the Levee until 1903 when she moved east and out of range.

Flossie Moore, of inflexible individuality, was the most success-ful footpad and black thief in Chicago. In four years, up to 1893, she stole over $125,000.

With a head for figures, as Flossie put it, "Any gal what can't make herself twenty thousand dollars a year in Chicago oughta be ashamed of herself." Marauding Flossie was a high liver. She had an indolent white lover, "Handsome Harry" Gray, who was on an allowance from her of twenty-five dollars a day for such stuff as cambric handkerchiefs, fancy booze, gambling.

Flossie, a hard-cash Valkyrie, carried a "bundle of the long green" in her stocking, and another stashed between her huge breasts. She favored the haute couture. When the black madams

and pimps held their balls and fetes, she always came in a five-hun-
dred-dollar gown on the arm of Handsome Harry. Her lawyer was
on a $125 monthly retainer to watch out for her legal safety—for
she was often arrested. Once, ten times in one day. In one year she
was held for trial thirty-six times, the bail bonds for her releases
adding up to thirty thousand dollars. One period of court appearances cost Flossie ten thousand dollars just in fines, which didn't
faze her; once when a judge fined her a hundred dollars, she yelled
at the bench, "You kin make that two hundred, cause I got money
to burn."

In 1893 she drew a three-year sentence at Joliet for holding up
an elderly farmer. She was no model prisoner with the possibility of
change for the better, but was instead a holy terror. Twice she tried
to kill a woman guard, and she once spent six months in solitary.
Released, she went east in 1900.

The hunter down of these women and other criminals, Detective Clifton W. Woolridge, had great confidence in his various disguises, although actually most criminals weren't always fooled by
him in his playacting. At times he favored dressing as a rich cattle-
man in a mangy buffalo-hide coat touching the ground, a Stetson
hat, and a white beard; as a flop-joint bum with a dirty face, turtle-
neck sweater, and beaten-up hat. But his pride was his aristocratic
society figure, one of the Gold Coast men-about-town, made up of a
polished high hat, boiled shirt and white tie, tailcoat, gloves and a
cane, his moustache twisted to points like a stage villain's, larded
hair parted in the middle and plastered down on either side of his
square skull. As a critic once said of some actor's Hamlet, "It was
funny without being vulgar." Hardly the figure to fool Mrs. Potter
Palmer, or either one of the Mrs. Fields.

> In Chicago originality still appears to be put above con-
> formity . . . I give you Chicago. It is not London-and-Har-
> vard. It is not Paris-and-buttermilk. It is American in every
> chitling and sparerib, and it is alive from snout to tail.
> H. L. MENCKEN

35

TROUBLE AT THE HAYMARKET

The ordinary man is an anarchist. He wants to do as he likes. . . . He is
mortally afraid of government officials and policemen.
GEORGE BERNARD SHAW, PRESS INTERVIEW, *c.* 1920

In 1887 the United States government built a military base, Fort
Sheridan, on land given for the purpose by the Commercial Club of
Chicago. Six hundred acres of lakefront. *Why* a Chicago fort? A
military post in the year 1887? The local Indian menace was long
gone; far to the west the Apache and Sioux were wailing their death
chants. War with Canada was very remote, and the soldiers and
their cannon could not proceed against the saloons, brothels, gambling houses of the city's sporting sections. Was it all a game of some
hallucinatory proportions, or military triviality?

The fort was seriously asked for by the city—and built for the
protection of those men of wealth in Chicago who feared a bloody,
murderous socialist, or anarchist, or nihilist uprising. Few of them
knew the differences between the political contents of these revolutionary ideals, but something disastrous called the Haymarket Riot
and its aftermath had frightened the good citizens of the city, suddenly aware of the impermanent nature of human hopes.

246

The beginning was the Panic of 1873; wages were cut, jobless men drifted around on the streets, loose and hungry, hopelessly unadjustable. A large immigrant population felt remote, cut off from the Anglo-Saxon rulers of Chicago. Poverty, hunger, exploitation increased and the politicians did nothing about it. The Welfare State was nearly a century away. Some of the immigrants were educated men, dreamers amidst the futility of personal hope; they tried to bring direct action.

To understand what the workers were up against in Chicago, one has only to reread some of the texts that Allan Pinkerton put into print. Pinkerton headed an early private FBI that was for hire, able not only to protect industry, but also to rent out protection, and search out elements that Pinkerton felt were harmful to the men who owned the nation. As he saw the workers' first organizations in 1879: "Never before in the history of our country had there come such a swift and far-reaching peril; nor had we record of any government being thus obliged to thus suddenly confront so overwhelming a danger."

As for ungrateful workers actually going on strike against their benefactors, Pinkerton could hardly make it strong enough. In his catchall of no-goods in his book, *Strikers, Communists, Tramps and Detectives*, he brings the true danger out into the open. "If members did not actually inaugurate the strikes, the strikes were the direct result of the communistic spirit spread through the ranks of railroad employees by the communistic leaders and their teachings. . . . At the back of the actors in the scenes I have to describe . . . will be found the inspiration . . . if nothing more tangible, of the Internationale —perhaps the identical blood-red figure who 'cried havoc and let slip the dogs of war.' "

The word *communist*, then as now, was the most effective term to destroy character and organizers, and frighten the bosses. Unions were as bad as communists. He wrote of the Brotherhood of Locomotive Engineers: "a huge political devilfish that feeds upon anything and everything necessary to satiate its appetite and give it power . . . animated by the vicious dictation of the Internationale . . . possessed with a greed for personal aggrandizement."

Pinkerton put his fists where his prose was; he was loyal to those who paid him, and he could take the measure of his opposition. Here he takes on P. M. Arthur, grand chief engineer of the

brotherhood. "I can best describe him by comparing him in personal appearance with the great evangelist, Mr. Moody, and with no disrespect to that eccentric individual. Take out of Moody's face, then, the low browed, sullen eyed, bulldog look . . . give him instead a fish-like expressionless dark eye, a bluish gray eye full of light and animation, and, at times, of jollity and merriment . . . and then give to every motion of his form and features determined, decisive action that reminds you of superb and finely governed machinery, and you have the man before you."

It can be seen that Pinkerton never underestimated the enemy, and that he liked his work. His goons and hoodlums, killers and wreckers, were aware the chief was always behind them. And behind him and the industrialists and utilities was always the threat of the U.S. Army to back them up against the damn workers.

Who, actually, were the leaders of the desperate men in the Chicago streets? Many were German radicals, others, native rebels with cranky Yankee mentalities, and an odd Englishman or two, loose in their social adjustments. Most were able speakers supporting a fiery German-language newspaper in Chicago, the *Arbeiter Zeitung.* It was a focal point of radical hopes, at first part socialist and later more or less anarchist, seeking camaraderie, and direct conflict by the hungry, sullen poor.

Railroad kings, aware of hard times, began to cut wages; too many workers wanted jobs. Ten-percent cuts were ordered in all railroads out of Chicago. (Strikers in other parts of the nation began to burn railcars and plants as far east as Pittsburgh.) Chicago socialists started to organize the workers to protest the wage cuts.

Five thousand men were put under arms by the city. Marshall Field delivery wagons were converted into troop carriers. Jeremiahs on street corners preached on human folly and doom to the city.

The people of the slums and factories organized The Workingman's Party of the United States. Street meetings were called for every night. Police, on orders, began to break up meetings, making bloodied martyrs of the poor. Free speech and vocal dissent were not acceptable in those days, any more than it was in Mayor Daley's Chicago of 1968. The crowds began throwing coal and other painful objects at the police—who opened rapid fire, killing sixteen of the crowd, badly injuring twenty-five. The city was groping toward a continuity of horror.

The mayor, with his enlisted five thousand citizens of a defense corps, set up headquarters in the Grand Pacific Hotel. Two companies of United States troops, suddenly withdrawn from the Indian wars in the West, trained into the city, carrying rifles, wearing full cartridge belts. Marching in worn uniforms, faded on the great span of the Western plains, they marched down Madison Street, were cheered, as they moved into the Exposition Building to set up camp.

The city built a cannon platform onto an express wagon, and rushed it about, threatening to blow the rebels into order. Rioting and fighting of a bloody meanness continued, police and U.S. troopers against the crowds along the train lines by the viaduct before the McCormick factory. Ten people in the crowd died; uncounted injured were carried off, bloody, dramatis personae wounded in an outbreak of despair.

Public meetings to point out the terror were attacked by the police in the halls. Turner's Hall, holding Poles and Bohemians in large numbers, was attacked by the police with an awesome fury—result: one dead, many wounded. The socialists took to the streets, carrying red flags. To some it was as romantic, and ridiculous, as a painting by Delacroix. Quickly passed laws soon prohibited marching in public.

Chicago's new Board of Trade Building was about to be opened. God and the stock market wait for no man, nor are they put off by street riots. A march was organized on the new building to mess up the dedication ceremonies of top hats and lyric prose. Marching with red flags ("The common blood of humanity") and black flags ("for starvation"), the crowds moved, singing English, German, and the original French version of "La Marseillaise." They moved en masse through the streets, about five hundred men and women, led by three revolutionaries, Sam Fielden, Albert Parsons, August Spies. Police in large numbers turned the marchers away from the ceremony.

Trolley-line strikes followed, walkouts at McCormick's reaper plant. Packinghouse and stockyard workers followed, for no living wage existed and misery was thick as fog among the poor.

Meetings of strikers were broken up, police instigated reactions, hoping hostile actions by the crowds would anger the nation and certainly cause the comfortable citizens of Chicago to turn against "the mobs of Hunkies and Bohunks!" In one riot, Mayor Harrison the First galloped out on his white Kentucky mare, but the strikers did not harm him. They knew he was a fair man, trapped by the powers that kept him in political office.

The *Arbeiter Zeitung*, hysterical, as were the police, the businessmen, factory owners, were also in no mood for calm. They issued, in their imbecile fury, senseless pamphlets calling for REVENGE! WORKERS TO ARMS!

There are always dreamers and fools ready to die for the fanatics of any revolutionary movement of the left or the right. Excruciating conditions bring on leaders to exploit chaos. The pamphlets cried out, *"They killed six of your brothers at McCormick's works this afternoon! To arms, we call you to arms* (signed) YOUR BROTHERS."

The poor are hopelessly inefficient and, once inflated to audacity, see life as soap operas. The saloons assisted their visions and were doing grand business. Both the strikers and the police and soldiers guzzled all they could get. Unlucky was a saloonkeeper named Weiskopf, in whose building the crowd's leaders often met. The anarchists in psychopathic mood called Weiskopf "a police informer," which perhaps he was. Detectives dressed as workers mingled with the crowds, cheering them on to deeds of violence. Weiskopf's saloon was wrecked and smashed to bits—barrels of beer and whiskey were rolled into the street, and it was free drinks for everybody. Hesitations and ambiguities drifted away—and the crowd leaders seemed heaven sent to make heaven *now,* right *now!*

The hopelessness of their situation grew among the workers as the leaders lost all sense of reality. The *Arbeiter Zeitung* never rested its presses . . . *"Rise in your might and level the existing robber rule with the dust."* Lenin and Trotsky would have found it too romantic a call, Hitler and Goebbels not high-pitched enough. The major call to get rid of bourgeois hang-ups was for a great mass meeting at the Haymarket on Randolph Street, between Halsted and Desplaines. *"Good speakers will be present to denounce the latest atrocious acts of the police . . . the shooting of our fellow working men."*

So after years of protest, riots, came Tuesday, May 8, 1886. Night fell, a hot night, muggy, dank clouds in a sky with not a star showing. Of the crowd that showed up (estimates put it at one thousand), most were serious, quiet. They were hungry, mostly jobless or poorly paid, and fully aware now that hope of any gains against the owners of the city was futile. Even the United States Army was mobilized against them, as was middle-class morality.

The police again intended to stir the mob to reaction. Two hundred cops waited at the Desplaines Police Station a block from the meeting. They were all issued new revolvers, said a report, and hickory skull-cracking clubs "extra long." Scores of detectives dressed as workers, as always, moved out to mingle with the crowd.

The speakers, coming late, found that the best place to speak from was a wagon left by the entrance of a factory. First was August Spies, German-born, publisher and editor of the *Arbeiter Zeitung* who made the first speech. It was revolutionary philosophy, smooth-worn now from overuse, like a pebble in a brook. Next came Albert Parsons, whose father had been a noted Confederate general. Last was Samuel Fielden, a devout Methodist, also a pious anarchist. He was a Lancaster Englishman. None of these men was an active ter-rorist, except in their speeches. Years of investigation later proved no acts of violence on their part.

Mayor Harrison, dismounted, was in the crowd, and he went and told the police: "I have no right to interfere with any peaceable meeting of the people. So long as they are orderly I will not inter-fere."

This was bad news for Inspector John Bonfield left in charge. He was a blowhard, an easily enraged man who was eager to en-gage the crowd. All he needed was a foolish statement by Sam Fielden telling the crowd: "The law must be throttled, killed and stabbed." That was enough. Bonfield, with a cheer, led his men and their extra-long clubs to break up the meeting.

They almost missed their chance as rain began to fall from the black skies and the soggy crowd began to drift apart and away. As a captain of police shouted for the already dissolving meeting to break up, someone threw a bomb with a sputtering fuse high over the heads of the crowd. It exploded in the middle of massed police in an archipelago of smoke, flame, and mangling horror.

We shall never know how many died. The crowd carried off its dead and wounded. Of the police, seven lay dead, often in frag-ments, and sixty were more or less injured.

Both sides, in unreason and in progressive degeneration of their senses, had been working toward the event. *Who threw the bomb?* The police and the city government had no trouble making up their minds. The city lay mesmerized, trembling in fear, or outrage. The word of the speakers, as reason for the deed, was good enough for them. The offices of the *Arbeiter Zeitung* were locked up. Claims were made that explosives were found there. (No proof was ever given for this being true. Stealthy faking of "evidence" was not beyond police methods.) Michael Schwab, George Engel, Adolph Fisher, Louis Lingg were all hauled in, as were the three Haymarket speakers, and all were accused of the bomb outrage. No connection could ever actually be found, but they were all bigmouth speakers, careless with words, and they would do, to hang.

Guilty or not, their imprecise trial was a farce. The verdict was in before the first day of court. Whoever threw the bomb, it was not any of the men convicted of murder on the grounds their speeches and publications had caused *someone* to make and throw a bomb.

Judge Joseph E. Gary, "owned" by the Steel Trust (according to Lincoln Steffens), sentenced all but a man named Neebe—a stockholder of the paper—to be hanged. Lingg blew himself up while in prison. The sentences of Schwab and Fielden were commuted to life imprisonment by Governor Richard Oglesby. The rest were hanged in November of 1887, making those usual tragic, brave speeches of rebels standing on the gallows.

Mass hysteria and fear caused the conviction of men who never had a fair trial or chance. They may have known of the bomb, its maker, and user—but no such legal evidence was ever produced in the court that tried them. Guilt must be proved on evidence—it never was.

Who threw the bomb? No one actually knows, even today. I have asked many people, mostly students of the Haymarket bombing: historians, Chicago editors, journalists, students of revolutionary movements. Here are three major possibilities given by most of the people I talked to.

1. The bomb was thrown by one Rudolph Schnaubelt, never accused, legally, a radical who ran off to Europe and died there, a natural death. There is no evidence that Schnaubelt threw the bomb. He just appears to have left Chicago in a hell of a hurry and was an anarchist.

2. The bomb was thrown by a police agent whose aim was bad. The police and those officials and business interests behind them had been trying to stir up the strikers and the unemployed to some desperate action, a major horrifying crime, so they could break the radical spirit and determination to keep resisting. (The Reichstag fire by the Nazis to blame on the communists comes to mind.) But

no one connected with the Chicago police ever came forward with any evidence of police involvement. It seems hardly likely that even the trigger-tempered Inspector Bonfield would act in such a manner and lead his own men to such a danger. But higher up?

3. Some fanatic threw the bomb, a loner most likely not too right in the head. Did it all alone to inflate his crippled ego, in the manner of the killers of the two Kennedy brothers and Martin Luther King, Jr. America has a history of assassination in public places—almost public ceremonies—by half-cracked messiahs. Most historians are inclined to this last theory, that of the reprehensible loner.

All the riots had one end result: a new fort to protect Chicago. For the strikers and the unemployed, there was no betterment of their miserable lives. "There is irony in posterity," a Chicago lawyer told me. "Today, the grandsons of the exploited crowds, if still workers, are reactionary, hard-hat unionists, members of Mafia-controlled unions, joiners of the Birch Society, all set strongly against socialists, anarchists, communists, and other unpopular groups."

36

THE BOYS IN THE BACK ROOMS

In Chicago there is a mysterious something that makes for individuality,
personality and charm . . . . a city which offers free play for prairie energy
. . . some imaginative equivalent for the stupendous activity they were bred
to.

H. L. MENCKEN, SMART SET

The male haunts in Chicago—where a man hunted privacy with
his own kind—were often odd, and by our modern standards of
what is wit and fun, sometimes grim. The Whitechapel Club was
founded in 1886. It was first set up in Newsboy Alley in a little dank
room under a slanting ceiling, and the decor was made up of
human skulls arranged on chandeliers and doorways. Most likely
the club members, to get these bone lampshades, knew medical students. There was a piano, and an assortment of swords, daggers, pistols, and hat pins. The police inspector, John Revere, helped the
dilettante members by bringing over hangmen's ropes, bloody shirts
of victims. The members of Whitechapel were *not* thugs or underworld characters, but the top literary figures Chicago had available,
a nonheroic aggrandizement against respectability. Members were
Finley Peter Dunne of "Mr. Dooley" fame, Brand Whitlock, to be
minister to Belgium, the humorist George Ade, Opie Read, a now
forgotten novelist, Alfred Henry Lewis, a neglected Western writer
of merit; people called Hobart Chatfield-Taylor, "Grizzly" Adams,

255

and "Tombstone" Thompson. None was given to self-abnegation, and they mostly took kindly to whiskey.

Among the other Chicago saloon attractions, there actually was a pickpocket and bar owner, of the Lone Star Saloon and Palm Garden, named Mickey Finn, situated at the south end of Whisky Row. To strangers he served the Mickey Finn Special and the M.F. Number Two. The Special was alcohol mixed with the juice of snuff and a white powder gotten from a voodoo doctor. Number Two used beer in place of the alcohol. But no matter what it contained, it would knock the drinker out for two or three days—if not kill him, which it often did. But alive or dead, the doped patrons were robbed, stripped in a back room, and tossed out into an alley. A street-corner preacher once chalked on Lone Star walls the words: The Unjust Prosper—The Just Are Sacrificed.

Mickey Finn wasn't big and he wasn't heavy; he stood five feet five, weighed 140 at his best. Yet he would go down in folk legend with Mike Fink, Davy Crockett, Paul Bunyan and Babe, his blue ox, Johnny Appleseed. For Mickey was the inventor or perfector of that dreadful poison, known by everyone as the Mickey Finn. He was as deadly with a bung starter as with his mixture, having knocked out an eye each of two customers with that weapon, the last time because the victim had argued over a sixty-cent bar bill. The police had little respect for the Lone Star which had political protection. They saw "a low dive . . . hangout for colored and white people of the lowest type." But being a barman and pickpocket still gave Mickey spare time, so he was also a notorious fence for stolen property. Some found Mickey's barbarity infinitely diverting.

Kate Roses Flynn, as mate to the Mickey, took care of the bar and the house girls who hustled the customer for drinks and were willing to engage in anything suggested in the line of convulsions of pleasure, at a price. Two of these girls were a strange pair, even for the permissive social license of a dive like Mickey Finn's.

"The Dummy" (Isablle Ffyffe) was a female version of Lennie in Steinbeck's *Of Mice and Men*. And "Gold Tooth Mary" Thornton feared for her soul; and knew what was going on with Mickey's knockout drinks. Dr. Hall, the black who provided the white powder (most likely a form of chloral hydrate), was no medical man—

his claim was that of a crime wizard, a voodoo witch doctor. No wonder Karl Marx wrote mockingly, "The function of criminals in society is to provide employment for policemen."

The police never did catch up with Mickey and Doc Hall. But there was later testimony of their deeds before a commission seeking information about aldermen grafting. Gold Tooth Mary, as a witness, related Mickey's delight with the power of the voodoo powder. He told her in a surge of anticipation, "See the nice bottle, Mary. We'll get the money with this. I give the doc an extra dollar to make it strong."

The drinks at Mickey's place did a lot of damage. Mickey proudly put up a sign behind the bar to encourage their sale.

TRY THE MICKEY FINN SPECIAL

The saloon help and the whores who circulated among the customers were told to sell the Special and get a cut of the price. The customer who drank a Special, as Gold Tooth Mary testified, "they get talkative, walk around in a restless manner, and they then fall into a deep sleep and you can't arouse them until . . . the drug wears off."

The drugged man, she said, was dragged into one of the back "operating rooms," and Mickey would don a derby hat and a clean white apron like a surgeon about to perform. He and Kate Roses peeled the victim to his skin, hunted for a money belt, and took everything of value, even his clothes if they were wearable, giving in exchange some rags. The drugged man was left on the floor until the next day when he was booted into an alley. The drug could numb a man for several days, but if he showed signs of life too soon, Mickey would tap him on the head with his favorite bung starter. Gold Tooth Mary testified that Mickey boasted he couldn't be touched by the law—he had the protection of aldermen.

Gold Tooth Mary told the commission she herself left the Lone Star saloon in 1903, when she felt Mickey was becoming too much of a brute. After a trainman, Billy Miller, came out of a stupor of twelve hours and demanded his gold watch and thirty-five dollars. . . . Miller was afterward found along the railroad tracks, his head cut off. "I was afraid I would be murdered for the two hundred dollars I had saved up, and I did not want to be a witness to any more of the horrible things I saw done there. I was afraid I would be arrested some time when some victims who had been fed on knockout drops would die. When I saw his wife put the drugged liquor to the lips of men I could not stand it, as bad as I am. Oh, it was just awful to see the way men were drugged and stripped of their clothing by Finn or his wife. Finn had an idea that most men wore belts about their waists to hide their money. He had robbed a man once who hid his money that way, and he never neglected searching the 'dead ones' to the skin."

Both Gold Tooth Mary and Dummy gave full testimony, but the commission—who could carry nonsense to magnificent extremes—decided that with no "specific complaints" they could not arrest Finn. Mickey left town for a few months while things cooled off—and, while traveling, sold his formula for "the genuine Mickey Finn," to whatever bartender or saloon owner was interested in bettering his take or stopping a rowdy customer in his tracks, often forever. No one has ever been able to fully count the dead the "Mickey" created, and that still pile up.

No matter how depraved, most whores had their awareness of some decency, as Gold Tooth Mary showed. The gold-hearted "dance hall girl" of popular films never existed, but there was an awareness in some of better values, for all their own apathy at times. They were not all sunk into a sense of inadequacy, but rather lived high when they could, and felt they served some biological scheme of nature. The more vigorous and vital girls became madams.

37

THE GREAT SAUSAGE MYSTERY

He ground her up
Into sausage meat
And Luetgert
Was his name.
CHICAGO STREET SONG, C. 1898

Adolph Luetgert was a bar patron, also a sausage maker in a brick building just west of Commercial Street (now Hermitage Avenue). In his fifties, with the belly of a beer drinker, Adolph was three hundred pounds, stood six feet tall, and figured he was still a dashing ladies' man. In all the neighborhood saloons of the 1890s, he was admired as the champion beer drinker of the district. A saloon was in the money when Adolph gathered a crowd of fellow guzzlers and a beer-drinking contest started.

Adolph neglected his wife and lived in his office at the sausage factory, where his various women—mostly street whores—visited him to make sexual play, among them the huge Tillie, a good beer drinker herself, built like a keg.

One day Adolph told the police his wife had disappeared. The police, finding no signs of her, set out to investigate, and found that the sausage maker had ordered four hundred pounds of caustic soda, which chemical even the worst sausage in the city did not contain. Scientific analysis had not made much progress in those days, but state's attorney, Charles B. Deneen, came to one conclusion. You don't use caustic potash in the making of sausages. "I think he boiled her up in the vat and burned her bones in the furnace." The hunt turned up corset steels, some bone fragments, and Mrs. Luetgert's wedding ring in the vat drain. But no corpus delicti, which worried Chicago sausage eaters. Though a body is not actually needed to convict in a murder case, the jury, off its feed, seemed confused, and Adolph was given a life term in Joliet penitentiary, where he died a few years later.

All the facts point to the conclusion that Adolph did *not* make his wife into sausages, yet "between the spring of 1897 and the summer of 1902, most families in Chicago did not eat local sausage," and sales of the item fell off even in the surrounding states. The question of *what* the population was eating or would eat remained an interesting question.

Jack London came to Chicago to lecture on socialism, and admitted he had lunched with cannibals in the South Seas on human flesh and found it "rather like chicken." (London's real father, whom he did not know, is said to have been an Irish, Chicago, street-corner grifter and fortune-teller.)

Sherwood Anderson once told a crowd of local literary figures lunching at Schlogl's that he had heard of a fox hunter "who was so enamored of riding to hounds, he had a fox's head marinated and ate it with relish."

In 1906, Upton Sinclair was to stir up the sausage eaters again by exposing revolting Chicago packinghouse practices in his novel, *The Jungle.*

38

THE BIG FAIR

From the very beginning our people have markedly combined practical capacity for affairs with power of devotion to an ideal.
THEODORE ROOSEVELT

Make no little plans, they have no magic. . . . . *Let your watchword be "order" and your beacon, "beauty."*
DANIEL H. BURNHAM

It all began in enthusiasm and sensibility in 1891 on one of those deadly gray, grim days Chicago has in January, on a run of beach seven miles south of the center of the city. Over a dozen architects stood there staring at the lake's wet push of soiled rollers meeting the snow on the gritty sands. The men stood shivering in their suede-topped shoes, eyeing the lake, the shore, sand ridges, and some mangy growths of bog oak. Their mufflers were tight around their necks, coat collars up, as they moved at last onto a pier and listened to a city official address Daniel H. Burnham,

"You really mean to say you propose to open a fair here by '93?"

"Yes, that's our intention."

"Can't be done," said the skeptical man, shivering, scowling.

"That point is settled. We open," said Mr. Burnham.

He was tall, full-faced, square-chinned (even showing a dimple), and the wind was playing havoc with his ample longhorn moustache. Burnham was the director of construction of the

World's Columbian Exposition to be. He led the party back to the city. He soon got the canals started, the lagoons dug, a wooden island built. He sent up workingmen to climb over the skeleton iron work of domes and towers. After all, the people said, Burnham's firm, organized just after the Great Fire, had put up the town's first really tall building, the Montauk Block, set it solidly on concrete and steel railroad iron, an innovation. But by 1891, Burnham had to work alone, with the fair staffs often dragging their feet.

The vicissitudes of turning the disheveled boggy shore into a fair piled up and up. A landscape designer, Frederick Law Olmsted, was given fifteen million dollars to do something rigorously to Jackson Park, so that the fair would at least be surrounded by something exciting and orderly in green. So mountains of sand and earth were moved, lake and river shores gave up native plants and flowering shrubs.

If any artist or planner ran a collision course with Burnham, there was no problem. Explained Mr. Burnham, "I told him that I saw it differently. He then said he would get out, and he did."

Those that stayed on enjoyed marvelous free lunches at the best restaurant in town: Kinsley's. Out of one lunch with a modicum of wine came the idea that *all* buildings must be white and *all* have the same cornice height. And the hope that the Classic forms were replacing the Romanesque and other less worthy styles of building. As Burnham put it with pride and in an incisive baritone, "During the storms of summer, through the frosts of winter . . . for two years, the little band of American boys ran the race for victory with Father Time, and won it." Hardly today's prose style or the jargon of IBM computers, but how much warmer and more human.

The winter of 1891–1892 was an icy hell. Bogs were menaces, and when a thaw came, workhorses sank nearly out of sight. Plank roads had to be built. Then a freeze and a storm, and roofs collapsed under the snow loads. Then one more thaw, new lakes appeared, rains came, and some buildings nearly were launched as ships into the big lake.

Seven thousand men worked on the project. In 1891 alone, eighteen were killed, seven hundred injured in accidents. But the conceptual dream went on. Not everything was ready on Dedication Day. The grounds were muddy, some of the bridges were still temporary and rickety. But there were on hand, count them, five thousand singers, and enough visitors to fill twenty-five acres. The ticket holders, thirty thousand of them, many of them made it to see what their money had bought. Gate-crashers came in droves. Some men and boys were hanging from the iron trusses, climbing higher. Theodore Thomas led the fair band in John K. Paine's "Columbian March." The singers launched into Haydn's "The Heavens Are Telling," then the "Hallelujah Chorus" rang out in hysterical ecstasy its nonstoic acceptance of mortality.

It was a day before public-address systems and microphones. Miss Harriet Monroe's "Columbian Ode" was hardly heard by anyone. Levi P. Morton (few can identify him today; he was the Vice President of the United States) muttered with dignity and compassion, "I dedicate these buildings to humanity."

Chauncey Depew, a noted after-dinner speaker, and teller of obscene stories to small private gatherings, made a cheerful talk of gay banality. The dedication was considered a bust by most—but for the lunch. What were called "light refreshments" were set out, and most everybody in the crowd susceptible to hunger made a rush for them. Of a hundred thousand people present, it was estimated seventy thousand got something to eat in the crush. As one newspaper reported it, curses, blows, mashed sandwiches flew; "it was all very inelegant. Dignity and pride were in momentary eclipse."

BOOK FOUR

HOW TO SEIZE A CITY

39

THE NEARLY WHITE CITY

Chicago sounds rough. . . . One comfort we have—Cincinnati sounds worse.

O. W. HOLMES, AT THE CHICAGO COMMERCIAL CLUB, 1880

To bring into being what one has imagined is the hardest miracle. So came 1893, and Chicago was ready to open formally its World's Fair to honor Columbus. Mrs. Potter Palmer, society leader of the city and president of the board of lady managers, invited as guest to the Palmer castle the Infanta Eulalia of Spain. The infanta of Spain, stepping from George M. Pullman's private palace car, heiress to the feeble minds and diseased nerve ends of a long line of royal imbeciles, said, "I prefer *not* to meet this innkeeper's wife." So adding bad manners to disrespect for the fabulous Palmer House hotel.

However, the infanta did show up at Palmer castle, after breakfasting with the Carter Harrisons and taking dinner with the Harlow Higgenbothams. There was a bitchy, cool exchange of small talk between princess and hostess. And when later, in Paris, Mrs. Palmer was invited to a fete to greet the infanta, Mrs. Palmer politely sent her regrets: "I cannot meet this bibulous representative of a degenerate monarchy."

It wasn't only European royalty that sneered at the prospects of a Chicago fair. The limp-wristed Ward McAllister, an effusive mediocrity, but in social power, who had claimed there were *only* "Four Hundred people" worth meeting in New York society, shot what he hoped was a blow to the hopes of the fair. "The contrast of New York and Chicago society during the World's Fair cannot help but open the eyes of our Western natives to *our* superiority. I do not wish to belittle Chicago in using the word 'superiority.' " He sniffed at the reporters listening to him and went on, "The society of Chicago is behind that of New York, but there is no reason why it should not eventually catch up." Then Ward tried for the knockout punch. "I could name *many* men and women who have been forced to spend a large part of their early lives in the West, but who have *nevertheless* established themselves in good positions in Eastern society. . . . I may say that it is not quantity but quality that society people here want. Hospitality which includes the whole human race is *not* desirable. . . . We, in New York, are familiar with the sharp character of the Chicago magnates."

Wrote one keeper of a private journal we have read: "Hardly a worthy remark, for as to sharpness, New York society was based on the Astor fur thieves, Commodore Vanderbilt's commercial shady manoeuvrings and known lecheries, Jay Gould's and Fisk's outright stealing and swindling of widows and orphans, J. P. Morgan's womanizing, clubbing of small companies, and stock kiting, and John D. Rockefeller's burning out rival oil fields, illegally breaking competitors and strikers—and with hiring Pinkerton for murder in Colorado. Chicago could produce pretty sharp characters, but none to match the unholy crew in flagrant abuse of honesty and integrity whose fortunes founded New York society."

But Ward McAllister was not through yet with the whole idea behind the Chicago fair. In irrelevant mocking words, he gave the insult directly to America's founder.

"Really, an exposition to honor *who?* Christopher Columbus? In a social way Columbus was an ordinary man."

Chicago responded with a calculated kiss-our-ass indifference. Somehow no one in Chicago cared about Columbus' standing with Mrs. Astor's list of acceptable dinner partners. Plans were made for

President Grover Cleveland to open the fair on a May day, as the World's Columbian Exposition, and four hundred thousand people were expected to cheer and enjoy the event. Mayor Carter Harrison, Sr., beamed at the hopes of the fair, and Marshall Field thought of the $250,000 his store had put into the fair's kitty.

Mr. Potter Palmer continued to have problems with Spain (our war with that nation was still five years away, and after all Columbus had sailed from Spain). Ahead was the moment when the duke and duchess of Veragua entered a carriage to ride at the fair, *and* a rush by some lady managers to sit with them. One lady left out raised an outcry of momentary grief crossed with public outrage. Mrs. Potter answered with dignity: "If it is *only* a struggle for few passing honors, and we are all torn up and pulling hair over an introduction to a Duchess, my time is *too* valuable . . . to be wasted this way."

A supporter of Mrs. Palmer rose to defend Manageress Mrs. Palmer. "I boldly say . . . that she [Mrs. Palmer] is the only woman that can lead me, and I bow to her character and amiability as it goes out to the world as *our* American Queen."

Mrs. Palmer, who seems to have come off very well in all exchanges, answered, "I am *not* calling for any personal endorsement."

The fair waiting for formal opening day (someone simple had named it "The White City") was six thousand acres, and it was hoped millions of people would enjoy its palaces, lagoons, classic white piles of buildings of plaster reflecting in the lagoon waters at night. In the night, even Richard Morris Hunt's big domed Administration Building, the Agricultural hulk, a last gasp of McKim, Mead & White, became electrically lighted fantasies after dark.

The only two adventurers in building ideas were Henry Ives Cobb's Fisheries Building, and Louis Sullivan's highly colored Transportation structure. The huge gathering of ordinary talents produced little that was original or daring. Each age prefers the safe solids of the previous age to its own pioneers. Saint-Gaudens, the sculptor, effusive, serene, and foolish, exclaimed, "Look, do you realize that this is the greatest meeting of artists since the fifteenth century?" The gathering of latter-day Michelangelos, Titians, and

Leonardo da Vincis, standing by in their top hats, derbies, and high-button shoes, bowed their heads modestly and could only privately agree. A flagrant abuse of fancy rhetoric filled most speeches at the fair.

However, the architectural critic, Russell Sturgis, thought most of the fair as "schoolboy work . . . merely the adoption of what was easiest and quickest done." Mostly the crowds were to remain indifferent or say *ah!* and go on to see Little Egypt do her famous belly dance, revolving her pelvis and revealing really a very ample navel. "The basic notions of the dance—tossing the head from side to side, gesturing smoothly with the arms, 'fluttering' the belly by deep and shallow breathing and shimmying the hips by changing weight distribution over the legs—appear relatively simple until you try it" *(Illustrated American)*.

Louis Sullivan sadly summed up the style of the buildings. "The damage wrought by the World's Fair will last for half a century . . . if not longer. It has penetrated deep into the . . . American mind, effecting lesions significant of dementia." And he left to get a drink of whiskey.

Sullivan, a great pioneer, was doing little work; no one wanted to hire him. His decline was tragic. Yet in one last burst, one final chance, he invented or perfected the modern steel skeleton skyscraper in the startling patterns of the Mayer Dry Goods Store on State Street (now the home of Carson, Pirie, Scott & Co.). Almost no one saw its merit, not when you could get Renaissance froufrou, Greek and Gothic Revival, and always there was Romanesque, and what bank could resist being a Roman temple?

One of Sullivan's best disciples, young Frank Lloyd Wright, wasn't blighted, or impressed by the fair's architectural katzenjammers, in whose area the Chicago underworld hoped to have pickpockets, its whores on parade, and shills among the hot sweet corn on the cob and the prize cattle. The bad element hoped to incite the folks to a friendly game of cards, or some high rolling crap shooting. As for sexual vice, hopes were high once the fair opened.

Wright had that self-confidence, that showmanship that genius must have, and the magic eye to freeze the rich of Oak Park, the West Side suburbs into commissioning him to design something called the Prairie Style. It was certainly starkly elegant and even

lovely, but hung with Aztec roofs and dark insides, broken-up inte-
riors. Later, as fame came to Wright, one owner of a Wright-built
house called him on the phone during a thunderstorm. "Mr.
Wright, that house you built for me. The roof leaks. I'm sitting here
getting wet. What shall I do?" "Move your chair."

On the fairground itself, already there were other complaints.
The area was a field day, even into the night, for confidence men,
all sorts of fakers, pea-shell and three card monte men, harpies,
floozies, and thieves of all kind. Some felt the dancers salacious, the
midway carnivals too brash and vulgar. Some out-of-town sports
wanted a hot time: they, too, could be taken care of, and taken, if
not on the grounds, there were the joints, cellar dives nearby. Newspapers (mostly out of town) reported robbings, muggings, stripping
of rubes, yokels, city folk, were to be common; country boys and city
slickers fell for loaded dice, marked cards, Mickey Finns, to the appeal of the feather-dressed whores, the lure of cafés and beer gardens. But most families planned to come with great packed lunch
baskets, and most hoped to walk the rounds among the great works
in the Arts Palace, with its "real oil paintings." Advice was to bring
umbrellas, easy comfortable shoes.

Official opening day came at last, May 1, 1893. President Grover Cleveland rode in front of twenty-three carriages drawn by the
best horseflesh in town, in the company of the city's solid citizens.
Marshall Field, of course. ("He was always every place; like Chicago water you couldn't avoid him"—Mr. Dooley.) Governor John
Altgeld, General Nelson Miles, the Indian killer. Mrs. Potter
Palmer, at last serene by the side of the duke and duchess of Veragua, and then loads of all those Spanish faces and names: the
Marquis de Harbales, Don Cristobel Colon y Aquilers, and doña of
the same name, and lots more. ("Hell, they look just like the Mexi-
can fieldhand come out here to hoe beans up in Michigan!")

Last in a splendid carriage, Mayor Carter Harrison, passing
through the Midway Plaisance, to cheering donkey boys, tom-tom
drummers, waiters, freaks, dancers, and lots of Chicagoans. Not to
forget the four roaring lions (trained to howl on order) of the Ha-
genbeck show.

Soon on the fairgrounds larger and larger unruly crowds milled around the main speech stand, as the "Columbian March"
again took over. Crushed children wept, women screamed as their

dresses were torn. Some fainted and were rescued before being stomped into the muddy lawns. Men, women, and children began to fall faster, lay about threshing underfoot. Some were unconscious. Some were pulled aside, some pushed, many cried out in horror. Ambulance and stretcher-bearers carried off the injured. Jane Addams of Hull House had her purse snatched by a thief in flagrant abuse of the event, but an officer of the Columbian Guard tripped up the thief with his sword to make a recovery.

A blind minister rose to recite a prayer. Then the President was told to press an electric key in a purple plush box. "When you touch this magic key, Mr. President, the ponderous machinery will start."

The Presidential high silk hat had been damaged in the crush. He laid it aside tenderly, like an injured small animal. He spoke over the din of disaster in the crowd, spoke the usual ceremonial words. "Stupendous . . . magnificent . . . American enterprise . . . Stimulation . . . Proud destiny . . . Exalted mission . . . Brotherhood . . ." He pressed the key with enthusiasm.

The flags of the United States and the red banner of Castile were run up their masts. Also, noted our journal keeper, "The white lettered banner of those murderous bigots, Ferdinand and Isabella." Frederick MacMonnies' fountain began to spurt water as near white as you could get it in Chicago. Liberty's statue was undressed as her shroud fell away, and almost everyone still on his feet who could manage it cried in awe at beauty and in copious gratitude, "Ah-h-h!"

The President's spark had started vast mysterious machines. And from the lake came the vehement *bang-bang* of the guns of the warships assembled there. Great flocks of gulls rose in panic at the sounds and circled the crowd with their screams; in the process some visitors reported bombing from the sky.

The fair was officially open. And the Midway began its grind of pleasure, the lovers of progress explained progress in steel, in wood carving. The spectacle of great art was available, and on a minor scale the tintype men produced, in a few minutes, pictures of visitors in frozen poses against white buildings.

Salesmen with guileful purpose touted the products of flour

mills, furniture makers, bottled drinks, tonics, watches, pickles, long underwear, machine processes, locomotives.

Little Egypt, the belly dancer, was for many the best remembered individual at the fair. To see how other dancers impressed the critic of the *Illustrated American* here is his own fervid prose on the Persian dancing girls: "The latter are very comely, but thick waisted and large footed after their kind, dancing with a grace that is heavy and languorous. They incline to plumpness, and are, verily 'sleek odalisques.' As the music begins to play, a handsome girl with a wealth of dark hair, on which is jauntily set a tiny silken cap, steps forward lazily, and smilingly bows to her vociferous admirers. Over a blue silk bodice she wears a red silk jacket, and her loose red trousers are girdled at the waist by a gold and yellow sash. Chains of brass coins hang from her girdle and heavy brass rings encircle the black hose at her ankles. Waving two scarlet handkerchiefs of silk, she moves slowly around, her white arms gleaming through her sleeves of gauze. Now she revolves and turns, her face assuming a dreamy smile, her painted eyes half closed, her white teeth showing between lips made redder and fuller by art. Now she begins the contortions that mark all the Oriental dances; her movements are snake-like and wanton, and she sinks lower and lower, wriggling, twisting, jerking, her face half veiled with her handkerchief, until she almost touches the stage, after the fashion which startled even Paris herself not so very long ago.

"At the close of the dance, the girl sits cross legged on the divan smoking cigarettes. After a moment's rest, she picks up a drum to tap, as a lithe beauty with long, black, silky hair rises to add her tribute to the entertainment. The girl is pretty and not more than sixteen years old. Her head is adorned with a gold cap and tassel. She wears a gold and yellow bodice, a brilliant red jacket, pale pink trousers, gorgeous sash, red boots, and trim black hose. Her Orientalism has a Parisian flavor. She is a great favorite and has many friends among the cigarette smokers in the audience. Her dancing has a vivacity that is unusual among her cult, and this Parisian of Teheran has absorbed all the terpsichorean devices and suggestiveness of all the lands through which she has passed on her pilgrimage from Persia to the Plaisance. One would suppose that her predecessor had exhausted all the possibilities of this kind of dancing; but this Persian now breaks into a whirling dance, and, gathering together the loose foldings of her trousers, springs in the air and comes down on the stage in the abominable 'split,' a libel on dancing from which the stage proper is far from free.

"Then comes a plump, slit-eyed girl, whose head is heavy with coils of brown hair and yellow chains of sequins, robed in trousers of gold and scarlet, belted with a yellow girdle, and whose bust is wrapped in red silk, over which she wears a blue jacket with loose sleeves of white, meshy gauze. She is the very incarnation of sleepy, lazy abandon, from the brown hair on her head to the thick, brass ringed ankles above her broad flat feet. She moves languorously into her convolutions to the music of the cumbrous guitar and the sounds of tambours and drums, stimulated by the cries of her fellow dancers. New Suggestiveness grows out of her physical snakiness. She contents herself with undulations in the descending and ascending scales, making a pretense of hiding her half closed eyes and mouth with her kerchief. The hats wave and the hall roars as the excited boys rain cigarettes at her feet and loudly demand a repetition. And throughout it all, the guitar player sits in his chair smoking, sneering, unmoved.

"The fourth girl is pretty and indecisive, though arrayed as gorgeously as any Circassian in a Padishah's seraglio. Her dance is tame and uninteresting after the audacious indecency of the other beauties.

"This closes the performance, and the dancing Delilahs jump from the dais to squat at the open windows of the theatre and ogle the streams of masculinity that flow by in the glaring white highway of the Plaisance below.

"In contrast to this exhibition of flagrant indecency, which should instantly be abolished from the Midway Plaisance, the risque dances of Cairo, Algiers and Constantinople, in the immediate neighbourhood, seem staid and respectable, and the frank nudity of Dahomey and Samoa, refreshing and natural."

40

CHICAGO'S PRIDE

It is the first requisite that a man be born in a famous city.
EURIPIDES, 415 B.C.

To most of us the great fair is a dim echo of some old aunt and uncle recalling a trip in more limber days. Or a relic: painted seashell, pot-metal pin box lettered WORLD'S COLUMBIAN EXPOSITION, 1893. Best of all is a scrapbook of old, yellowing, crumbling newspaper clippings from various sources describing the fair fresh in the eye of the beholder:

"Uncle Sam has a handsome and commodious building at the World's Fair that cost him $400,000. It is modelled somewhat after the Capitol in Washington, having a central rotunda surmounted by a great dome; and the several departments of the Government exhibits radiate from this central hall. Its exterior is plain, differing in this wise from the other Fair buildings, though the portals, piers and cornices are surmounted by historical and allegorical figures.

"A tremendous array of the implements of war is shown, torpedoes, siege guns, mortars, field pieces, rifles, bayonets, and such wholesale destroyers as the Maxim, Gatling and Gardner machine guns. On the walls, are the clumsy engines of death of a past age,

277

muskets, blunderbusses and kindred weapons, dangerous alike to friends and foes; and close by is a rack filled with rifles picked up from the field of the civil war, rusty, twisted, and bullet splintered.

"The arsenals of the United States have an exhibit of their own, showing the whole art of making a rifle, from the steel bar and the wooden log to the shining deadly instrument that makes armies potent. Reduced to its simplest elements, as observed here, the making of a rifle is merely the operation described by the Irishman: 'First get a hole; then put your iron round it, and there's your rifle.' The food of the rifle, the copper cartridge, is being made next to the gun itself, by machinery that is almost human in its working.

"This particular section has a horrible fascination for men and women and children, who linger around the machines watching every detail with the keenest interest."

Advertising with class was also present:

The Parfumerie Ed Pinaud.

"To the immediate east of the magnificent pavilion, that the French Government has erected to house its Gobelin tapestries and Sèvres ware, stands the dainty exhibit of the Parfumerie ED PINAUD, whose eau de quinine, soaps and perfumes are known the world over. It is a salon of the purest style Louis XV., exquisite in design, appointment, finish; furnished with cabinets and carved tables that follow with absolute fidelity the art of that historic era."

The common man and family got a few lines:
"The laboring man from the city, who sacrifices his day and his pay because of his pietistic, Sabbatarian neighbour's unchristian prejudices, comes with his wife, family, and big lunch and enjoys it all hugely. It is a new and magnificent world to him; the kingdoms of the earth and the glories thereof are his for this day; the glory and genius of the sculptor and painter touch his heart, and he goes home happy, satisfied and weary, with a pleasure more arduous than work."

The kind of high-class shows the fair attempted can be seen from a notice of the fair's *Grand Spectacle.*

A SUPERB SPECTACLE
"AMERICA" ON THE STAGE

"America" is by far the most superb stage spectacle of the day. London cannot show anything to equal it. Paris cannot rival it. This production is at once magnificent and instructive. It is a gorgeous and beautiful pageant, and it is thoroughly interesting into the bargain. It delights the eye and ear, the while it refreshes and informs the mind. It is a colossal and thoughtful Empire entertainment. Even that famed home of dress and dance has not done anything to eclipse this ambitious accomplishment. Nor has London's other great house of spectacular display, the Alhambra of brilliant memory, come near to this lovely production. This is not a case of a single ballet, or of one elaborate procession. "America" lasts throughout the entire evening. It embraces three ballets of exceptional elegance, and marches and processions innumerable. It captivates the senses by its harmony. This, I think, is the keynote to its success. There is no jarring note in the whole thing. It is full of movement, life, color, but everything harmonizes—story, music, dance, pageant, dress, all suit each other perfectly. The prologue is descriptive of the setting out of Columbus, of the voyage, of the discovery of America and of the return to Spain. The Plymouth Plantation of 1621 serves as an opportunity for the introduction of a Maypole dance, a characteristic and quaintly dressed scene which appeals to all who love color and life and which affords a happy contrast to the costumes and scenes which succeed it. In the second act, there are various historical scenes, such as that of Washington crossing the Delaware and the surrender of Yorktown, all carried out with excellent dramatic effect, the whole terminating with an unusually interesting representation of various allegorical figures and a grand ballet illustrative of the arts and sciences.

This dance of Arts and Sciences is one of the most magnificent things of its kind which I can recall. It is clever in design and in detail, but it is chiefly distinguished by the rare loveliness of the dresses. "America" is not to be named in the same breath with the "farce-comedies" and wrongly called comic operas with which the stage of this country is flooded. It is vastly superior to all these productions of a vitiated taste. They disgrace the stage; "America" honors the theatre.

Some visitors paid Chicago compliments. An English author did the proper thing. In a letter written on the eve of his departure from the city of the World's Fair, Mr. Walter Besant said, "I carry away a delightful memory—not so much of a Chicago, rich, daring, young and confident—as of a Chicago which has conceived and carried into execution the most beautiful and poetic dream—a palace surpassing the imagination of man, as man is commonly found—and a Chicago loving the old literature discerning and proving that which is new, and laying the foundations for that which is to come. A Chicago which is destined to become the centre of American literature in the future."

But the Midway was not interested in American literature, then or in future. It liked entertainers like Maggie Cline, a mountain-sized singer who delighted the Irish.

> Did ye ever hear tell of McGarry—
> Mick McGarry? Comes from Darry?
> When he got half tight he was sparry—
>   Oh, he was such a divil to fight!
> Sure he'd fall out wid soldier or sailor,
> Or a nailer or a tailor;
> Be jabers! he'd tackle a jailer.
>   He was dyin' to fight ev'ry night.

The audience loved it, and howled with glee at the spirit of McGarry.

> So one day through the streets he wint rowlin':
> He was prowlin', he was growlin',
> "Will nobody fight? he was howlin',
> Till he met with a very tough gang.
> Says he, "Be the pow'rs! I can bate ye!
> I can ate ye! I can slate ye!
> Stand there and I will massacre ye!"
>   When one of the gang went—Biff!!!

Reports of other doings at the fair were not as amusing:
"The country is flooded with genuine counterfeit silver dollars. These paradoxical coins contain sixty cents' worth of silver—the

same amount as the dollar of the Government mint—and are un-distinguishable from the mint issue. In former times, when a silver dollar was worth one hundred cents, counterfeiters had to use baser metals, which soon led to their detection. But when the Government itself gives a fictitious value to the coinage of the country, there is nothing to prevent the counterfeiters from taking advantage of the situation."

41

ALL FOR COLUMBUS

A financier is a pawnbroker with imagination.
A. W. PINERO

Among its other problems, the fair faced a panic on Wall Street and bad times in the nation. Wall Street, that New York monster, frightened many Midwesterners into bewilderment and desolation. Kept them from the fair.

The Chemical National Bank with a branch at the fair, eight days after the grand opening, failed, and also its mother bank in Chicago. A lot of phoning was done. (Already the telephone was disturbing American life in reality and song: "Hello, Central, Give Me Heaven, Because My Mother's There.") Phoning done by managers of the fair to reassure the European exhibitions with money in the bank. It was guaranteed there would be no losses for them.

The other big problem was Sunday, a day, by tradition, of churchgoing and prayers, the Pilgrim Fathers had said. And the nation was still in the grip of the puritan morality, and certain nuances of discomfort as faith—at least on the idea that Sunday was sacred to boredom and no time for pleasures, amusements, having

283

fun. Congress had voted two and a half million dollars to be minted as Columbian coins to help pay for the fair, and had added the snide provision the gates of the fair *must* be locked tight on Sundays, as the church bells rang out over Chicago. Here was a formidable, slippery problem.

However, some sly person discovered a loophole; Congress had drawn off some of the money to be used to pay for awards, which gave the fair managers an excuse that the contract had been voided by that action, and the gates were thrown open on Sunday. The severe, solemn God-lovers rose off their knees. Preachers cried out at this "hedonist example of law breaking." As a sop, most of the gay places and carnival shows were kept closed. The result was the public stayed away in droves at this example of curtailed showmanship. The courts first ordered them to close, then to open, then to close, and for a time it was a disagreeable experience for the fair's backers to watch the jabberwocky of legal nonsense.

Commercialism had, of course, already reared its sinister head, and the tones of Pecksniff mixed with the band music. Steinway pianos having bought no space at the fair, the Steinway was barred *anyplace* on the grounds. However, the bushy-haired Paderewski, trailed by admiring women, had been booked to perform; he may not have been the world's greatest piano player, but his cult reached the proportions of mania and he was a master showman; he insisted he could *not* play on anything but a Steinway grand. The fair managers remained firm with ludicrous determination, but a Steinway was smuggled in for the maître. The director of music, Theodore Thomas, was dragged before the Fair Commission to explain this early example of payola. He pleaded his case as a noncorruptible individual. "I am an old man, sixty years old, and nearing the end of my course. . . . I value my reputation as a musician and leader more than any pecuniary benefit I might derive from aiding any piano firm."

The fair managers stood firm like Spartans at Thermopylae, and Thomas was asked to resign. He didn't, and then gave up in despair when his type of good classical music failed to draw the expected crowds.

Then the waiters went on strike, demanding the high salary of fifteen dollars a week, and got it. "The country is going to hell in a hack!"

The Jewelry Exhibition, a supposedly impregnable repository, was broken into by expert yeggs, and was robbed of two diamonds set in a riding whip owned by King Leopold of the Belgians. Since the king was murdering hundreds of thousands of natives in the Belgian Congo for not collecting rubber fast enough, and lopping off the hands and feet of those who tried to flee his tax collectors, the bar joke at the Palmer House by some reporter was that "the King

needed the whip to flog his darkies." It was a jest not at all amusing to the fair managers.

In Chicago, fire was always a simple certainty. Tragedy struck with flame at the fair in July. The Cold Storage Building decorated with three unnecessary towers burst into flames and a crew of firemen foolishly, bravely, climbed one of the towers. Suddenly, flames enveloped them as 130,000 people watched. Seventeen of the doomed firemen slid or leaped to their deaths directly into the fire. It added a creepy attraction to the fair. The admission price was fifty cents, and the month of May saw several hundred thousand customers and visitors who had come and seen, stared and enjoyed. It was a simpler age, and in a nation more given to farming life, the sights amazed the visitors. A ferris wheel 264 feet high; movable sidewalks; the Yerkes telescope, still waiting to be installed at the University of Chicago; unhistoric replicas of the three ships of Columbus that had actually in 1892 sailed to the fair from Spain; the great stamp hammer with which the House of Krupp had already been beating out some of the Guns of August, 1914. For the fun lovers, besides Little Egypt's gyrating belly button in the Street of Cairo, there was the Irish Village, Blarney Castle (a fake Blarney Stone—a Chicago paving block), and Donegal Castle, *Alt Wien,* which one reporter mistranslated as "Old Wine." One could walk with Arabs, American Indians, Laplanders among the 50,000 roses, more or less, carpeting the Wooded Island. Montana sent a solid silver statue of a politician—and Nikola Tesla had high-tension current available that powered a long-distance phone line to New York City. It all seemed a reaffirmation of progress.

Parisian fashions were on display and showed Worth and other designers on wax figures; the parading of hip-swaying models was not yet acceptable. You could see Miles Standish's pipe, Mount Vernon (full sized), and even the Liberty Bell, crack and all. Every place wheelchairs were pushed, gondolas moved on the tepid, murky waters, Columbian Guards patrolled the fair, guarding spurious antiques. Women's rights and morals were taken care of by the appearance of Susan B. Anthony who cherished a hopeless dream of women voting and so purifying politics. Temperance shouters were laughed at when they predicted they would pray the nation dry. The archbishop of Ireland came with a set of rolling Rs in his brogue. (The archbishop of Canterbury refused an invitation from the colonials.)

On "Chicago Day" 700,000 people came. It seemed to be a splendid time for Chicago. Mayor Carter Harrison felt so and he was held in affection by what were called "the lower classes of Chicago." The *Illustrated American* found this distasteful, also the habits of his followers:

"The Fourth of July this year was productive of more than the usual number of accidents and catastrophes. There were tragic disasters resulting from the drunkenness of motor men on trolley and cable cars, and of the drivers of street cars and cabs, but, perhaps, no sadder sight has ever been witnessed in this country than that presented by that unspeakable rogue and demagogue Carter Harrison, the Mayor of Chicago, who, standing on the steps of the Administration Building, at Jackson Park, called upon men and women to kiss the sword of Jackson in token of their fidelity to the Union. Never before, perhaps, has the Fourth of July been disgraced in a community by an act of such vicious taste and rank hypocrisy performed by the very man who was the chief agent in securing the release from prison of the guzzling, unwashed foreigners who lately took up arms against the peace and order of an American community. There is trouble in store for the nation from creatures like Carter Harrison and his kind."

The fear of "the unwashed," usually suspected of being bomb throwers, was a good club with which the enemy press libeled the mayor, as this quote from a contemporary magazine shows:

"No one with the slightest knowledge of the career and character of Carter Harrison, the Mayor of Chicago, was at all surprised at the conduct of the knave in suggesting to the lawless element of his domain that riots and revolts would enlist his sympathy and interest. Harrison proved himself during Chicago's troubles with the Haymarket murderers, to be not only an unblushing demagogue, but a cowardly, sneaking traitor, who fled from the scenes of carnage and rapine that he predicted would follow upon any attempt of the authorities to inflict the death sentences passed upon the chief culprits in the Haymarket tragedy. That such a creature should be again advanced to the highest position in the gift of his fellow citizens is understandable only in view of the monstrous license of our suffrage laws, which permit the offal of European population to equal power at the ballot box with the pink of native respectability. . . ."

The WASP idealists and the Know-Nothing Yahoos expressed themselves freely in those days. Harrison was Southern born; "Kentucky, sir," a claimed descendant of Pocahontas and a Robert Carter. The mayor, a lover of clabber, and watermelon, weighing 225 pounds, was about to take a third wife, a dashing young charmer from New Orleans, Miss Annie Howard. He was a mayor who pleased Chicago; the underworld operated freely and paid for protection, but the mayor did not share in it. All he demanded of criminals was their vote. He liked a lively city and he was for its growth and progress, with not too much pressure to be good, or channel off its extravagant ways. He was gray bearded now, and liked his carriage to be cheered as he drove by.

At his home, soon after Chicago Day, he had a visitor. He cheerfully encouraged visitors. This one was a man named Prendergast who rang the doorbell, and when the mayor was called, Prendergast fired three revolver shots at Harrison, visible at the door to the dining room. And ran for it. The assassin was sure he should have been made head of the Corporation Council of Chicago; denied the post, he had come to kill. The mayor died in fifteen minutes.

The killer was declared insane because he had no fitness for the city job. But as Ben Hecht was to explain it in a conversation I had with him: "Which was a poor excuse. Most of the people who held office in Chicago were feeble-minded, crazy, or dishonest—and most all were and *are* unfit for public office—so labeling Prendergast mad for seeking a city position he wasn't fitted for was a poor farce of an excuse. Whoever was fit in Chicago's highest offices?"

The fair flags were lowered to half-mast at news of the murder. But on the Midway Plaisance, a rowdy crowd of thrill seekers, criminals, nihilistic characters broke into song, pantomime, created a drunken riot, as whiskey bottles were emptied, the empties then flung to burst in shards on the facades of the white buildings. Lewd and mocking signs were marked out, graffiti appeared, and until near dawn the carousing, howling, and drunken revels held the fairgrounds of the Midway.

In his last speech on the day of his assassination, the mayor, addressing a meeting of visiting mayors, had articulated a hope and a reassurance: "Genius is but audacity, and the audacity of the wild and woolly West and of Chicago has chosen a star, has looked upward to it and knows nothing that it cannot accomplish."

Not since Abraham Lincoln's funeral train had stopped over in Chicago had there been such a weeping, pushing, wild procession of mourners as when the mayor lay in state at City Hall.

It seemed a fitting climax, somehow, to the soon-closing fair.

Not all the mayor's obituaries were kind. The *Illustrated American* said:

"And so Carter Harrison is foully murdered and thereby gains a world-wide fame. Chicago regrets the loss of a genial friend, the United States an erratic citizen, and the world a remarkable man.

"We are not by nature a picturesque people, and our politicians make an ugly foreground in the portrait of the nation. But Carter Harrison was a picturesque politician. He was a demagogue of the worst kind, and though his bark was worse than his bite, did an infinite amount of harm, but he always carried with him a richness of color that warmed his crude surroundings. . . .

"In 1879 he was elected Mayor of Chicago, and many times since has he been elected to the same position. As Mayor he showed how much better a man of common sense can deal with vice than a preacher of theoretical impossibilities. He could not make Chicago a moral town, but he made it a decent city where vice is not flaunted in the faces of those who don't want to see it.

"Carter Harrison and the ex-President's grandfather were brothers. They were not descended from the 'regicide' Harrison as is generally supposed, but from the brother of the man who signed Charles I.'s death warrant.

"Mr. Harrison's wife, who was a Miss Preston, died in Europe in 1876. In 1882 he married a Miss Stearns. She died in 1887. At the time of his murder, Mr. Harrison was engaged to be married to Miss Annie Howard of New Orleans."

The mayor had closed his eyes to the conduct at the fair of the more criminal elements, and this brought sharp comment from some of the press:

"Now that the World's Fair has come to an end Chicago can

afford to acknowledge the ugly truth regarding the rampant disorder that prevails in that city. The reports of the parlous conditions existing in the crude metropolis of the West would be incredible if they were not corroborated by the circumstances of their official source. Murders, robberies, burglaries and 'hold-ups' have become of such frequent, almost continual occurrence, as to scarcely attract the notice of the public or the concern of the police. The horde of malefactors that have literally taken possession of the town are absolutely fearless. They stop at nothing to accomplish their purposes of plunder, and murder is as commonplace out there as robbery. As the first step toward reforming the frightful state of matters the Superintendent of Police has issued orders that any person found on the streets after one o'clock in the morning must be prepared to give an account of himself and to explain his being abroad at such an hour to the satisfaction of the police. Of course, in the abstract, this seems rather a high-handed proceeding, but it is as the Superintendent says: 'No good citizen will take offense at this. The officers are specially instructed to be polite, to use no rough language and to refrain from violence, and to announce in every instance where they halt a citizen that they are officers. While this extraordinary patrol duty is being performed all officers must be very careful in their manner of halting persons, and any officer who is guilty of discourteous or abusive language to the citizen will be instantly discharged from the force.'

"Under such circumstances the somewhat autocratic and imperial restrictions put upon the personal liberty of citizens will be quite tolerable."

Another report, from the *New York Herald*, indicates that the criminals at the fair did make some change in the safety of Chicagoans:

"Latest reports indicate no improvement in the almost incredible conditions of disorder . . . Murder, burglary and highway robbery are still of nightly and daily occurrence. The semblance of martial law that was counted to prevent in part at least these crimes, has proved quite ineffective.

"An amusing feature of the affair is that while the criminals who are now worrying the natives occupied themselves almost exclusively with the outsiders who came to the World's Fair, no effort was made to drive them from the city or to suppress their activities.

One of the police officials of Chicago naively admits this. 'While the Exposition lasted,' he says, 'they managed to pick up a living without annoying our townspeople. Now, however, they are bothering some of our best citizens and it's got to be stopped.' "

With the fair closing, moralists worried about the release of its more rougher entertainment into the country. Brooded the *Buffalo Express*:

"The Midway Plaisance is being scattered piecemeal among the variety shows and museum circuits of the country. No fault is to be found with this so long as the performers are what they purport to be, foreigners exhibiting their own native dances, musical performances, etc. But of all the abominations yet invented, the worst is an American dancing woman trying to give the Oriental body dances. This exhibition was to be seen in certain Chicago resorts during the summer, but we hope that the theatre managers of the East will be so discreet as not to impose it upon their patrons this winter."

Little Egypt's imitators were soon to be on the loose—every small-time carny midway was to feature "the Original Little Egypt direct from the Chicago Exposition!"

How had the fair fared on the money side? An unofficial report circulated among the newspapers:

"It is estimated that the gate receipts of the World's Fair at Chicago will approximate $10,500,000 and the concession receipts $4,000,000. From souvenir coins and premiums the Exposition has drawn almost $2,500,000. Interest on deposits has brought $100,000 more, and from various other sources, entered in the books as miscellaneous receipts, is a credit of about $700,000. To these amounts must be added $10,600,000 of capital stock from individual subscribers and the city of Chicago, and the total amount of money that has come to the Exposition will be found to be approximately $28,400,000. It is believed that about $3,000,000 will be left to divide among the stockholders."

To peer a little into the future, in time Chicago elected Carter Harrison, Jr., to be its mayor in place of his father—he refused that half-million dollar bribe from Yerkes for a trolley line swindle, rode no white horse or wore no slouch hat like his father. He was a solid, chunky citizen with a splendid black moustache. He ran the city a little tighter than his father, arrested some notorious characters, tried to enforce a few gambling laws, raided a few madams, badgered some hustlers. But Chicago being Chicago, the city ran nearly as wild as it had in the past. Harrison backed the Mueller Municipal Ownership Law that gave the city some control over the monopolists of the past. He never reformed the aldermen, boodle, and graft, bought votes remained a city tradition.

When, after five terms, Carter Harrison, Jr., left the mayor's office, someone wrote a verse, "Harrison's Farewell," to the tune of "Tipperary":

> *It's goodbye Old Chicago, farewell to City Hall.*
> *Sorry I've got to leave you, but it's written on the wall . . .*

Then the Republicans, looking for someone with the color, they hoped, of the Harrisons, put up a variegated young man from a wealthy family background, a big-muscled chap, apathetic to culture, an athlete who had banged around in football togs, done duty as a yachtsman, and at thirty, with heavy good looks, was willing to stand for public office.

The master minds of the Republican party liked what they saw. One member felt that as a candidate, the athlete was harmless. "Worst you can say about him is that he's stupid."

The athlete was William Hale Thompson, better known later as "Big Bill." While he belongs to the Chicago of the twenties as a major figure, he can be outlined here as a new breed of political figure who did not, as in the past, merely "make the eagle scream," but based his herd popularity on pleasing the voters by taking as targets world-famous figures—such as attacking the king of England to please the British-hating Chicago Irish. He was to attract national attention by offering to punch royal noses, and made clever use of the newer art of public relations.

42

THE EVERLEIGH CLUB

Every girl . . . is sitting on her fortune.
NELL KIMBALL: HER LIFE AS AN AMERICAN MADAM

The most famous sporting house in America was the Everleigh Club in Chicago. More myths and legends have come down to us about it than any other bordello in America. What the place was really like is told in an amazing volume of contemporary memoirs called *Nell Kimball: Her Life as an American Madam, by Herself.*

Came June of 1901 . . . I took off east for Chicago . . . I always give a big horselaugh when people start talking about the Everleigh Club, the wonderful whorehouse madams, the Everleigh sisters, Aida and Minna, and their world famous whorehouse in Chicago, their two dozen or thirty beautiful whores. I knew the Everleigh girls as well as I knew most of the important madams in America, and beyond the fact that they ran a first class house and knew how to get talked about, their house was no better as a knocking shop with beautiful girls than a half dozen sporting houses in half a dozen big cities. It was overpriced for what could be had elsewhere.

While in Chicago I decided to visit the Everleigh Club to

see what was the newest thing in whorehouse decor—outside of girls and beds—which never changed. I had been in contact with the sisters—there is a kind of underground railroad at work between madams—the exchange of information of the trade, the recommending of good girls, or warnings against big spenders whose checks are rubber, or those who were trouble-makers among the traveling johns and should be barred at the front door.

Around 1899 my friend, Cleo Maitland, the Washington, D.C. madam who catered to the cocksmen in Congress and the Senate, told Aida and Minna Everleigh the place to open a fancy whorehouse was Chicago. The sisters were loaded, hav-ing run a cathouse near the Trans-Mississippi Exposition in Omaha. When the exposition closed, they had around $80,000, and so they moved on the advice of Cleo Maitland, who knew of a house available in Chicago's 1st Ward—sporting country known as the Levee.

It was two big structures made of three-story houses knocked together. When I saw it, it had fifty rooms and a fancy set of stairs up from the street. Lizzie Allen, the old madam, had knocked it together as a high toned whorehouse for the 1890 [sic] Columbian Exposition. The talk was it had cost Liz-zie—a dreadful liar—around $200,000 to rebuild; cut that in half and you were nearer the truth. Effie Hankins, another madam I knew, bought out Lizzie after the fair. The Everleigh sisters made a deal with Effie to take over the place, lock, stock (whores and furniture) and barrel; $55,000 for the furniture, crockery, silverware, art work and carpeting, and to pay a rent—long term—of $500 a month.

I'd have dickered on the cost of the furniture—as a madam I always knew that on the furniture you can save a lot by just saying, "Get your old junk out of here. I don't want it around."

The girls opened for trade on the first of February, and also for the first time as the Everleigh Sisters; before that they spelled it Everly in the whorehouse trade. And that was the true form of it. They had a trained staff of darkies, a better class of whores, and they paid attention to the food and whisky and wine. And getting talked about.

It was a cold night, but trade was brisk. I never believed Aida's story that a senator from Washington sent them a mes-sage of good luck and flowers on opening night, or that the take

that night was over a thousand dollars. But business was good. And the place had class and taste—the two aren't always the same thing. Class is cost, taste is where cost doesn't show.

Who were these two sisters, leaving out the crap the newspapers printed about them? And the boasting the studs did, added to what lies the sisters told? It's not hard to put together the true facts; no madam has too secret a life if she stays in business long enough.

Aida and Minna Everly were born in Kentucky, the first in 1876, the second in 1878. Their father was a lawyer, how successful or how much of a shyster, I don't know. Before they were twenty years of age they married two brothers, always referred to as Southern Gentlemen—which doesn't mean a damn thing, as the girls found out. The men, so the sisters claimed, were brutes, knocking them about and in general mistreating them; that is their story. My opinion is they just found marriage a great bore.

The sisters ran off to Washington, D.C., a town full of Southern Gentlemen. They became actresses—which means just that they went out on tour with players and most likely were already peddling their tail on the side as most actresses did in those dingy little one night stands, always broke, always hungry, and somebody attaching the ticket sales. I know actresses don't like to hear this kind of talk, but I only knew of two actresses who didn't screw for fun or money while on tour. One had a cork leg, the other was a Mormon.

In Omaha for the Exposition, the sisters were informed their father was dead and had left them a bundle; the sisters always claimed it was $35,000. I'd shave that a bit, shave it a lot. They tried to get into local Omaha society, but the local wives soon found out their menfolk were laying the sisters—at first on an amateur basis for little gifts and suchlike things. Later the sisters gave out they had decided to turn against this respectable society and turn to whoring to revenge themselves for the brutality of their now forgotten husbands. You can take that with a grain of salt as big as the Woolworth Building. People become whores to make money. They were already whores by the time their father died, and their success with a house in Omaha showed they weren't Miss Alcott's LITTLE WOMEN even if only aged twenty-two and twenty-four.

So from Everly to Everleigh—from hotel bedrooms with small town johns to Chicago's Everleigh Club they became madams.

They were pleased to see me. Minna showed me through the club—she had done the place over and planned the decoration. She rattled off names for me as we scooted from room to room. "Silver Room, Gold Room, Moore's Room, Rose and Red Room, Chinese Room, Blue Room, Egyptian Room," and a dozen I no longer can remember. They were very elegant rooms, over-ripe, very much crowded with exotic looking stuff. I remember the Gold Room had fish bowls on gold stands, solid gold spittoons at $700 each, and a gold piano priced at $15,000. Again those costs told me didn't mean they were true. There were Oriental carpets by the acre, all "priceless" which doesn't mean you couldn't buy them in any good rug peddler's den. I saw lots of the place stank of incense, was full of brass Arab furniture, copies of Gibson Girl drawings and college colors and banners. It was a costly mish mash of what some kind of men think is the McCoy of luxury. The art gallery was the usual whorehouse collection of pictures in fine frames. The library held a lot of books in leather bindings. The dining room had silver and fine china services and the ballroom—"Turkish," Minna told me, "real Turkish," also had a real spouting water fountain. She turned it on and off for me. (Any running water in a house was a treat to many folk.)

I asked to see the details in the bedrooms—that's where history is made in a whorehouse, not among marble statues or palms in gold pots and gaboons.

Minna said, "We have thirty boudoirs for our ladies." The rooms were mostly the same, mirrors on the ceiling for easy viewing of the guest at his games, a big bouncy brass bed—the same as in my places—oil paintings of the usual subjects—fun in the woods and lots of flesh being chased. And a bathtub that was gold colored and Minna claimed was eighteen karat gold plated. Divans, spotlights, buttons for bringing wine or food, perfume sprayers; all could be had in most of the rooms.

Minna added, "And on some nights we let loose boxes of live butterflies in the parlors and boudoirs." The sisters had spent and spent, even for flying bugs.

I said I could see they were sparing no expense. I also saw, but didn't say, the girls were smart operators. All the gingerbread, fancy truck and the butterflies got the place talked about. As Cleo Maitland once said to me, "No man for sure is going to forget he got his balls fanned by a butterfly at the Everleigh Club."

The guest knew in advance a night visit to the club would set him back at least fifty dollars for the evening. Usually the tab came to much more.

Minna said, "Wine is twelve dollars a bottle downstairs, fifteen in bed." The four piece orchestra favored *Dear Midnight of Love*, said to have been written by some local ward heeler who took it out in trade at the club.

"Lots of guests stay for a late dinner, cost fifty dollars, ladies and wine extra, of course."

The price for a lay—extra—was fifty dollars—tipping the whore also came as extra. The whore gave half of her fee to the sisters. Many houses let the whore collect the fee upstairs. I always collected myself.

Aida told me she picked the girls as carefully as they pick a cadet at West Point. Experienced whores only—no amateurs or virgins. They had to be lookers, healthy, knowing all the varieties of sex a john might favor. Classy dressers, too, no slobs, drunks or dope takers. The whores were just as eager to get into the club as the johns were, so there was a waiting list of girls willing and able. Actually the Everleigh Club girls were no more skilled or better looking than whores in most high class sporting houses. They were trained to dress, make up their faces, do their hair—and maybe forced to read a book. I doubt the last. Bet-a-Million Gates once said to me of the club's book collection, "That's educating the wrong end of a whore."

Some guests stayed for weekends of specially appetizing food, drink and quiff. It cost around $500 for a full weekend spree.

With the years lots of famous men came to the club to get their ashes hauled or just to brag later they had been there. John Barrymore, a noted whoremaster, Bet-a-Million Gates, James Corbett, Stan Ketchell never got tired talking of their visits to the club. A Congress Investigation Committee sent to Chicago spent its nights—almost to a man—every night at the club.

The club was involved over the years in two murders. In 1905 Marshall Field's son was shot in the stomach at the club. Some say by a gambler, some say by a whore . . . the body was rushed out and he was found dead in his home—the police, on the take, said it was suicide or a "self inflicted accident."

A few years later a Nat Moore, son of a railroad nabob, died from aphrodisiac knock-out drops and plans were made to burn up the body in the club furnace. The sisters always claimed Nat Moore had died in another whorehouse and they were trying to plant him at the club to ruin the sisters' business.

Years later, meeting me at a spa, Minna told me Chicago whorehouses paid a million and a half dollars a year to police and city officials for protection. "We paid $130,000 ourselves over those years besides what we handed out to the legislators in Springfield to vote against bills unfavorable to our business."

I asked her what their take was. Minna said, "A good year, $125,000 to $150,000." I don't think she was lying by much.

What ruined the club was that the sisters made a habit of getting talked about; it made the club, and closed it. A fancy brochure they put out in 1910 praising their place and the comforts there, the delights of the guests, all were set down, including the address, 2131 Dearborn Street. It was read to a blue nose reform mayor, Carter Harrison. He blew his cork and ordered the chief of police to close the Everleigh Club. Secretly the sisters were told that $20,000 could keep delaying the order. But according to Minna, they said no and they closed the club.

No madam in America believed that part of the story. The truth most likely was that the reform wave was too strong just then to buck, and the sisters had to close or get raided and jailed. In 1912 they tried setting up a new club in the West Side of Chicago, but reform was still in power, and the pay-off price of $40,000 was too high. Reform is great for grafters—it raises the cost of protection and increases their incomes.

The sisters did pretty good when they retired in their late 30's. The talk in whorehouse circles, always with a good eye to values and a head for figures, was the sisters got out with $200,000 in diamonds and other jewels and $150,000 in household stuff. For all their claims of being high toned Kentucky born, they ran out on some unpaid bills. They also claimed guests owed them $25,000 for services of the house girls. That sounds fishy. Whorehouse credit doesn't extend that high. Most likely some famous johns got free lays—or expected them for free with free drinks and food—and the sisters listed this entertaining as debts.

The girls retired or tried to. From time to time they'd be back in the news. Bones of a skeleton were found in the back yard of their club—but no one could prove it was a guest's or a whore's remains. There was talk of a girl who died aborting in the club, but no one connected it with the bones. One of their girls was murdered later in New Orleans, her hands cut off to get her rings besides all the jewels she carried. This brought the Everleigh sisters back as news. I knew the whore. I knew who killed her, but it doesn't matter at this late date.

The last item I ever saw about the sisters was when a millionaire named Stokes in a divorce case claimed his wife had been an Everleigh Club whore at one time and he had married used merchandise.

I was impressed by my visit to the Everleigh Club. One couldn't help being. The girls knew how to attract attention. I came away with a few ideas for decoration, ways for impressing the guests, but nothing really world-shaking. No one has done anything to change . . . games much since the start of there being two sexes. And when you can't change the basic pattern or dance, you just add to the trimmings, the comforts, and always to the costs. That, to me, was the main discovery of the sisters—that men with money are impressed when they have to spend a lot of it for their pleasures. The difference between the two dollar hooker and the fifty dollar tart is just the surroundings and a myth—a mist like the one the sisters sprayed their bedrooms with.

Minna and Aida also found out something I discovered early in the trade—men don't really find sex the most dominating drive in their lives; they like the idea of sin and the freedom of the whorehouse, the company released from the lies of social position, the blinders society puts on itself. Man to man they like each other's company, drinking, smoking, bawdy comradeship. As Minna told me, "It's not the ladies they like best really. They like cards, they like dice, horse racing best. If it wasn't unmanly to admit it, they'd rather most of the time gamble than screw."

The Everleigh Club existed in its voluptuous setting until 1911, and numbered among its special guests, who can be mentioned here without upsetting the descendants of important American families, Prince Henry of Prussia. The prince, in March of 1902 on tour of the nation, gave himself three hours to enjoy the jollies of the Everleigh Club, including a fancy supper after spot testing the other product. Toasts, he reported, were drunk to his cousin the kaiser "from the courtesans' slippers." (The kaiser, when this was reported to him, promptly asked his cousin, "*What* was the vintage?" Certainly the height of nuances in wine snobbery.)

The sisters, after closing their club, retired to Riverside Drive in New York City with the best of their club furniture. They played their gold-plated piano, served champagne and planked shad to guests who came visiting, and to recall, as old roués will, the past in Chicago. And it was agreed most of the guests now had more toes than teeth.

What ended the glory of the American sporting house was the breakdown of the exclusiveness of society, when the Four Hundred became no longer the goal of the intelligent rich. Also there was the freedom given to women after World War I, so that a sexual escape from marital fidelity, or virginity, began to widen the acceptance of fornication as an individual's free choice, and the gulf between the free-living women and the inmates of whorehouses narrowed down to sex for pleasure or gain. With the Mafia in power and the gangster eras after the Great War, the hoodlums entered politics, bought police and Federal forces, the courts, so that the best sporting houses without gangster protection were forced out of business; those that accepted gang protection degenerated into mere whorehouses of no taste.

43

CHICAGO'S OWN WIZARD

Witchcraft . . . has driven many poor people to despair and persecuted their minds . . . has made them ever run distracted with terror.
COTTON MATHER, 1692, COLLECTED WORKS

In the early 1970s, the nation was shocked by the multiple, cultlike murders by a group called by the press, and perhaps by themselves, the Manson family. Their messiah leader, or crime guru, was one Charles Manson, who had spent much of his mature life in prison, and had for his followers, mostly young girls from good middle-class homes, a charisma worthy of a modern political figure. What was most shocking beyond the actual senseless brutality of their crimes, the butcheries of the Manson family, was the intriguing subtleties of power the little shaggy criminal leader seemed to have over his followers. Like some satanic cult founder, he was to his group God Himself; some even called him Jesus.

It was not merely physical gratification he offered, even if Charles Manson was said to have the stud quality of a Casanova or a Don Juan. The ultimate accolade of his mesmeric success was the spiritual hallucinations he induced in his followers, not just with sex and drugs, music (he was a poor ballad monger of sorts), but his control was actually hypnotic among his maladroit young sluts, so that in the months of a long-drawn-out trial for mass murder, he seemed to control their every action by a glance, and produced in them confessions, bursts of frenzy that outraged the court. Offering bizarre full confessions of their homicides to the jury deciding on their punishment, even to admitting details to murder that somehow they hoped would clear Charles Manson. He seemed to have for his followers, in their paranoia and narcissism, the awesome powers of the prophets.

All this metaphysical change of "nice" girls into monsters shocked the public, unaware that such a kind of mass hysteria, unconditional surrender of mind and body and sense to one man, had actually taken place in Chicago. Over a Herman Billik, just past the turn of the century, and pathologically had gone much beyond a handful of benumbed followers, had for the Chicago witch doctor or seer resulted in huge public mass meetings after his conviction, and outcries like those created for Lieutenant Calley, even brought in the wary Church to defend him, caused the signing of petitions, created street mobs as excited as any to some warped emotional, national cause, unreasonable and sick.

The incredulity and contempt a section of a city or nation can have for logic and justice was proved by Herman Billik in 1904, in Chicago. The illogicalness of city life made a martyr of a mass murderer.

Herman Billik claimed mystic and great occult powers, received from his mother who, he claimed, was a working witch in Cleveland. She could, as an urgent phenomenon, foresee the future, tell one's destiny by cards; and seems actually to have been a store-front fortune-teller. Herman with absurd arrogance also laid out the cards, mapped the future at the small cost of twenty-five cents a shuffle. Love charms, too, were his stock in trade, potions for the jealous, surefire results for the sex hunters. He dabbled in the art of the hypnotist, and had, as Charles Manson was to have, the ability to gather around him sublimated followers who did not question his demands or his desires. Herman Billik, even if a bit on the plump side, was handsome, with the piercing, stabbing eyes of a warlock that caused many to feel he had miraculous strange powers.

Billik was of Bohemian stock who, unlike most of his fellow countrymen, did not go into the stockyards, packinghouses, or factories. His trade was magic, his skill descended, he told all, from a genuine hierarchy through a witch mother. Billik was his ritual name. He had been born Vajicek.

His cards read simply, THE GREAT BILLIK, CARD READER AND SEER. In 1904 he left Mama's side and came to Chicago to create his own earthly realm. He came with his family, a wife, three children, none of whom appeared to have his powers, his direct psychological drive to impress peasant immigrants.

His den of mystery was a plain little rented house on West Nineteenth Street. Not merely a lack of cash brought the seer to such a humble address. Billik had scouted and cased the Bohemian section of Chicago. Near his new address lived the Martin Vzrals, the husband and father a prosperous dealer in milk. There was Rose Vzral, the wife—solid, yet credulous, pious, yet sensual—and seven children of all ages from eighteen to two.

People spoke of Martin Vzral as a well-off Bohemian, "a rich fella." He actually had two thousand dollars in a bank! Owned his own house, and the milk business brought him from eighty to one hundred dollars a week income. In the early 1900s, all that was solid success among the immigrant quarters of Chicago.

Families like the Billiks (without the card readings) and the Vzrals (few with business success) were part of a great migration of first-generation newcomers, Europeans who made up so much of Chicago in the decade before the turn of the century and the decade after. The largest number of Bohemians, Dutch, Slovaks, Croatians, Danes, Norwegians, Lithuanians, and Greeks to be found in any American city were settled in Chicago. It was the second-largest Bohemian city in the entire world. Germans, Swedes, and Poles were there by the thousands. Italians, too, settled in a city of nearly twenty-two square miles, and a population of over 2,200,000. Chicago was second to New York City, and had passed Philadelphia in population with ease.

The foreign-born population in their ghetto enclaves stuck to their own music, festivals, costumes, native cuisine. They feared the inefficient and corrupt police, took advantage of lax building laws, soon knew that graft and payoffs could get one nearly anything officially approved, above or below board. The polyglot population, like the rest of the city, fudged on the fire laws. In 1903 over six hundred people died in the Iroquois Theatre fire, and the burning of the city again was spoken of with a shrug. Slums and near slums brought in good rents, money was progress, "progress was getting things done." Mostly the immigrants were hardworking, frugal, but some came over as criminals, full of Old World vendettas, reprisals, and codes of revenge.

The Bohemians were easy prey for Herman Billik. Billik the wizard, the Seer, talked magic, muttered strange lines, blazed out his hawk's stare at the citizens with his dark piercing eyes, and spread it around he was the true son of a witch, able to fathom and aid esoteric fantasies.

In a few days after moving in and settling down, Billik appeared at the Vzral milk depot, it smelling pleasantly of that cheesy odor of a well-run milk depot. He asked for a can of milk (the milk bottle was not yet in much general use).

As the Seer took up the can of milk, he put his eyes to full focus on the milk dealer Vzral, made a few gestures, muttered some magic, incomprehensible secret language, then spoke some kind of sense to the staring milk dealer.

"You have an enemy . . . I see him. . . . He is trying to destroy you, this enemy."

Then he took up his milk and left. Vzral, a simple man, brooded over this remark for a few days, then was earnestly worried. The great Billik appeared for a fresh can of milk. He now explained to the frightened milk dealer that his enemy was simple to sniff out, by one with true occult gifts; the enemy was the rival milk dealer across the street. Billik offered, as a helpful gesture, to put in play his powerful gifts against all enemies for the benefit of the Vzrals. His best spells, he added, those with diabolic ferocity, were done at midnight. Vzral invited the Seer to come over at that hour and go to work.

In his desperate disquietude, the milk dealer, a simple and hardworking man, not at all stupid, was no student of the true actualities of life. In panic, with no mistrust of this splendid fellow Bohemian, Herman Billik, he began to anticipate hopes in the magic, the casting out of his enemy's evil intent. The Seer at midnight began his task with a laconic direct candor, spoke more magic words as the nine Vzrals—the solid adolescent daughters among them—all shivered and watched the witch's son go into his protective language. On the kitchen stove stoked with extra coal, he mixed and brewed a mess that stank nasty, and so suggested the cauterizing power it contained to stop an enemy's plans. Taking the pot and crossing the street, reciting the gibberish of his mumbo jumbo, the Seer anointed and then splashed and drenched the front steps of the enemy milk dealer.

To the bedazzled Vzrals he returned and announced, "Now you will certainly prosper, for now *he* cannot harm you."

When payment was offered, Billik shook his head, "No, no," but he could be overwhelmed by gratitude to accept twenty dollars with the understanding it was only a loan!

So began the immutable course of tragic events.

Vzral continued to believe in the Seer—his business was good. It got better, not because of magic but because he worked hard and sold a fresh, clean product. The Seer took no umbrage—smiled and pointed out how effective *his* magic had been. Of course it was a minor spell of witchcraft. He had, he said, done greater deeds against evil. His aura had solved major crises of evil, doubts, fears, of some insistent, dangerous specter.

The Seer's hold on the Bohemian family grew stronger. Good Catholics, but of peasant stock that still relished superstition, remembered ancient tales of werewolves and vampires, haunted castles and witchcraft; all the folk talk from the old country. They were easy prey for the Billik touch and his refresher courses in the knowledge and secrets stored up by his mother, the witch. If warned by neighbors against the Seer, they took it as envy of their good luck.

The Vzrals, in time, trapped in sinuous prophetic utterances, became little more than zombies. The Seer was in and out of their house at all hours, dominating adults and children. The fleshy side of life appealed to him. Later reports were, "He made love to Mrs. Vzral and her daughters under the beaming eyes of their husband and father." Submission to his lusts by the women in a most revolting, casual manner—as a family spectacle—could not go much further. Mrs. Vzral seems to have lost her senses completely as love slave of the Seer—at times not daring to go out so that no matter when Billik appeared she would be available for his convivial needs. In the sexual and mental control that Billik held over these people, we come closest to the Charles Manson Syndrome of fully willing, enthralled, manipulated slaves, going to any physical extremes in their acceptance of their dominator's fantasies. However, this Chicago Rasputin did not demand of them they go out and murder as the Manson family did. His inordinate passion was for money.

Billik ruined Martin Vzral. He had long since "borrowed" the entire bank account of the milk dealer; actually he had confiscated it as their protector, their worker in the exorcism of ghosts.

In consequence of complete commitment to the Seer, whatever the milk business was making, Billik took over, and soon it was clear the once prosperous business was being destroyed. Still Billik demanded more cash. So some of the older Vzral girls, three of them, were sent out to become maids and house servants. Willingly they turned over their earnings, and more, to the Seer. Mama and Papa did not object. Their ardor, their unreal life continued as if in some bad yet fascinating dream.

The Billik family began to live in style. The Seer became a dude, dressing in the height of his idea of fashion, picking up for himself a good horse and a shiny carriage, thinking of widening his version of the great fine nation—see more of it—at least go wandering with Vzral money in his pocket, go to inspect New York City, move up to watch the high life in Saratoga. And in one bold push, even reaching California on Vzral funds. What a future—if he had stayed on—he could have had in that sun-kissed land of cults, odd faiths, messiahs by the dozens.

But back in Chicago, the Seer became greedy for more. Lump sums of big money were perhaps foretold on his deck of fortune-telling cards. He expanded his schemes. Mrs. Vzral in sexual thralldom was induced to insure her husband and most of her grown daughters for sums from $105 to $2000. The charlatan Merlin, however, was losing his grip on Martin Vzral. The Seer had moved too quickly, pressed too hard the troubled milkman. Martin Vzral was beginning to mutter out loud about all the money going to Billik, about how run down the milk business was. The hypnotized figure was beginning to think normally. His eyes no longer were blanks. Once, when Billik asked for more money, the exploited milk dealer had doubts about extending another "loan." But the sharp steely look in the Seer's eyes soon gave doubt, and he handed over the money. It was clear, however, Martin Vzral needed some special magic attention. Billik, while locked in amorous play with Mrs. Vzral, whispered into her attentive ear that he would give her a white powder to put into Martin's food, just a charm to keep the man safe under the Seer's control. Did she suspect more? Was she even aware the game was to be played with the death card?

Soon Martin Vzral said he had fearful belly pains, and Billik said it could mean serious stomach trouble—every bed is waiting to be a death bed—unless he took some of the Seer's special brew, and so Vzral drank from the whiskey bottle which the Seer had filled with one of his magic potions, mostly a dissolved white powder.

By March of 1905, Martin Vzral, with no vacillating, was dead and his wife Rose collected the two thousand dollars life insurance, and humbly and proudly turned it over to the consoling Seer. He graciously returned a hundred dollars for burial costs and full church rites for the departed head of the family.

44

THE WIZARD AT BAY

The wicked flee.
PROVERBS, 28:1

The success of the white powder in solution (it was pure arsenic) and the insurance money decided Billik that he had hit pay dirt in the American insurance business. Meanwhile, not to hurry things, he toured the countryside in a tent, telling fortunes. The Vzral girls, Emma and Mary, came to see their dear maker of magic, so alert to the sensibilities of young girls. He showed them a specially marked playing card that held some intimations of coming events.

"This is the card of death. Soon Mary will die."

It was not pleasant news to the simple girls.

"Stomach trouble" soon killed Mary, and Billik took over the eight hundred dollars her death brought from the insurance company, but again in a proper attitude, he returned one hundred to pay for the full Catholic burial and a Mass. Mary's brother Jerry, however, was beginning to suspect all wasn't as Billik claimed. Some acute irritation, suspicious thoughts irked the boy. His mother's hedonistic attention to the Seer, he was also beginning to find

311

revolting. Mrs. Vzral told her son she'd arrange it so that Jerry would not be bothered by the Seer's presence anymore. Two days later, Jerry was down with rolling, stabbing stomach trouble. A doctor was brought in and the boy came back to health, pale and fearful. It was the Seer's doing.

The gossip later was the Seer was showing the boy some of his magic, not giving him enough white powder to kill, just to cause pain. Actually, Jerry was one of the two Vzral children not insured. But the eighteen-year-old daughter Tillie was, and in December of 1905 she died of that persistent Vzral stomach trouble—$620 was collected on her.

It would be just murderous bookkeeping to list other deaths. The score: Rose, fifteen, dead; result, $300 collected. Ella, twelve; result, $105 collected. However, Herman Billik always gave Mrs. Vzral enough back for decent burial of her children.

There were no more insured Vzral victims to feed the powder to. The milk business was gone to creditors. The Seer came up with a splendid idea; why burden Mrs. Vzral with her house? It was incongruous to her needs, too big. She certainly did not want all that room now. It brought $2,900 to Billik, and he thanked Mrs. Vzral and told her he was about to visit Cleveland and "take care" of his mother the witch and so inherit *her* great fortune. It seems reasonable that by now the love-bemused, sexually drugged Mrs. Vzral was aware of some of what Billik had done to her family, the voracious and evil man he was. But she was too far gone in her passion, well down the fantasy trail, to attempt to come back, to shrink with horror from her demon lover. Besides, could she interfere between witch and wizard? Billik, with his funds from the Vzral house sale, took a delightful journey first to see the falls at Niagara, and to visit Buffalo.

If he did go to visit his mother in Cleveland, he certainly did not try his deadly powers on her. Or her black magic was stronger than his. He returned to Chicago with no fortune, again in need of money. Billik was an easy spender. But the insurance gold mine was closed—the remaining Vzrals were sucked dry, and about to be tossed out of a house they no longer owned. They lacked the money to buy food.

The night of his return to Chicago, Billik visited Mrs. Vzral, most likely in the role of the returning lover. At four in the morning he withdrew, and an hour later the deluded, infatuated woman was dead of a dose of arsenic.

One is amazed at how easily Billik got away with his long list of killings of one family—all healthy peasant stock, rosy with life. The true medical skill in Chicago, available for the middle class, was no better or much worse than today. And that in those long-gone days when medical men made house calls and had no Wednesdays off for golf, the tired doctor, most likely years behind in any advances made in medicine, or poison detection, was more than willing to report any "stomach pain" as pathologically possible to cause death. The police had little personal dealings with ethnic neighborhoods—black, Italian, German, Jewish, each avoided trouble, herded under its own umbrella of language, cooking, holidays, and only timidly peered out into the outside world of the native-born Americans. Their isolation could be as solid as behind the Great Wall of China. And hide a murderer like Billik.

But chance, God's irony, who knows anyone's road of destiny by any sure road map? The Seer came to trouble because a Bohemian servant girl was overheard in iniquitous gossip with another servant girl by her mistress. "Say, somebody should for sure look into all them deaths in that Vzral family."

Questions brought out the fact the girl had known Mary Vzral, and Mary had confessed to her that much as she feared for her life with Herman Billik, she just had no willpower to resist the man. The girl's mistress at supper that night told her husband what she had found out, and he went to a policeman he knew in the neighborhood, who wrote it down—the gossip of so many deaths—in his day's report. This report went to the desk of Inspector George M. Shippy, and so by this precarious path the outer world heard of the Seer and an unlucky family.

The inspector did not discard it as just gossip, but set his detectives to look into affairs in the Bohemian district of Chicago, and see what was up with Billik and his strange friendship with an unfortunate family taken with so many sudden deaths.

The detectives listened, snooped, and some days later Mary Vzral's body was exhumed and lay on a morgue table. An autopsy showed her stomach contained five grains of arsenic. Billik was arrested for the crime of murder by poisoning; motive, to gain insurance money.

In the summer of 1907, the Seer stood trial, evidence was clear and strong. The jury had no problems in finding him guilty of first-degree murder, and in July he was sentenced to be hanged by the neck until dead. This should have ended the sordid matter. But under sentence of death, Billik's fine dark eyes, that charisma of the Seer to influence people, was to expand its area of action, and stir up not a mere simple family in his favor, but a whole community, even a city, to believe him innocent, a God-gifted man of special spiritual content. The governor of the state, under ward politics pressure, reprieved him from the rope. In the next two years there were various appeals to higher courts—and a final grandstand play of the case before the Supreme Court of the United States, in Washington, D.C.

Billik had not lost his touch. In Cook County Jail prisoners and guards alike came under the Seer's witchcraft or charm. He was the special-care prisoner, popular, cherished by all, voted the most wronged man ever put in a cell there. With persistent intensity his supporters assaulted the jury's findings, the state's evidence.

A great spiritual power on earth had come to Billik's aid. The Catholic Church in America, its Chicago parishes, had put itself behind his defense, cried out for a pardon, led by Father P. J. O'Callaghan of the Paulist Fathers, well and vocally aided by a nun, Sister Rose, of the Order of the Sacred Heart. Looking over the records, we today can understand mass hysteria, this illogical rally to a murderer. Even if we have not stood before the blazing charm of Herman Billik, the Seer, he must have had power, maniacal, impressive power. Certainly he had hypnotic skills to use on the priest and nun, for they organized great mass meetings in Chicago and elsewhere, raised the large sums of money by solicitation, public and private, for the many appeals and legal costs to keep Billik from hanging.

When it came time for the appeal to come before the Supreme Court in June of 1908, Father O'Callaghan was at the Cook County Jail leading the four hundred prisoners there, all on their knees, in loud prayer, asking God to intercede and save Herman

Billik from the hangman's noose. The scene was like something out of a Goya painting depicting a scene from the Inquisition, or a smoldering Callot print of the horrors of religious warfare in all its copious frenzy. It hardly belongs at this stage in the twentieth century, but an anachronism recalling, rather, a trial for witchcraft at Salem, or the burning of some old crone and her tomcat during the period of the Black Death.

Two days later an even bigger orgy was held at the jail—the party bosses were involved; the politicians were not going to offend any would-be voter by saying no to any meeting shouting for a pardon for the Seer. At this most massive pious jamboree for Billik, Father O'Callaghan again led in loud, vocal community prayer, aided by a repentant or frightened Jerry Vzral, one of the surviving members of his family (the baby being too young for an orgy). He was flanked by Mrs. Billik and the couple's ten-year-old daughter. Billik himself joined the prisoners and guests in the weeping, moaning prayer meeting.

Billik's cell mate at the jail was a hard-shell burglar named Milwauski, but he too came back to the faith of his childhood on his knees, grabbed Billik in a bear hug, and began to kiss the Seer again and again, wept, and cried out during the prayers of a long, long session asking for God's and Chicago's aid. None of the prisoners felt left out in this outbreak of naked public emotions. They all gave their mite of silver coins to buy flowers which were presented to the jail warden, to Father O'Callaghan, and to Sister Rose. "Billy Graham would not have done it better" (private conversation with a bishop).

By June 10, twenty thousand citizens of Chicago and the surrounding territory had signed a petition asking not to hang Billik, and it was presented to the State Board of Pardons. SAVE BILLIK mass meetings were going on in the streets of Chicago and large halls. Action meetings took place. They were hysterical outbreaks that reminded some of the Dancing Sickness of the Middle Ages. Hundreds of girls and women screamed and wept, rolled on the dusty floors, plucked at their clothes. One prominent physician of the period in a private letter wrote of one such gathering: "It is clear to any knowing observer that much of the female emotional carrying on has a sexual content, known or unknown to these foolish women. They toss around to indecent lengths in their caterwauling, weeping for this murderer as if they were again raising a god on a cross. I find it most revolting . . . this public display of raw emotions demanding this fellow Billik shall not hang. How can the Church permit this priest, O'Gallaghan [sic] and an addled nun, to be the main speakers at these sickening mob meetings?"

It was not alone women who seemed to have lost their senses. The boy, Jerry Vzral, who had disliked the Seer and had testified against him in court, now spoke in repentance at the meetings, crying out, tears in his eyes, streaming down his face, shouting that he had lied, committed perjury against Billik at the trial. For all their harsh clamor, the meetings turned into immensely congenial gatherings.

The police could only try to keep order at the delirium of the meetings. Police Chief Shippy, like the letter-writing doctor, was revolted at the sick, perverted emotions the priest and nun produced at the mass meetings. "Billik is a cold-blooded murderer of the worst type, and is simply deceiving the people who are working in his behalf."

Even if true, the mass meetings did their work to change the picture. Governor Charles S. Deneen in January, 1909, commuted Billik's death sentence, with a quick slash of a pen, to life imprisonment, "on the recommendations of the Board of Pardons." The board and the governor were practical opportunists, seeking votes, and the retaining of their positions. The people, the whipped-up mobs had spoken, and Chicago politicians always listened to humanitarians and hand wringers—and, if of value to themselves, acted.

By February 1, Billik was settled down in the state penitentiary at Joliet. Eight years later, in 1917, the murderer of nearly an entire family by poison was pardoned by Governor Edward F. Dunne, and set free. The Church, which had never let up its crusade for him, headed a huge voting bloc in Chicago politics, and the governor was never one to ignore any large group that voted solidly in the city and state elections.

Of Herman Billik's life after his release, we have found no record. Did he go back to the fortune-telling cards and his mother, the witch? Our interest in him is mostly in the vehement passion he could arouse in some section of the city's population, that section of it, which in undisciplined pathos and in their prayers and howling saved his life, no matter what mordant stench his crimes left on the scales of justice. Billik was able, like some political figures in our time, to arouse a faithful following beyond reason or logic. A personality able to stroke the amorphous mass into action and adoration. It is too easy to see it all—the Billik meetings for a pardon—as some Dostoevskian apocalypse; this perhaps is too strong. Was it just the naïveté of emotions rushing into unthinking action? Small minds that pushed nonsense into power to change society's mind? We still live in danger of such power of the mass mind made frivolous and dangerous.

45

THE GOOD LIFE

Never speak disrespectfully of society. Only people who can't get into it, do that.
OSCAR WILDE

It would be a common error to imagine that the crime and the political shenanigans of Chicago dominated the entire life of the city, and the existence of all of its citizens. Or that the boiling, greasy slums that produced so much misery escaped their boundaries to soil the community. Rather, in the larger part of Chicago, its well-off citizens led full and pleasant lives, and those rich—by their standards—lived in a style even many of today's wealthy cannot reach. Where are now the servants of extreme filial affection—at five dollars a week?

In the decade *before*, and the decade *after*, 1900, the well-off householder and his family were deep in security, respectability, and comfort. No matter if Papa was "in trade"; ran a meat-packing plant for Mr. Armour, or was involved with wheat futures on La-Salle Street, managed a fine hotel or splendid store.

Christmas—not yet as commercialized as ours—brought out the gold and silver dishes, the sleds and belled horses at the door,

319

and the drinking of hot toddies and eggnogs, the singing of "Stille Nacht, heilige Nacht." Spring in the parks saw the children from Prairie Avenue with their governesses, in sailor or Buster Brown suits; coming back from play to find Mama at tea with other ladies, her pompadour done up with "rats," all talking of the poetry of Browning, confinements (as pregnancies were called), or scandal.

They ate well, and the Chicago upper-middle-class families sat down to breakfast of cracked wheat, lamb hash with creamed potatoes, broiled salt mackerel with baked potatoes. Forget calories, which no one had heard of anyway—and orange juice had not yet come to make acid the American stomach. Lunch (called *dinner;* what we call *dinner* now was the *supper*) would be pigs' feet, hot breads, beefsteaks, and chops. And the suppers of six to eight courses were hardly to be believed—eaten around golden oak tables, with napkin rings and a container of toothpicks for direct use after meals.

Papa was a member of the Chicago, or Calumet Club, and Mama drove mornings in her carriage (Irish coachman—two matched bays) to leave calling cards. The top hat was the proper headgear, and dyspepsia a sign one was living well. The house had to show style even if only in a spiky iron fence, a stable out back, and to indicate one had taste, a porte cochere. In the cellar a great hot air furnace devoured coal, upstairs, books were locked up behind glass doors (Scott, Doré illustrated texts, Louisa Alcott, *Idylls of the King*, Zola in yellow paper cover—and in French). Some parents never encouraged too much readings among the young. ("Makes damn bookworms of 'em, you know.")

The servants. Our past is inadequate without them, unreal. A well-run ménage would have a butler and a cook (usually Irish), a second man, a coachman (Celt or British), a groom, laundry worker, parlormaid, chambermaid, kitchenmaid, and if Mama was fussy, martyred by buttons, hooks and eyes, hair brushings—her own personal maid. In a more fertile epoch, among the well-off there were many children. ("Birth control was a shot-gun by the bed.") So two or three governesses were the rule, usually English, French, or German. ("Fraulein, Willie swallowed *my* frog.")

In 1905, the Washington Park racecourse was closed as betting was declared illegal (but Chicago remained the horse bettors' and bookmakers' heaven in the nation). So the horse remained only for the carriages and drays. But already complaisant satellites of pleasure talked of the autocar smoking up the brick street surfaces. Among the first cars were French imports like the Tony Huber and a hundred makes now only forgotten names. The simpering electric car was only for timid ladies; no man would sit at its control levers. The best houses had a Pekingese, usually called Ming Toy, or a Victorian pug with a knotted tail—and a spotted coach dog who lived with the groom and coachman over the stables.

The best people began to migrate at the century's turn to the North Side, a regular exodus of gold picture frames, double beds, hatboxes, cut glass. Streets for social standing were either *du dernier chic* or not. God, too, had to be approached properly in Chicago, and one went, or hoped to, either to the North Presbyterian or the St. James Episcopal. Church Street, which in a later Godless age became Washington Street, once held the First and Second Presbyterian, Baptist, Methodist, Universalist, Unitarian, and Trinity Episcopal churches. Popery was knavery and escaped nuns, and the Hebrews had cabalistic rites and wore hats indoors.

There was no style one could not dig up or invent for one's house. One's house decided one's milieu. Queen Anne, Georgian would do for some. *Alt Deutsche* castles for others. Gothic cottages and primroses and stone trolls. Stained glass, cupolas, houses with Mississippi steamboat gingerbread. Away from home, one shopped from one's carriage or sent the butler to the markets. Tebbett's on Prairie Avenue and Garland's on Wabash were fashionable markets. The holy three for entertaining were as usual Johnny Hand when you needed an orchestra, Weeks when you desired a dressmaker, and, of course, Kinsley for catering.

But there were flaws, cracks, sounds in the night, slammed doors, professional visits with little black bags. All calm and dignified on the surface, some houses had alcoholics in some upper rooms, or a drooling idiot and an attendant. And what if Papa went to the Everleigh Club for philandering with his favorite whore? Or the groom corrupted the boys with Sweet Caporal cigarettes and encouraged mutual masturbation? There is still coherent optimism in the faces that show up in the *fancy* good clothes in photographs taken in Steffen's studios, all who may have skated in the rink and taken dancing lessons at Bournique's. One must not get too close there to Catholic girls.

And what could one do when next door a Jewish family built a fine house, a Levi Leiter, Leschetizky, Rosenwald; some Venetian palazzo or Second Empire facade? Well, they were people too ("and anyone, Maude, who can afford to buy or build in *this* neighborhood can't become a problem . . ."). After all, their nurses pushed the babies in their perambulators with the ermine spreads like everyone else, and there were no signs of tails or horns on the Hebrew children in their fur tippets or Eton jackets.

One could even in time, as they grew into adolescents, invite them to hear the Swiss music box that played the "Druids' March" from *Norma*, or Dinorth's "Shadow Song."

On wide-screened porches (those pesky insects) one could whisper about the goings-on in the gambling dens and the bordellos ("never say whorehouse"), where some cousin or uncle was seen "consorting and pixilated."

But as for Mr. Marshall Field, his domestic life, that could be talked over in detail as teacups clashed. It was no secret the first Mrs. Field led Marshall Field a hell-on-earth life. Their loud, excruciatingly shrill battling scenes (even before the servants) were really something no good society would expect of them; so violent, such malice. Mrs. Field not only had actors and singers in as friends, those devastatingly common Bohemians, but she was the first respectable woman to wear a tea gown. Mr. Field got the harsh side of her tongue when he objected. The scenes became so violent that it was clear the Fieldses were destroying their marriage. No divorce, of course, but Mrs. Field went off to live in France—that profligate nation—where she died before 1900.

Mr. Field fell in love, and with a married woman, Mrs. Arthur (Delia) Caton, a large beautiful woman of "comfortable embonpoint." She entertained in a big house on Calumet Avenue and was married to the son of a chief justice of the state's Supreme Court. (He is not identified beyond this.) The parties and dinners only made Mrs. Caton wider and more desirable in an age when the Rubens ideal of pink, meat-pie women was the style. She had, one social historian records, "a friendly heart." She fed guests well: Bodense felchen trout, pâtés, Westphalian ham, game birds, venison, beef Wellington.

There is evidence that Marshall Field and Mrs. Caton became sexual intimates—"lechery without levity," as one letter writer put down. No one is sure just when the affair began—but as she was married and, as usual, the idea of divorce was not to be thought of, so the staid merchant widower and the wide hostess carried on a rigorously discreet affair that was whispered about and almost respectable. There was talk of a tunnel connecting the Field house on Prairie with the Caton house on Calumet. One wonders if such a tunnel actually existed, or if later Chicago historians ever hunted for it.

In a day when pretentious psychiatry did not exist, no one saw the Freudian implication of the tunnel gossip.

The most interesting story of Mrs. Caton and Field was when they were still only lovers. It was at a dinner she gave, and everyone made a speech but Field, who didn't make speeches. So Delia Caton made one for him. "Mr. Field just wants me to remind you that the White Sale starts next Monday."

What Mr. Caton thought of all this—he must have heard the town talk—we don't know. He took a long, casual time dying, not departing until 1904. With only a short wait, Field and the widow rushed to London and were married. Happiness was to be of short duration for Field. His son, shot by a whore or by his own hand. Field, himself, died soon after that tragedy. He left his estate to his children, and the town shook its head, for "Delia was cut off with a million." Delia took the million and moved to Washington, D.C., to entertain diplomatic society. Even if the crème de la crème of Chicago's society had accepted Field and his mistress with very little brouhaha.

Those females who didn't divert their lives from rigid morality spent their excess drives—if we believe social notes—in growing plants in Sung pots, planning shrubbery, flowers, terracing, erecting pergolas, a pond for imported rare ducks, a playhouse or tree house for the children.

Many people talked of the Gold Coast of Chicago, where the best and richest people lived, as a kind of combination of Valhalla, Palm Beach, and bits of Buckingham Palace and the U.S. Mint. Few could fully define its boundaries or its heterogeneous nature. On the city map, in part it was the section of the Lake Shore Drive just south of Lincoln Park, also North Michigan Avenue from Oak Street to Chicago Avenue, and streets parallel to the Drive, North State, Astor, and North Dearborn parkways, a section called Streetville. These were the prime locations to build your Rhine castles, your medieval watchtowers, your French fortresses. Certainly there were many craggy greystone *castellinos* on the streets connecting Bellevue and Burton, stables smelling of the best horses.

By 1914, there would be a change, a lightning of social diversions—the Casino would be built where there was a Parisian chef, at least a continental menu, and the chief stewards knew *who* was *who* in Chicago society (Money and Old Family) and who was not entitled to the fried perch with cucumbers, filet mignon, and the gastronomic height of sinning, the lobster thermidor; suggesting to the city's youth the sins of Eastern hedonists like Stanford White— naked show girls in a cake, and wine drunk from a slipper. The dance floor was active, but cutting in was a problem, and there was a shortage of acceptable young men. The smart younger set talked of the soirees of some of the McCormicks at the Drake, the walls hung with mountain laurel shipped from North Carolina, and dance steps by Mr. and Mrs. Vernon Castle.

Mrs. Potter Palmer still reigned among the older folk, no more like her painting by Zorn (John Singer Sargent never mixed paint to capture her in her prime), she in youth and crown and scepter as Titania. Her hair had gone gray and was marcelled, the dog collar of pearls hiding the wrinkles of time, she still trying to keep Chicago from being Gomorrah-on-the-Lake. Potter Palmer to the end always called her "Miz Palmer," and spent all of his twenty million dollars she wanted. When Mrs. Palmer died in 1918, there was no one of her style, grace, or power to replace her. The *fêtes champêtres* of others lacked her flavor, the tranquil plaintive face; the *bosquet* of lilacs did not smell the same.

Styles were already changing as the new century began. One of the pacesetters had been Rue Winterbotham Carpenter, whose husband John Alden Carpenter is remembered for one musical composition: "Adventures of a Perambulator." Some called Rue "an original genius, one of the most important decorators in the early 1900s in America." What she was, actually, was an interior designer with some taste and originality. She began to import and sell Biedermeier furniture, Directoire, Empire fittings, a mode of taffeta curtains. She made the fortune of dealers in Aubusson carpets, striped wallpaper (after her cut). She mixed periods (a great sin at the time) and liked opaline glass. She got rich women to eat umbrage like cake as she did over their houses. She decorated the two Casinos, the Fortnightly Club on Bellevue Place, made the old Chicago Auditorium, built on Michigan Avenue and Congress Street, ready for opera. She was avant-garde when the word was unknown in Chicago. She expressed the opinion that in decor, "courage is the right choice between alternatives."

The lurch toward culture among the Chicago women led to forming clubs like the Scribblers, the Fortnightly, the Friday Club, and a hundred copies of these. Rue Carpenter, like most dictators of style to willing victims, was at times bad-tempered, ruthless with fools and bores, unless they flattered. She was jealous of rivals, and could be unfair in destroying social standings. Rue's parties were remembered with delight as informal floor sittings, at times given to catch-as-catch-can costumes, and the serving of casserole of veal, and gin and lemon juice between the gregarious charades. One who knew her wrote with complete insensitivity—of "her kindness to the humble." An expression that no one would dare make today in the Welfare State.

Like so many Chicago hostesses, Rue Carpenter snared passing celebrities and spoke knowingly of the work and ideas of people she first-name-called Igor, Pablo, André, Leonide, Artur, Jascha, Vladimir, and Mary (that last person was a hard one to guess, as there were too many Marys; she meant Mary Garden, the city's favorite opera star).

The more stiffly settled well-off people had the best dinners and the yellow Chartreuse, Benedictine, old Kummel, Anisette and Danziger Goldwasser, with the usual Mumms. One overwined guest was even heard to say, "Plato conceived of an unexciting form of love."

Something should be said of opera and Chicago. It was *the* social item that separated the goats from the best people, from the would-like-to-bes from the arrived. How much one raised for the opera, what box one held like Verdun, with *whom* one was photographed in the lobby at openings, *that* was making it. The most notorious female figure around was a Polish woman, handsome, wide, solidly built: Ganna Walska, who claimed to be an opera singer. No one ever admitted that after hearing her sing. She was married seven or eight times, her biggest catch—for a short time—being Chicago's Harold McCormick, ludicrous and susceptible in his adoration of the Amazon. He spent millions on her. On one early trip across the Atlantic, Ganna claimed that three millionaires, Harold McCormick, a Mr. Alexander Cochran, and Richard Crane (the plumbing czar), offered her marriage. She admitted "Every man proposes to me the second he meets me." Jane Cowl, present at one confession, is said to have answered, "Yes, but *what* does he propose?"

A more charming singer, a soprano of very great talent, was Edith Polacco, who, it seemed, also was always getting married. When asked by a Chicago hostess *why* she married so often, and for no really romantic reason, Edith answered, "Honestly . . . I don't know. I just guess all my will power goes into my singing." Unlike Mary Garden whose favorite lines of poetry were:

In the cooling of nights of love,
What beget you, where you beget,
A sense of strangeness overcomes you
When the silent candle shines.

As Chicago produced greater desires for social status, from 1880 to 1910 more books appeared to help the well-heeled hopefuls, mostly for the women. Wrote a Mrs. Sherwood, "The well mannered and well behaved American woman . . . is the queen of the man who loves her. . . . She must be first servant-trainer, then housekeeper, wife, mother, conversationalist . . . keep up with the advancing spirit of the times . . . be beautifully dressed, play the piano . . . be charitable, thoughtful . . . a student of good taste and good manners, make a home luxurious, ornamental, cheerful and restful . . . dress and entertain in perfect accord with her station, her means, and her husband's position . . . she must go to the cooking lecture, come home and visit the kitchen . . . she must steer her ship through stormy seas, and she must also learn to enjoy Wagner's music."

Books like *The Correct Thing in Good Society and Social Customs* were popular: "Where society is divided into certain cliques or sets,

as is often the case in our cities, a lady belonging to the less fashionable clique should hesitate long before calling upon one of a more
fashionable circle, even though she may have been introduced to
the other lady."

Illustrated Manners insisted that, "Married couples were to avoid
dancing together. A married man pays his court to other ladies, his
wife accepts the attentions of other gentlemen; and the married
couple who should be seen dancing or talking much with each
other, would become subjects of general ridicule . . . husbands and
wives do not even go to the same parties unless they prefer to do so.
It is presumed that they have enough of each other's society in private." But few couples were really that advanced.

"A lady in her own house can in these United States do pretty
much as she pleases, but there is one thing in which our cultivated
and exclusive fashionable city society seems agreed, and that is that
she must not introduce two ladies who reside in the same town . . .
how the new acquaintance would be received, whether or not it is
desirable to both parties to know each other . . . good natured desire of a sympathetic person that the people whom she knows well
should know each other sometimes went wrong. She strives to bring
them together at lunch or dinner, but perhaps finds out afterwards
that one of the ladies has particular objections to knowing the other.
. . . The disaffected lady shows her displeasure by being impolite to
the pushing lady, as she may consider her. Had no introduction
taken place . . . she might have still enjoyed a reputation for politeness. Wary women of the world are therefore very shy of introducing two women to each other" *(Illustrated Manners)*.

(Americans could amaze visitors. The English journalist,
George Augustus Sala, before World War I, was amused to see a
pretty young lady "dexterously twirl a corn-cob till she had nibbled
off all the grains . . . without soiling her fingers or her symmetrical
chin.")

But unlike Mrs. Sherwood, Miss Harland was a tough teacher,
saw her readers to be "people of rude upbringing . . . who have
longings and taste for gentlehood . . . to whom changed circumstances or removal . . . to a fashionable neighbourhood involved
the necessity of altered habits . . . her natural desire to mingle on
equal terms with the better sort of rich people . . . Mrs. Newlyrich
and her Social Duties . . . a woman of worthy aspirations and in-

nate refinement, raised by the whirl of fortune's wheel from decent poverty to actual wealth . . . men, as a whole, do not take polish readily. Unless John Newlyrich wore a dress-coat before he was twenty-one, he is not quite at ease in a 'swallow-tail' at forty. . . . He butters a whole slice of bread, using his knife trowel-wise. . . . He cuts up his salad. . . . He never gets over the habit of speaking of dinner as 'supper.' " But Chicagoans desiring the upper life were quick learners.

46

THE SECRET CORNERS

Lots of women are just naturally unchaste.
STEPHEN CRANE, IN A LETTER

They stare at us from old photographs, from the solid stone houses, their overdraped windows; the people are there in their best, looking down from their wide verandas, the children on the walk, with a hoop or a ball, frozen for time by silver bromide on browning paper capturing the shadows of light.

These well-dressed matrons, young girls in their first corsets, seem ready to exalt or deplore—as the groom leads out the carriage team for shopping in the heart of the city, or to go see Eddie Foy make comic gestures, even to brave the naughty satire of Gilbert and Sullivan. Dinner perhaps later at the Richelieu or Palmer House, even (if the season was right) to the opera to see McCormick jewels and the spectacle of people one approved of gathered together.

But this was all social veneer. Under it, these women (wider than our own time admires), the maidens with their tasseled shoes, Gibson hairdos, so demure in look or wry smile, *what* were they really like?

The lives of the wives in the well-to-do families of the city followed a pattern that can be traced, in social notes, private journals, and letters, like footprints on Robinson Crusoe's island. The society mostly followed the text that the philosopher Thorstein Veblen put down: "Prosperity required respectable women to be free from any taint of utility . . ." outside of the home, of course.

Somehow, the idea that a respectable woman had fewer sexual desires and drives than the lower-class female seeped into the culture, and the women of Prairie Avenue, Lake Park Avenue, Oakwood Boulevard, the Gold Coast, Lake Forest were held, in public print at least, of lesser sensual impulses. Just before the Civil War, Dr. William W. Sanger had written, "But it must be repeated and most decidedly, that without these or some other equally stimulating cause (such as destitution, drink or seduction and abandonment,) the full force of sexual desire is seldom known to a virtuous woman. In the male sex, nature has provided a more susceptible organization than in the females, apparently with the beneficent design of repressing those evils which must result from mutual appetite equally felt by both."

Some Chicago husbands agreed with the doctor and went down to the Levee for women who felt "the full force of sexual desire," or acted the part for pay. Dr. William Alcott—friend of the Sylvester Graham who invented the cracker—went even further in his advice to Chicago husbands and wives who read his magazine, *Moral Reformer*. He came out against, "Fermented liquor, tobacco, and tight corsets, gambling, late parties, coffee, tea, condiments, confections." His opposition to condiments was related to rich and spicy foods, lard, butter, sugar, eggs, pepper, gravies, ginger, even salt leading to disease . . . to vice. "No man has ever become an adulterer, a fornicator, or an idolater eating simples such as plain wheat, corn, rye, potatoes, rice, peas, beans, turnips, apples." He made clear in *The Moral Philosophy of Courtship and Marriage* that indulgence in sexual activity before the age of twenty-five in a man, or twenty-one in a woman, depleted the vital juices. He quoted a British author who said that for every year of married life before twenty-two, the woman risks shortening her life by three years.

A wife who took this nonsense seriously could only act as an excessive influence—a recruiting agent for the Everleigh Club, the Levee whores.

Mark Twain was a popular visitor in Chicago and in the surrounding country. In public he played the clown for the puritanical
matriarchy that enjoyed lectures. Only in private, with a hand
holding a glass of bourbon at the bar of the Palmer House or at
some unbuttoned male gathering, would he talk out his ideas of the
sexual relationship of American women and their husbands. Some
of this talk about man's law against adultery, because of male temp-

tation and temperament, later got into some of his manuscripts, those unpublished during his lifetime (as in *Letters from Earth*): "Many men can't help committing adultery when they get the chance." As for the female, as a sexual gamester—he would today be the darling of Women's Lib when he gets on the subject of women and their sex patterns as he saw them. "During twenty-three days in every month . . . till she dies of old age, she is ready for action and competent. As competent as the candlestick is to receive the candle. Competent every day, competent every night. Also, she wants that candle—yearns for it, longs for it, hankers after it, as commanded by the law of God in her heart. Man is competent only from the age of sixteen for about thirty-five years. After fifty, his performance is of poor quality . . . whereas his great-grand-mother is as good as new . . . Her candlestick is as firm as ever, whereas his candle is increasingly softened and weakened . . . until at last it can no longer stand, and is mournfully laid to rest. . . . Man knows . . . he will never see the day that she can't overwork, and defeat, and put out of commission any ten masculine plants . . . put to bed with her. The Creator intended the woman to be restricted to one man . . . without consulting woman though she has more at stake being capable of at least 150,000 refreshments in her life, where he (man) is good for only five thousand."

But Mark Twain on tour didn't go around shouting any of this in mixed Chicago company.

One has to hunt out old journals and letters, the private papers of doctors, to find any hint of actual sexual problems, beyond dalliance and initiation, that plagued the best people of Chicago. The brothels solved some of them for the men—also the *tableaux vivants,* the *poses plastiques,* where lightly draped girls in risqué art poses served for many as a peep show thrill. Sometimes there were even naked girls behind gauze onstage, until the police raided them. A newspaper poet could write:

> *Those nice tableaux vivants*
> *Of beautiful young ladies, sans*
> *Both petticoats and pants,*
> *Who, scorning fashion's shifts and whims,*
> *Did nightly crowds delight,*
> *By showing up their handsome limbs,*
> *At fifty cents a sight.*

Chicago still retains its strippers—but fifty cents is no longer the cost of the entertainment. The shimmy, the hotsy-totsy have given way to the topless and bottomless.

Many married couples worked out their sexual patterns to their own mutual satisfaction in the nineteenth century. But of those women, who under the prudery and fears and wrong advice (when Victoria reigned morally in America) were sometimes sexually and emotionally involved with their own sex, little can be found on record. But a rare glimpse of it turns up from time to time: some female attachments in Chicago's best circles, denting the aggrandizements of respectability by some secret delinquencies. Only a European traveling or settled in America dared report on this. Early in the nineteenth century, a Frenchman, Médéric Moreau de Saint-Méry, could frankly admit about respectable American women— "I am going to say something that is almost unbelievable. These women without real love and without real passions, give themselves up at an early age to the enjoyment of themselves; and they are not at all strangers to being willing to seek unnatural pleasures with persons of their own sex."

Margaret Fuller, the first great fighter for women's rights in America, was bolder in her statements that, to her, "a woman may be in love with a woman, and a man with a man. . . . I loved . . . for a time with as much passion as I was then strong enough to feel. . . . She loved me, for I well remember her suffering when she first could feel my faults."

Chicago was often the lecture-platform meeting ground for the women's rights group led by Susan B. Anthony, the great suffragist pioneer. That Miss Anthony was more than a force and symbol was clear in her letters to Anna Dickinson, a young beauty, letters as clear as glass about her sexual drives. One finds many—"Dicky darling Anna." "Dear Chick a dee dee." "Wanting to give you one awful long squeeze . . . promise not to marry a man . . . I have plain quarters . . . double bed—and big enough and good enough to take you in— So come and see me." And, "I do so long for the scolding and pinched ears and everything I know awaits me. . . . What worlds of experience since I last snuggled the wee child in my long arms." Susan Anthony wrote that she had had many "Anna girls . . . nieces . . . but not like her first Anna." It is all so direct, there is no psychological puzzle.

The Lucy Stone movement, preaching for women to retain their maiden names and not use their husbands', was strong in Chicago, and both Miss Stone and her divinity student friend at Oberlin, Antoinette Brown, were on the platform as feminists, preaching the good cause. When Miss Brown became a minister, she wrote to Lucy a frank letter which has survived, addressing Lucy Stone as "my dearest little cowboy . . . I love you Lucy any way, and if you would only come and take a nap with me here on my bed my head would get rested a great deal faster, for it is aching now."

Dr. Henry N. Guernsey, a popular advice giver, wrote that "The deadly habit of self-abuse is common among girls. It is true that some young ladies, the sweetest and fairest of our race, play with one another in an immodest and indecent way, teaching immorality to the pure and innocent."

The private papers we have read of another doctor in Chicago in the 1890s record the following:

"Mrs. E. G. of Lake Park Avenue, 42, infatuated with her housemaid Kate B., now being blackmailed. Actions sexual were very physical, maid and Mrs. G. bathing together naked, cat-napping in bed in daytime—acts of sexual deviations are sexual mouthings of their parts, impetuosity of E.G. beyond control at times, begging Kate to punish her and treat her as a cruel husband would a wife. Advised confession to husband, Mr. G., and call the police against extorting servant. Ein unglick kommtselten allein."

It has been noted that the bathtub as a setting for sinning was mentioned in the affair of E. G. and Kate B. in the doctor's notes. A sure sign of being well off for most Chicago homes was indoor plumbing—the rest of the city regarded a bathtub as a sign of wealth, and, to many, a daily bath was something the devil invented. Early texts, still found in the rare-book sections of Chicago libraries, warn the water fiend of his road to ruin. A warning came in 1873 in a printed text from Catharine Beecher: "It has been supposed that large bathtubs for immersing the whole person are indispensable to the proper cleaning of the skin . . . A wet towel applied every morning to the skin, followed by friction in pure air, is *all* that is absolutely needed . . . a full bath is a great luxury." In opposition was Emily Thornwell, of *The Lady's Guide to Perfect Gentility*: "What must we think of those genteel people who never use the bath, or only once or twice a year wash themselves all over, though they change their linen daily? . . . In plain English, they are filthy gentry."

And, the *Guide* added, those who do not choose to bathe gave off personal odors, "who have enough of this odor about them to be perceptible to others . . . are often unconscious of it themselves . . . at least to wash armpits and feet regularly . . . a sponge bath can do little harm and almost always some good . . . the part of the body which should first be attacked is the stomach."

Said one worried moralist: "All this washing and handling of ones private parts could only lead to sexual experimenting on ones self, and to thoughts of copulation and seduction of others." Recorded one hellfire preacher, Ira Williams, in a letter: "Oh the water and soaping is leading lads to the pulling of their own pudding, and the hot water to day dreaming of the openings in women and dipping their pecker there. As for the young gurls [*sic*] hot baths behind a locked door is a sure road to the whore house" (Bronson Scrapbook).

Another case in the Chicago doctor's records: "P.J. age 28, Astor Ave—married six years, two children, husband on board of A——, travels in Europe for market reasons. P.J. and M.B., 32, Drexel Blvd., married, no children, husband heavy drinker. Talked to both women today, confessed they have had much physical contact for two years. M.B. owns rubber penis and acts out the male. Both (Catholics) confess fear of damnation but cannot resist great sexual satisfactions by their 'games.' I have known P.J. since she was a child, confesses her love for M.B. is true physical passion, greater than the love she bears husband. M.B. of independent means admits she suggested they together go off to Paris to live. Will take up the serious matter with Father S—— on Sunday."

We are left with an unfinished drama. Did the two Chicago matrons go off to Paris together? Join the colony of other American lesbians there? We don't know. The doctor's notes do not mention them again, and he seems much beyond his depth, almost in a paralysis of his faculties facing these two situations.

Chicago was dotted with bathhouses in a day when private baths were not available in homes. Mostly they were cheerful places for bathing, sobering up, and organizing politics. But a few caused mention in some journals as places where men could meet men, for what was to be called "the love that could not tell its name."

Male homosexuality thrived in Chicago. Male prostitutes catered to their needs. But we know more about female whores who often formed passionate attachments to other members of their profession. Of the genteel society, the respectable, well-off woman who turned to other women for sex and love, we have little beyond the old letters and the few medical notes.

Oscar Wilde, lecturing in Chicago, got some amused laughter by his talk on interior decorating. He also toured the Levee and made some contact with the local homosexual scene. However, Henry James, trapped in Chicago while crossing the continent in 1870, could hardly wait to move on west, nervously pacing the Dearborn Station until his train was ready. He was finding America, its rectangular cities, not to his taste. "To make so much money that you won't, that you don't 'mind,' don't mind anything—that is absolutely, I think, the main America formula." Chicago certainly was all talk of money and making money. The sooner he got out, the better. Yet writing love letters to the young sculptor Hendrik Andersen, he was not free of the vices that existed even in Chicago:

"Dearest, dearest boy, more tenderly embraced than I can say . . . lean on me as a lover. . . . Your terribly tender old friend . . ." (published letter).

Publicly, Henry James never wrote of his private passions, bland or buried in a chaotic absurdity of feared emotions. He could only hint: "Experience is never limited, and it is never complete; it is an immense sensibility, a kind of huge chamber of consciousness, and catching every air-borne particle in its tissues."

It is to be regretted someone did not drag Henry James to the Everleigh Club, so we could, perhaps, have gotten his impression of it, in his involved mandarin prose.

MR. DOOLEY AND MR. DUNNE

History is a post-mortem. It tells ye what a counthry died iv. But I'd like to know what it lived iv.

MR. DOOLEY

The world as a spectacle has few folksy, amusing historians who also know how to pontificate properly.

The one man who took the measure of the politicians of Chicago, their boodle-grabbing, their use of the voter to defeat himself, was a journalist named Finley Peter Dunne, who created a sly, acid-tongued, Irish saloonkeeper of Archy Road, named Mr. Dooley, who in a thick brogue (and teeth-breaking phonetic spelling) commented on the daily doings of the city, the nation, and tested the moral weather, its storm warnings, all to the delight in time of millions of newspaper readers.

It is to be regretted that Mr. Dooley, a wiser Gulliver, is not read today, the main reason being that Dunne wrote his turn-of-the-century monologues in a thick and now-out-of-date Pat and Mike Irish dialect that needs some effort to penetrate, even when what he said of the Democratic party is still true. "Tis niver so good as whin 'tis broke, whin rayspictable people speak of it in whispers, and whin it has no leaders an' on'y wan principle, to go in an' take it away fr'm th' other fellows."

He knew the consequence of errors by the true rulers of the nation, the ward heelers who got out or stole the vote. "No matter whether the Constitution follows th' flag or not, th' Supreme Coort follows th' iliction returns."

Finley Peter Dunne was born in 1867. At nineteen, he was already a city editor on a local paper, as no journalism college courses existed.

On the *Chicago Post* he began writing the sayings and comments of the jocular Mr. Dooley for the ten dollars extra pay a week he got for creating the Irish barkeeper, who, in years to come, was to entertain readers like Theodore Roosevelt, William Jennings Bryan, Samuel Gompers, Senator Frederick Hale of Maine, Eugene Debs, Elihu Root, Winston S. Churchill, Henry Cabot Lodge, and President Charles William Eliot of Harvard: an impressive spread. Also a great many people whose names meant nothing to historians of the period. Mr. Dooley didn't much care for heroes, anyway. His recipe for designing a triumphal arch for a hero was to build it out of bricks "so th' people will have somethin' convenient to throw at him as he passes through."

He wrote the first Dooley texts, trying to cauterize the city's wounds, to expose the thieves and grafters on the City Council, but soon was aware he could only inflict pinpricks on the hard elephant hides of the aldermen, the political hangers-on, and freeloaders. Into the pinpricks he rubbed acid wit, and people read him, laughed, agreed, and the corruption went on. He saw the cause of greed, of most wrongdoing in politics, in business, was money as king. "Tis as har-rd fr a rich man to enter the Kingdom of Hivven as it is fr a poor man to get out of Purgatory. . . . Onaisy is the head that wears a crown. Other heads are onaisy too, but ye don't hear iv thim."

He went after the Yerkeses and the Rockefellers, the great devouring, greedy men who dominated their time. He knew "Prometheus was impressive as a fighter, but it was the eagle who ate the liver" (from an unpublished letter).

Of the rich man and his methods he wrote: "His heart was pure, seein' that he had niver done wrong save in th' way of business. . . . I care not who makes th' laws of th' nation if I can get out

an injunction . . . if greatness an' goodness went hand in hand, 'tis small chance anny of us wud have iv seein' our pitcher in th' paapers. . . . Th' reason ye have no money is because ye don't love it f'r itself alone. Money won't iver surrendher to such a flirt."

His scorn for the rich and powerful, the asinine, was balanced by his compassion for the hopelessness of the poor.

Dunne's own life pattern was simple. He found writing hard, and tried to avoid it. The people he liked and got to know well, oddly enough, were wealthy and Republicans. Dunne, in time, joined Thorstein Veblen's "predatory society," voted for Hughes, Harding, and Coolidge, as well as for Theodore Roosevelt. He was a member of several country clubs, yet Dunne, with his work on magazines, was associated with the foremost muckrakers and reformers. He was listed as one with Ida M. Tarbell, Lincoln Steffens, William Allen White.

Writing had always been a struggle. Dunne was lazy, he wrote only when he had to, sought excuses to avoid writing. He used to count flowers on the wallpaper in preference to writing, a Don Quixote, thrusting his Irish spear at such windmills as the Gas, Ice and Coal trusts, the Chicago vice problems. The trouble was in getting ideas. The formula of Mr. Dooley made things difficult. The longer he wrote, the more subjects were exhausted. He would quit writing, take a vacation, and start again. The vacations grew longer, periods of writing shorter. The stimulation was financial. Late in life, Dunne inherited a half-million dollars. It was the end of his writing. "If a man is wise, he gets rich an' if he gets rich, he gets foolish, or his wife does. That's what keeps th' money movin' around."

Let Mr. Dooley and his kind be critical. The city itself was infected with no self-deprecation—it had a rendezvous with something called progress and "git up and go!"

Chicago continued to smell; it always smelled of the stockyards where cattle waited for the icebox cars, and pigs grunted as they marched up the gangways to the butchers' throat thrusts. The packers were too powerful to worry much over sanitary laws, pure food acts, workingmen's rights. The teeth and belly of the nation were waiting for pork chops and sausages, for "smoked" meats, for by-products. Those in control saw profits in every part of a carcass, and felt stronger than the Federal government—much of it on their payroll.

In 1906, Upton Sinclair was to open the horrors of the packing plants to the eyes (and stomach) of the nation with his novel, *The Jungle*. To the packers, this depressing text was an attack on free enterprise, on the American way of life where every boy could become a millionaire. What mattered if every now and then—as Sinclair claimed—a Polack or Hunky worker fell into the sausage machine and came out in links as prime smoked sausage, or pound cans of pure leaf lard? Or if tubercular cattle were passed as "fit" by bribed inspectors, or if "smoked" meats were actually merely chemically treated with dangerous or even poisonous compounds?

There had, of course, been a Senate investigation in the 1890s of the packing industry, investigating diseased meat, and the nonsense of government regulation was threatened. "Yes," said witnesses from packinghouses, "they slaughter diseased cattle cancerous with running sores." Or medical testimony: "Yes, in the Spanish-American War condemned beef sold to the army killed more soldiers than the enemy." Teddy Roosevelt testified, "The cans showed on top . . . a layer of slime . . ." General Nelson A. Miles testified, "The embalmed beef was treated with chemicals to preserve it . . . nauseating . . . if swallowed it could not be kept on the stomach." Another witness. "Hundreds of graves tell the hideous story of chemically prepared beef." General Miles summed up: "I believe that three thousand soldiers lost their lives because of adulterated, impure, poisonous meat."

The first packinghouse investigation was smothered by friendly Senators, some suddenly a bit richer. Yet even when scientific journals had gotten to reporting the poisonous conditions of Chicago packinghouses, none of the firms took on much alarm. After all, who read the British medical publication, *The Lancet*, which in a series wrote in detail of unsanitary conditions at Armour's and Swift's and other packers; wrote of those "nooks and corners where blood, the splashing of offal, and the sputum of tubercular workers can accumulate for weeks, months and years."

Yet somehow, perhaps because it made meat eaters ill, Upton Sinclair's *The Jungle* did become a best seller. Senator Albert Beveridge did try again for a law for a rigid inspection, a Federal inspection, of all meats. (It might be of interest as this book goes to press that there is still no Federal inspection of *all* packing plants in the United States, only on meat that crosses state borders.)

President Teddy Roosevelt released a government report on the Chicago packinghouses to help the Senator's bill, but it had most of its teeth drawn by the Congress and Senate with so many members "friendly to the packers." The report made the nation sick, telling of dead hogs rotting outside plants, killing rooms floored in slime and workers' urine (time out for nature's needs being frowned upon), of meat left to lie on decaying wooden floors, "bodies of cattle hauled out of privies and hung, unwashed, in cooling rooms."

Defenders, familiar with politics and how to kill laws, rose in Washington to protest the treatment of the packers. "The packers have done more for this country than any other body of men." As for those who wanted Federally controlled examination of meat fit to eat, "They are most dangerous. . . . We have anarchists, but they are positively more destructive . . . they . . . would destroy the foundations of the Republican government." No one would want that, so the crisis passed.

Federal health controls of packinghouses were never solidly set or, when too rigid, fully enforced. America was a meat-eating nation, when it could get it. It had grown up as part hunter, filling the pot with wild game, Chicago packers pointed out, fed on the varmints that fell to the Kentuck' rifle. The homesteader, too, still fed his family part of the season on wild ducks, jackrabbits, and whatever was hit by his shotgun. So it would be onerous to tamper with a need for meat. The packinghouses had the demand and also the supplies. Europeans were amazed at the American demand for meat.

The most poverty-stricken sharecropper—seeking work in Chicago—had a spider skillet, and, if able, three times a day fed on fried meat and grease sopped up in corn bread. Europeans, immigrants, who thought the humble sausage a treat, were amazed at the pounds of meat eaten, the love of animal flesh, and the amount desired even by the Chicago poor. In 1962 appearing with Upton Sinclair on TV in Los Angeles, he told me that in the eighteenth century J. J. Rousseau had written: "It is a fact that great eaters of meat are in general more cruel and ferocious than other men . . . the barbarism of the English is well known." I replied that, like

Rousseau's nonsense about the Happy Savage being a happy man, this remark was to cause a great deal of unhappiness and the growth of cults trying to disguise a fact that Armour and Swift knew: man is of the order *Carnivora*.

48

BATHHOUSE JOHN

*I don't expict to gather calla lilies in Hogan's turnip patch. Why shud I
expict to pick bunches iv spotless statesmen fr'm th' gradooation class iv th'
house iv correction?*

MR. DOOLEY, ON CORRUPTION IN POLITICS

No dweller of the Gold Coast of Chicago was Bathhouse John. The
father of John Coughlin came over "bare-arse-poor" from County
Roscommon in Ireland, and in 1867 settled in the 1st Ward of Chicago, a domain his son was to dominate for many years with his impulsive vitality. John, himself, was born in 1860, his mother having
been a Johanna Hanley from County Limerick. The father ran a
small grocery store at Taylor and Miller streets, which burned
down quickly in the Great Fire. Bathhouse John always saw this
disaster as a good thing—an exemplary sign of fortune—a monu-
mental chapter in his life. "I'm glad the fire came along and burned
the auld store. Say, if not fer that bonfire, I might have been a rich
man's son and gone to Yale—and never amounted to much."

John, at the Jones School for boys, was the janitor's assistant
and was called "Dusty John" because of the soiled condition of himself and his clothes after handling the school's coal bin. He played
at boys' sports, and as a cheerful adolescent was a member of the

Phoenix Club which took trips around town, visited the stockyards, the oversaturated river, and the lakefront. The boys even took a look at vice on notorious Biler Avenue. John left the Jones School at thirteen, spent two more years at the Christian Brothers' Industrial School, and then felt that was all the education he wanted to carry. Greenhorns who lacked his moxie might need laws of adverbs and geometry, but not he.

Tall for his age, at fifteen he was close to six feet already, with wide shoulders, powerful arms, thick-necked as a wrestler, a face and head hard to forget, dominated by deep blue eyes. It was blatantly obvious he knew his worth. He took what work there was for the son of an Irish grocer: water boy to a railroad gang, butcher's delivery lad, "helping out in the family store among the mackerel snappers and buyers of packets of butter and a can of coal oil," as a ward heeler stated to a local newspaper. There was always a lot of love of theater in him, and at eighteen he was acting in a dramatic club set up in a second-floor loft at Halsted and De Koven streets. His voice was strong but melodious, his laugh infectious.

He also had a job at a local racetrack, and didn't waste time, soon becoming a skilled handicapper of the sorry nags that ran there. John was expanding his world among the sleek, hard-living people who knew and liked him, he meeting important political figures and making a bit of money betting, often on sure things, fixed races, beating his fists together like cymbals in his glee.

His friends were like himself boisterous and given to saloon jests and hanging out in bathhouses, where an infinite diversity of life existed. It was an age when plumbing and bathtubs were rare in most of the city. So in the steam of bathhouses, a whole society existed of nude males in normal friendships: boxers, jockeys, drunks steaming out alcohol, political ward heelers, precinct captains, aldermen, talking of losing weight, schemes for stealing elections and boodle. John found a life-style he liked of conditioned action, of the main chance. He didn't aspire at first to the fancy bath establishment at the Palmer House, the first one in Chicago, where the rich and the sinful boiled their pores clean in fancy settings and planned visits to the gay brothels and scented whores of the Levee.

At first, John Coughlin stuck to the bathhouses of his district, one of his favorites being the one at 205 Clark Street where the greats of the First Ward steamed and talked avidly of election frauds. Then one day he came home all excited. "I got a real job, I'm a rubber in a Turkish bathhouse. Now ain't that a *real* job!" Gone delivery boy chores, slicing rat cheese. He reveled in his work on the fat overweight bodies, whacking and laughing at his trade. It was true, as he later said to reporters, of his coming of age in bathhouses, "I formed my phio—philosophy . . . I met 'em all, big and little, from La Salle Street to Armour Street. You can learn from everybody. There isn't much difference between the big man and the little man. One's lucky, that's all."

Luck, and plenty of charm, and a way of letting the other feller make you an offer for what you could do for him. That was the way he was to see life, make the best of venality of human existence. He entered at last the Palmer House baths, as the head rubber, and here he pounded the flesh of Senators, Congressmen, businessmen, actors, meat-packers. Even the flanks of the great Marshall Field came under his large skilled hands, to pound the melancholy of domestic battles with his wife from the great merchant's body.

A First Ward saloonkeeper and vote getter, John Morris, in 1882, lent John Coughlin eight hundred dollars to help him get his own bathhouse on East Madison Street. He told his family, "I'm me own boss. I got me own bathhouse!" He was so carried away, he went down to St. John's Church on Eighteenth Street, fell to his strong knees, and offered up a prayer at his good fortune. He was a mixture of the parochial and the wise knowledge of the streets. Soon he did so well he opened another bathhouse at the stylish Hotel Brevort, and had a staff of rubbers and other help to do the pounding. But he always came in early to check the cash, and greet the drunks and hedonists after they arose from sleeping off a gay night in the beds he provided in his bathhouses. Sexual lions were turned to scuffling stoats in the morning.

John's moustache grew with his prosperity; his sideburns had the dignity of a bishop's. He combed his hair upward in the pompadour of a Princeton fullback, and he became known from then on as "Bathhouse John" Coughlin, or just Bathhouse.

He wrote out his own signs and saw them placed on the walls of his establishments.

GOOD HEALTH IS PRICELESS
CLEANLINESS GIVES HEALTH

HEALTH IS RICHES   HEALTH IS LIFE
THERE'S HEALTH IN COUGHLIN'S BATHS!

The young sport in his stable, transitory phase as a bathhouse owner was popular, and, within the range of his world, he was considered a man of his word. As one of the watching politicians of the First Ward put it, "John's not very bright, but once he gives his word you kin count on him." Bright, or not, he had a shrewd sense of self-preservation—and perhaps a prolonged adolescence.

Bathhouse early joined the First Ward Democratic Club and was soon Democratic captain of the precinct. The job of a captain was to get out the vote, to find voters where none existed, to vote floaters: tramps and drunkards brought in, often paid as high as five dollars each for voting, and as little as twenty-five cents—often satisfied with a pint of raw whiskey. To do good for one's ward, to get out all one could of one's district voters, *and* put aside a little for one's self, that was politics. Loyalty to the party boss, the party; never to abstractions called the city, the nation, the ideals of government some chowderhead would talk about. It was too hard a world, too cynical a system, to go beyond giving your word and keeping it. And hand out a few silver coins to some skid-row bum needing a ball, a beggar, his handout. No self-scrutiny; just be loyal, deliver, keep your eyes open.

Bathhouse in his relationship to man put it simply: "That guy might have been somebody once, might be somebody again. It don't pay in this world to think you're better than the next feller just 'cause you happen to be on top and he ain't." It was the kind of sympathy and thinking that could only lead to public office, from precinct captain upward with the Democrats. His was not the mere attitude of a stereotype or a depersonalized stooge; he cared. He was alive. "A Republican, now, is a man what wants you t' go t' church every Sunday. A democrat says if a man he wants t' have a glass of beer on Sunday, he kin have it. Be a Democrat unless you want t' to be tied t' a church . . . or a Sunday School."

Power struck a deep responsive chord in him: its use, its getting and keeping it. It was also fun.

He became a fan of the horse races run at Washington Park.

The fee for a new club member was $150. The grandstand had cost $40,000, the clubhouse $50,000. The American Derby was the big social event for the high-flying sporting men of society, city officials, and First Ward people, all cheering the horses. Bathhouse John began to cultivate the jockeys, the trainers chewing on a straw. He was given tips of arranged races, called "boat rides." But keeping his bets down to two dollars.

Meanwhile, John was falling in love with someone he had known from childhood. Mary Kiley was from his neighborhood, his station in life, and social scene. She was neither above him nor below him. He was a big, bumbling shy lover, slow in his ways, either in gaucherie or braggadocio. Mary tried to change his sense of grammar, repair it, for she hoped to be a schoolteacher. To show his love, John bought a racehorse and told her he was calling it My Queen. To the track crowd he announced, "I'm naming her for Mary."

Bathhouse, in moist nervousness, even got around to proposing, and they were married in 1886, at St. John's Church. Skipping a honeymoon they settled into a flat on Michigan Avenue. No braised partridge and claret—but he was for corned beef and cabbage and beer.

Bathhouse was a happy man, not a skirt chaser but a loyal husband, a fancy dresser, a smoker of good cigars, mostly gifts, a fine figure of a man like "Sandow, the strong feller"—leading the Democratic Marching Club with a good stride, a bull's voice. A teller of ribald jests in saloons, smelling of the best sour mash whiskey, malt beer, he reaching his mitt into the jar of pickled hard-boiled eggs or pigs' feet on the bar, paying for a round. "Bellies to the bar, boys!"

Bathhouse John was a coming man. But he was wondering *when*. The big boys smiled and patted his shoulder, gave him half-dollar butts. He was four times president of the First Ward Club. What else? "We're keepin' you in mind, Jawn boy. Yer a comer." He could almost taste the City Council chambers. But still the bosses shook their heads and took him to Boyle's Chop House. "Easy, Jawnny, easy lad. Yer time will come one of these days. Yer young" (Bronson Scrapbook).

Boyle's Chop House. Bathhouse John loved the place where the party's great and powerful gathered to swallow the salt pork and truffles, the fine rare chops. To sit with Senators, lawyers, both criminal and civil, with men who controlled the graft, the boodle that came out of the brothels, the payoffs of the gambling houses, the city utilities boodle men who said *who* would, who would *not* hold office. "Meet Bathhouse—the coming man of the 1st Ward."

Boyle's was Bathhouse's Mermaid Tavern, the paneling thick in Havana cigar smoke. It was the heir of ancient Greek town meetings, and Billy Boyle kept out those whom he did not think belonged. For them crumbums, he had a fake menu printed. French Peas $1.25, Potatoes $1.10, Coffee 50¢, Pigs Feet $4.30. It not only kept out those moochers who wanted to plague the great men, but also the nigras. Once, Billy handed his special chasing-out menu to two well-dressed blacks who just smiled and ordered a huge meal, and smiled again at the bill of thirty-two dollars. They ordered two-dollar cigars, paid up, left a good tip, lit their H. Uppmanns and went out *still* smiling. Billy couldn't get over it. "You'd think they was human, like white men!!" (Bronson Scrapbook).

As for the First Ward, the word went out Bathhouse John was going to run for City Council. His wife watching him cheerfully at breakfast was worried. He was not neat. The half-dozen fried eggs had left spots on his waistcoat, and the several thick slices of ham had added some red-eye gravy. He was also free and easy with his spitting after savoring a good length of his pungent cigar.

"John, dear, if you're going to be the alderman, you must talk and *act* like one."

He asked what she meant.

Her first political contribution was a large porcelain spittoon. Taking this art object (today a rare antique) to an art school, she asked if one of the students could "decorate it with some pretty flowers . . . red ones and blue ones? Mr. Coughlin is fond of flowers."

There were tougher critics of Bathhouse than Mary.

The *Journal* wrote, "Coughlin, the Democratic candidate, is in every way unfit." Said a barroom political expert reading that: "As fit as the fellow he's running against, or as unfit."

The *Mail* wrote, "Bathhouse John would use his vote and influence so as not to interfere with the gamblers." They also noted that the sporting-house circles were solidly behind him.

Running easy with no expenditure of extra energy, Bathhouse won office with 1,603 votes, and a plurality of 768.

The new alderman was kept stainless by his wife, and one evening he entered the City Hall Council Chamber in all his glory. Matching coat and pants of fawn gray, his racing colors of green and white on his waistcoat, a batiste cravat under a wing collar, his moustache waxed sharp as spurs, his hair standing at attention. He was a man taller than most, sweating more. He dabbed at his face and neck with a silk handkerchief, and he was made welcome and took his seat. As a newspaper reported, "There was a good natured cheer for Bathhouse John." Said an alderman, "He was as pretty as a little red wagon."

It was time to get down to the rewards of office, the boodle. There was a fund to be collected from the whorehouses, the gamblers, the disorderly saloons, to explain with flamboyant plausibility it was a fund to see that the city officials didn't get too pious or pass laws to hurt their business. After all, aldermen were only paid three dollars a council meeting, and most of the good men owned mansions, racing stables, Goodart buggies, broughams, country estates. If some voter or reformer asked how they lived so well on three dollars a meeting, it was wise to say, "On good investments." So those who needed the aid of the council came to them with gifts. In cash.

C. C. Thompson of the Chamber of Commerce put it bluntly: "If you want to get anything out of the council, the quickest way is to pay for it—not to the city, but to the aldermen."

Bathhouse John was to help extend and refine the process of office.

49

COME TO THE LEVEE

*Chicago presents more splendid attractions and more hideous repulsions
close together than any place known to me. It takes elaborate care to present
its worst side first to the stranger. It makes a more amazing open display of
evil than any other city known to me. Other places hide their blackness out
of sight; Chicago treasures it in the heart of the business quarter and gives
it a veneer.*

LONDON DAILY MAIL CORRESPONDENT

Home of Bathhouse John and of the First Ward Ball was "that
wildest part of town called the Levee," and in space it ran from
Twelfth Street to Van Buren Street, and from State Street to Pacific
Avenue. Part of the First Ward, it paid for protection and ran wide
open. It was called the Levee from the fact that, even before the
Civil War, gamblers from the South had come there off the big
packets, the steamboats out of Mark Twain, to play games of
chance, to enjoy, to orgy. Always it was the Levee—up to about
1910—that was spoken of as the city's wildest entertainment for
those seeking gambling places, dance halls, barrelhouse joints, hock
shops, tintype picture galleries, penny arcades, voodoo goofer dust,
charms, gyp auctions, livery stables, a blacksmith, yellow girls, or
an all-night oyster bar where they were shucked fresh and served
with a hot sauce and a half of lemon. "The Levee accepted the rest
of the universe," said one reformer, "but reluctantly."

The Levee was just a few blocks square, but two hundred

whorehouses managed to crowd in; some were almost honest flesh peddlers, and some were low dives. And on top were the really fancy luxury brothels, all gilt chamber pots and red velvet drapes with art collections, wine in fairly good bottles. There was an absence of morals bordering on genius.

A gentleman and his male guests going down the line (touring the Levee) could be assured in the better brothels that he and his wallet were fairly safe, and the girls not recently diseased, and the piano player knew all of Stephen Foster, ragtime, and coon songs. Some places, like the French Elm, had walls *all* mirrors, even on the ceilings. For the jaded male, the House of All Nations furnished women of all shades, colors, and dialects, but mostly the exotic touted girls were natives of Chicago. Private wine rooms at eating places, and boxes at the Park Theatre, gave the guest the privilege of bringing his own women, or being entertained by the house hostesses, waitress girls, or actresses; amused, serviced with some sexual form of what were proudly called "perverted acts to watch, or join in."

The foot-shaking, beating center of the Levee was Freiberg's Dance Hall, with Ike Bloom running things; he took a share of what the girls made, and insisted the dancing have some decorum. Reformers, disoriented by all the vice around, always came to the Freiberg Dance Hall first; it was good publicity all around—for the reformers and the hall. Ike would welcome the reformers, usually moving about in a party as if for protection. As Ike explained to a reporter: "I give 'em the freedom of the tables, I order the drinks all around—lemonade, and when they asks for the center of the dance floor to kneel down and pray, and sing, 'Washed in the Blood of The Lamb,' I gives it to 'em. I even give 'em my jazz band too, which plays their accompaniment and plays it mighty damn well. One of the papers carried a story . . . that was all straight except where it says I kneel and sing with 'em. That was an error, I *don't* sing."

The most publicized reformer was an Englishman, William T. Stead, who came for the Columbian Exposition and wandered into the Levee, and all its *fin-de-siècle* decadence. He held meetings and wrote a book, *If Christ came to Chicago*, pointing out that the morality of the city would have shocked Him. Stead stated, "Here we have assessed in its baldest and plainest form the working principle on which the smart man of Chicago acts. Everything that is not illegal is assumed by him to be right . . . as long as permitted by law or so long as they can evade the law by any subterfuge, they consider they are doing perfectly all right. They believe in the state; they have ceased to believe in God."

He found that the Democratic party had replaced the church as a religion, with a "faith built on bribery, intimidation, bulldozing of every kind, knifing, shooting and the whole swimming in whisky . . . the recognition of human obligation, set in motion . . . for party reasons and from a desire to control votes rather than save souls." He admitted it set in off the "molding into one, heterogeneous elements of various races, nationalities and religions who are gathered together in Chicago." Even with a fraternizing at times *en déshabillé*.

Mayor Carter Harrison, Jr., when he came to face realities, explained in an interview that these unifiers "a motley crew . . . saloon keepers, proprietors of gambling houses and undertakers . . . Chicago in the 90s, whose citizens . . . had permitted the control of public affairs to be the exclusive appendage of a lowbrowed, dull witted, base minded gang of plug-uglies with . . . an unquenchable lust for money . . . with a certain physical courage which enabled each to dominate his individual barnyard . . . the average Democratic representative is a tramp if not worse."

An alderman, Nathan T. Brenner of the Ninth Ward, with prodigious curiosity, stated, "There are only three aldermen in the entire sixty-eight who are not able and willing to steal a red hot stove." (This phrase became the core much later of a famous W. C. Fields' skit, his pool table routine when asked, "Why do they call you Honest John?")

The Civic Federation—a reform group—figured out that only fifty-seven out of the sixty-eight aldermen were thieves and grafters, but they did not know the group as Brenner knew it, from the inside. The take of a grafting alderman was set at from $15,000 to $30,000 a year, besides such favors as cigars and whiskey, "a piece of ass," and freeloading on huge meals. An important city ordinance, like a utility franchise, could bring an alderman with the right-needed vote, $25,000, and those trailing him at least $8000 each. Any payoffs for minor favors cost from $300 to $400. Calculable powers, with precise bookkeeping as dependable as the tides.

Aldermen would also set up dummy companies to buy up street rights and then sell the rights to the companies seeking franchises, at *very* inflated prices. (It is still being done by politicians around airports in California.) Any changeover from horsecars to cable cars, to electric trolleys, was a good time for graft, as *each* move had to get new city franchises.

Prime examples of the aldermen with a hold on the big boodle were the two who controlled the votes and graft in the First Ward and the Levee, Bathhouse John Coughlin and Hinky Dink Michael Kenna. Bathhouse John, a big brute of a fellow with a well-filled paunch, and Hinky Dink, slim, neat with a small moustache; they made a marvelous team. They believed one must never depend on the kindness of strangers, and every friend will vote right. The two boodle hounds kept the First Ward and the Levee solidly Democratic; they delivered as always on election days an amazing number of votes, often more than there were voters. Some claimed they were the first to vote the dead, copying off names from gravestones. They cultivated their huge population of barflies and moochers, all ready to cast as many votes each, as were needed, each visit to the polls worth often two dollars and a pint of rotgut. Chain voting was Hinky Dink's job, also seeing that the police didn't harass the whorehouses, that they merely collected the protection money from the madams. The cops demanded loyalties, not scruples or qualms.

Bathhouse had opened a saloon called The Silver Dollar after hearing William Jennings Bryan give his "Cross of Gold" speech defending free silver coinage. The ceiling and walls of the saloon had huge replicas of silver cartwheels (as dollars were called). The alderman put the state Democratic party behind the free silver issue. As one newspaper put it, "16 to 1—sixteen parts whisky and one part water."

Greeter of patrons at The Silver Dollar was "One-Eye Jimmy" Connelly, whose call to fame was that he was a notorious gate-crasher and served later as W. C. Fields' stooge. One-Eye would point to a big silver dollar on the saloon wall: "Now, *E. Pluribus Unum*, to read it right, it's, He brews us new rum." It was best to laugh at the feeble jest before One-Eye reached for the bung starter.

Bathhouse John remained a dude, a fashion horse. At his showing up for any public event, he might have on a dove gray tailcoat, matching pants, a Kelly green vest with white checks, brown silk shirt, yellow bulldog-toed shoes. His cutaways were usually Irish green, striped Prince Albert, a plaid waistcoat with white buttons. In reserve were six spare vests of various patterns, a four-button, hammer-tailed coat, patent-leather dancing pumps with green tops. He was always willing, with a serious precision, to give his views on the well-dressed male, as he did in this interview: "I'll show 'em a thing or two in dress for the masculine gender. I gotta be strictly original. I think the Prince of Wales is a lobster in his taste . . . all right fer playin' baccarat and puttin' his coins on the right hoss at the races. But when it come down to mappin' out style for well-dressed Americans, he's simply a faded two-spot in the big deck of fashion. People, they been followin' his lead 'cause no other guy has the nerve to challenge him for the championship . . . now I'm out fer first place and you'll see his percentage drop."

The First Ward balls were always run for raising money for the party, but somehow most of it stayed stuck with Hinky Dink and Bathhouse who had extraordinary abilities for smelling out loot.

The benefit ball really got its start on the Levee when Carrie Watson, the popular madam, began to give benefits for her pet violin player, "Lame Jimmy." Every year for fifteen years, gimpy Jimmy had a benefit ball. The police were always in attendance, dancing and drinking. One year, two harness bulls got into a fight over a whore, lost their complacency, and one cop drew his police special, badly injuring the other. The lid was on Lame Jimmy's benefits after that.

Bathhouse John was sorry to see the event go; he figured the four or five hundred people who came to Jimmy's balls were nothing to what the First Ward bosses could crowd into the 7th Regiment Armory if they took over the idea of a yearly ball. The whole Levee would be happy to show its patronage of a Bathhouse John and Hinky Dink shindig. Every saloonkeeper, crib pimp, cathouse madam would be invited, and no one would dare not buy a batch of tickets. Neither could refusal come from the distilleries, beer brewers, wine salesmen, all of whom knew if they wanted to stay in business in the First Ward and on the Levee, they had better pony up. Free likker, the foodstuff at special low prices, was provided for the

First Ward Ball. The waiters, hundreds of them, were not paid, but had to shell out five dollars each to get a job, for the tips would be big from the madams and the sports.

Tights on the ladies were barred, but short skirts were encouraged, the idea it being "bad form to wear anything that would collect germs from the floor." The women had police escorts, and the floozies and Levee girls were in costume, the less the better, Indian and Egyptian sheer clothing being popular on geishas, gypsies, who came in large numbers to wriggle to the blare of loud music. That it was all "for the good of the Democratic party" was an added piquancy.

After the first successful ball, more room was needed, and so it was moved to the Coliseum, and one could come in costume or not. Fifteen hundred people tried to crowd into the place. The traffic of hansoms and carriages and hacks could not move for blocks. The people, once inside, were so packed together that the *Record* reported "those already drunk were forced to stand erect." Fights, broken tables, smashed glasses tried to outsound the music. The Grand March started just on time, with fifty guests lying knocked out in the alley. Bathhouse John and Hinky Dink properly led off, each escorting an Everleigh sister on his arm, followed respectfully by the First Ward Democratic Club, twenty-six across. Outside, gate-crashers fought police, and the cops charged the mob again and again, clubs and fists beating away. It was a grand slugging brannigan.

Hinky Dink, with petulant self-satisfaction, looking over the vast gathering of madams, police captains, saloonkeepers, dips, and second-story workers, whores and sweating waiters, while outside the sound of the excluded grew louder, said with pride, "It's a lollapalooza! There are more here than ever before . . . all the big people. Chicago *ain't* no sissy town" (as reported in the *Chicago Tribune*).

One frowning face in a corner box belonged to Dean Walter Sumner of the Episcopalian Saints Peter and Paul Cathedral, who reported on the event to the mayor: "The ball is a disgrace. Chicago is unique in holding this revel of the underworld."

BOOK FIVE

SOCIETY UPSTAIRS AND DOWN

50

HINKY DINK

"A reformer tries to get into office on a flyin' machine. He succeeds now and thin, but th' odds are a hundhred to wan on the la-ad that tunnels through."

MR. DOOLEY

They made a great team, Bathhouse and the Dink, the reason being perhaps they were so different, so that the combination would seem comic, and what is comic seems harmless and is usually trusted, even if one knows the worst about it. Michael Kenna was glum and given to sour expressions on the disintegrating of social homogeneity—while Bathhouse John was an extrovert given to loud sound and much laughter over pleasures or indignities. Kenna was a small man with the delicate bones of a dove. Bathhouse was built over life-size, solid "like a brick privy," and strong enough to do amazing physical deeds. Kenna didn't, by his look, trust the world, and he didn't believe much in what anyone said—so speech was one thing to avoid, and to use merely to ask the way to the men's room or to demand a vote tally. Bathhouse John, with a bulldog countenance of power, was a friendly man, called the world a happy place but for a few hundred thousand Republicans, reformers, investigators. Bathhouse was not given to order, to neatness, except for dress events, and he would fumble and yawn at times when keen attention was needed. Kenna, in perpetual agitation at elections, was a doer, a watcher, a maker of order, and a giver of short crisp commands. What he shared with John Coughlin was an itch for power, an avid desire for money, big money, large sums of it, and, as he said in a speech, "don't be asking to closely how its gotten or you'll get your moustache pushed into your nose."

Bathhouse may have been mistaken for a buffoon and Kenna for a mountebank, but both were master politicians.

Michael Kenna was born in a wintery 1858, in a shanty at Polk and Sholto streets, at the edge of the disrespectable district called the Patch. He wasn't a healthy baby; puny as he was, his mother felt this little mick must have his chance of heaven—not die unbaptized. She wrapped him up and carried him across the sleet and ice-rimmed streets to Father Damien's church at Eleventh and May streets, for him, in Jaysus' name, to baptize the little creature. He grew up in a nest of uncertainty and poverty—under a God for whom the rich practiced charity, the poor humility.

Mike's boyhood was as hard as most of the Irish who came from families where there was never enough "and only the priest had an egg regular for breakfast." By the time Mike was ten—sly but not gauche—he had done with school, not that he didn't have the mind for it and wasn't outsmarting the rest of the class. It was the outside world of Chicago, its streets, saloons, busy corners that attracted him. So in the streets he took to selling newspapers, pleading, yelling the headlines in saloons, restaurants, not being chased out but making friends, running errands for wide folk, for barmen and whorehouse madams, hookers and saloon hostesses. Mike was learning how the world lived, his part of it, and its irreconcilable contradictions. He heard the gambler talk of a rich take on the riverboats, a tart explain the lifting of a wallet from one of the Gold Coast swells, he saw he was a *disjecta membra* of his society. And he decided to make his mark, his pile—show that a little fellow could outthink the big ones.

Mike was twelve when he went into business, on fifty dollars borrowed from an admiring bartender. He bought the rights to a newspaper stand at Dearborn and Monroe streets, just outside the old *Tribune* building, and he sold papers so well he could repay the loan almost at once. How did he become "Hinky Dink"? The legend is that Joseph Medill of the *Tribune*, himself noticed the wise-looking little newsboy and said, "I'm going to call you Hinky Dink, because you're such a little fellow."

Mike himself said the truth was he got the name from boys kidding him at some river swimming spot as a hinky dink, for his size. Certainly Medill wasn't a man to go pat a newsboy's head and give him a name; all he would care about was that the miserable little tad sell the *Tribune*. But Hinky Dink it was, however come by his name, all of his life. He went on outselling all the other newsboys, right up to the Great Fire. At thirteen he rented a lean-to where the Matteson Hotel had stood before the flames came. The Dink set up a coffee and lunch counter, popularly called a "greasy-spoon joint." It failed, as he admitted, because "cash registers hadn't come into style yet at the time, and the man who worked for me knew it."

In 1880, he cut his umbilical cord with Chicago, tried the West of the dime novel, going out to Leadville, Colorado, a tough mining town, where he worked on a newspaper, *The Lake County Reveille*, with title of "circulation manager," which was really little more than forcing the sale, getting the paper sold on the streets, pushing the newsboys to greater energy. Two years later—the West too raw —given to derision of small men—he was back in Chicago. He was twenty-four and "no bigger than a pump handle, knee-high to a grasshopper."

Through the newspaper business—not one to shrink from the coarse flavor of life—he became a saloonkeeper and one of a dozen promising political small fry of the First Ward Democratic Club. His work in getting out the vote for Grover Cleveland in 1884 was fine—and had him appointed precinct captain of his saloon district. Some of the club went to jail for county vote frauds, but not Hinky Dink. He avoided incompetence. He had already met Bathhouse John, but the combination was yet to become formidable, and they were still not comrades-in-arms, merging their comprehensive image of their world.

Mike married Catherine Devro; he was loyal to the Irish, but Catherine was a wife who did not share in her husband's political activities, being a devout churchgoer and working within the temperance movement—and *her* husband running a saloon, the priest said. As the First Ward saying was, Dink reminded people, "The church is for women, God is for men." Not that Hinky Dink did more than tip his hat to either. Mrs. Kenna was not like Mrs. Bathhouse John, lace-curtain Irish, who hated the name Bathhouse, and insisted he was a gentleman. Mrs. Kenna didn't give a damn about grammar, and didn't see anything wrong in people calling Mike "The Boss."

Both Bathhouse and Hinky Dink took their orders from "Chesterfield Joe" Macklin, and the First Ward was their home base, aware no one is independent of his external surroundings. Hinky Dink had an Achilles' heel; he was a gambling man. He also ran, so he claimed, "an honest game" over the saloon and didn't approve of Mayor Harrison closing it, as he did so many places when a patch of reform occurred, as it did from time to time.

Hinky Dink called in Bathhouse and offered an alliance to make gambling safe.

"John, things are movin' fast . . . we got a good thing and want to hold on. Let's stick together and we'll rule the roost some day."

"I'm wit you Mike, I'm wit you. Why together we . . ."

"We got work to do."

So was formed a famous, notorious partnership in Chicago politics that was to run the Levee for many years; but that was still in the future. Bathhouse, to preserve gambling, went courting the mayor. He and Hinky Dink controlled votes, they were there to explain how coteries of ward boys held elections, could steer them votes—*here*—*there*—eh? The mayor nodded. "You do your work, Alderman Coughlin, and there'll be no trouble."

It was the wink that said the political boys in City Hall would turn the other way while the First Ward collected money for the Democratic party from gambling houses and whorehouses, and let the district run wide open. Bathhouse gave Hinky Dink the good news from City Hall, "Go ahead, Mike."

Hinky Dink went ahead. He set up a collection system, he built a power organization, and a defense fund for the protection of the vice crowd who had the money and were willing to shell out. Any of Bathhouse John's and Hinky Dink's followers who got into a jam would have legal aid and political pressure on their side. Two lawyers went on full pay at ten thousand dollars a year; they had to be handy with habeas corpus writs. It was noted—later—that the two ward heelers paid themselves the *first* ten thousand dollars in the kitty. The talk was that even rape and murder could be fixed in the First Ward. More importantly for the Levee, the gambling raids petered out.

The Levee, a voyeur's world, was the titillative district visitors in the 1890s and the 1900s liked to visit. "Going down the line" was a must for many out-of-towners. It became a prosperous protected district. Bathhouse and the Dink were treated as ministers plenipotentiary of a rich country.

Vice ran wild and wide open on the Levee; depraved brothels, obscene concert saloons flourished. South of the Levee was created the Tenderloin, between Eighteenth and Twenty-second streets. Gambling reached new heights. The King of the Bunco Artists, Tom O'Brien, in a few months had profits of half a million dollars. The whorehouses ran double shifts, and the girls displayed themselves as window showcases. Streetwalkers moved freely through the section in infectious exuberance. In a sermon it was said that "Chicago is again the wickedest wide open town in America."

Bathhouse and Hinky Dink were the leaders of the district. Mayor Harrison had honored Bathhouse by putting him at the head of the World's Fair Reception Committee, greeting the honored dignitaries from all over the world. Hinky Dink didn't want much public attention—but as for Bathhouse, the crowds had looked over the big man with medals and badges, big in his Prince Albert coat and high hat, and cried out, "That's *the* Bathhouse!"

He greeted, in his impassioned eloquence, Lillian Russell in her box at the Washington Park track on the day of the running of the American Derby, offering her the freedom of the city and its pleasures. Girls from Ike Bloom's dance hall, done up in organdy and big hats for the day, cheered and applauded the two, big, handsome man and woman. Lillian was no slim nymph.

On the Levee, Bathhouse John would greet strangers with "Come on, I'll buy you a beer." Hinky Dink merely saw to the running of his saloon and the building up of the political power of the two of them. He continued the collecting of the defense and protection money from the houses and bars.

In time, Hinky Dink seemed sure of election as an alderman himself. He had supported Bathhouse at elections and felt such an office might be his, too. He ran for alderman. The Municipal Voters' League issued a report that Michael Kenna, the Dink, "was intimately associated with the gambling element." Hardly news, he shrugged it off. "Sure I associate with gamblers. Why now shouldn't I? I like a good game myself."

Election day in the First Ward was a madness of activity and fraud. Bathhouse, Hinky Dink, and all their aides moved from poll to poll, heavy-laden with sacks of silver coins, pockets loaded with silver dollars. They paid for votes on the spot. Hinky Dink was elected alderman, 4373 votes to his rival's 1811. The silver message had been heard.

The newspapers reported the First Ward had gone mad the night before the election. The Star League, a voters' pressure group, paraded with dangerous flaring torches. Last speeches and curses were hurled at rival candidates, and the saloons didn't close that night, and the whorehouses let no girl sleep or have much time to sit on a *boîte de nuit*.

Election night, *after* victory, again the streets were wild. Again women and men in all stages of drunkenness packed the streets of the Levee. Huge bonfires burned, made up of barrels, storefronts, signs, stairways, awnings, anything that could be torn free and put to the blaze. Hoodlums and young gangs began to set off fireworks, flinging them under the bellies of carriage horses and the wheels of the streetcars.

The Republican headquarters remained in silent darkness, took no part in the spectacle of their defeat. The jeering, mocking pimps, whores, gamblers, sightseers paraded by, cheering and passing bottles. Great mobs of them decided to visit Hinky Dink's saloon "to wish the little fella the best of it, and God bless." But the lights were out there, too, and the blinds pulled down. The Dink was at the mayor's headquarters being patted on his slim shoulders at his own successes, and the so many votes he had turned out for a grateful Mayor Harrison.

Hinky Dink was a sharer. On his mind were the strange voters he had had to shelter and feed: the drifters, floaters, down-and-outers who were so important on election day. They were so much a part of his political machine, producers of the ballots he could deliver. On Clark Street, south of Van Buren, in the 1890s, he set up the Workingmen's Exchange, where for over thirty years he fed and lodged the moochers, tramps, hobos, the out-of-lucks, the jobless. They could have a free lunch, and for a nickel, a schooner of beer which was, as the sign outside said,

THE LARGEST AND COOLEST IN THE CITY.

Over the exchange was the Alaska Hotel, a skid-row flophouse, where three hundred men a night could sleep and scratch in a fog of their own strong odors. And where, before an election, Hinky Dink could crowd in three hundred extra floaters, all with a vote, or two, or three, or more.

The Dink, with the position of alderman, had more graft than ever pouring in; another man might have bought a mansion, a string of racehorses, even a false Rembrandt or Corot. But Hinky Dink just opened another saloon, *his* idea of social status on the Levee. It was a plush place, at 307 Clark Street. Here was Hinky Dink's private little office, out back, where special visitors were admitted to sip the brew, or be taken out front to inspect the grand bar over whose mirror was set the Latin phrase:

IN VINO VERITAS

The Dink, chewing on a cigar, would grin. "Now that there means when you get yer snoot full, you'll tell yer right name."

"In wine there is truth," translated one *Tribune* reporter, adding, "but hardly ever in 1st Ward politics."

Waiting for an election at the Alaska Hotel was a nest of down-and-outers, lushes, broken men, hobos wintering in Chicago, scratching their fleas, singing:

> *Beside a rail-road water tank on a cold and wintery day,*
> *In an open box-car a dying hobo lay.*
>
> *His partner sat beside him, with low and droopin' head,*
> *Listening to the last words the dying hobo said:*
>
> *"I'm going," said the hobo, "to a land that's clear and bright,*
> *Where hammocks grow on bushes, and people stay out all night.*

You do not have to work at all, not even change your socks,
And little drops of alcohol came trickling down the rocks."
FOLK SONG

So, fed with Dink's stew—with a mooched jit for a beer—how could they not be loyal to the First Ward while outside a cold wind blew from the lake and "they were bringin' the brass monkeys, it was that freezin'."

The Republicans never understand the human element that so often decide elections because of a gratitude.

"Oh, tell my gal in Chicago, no more I'm gonna roam;
I hear the fast mail coming, I'm on my way back home
I hear the fast mail coming, I'll catch it bye and bye,
Oh, gal o' mine, oh, gal o' mine, it ain't so hard to die."

His head fell back, his eyes fell in
As he breathed this last refrain,
His partner swiped his shoes and socks . . .
HOBO SONG BOOK, C. 1907

51

THE CAR BARN BANDITS

The criminals . . . shoot quicker and with less provocation . . . and the detective who pits himself against these desperadoes and hopes to come out with a whole skin must be nervy to a degree and as quick as chain lightning in handling a gun.
TEST FOR APPLICANTS TO THE CHICAGO DETECTIVE FORCE

It was no wonder the police, the detectives, were cynical about the desire of the city officials really to stop criminal activities. The *Record Herald* could report on one period of raids in the first decade of the twentieth century to close the whorehouses: "Five minutes of real police activity, which gives a rough idea of how such matters can be handled when they want them handled, wiped out the South Side Levee district in Chicago. It ceased to exist as if by magic, not because of enforcement of the law, but because of the apprehension of it. A few minutes before six o'clock last evening policemen began nailing the doors of Tommy Owens' cafe 2033–35 Armour Avenue. They were acting on the orders of Mayor Harrison, delivered at last in an unmistakable manner. Echoes of the blows of their hammers had hardly died away before the entire district was deserted. By six o'clock not a woman was to be found in it."

But the paper knew payoffs would reopen the dives soon. Protection just cost more. As the Illinois Crime Survey found out, "The fact dive-keepers were willing to pay so much gave evidence of the profitableness to the police of the old segregated district."

The gang of the early 1900s best remembered today by old Chicagoans was the Car Barn Bandits. Gustave Marx, Harvey Van Dine, Peter Neidermeyer liked to think of themselves as the Automatic Trio rather than by the title the newspapers gave them, the Car Barn Bandits. The stooge of the gang was Emil Roeski, whom they paid off in nickels after a job.

The boys of the gang, scabrous, malicious, mean, grew up near the freight yards of the Northwestern Railroad, a fearful slum of diseased brick, smoke, Dickensian hard times. The families of the boys were poor, but toilers: farmers, working stiffs trapped in dull routine, fertile, overbreeding. The gang had the rare privilege of graduating from grammar school. Roeski got a job in a brewery, the rest, Gus, Harv, Pete, joined a criminal gang with the title of the Monticello Pleasure and Athletic Club.

The three soon dominated the club by their daring and their powerhouse drive to shameless street crimes, beginning as fruit robbers, wagon thieves. They stole brass and lead pipes from buildings. Growing older, they began boldly to hold up people under streetlights, break into houses and stores, snatch at a purse, try picking a pocket, rolling a drunk, coshing a late-hour traveler.

In 1903, the gang, now in their early twenties, felt they were ready for big-time crime. They found a gang hideout in a cave in the Indiana sand dunes, near a railroad track by Miller's Station. They acquired a dozen six-shooters and a few hundred rounds of ammunition. Roeski, the dunce, they debauched. He said later he joined them because he didn't like his job, "and they fixed me out with guns." On a hot July day they got seventy dollars holding up the Clybourne Junction of the Northwestern Railroad, shooting the stationmaster, but not mortally. They were set as entrepreneurs of violence for hard cash. Next day they jumped in to heist the patrons of Ernest Spires' saloon on North Ashland Avenue, killing a boy who panicked and ran for it. As Van Dine was later to explain, "We cleared $2.35 . . . shootin' came cheap." In the next few days they held up two more Chicago saloons for the paltry sum of twenty-five dollars. From then on, saloons were held up every few days. Killings, with no rhetorical pretensions, just happened. "I had two guns in my hands," said Van Dine, "and covered two bystanders named LaGross and Johnson. I let 'em have both guns at once and Johnson fell hit in the stomach. LaGross got to the door and I gave him another shot. He dropped in the doorway. Then I went home. I slept fine. We got eight dollars out of that haul. We killed two men—four dollars apiece."

The big haul came at the end of August when they got $2250 in a holdup of the Chicago City Railway Company, murdering a motorman named James Johnson and a clerk, Francis Stewart, during the trigger-happy event. They divided the take in Jackson Park, Roeski's share being five dollars.

The Car Barn Killers, as they were now called, were not original in spending their criminal take; it went for whiskey and for whores. The police, moved by the press outcry at the senseless murders, began looking for young hoodlums who had no jobs, had reputations of being hard guys in their neighborhood, and—in inebriated juxtaposition—suddenly had lots of money to spend in bars and on entertaining tarts. It was that easy to identify the gang as suspects. By November the police decided to take in Marx, Van Dine, and Neidermeyer for questioning. Orders for arrests went out.

Detectives Quinn and Blake found Marx in a boozer on Addison Street. Quinn put a hand to the young gunzel's shoulder. "Chief wants to talk to you."

Marx, in direct reflex action, pulled two guns and began firing, killing Quinn at once. Blake pulled his own weapon and hit Marx in the right leg. At this sudden shock of return fire, Marx tossed down his guns and meekly held up his hands. At the Sheffield Avenue Police lockup, recovering somewhat, he cried out in protest: "You can't do nothin' to me. I only shot a cop. Anybody got a right to shoot a cop!"

It seemed to the police a poor idea of law, and less logic, as they slapped Marx around. Neidermeyer and Van Dine, still free, made plans to dynamite the police station to free their pal. But on November 25, the newspapers carried banner stories that Marx had confessed and ratted on his pals. So much for the honor among thieves. The boys rented a room across the street that had a direct view of the entrance to the police station in Van Dine's line of aim. He intended to shoot that fink stoolie Marx when he was moved to police headquarters . . . shoot him as a "dirty squealer."

Their blasé, fearless days seemed over. In sudden fear, they gave up the assassination idea and, with Roeski, went to their sanddune hideout, leaving town by an electric trolley car bound for East Chicago, then walking. It was still in the days before going on the lam was done with a stolen high-powered car.

The boys had forgotten, or overlooked the fact, that Marx knew of the hideout. He had been worked over in the station house, "eating knuckles," and told the police of the dunes cave. One morning, ten plainclothes men and harness bulls of the Chicago police showed up on the dunes—armed with rifles and police specials. They had crossed the state line into Indiana, niceties of states' rights not being of importance just then. Some civilian posses soon formed, farmers and loafers at loose ends among the Hoosiers. Nine A.M. was zero hour as the police closed in and firing began from both sides. In the curtain of gunfire, the three gangsters were hit, as well as two detectives badly bloodied, one of whom, Joseph Driscoll, died a few days later from gunshot wounds.

Some fifty rounds had been fired when the three bleeding bandits came out, firing two pistols each. They scrambled and got into a patch of woods, cops and yipping posses hightailing after them. Firing all the time. It seemed to the man hunters too dangerous to go in after the bandits. Roeski, however, was out of the fight with a slug in his belly. He wandered off alone down the tracks to Aetna, collapsed there, and, moaning, waited for his arrest and hopes of medical aid.

Van Dine and Neidermeyer managed to shake off the wary hunters in the woods, and thrashed their way to East Tolleston, where they came across a gravel train standing still, steaming up for rolling while the engine crew was drinking coffee. The two gangsters climbed into the engine cab with pistols showing; the engineer and fireman stared openmouthed. A brakeman came in over the tender to see what was up, and Neidermeyer killed him with one shot. His excuse later was, "He tried to take my gun away. . . . I'm a bad man if anyone tried to do that."

The two desperate, wounded outlaws had the locomotive uncoupled and the engine run down the line two miles to East Liverpool. Here progress was stopped by a locked switch. They couldn't smash the switch open. They ran for it, right into a cornfield, into the arms of a posse out with shotguns. The gangsters gave up—not trying to shoot it out. They were turned over to the Chicago police.

Mayor Harrison, Jr., a face reaffirmed by a large curled moustache, was in need of good press coverage, so he had the captured men brought to the office of Police Chief Francis O'Neill at City Hall. Escorted by two patrol wagons filled with the law, the deed was done. A crowd of several thousand had collected on the news that the Car Barn Bandits were being brought in after a daring battle and capture. As a French traveler wrote home, the criminals' lives were in Chicago . . . "Sports et divertissements."

The chief's office became a production number of Law's Victory, starring the mayor, the chief, the bandits, played for a group of reporters and city officials. It was all very formal, yet happy; all present had a sense of participation, the boys being introduced to the mayor, and to the chief of police. The chief, himself, washed Van Dine's face clean for posing for the primitive news cameras of the period. The detectives, refreshed at saloons, entered into the spirit of the thing, talking of Van Dine's skill with a pistol, ". . . a great shot. An officer named Zimmer was behind a tree. . . . Van Dine got him *twice.*"

It was clear the bandits were getting the royal-celebrities treatment as folk heroes, and the mayor was getting public notice. Van Dine, modestly, in the manner of a later film actor, Gary Cooper, just said, "Could'a killed a dozen men . . . if there hadda been any pleasure in it."

Like Dostoevski's hero in *Crime and Punishment*, the boys were happy to detail their guilt. They talked of their careers in crime. The trial was held in January of 1904, and was a grand show. Van Dine was the star, giving a good performance as a contemporary folk hero and dead shot. He was right out of a trashy Western novel. For the press, after the death sentence, he did a drawing of the gravestone and added the texts of those to be buried there.

HERE LIES THE NOTORIAS GUS MARX, DESPERADO
DIED MAR. IST, 1904.

HERE LIES THE FAMOUS DEAD SHOT, PETER NEIDERMEYER,
AGED 23, DIED MAR. IST, 1904.

HERE LIES THE RED CROOK, HARVEY VAN DINE,
AGED 21, DIED WITH HIS BOOTS ON, MAR. IST, 1904.

Only the dates were wrong when they went to the gallows in the county jail, "to dance on air at the end of a rope." And, as usual, nobody thought of Roeski, who had a separate trial and was sent to Joliet for life. (Mrs. Marx blamed the bad destiny of her son Gustave on "dime novels, whisky, cigars, cigarets [*Tribune* spelling] and evil associates." No gangster died without a mother, if available to the press, telling that her son was really a good boy, led astray.)

Certainly the reception the Car Barn Gang got at City Hall after their capture seemed glamorous to many other young hoodlums—no matter how young. The *Tribune* reported: "It is not un-usual for a boy six years old to be arrested for a serious offence. Boys who should be at home learning their ABC's are often found armed with cheap revolvers and knives. At Maxwell Street station the ar-rests of boys under sixteen average nearly sixty a month. Most of these arrests are for larceny and burglary. Some for holdups." And almost proudly, hysterically, an editor would warn that "Chicago is terrorized by . . . criminals who have helped to make the name 'Chicago' a byword for crime breeding throughout the country."

Killing a man seemed to set up a slum boy equal with Buffalo Bill, Kit Carson, Billy the Kid, the heroes of the dime novels they read while moving their lips. It was too early to blame the motion pictures, the senseless cant of television. Still there was the Formby gang of three boys—ages sixteen, seventeen, and eighteen. Formby killed a streetcar conductor in 1904. Dulfer killed two men when robbing a saloon. He said that he had "shot both at the same time."

From the 1890s into the first decade of the twentieth century, Chicago never stopped growing and the crime rate never stopped climbing. A sort of underworld Parkinson's Law was significantly present. The city was in size two hundred square miles of territory, and the population was to go over two million. Taxes for the rich, not too highly or fairly estimated, stood at two and a half billion dollars, and the daily bank clearances were forty million dollars a day. No wonder the city was proud of its vitality; men act out their times; there is no alternative.

Crime figures—nearly correct—were hard to come by. And now for commissions to ponder, there were the immigrants, mostly hardworking, ignorant, often piously bigoted, but eager, trying to better themselves. They, too, were often contributing to the rising crime rate, and diluting the native American and the Irish-Ameri-can thieves, the black criminals that had been around in succeeding assaults on society almost since the founding of the city. The alli-ance of whorehouse keepers, gamblers, ward heelers, and city officials had grown more corrupt, for there was more to steal, to col-lect graft from, and the aldermen had more to offer in return, better protection, bigger city contracts, trolley rights, licenses, favors.

By the beginning of the new century, there was a robbery every three hours, a stickup every six hours, and murder every day. Compared to the vast, rising crime figures of the 1970s, today's lawlessness and the hatred in the minorities' ghettos, it is not impressive. The early 1900s were to many people a more peaceful, innocent age (in most of Chicago's streets in middle-class neighborhoods, it was safe to walk at night). These figures shocked a nation then, a country still in a horse-and-buggy state of being and mind. The juries— even the sensational murder trials lasted but a few days—convicted criminals in county sites without the courts pampering the thief and murderer. Only in the big cities—and only when aided by city officials—was the criminal as yet able to make a mockery of the courts, and lawyers and defendants, create circuses.

The result in Chicago, battling of crime in the 1900s was usually a "Committee of Twenty-Five," or a "Citizens' Association," dedicated to "eradicating crime in Chicago."

This talk was nonsense to those who knew the score. One hundred fifty indictments against Chicago bosses of policy games in 1900 resulted in not *one* conviction. No clear rationalization of justice being effective was possible. Mayor Carter Harrison, Jr., was a chip off the old live-and-let-live block. Like his father, he listened to reason as offered by the ward bosses who controlled the votes. In six weeks he pardoned—many records show, at the request of aldermen—110 criminals, all sentenced for robbery and other criminal acts. The mayor, when his attention was called to the climbing crime rate, suggested—with peculiar awareness—that citizens might "carry revolvers strapped outside their clothing." That fashion hint did not catch on.

The grafting aldermen had decided in 1903 to take the heat off their own boodle-grabbing by investigating the police department and its unholy connections with saloon owners, brothels, and gambling houses. It was a snow job. After millions of words and sittings of weeks, the police promised "every criminal known to us would be run out of town." However, nothing much changed; the inherent failing of human nature that produced profits was untamable. To get a more honest picture of Chicago's police connection with crime, a former U.S. army officer, Captain Alexander Piper, aided by a secret squad of New York City detectives, did his own investigating and finally submitted his report.

The city, it showed, did have some honest, hardworking police, men of integrity and intelligence. But, the report went on, "as a whole the force was inefficient, insufficient, ten percent of it decrepit or too fat for service, another hundred unfit because of viciousness, bad habits. Practically no discipline, no protection given pedestrians, no proper handling of traffic. Many police were afraid of thieves, many lacked intelligence to cope with crime, many shirked duty. The entire force was slack in appearance, many loafed, drank in saloons while on duty, many were in collusion with saloon keepers. Of all of those found drinking, just one paid for his drink. The report recommended a thousand men between the ages of twenty-one and twenty-five be added to the police immediately, another thousand within two years."

The report was filed away with other reformers' texts.

Mr. Dooley remained doubtful about reports and reformers: "A man that wud expict to thrain lobsthers to fly is called a lunatic; but a man that thinks men can be turned into angels by an iliction is called a rayformer and r-remains at large."

The average slum dweller had his own idea of the system and the police.

> *If I was to work, and save all I earn,*
> *I could buy me a bar and have money to burn.*
>
> *I passed by a saloon, and heard someone snore,*
> *And I found the bartender asleep on the floor.*
>
> *I stayed there and drank till a copper came in,*
> *And he put me asleep with a slap on the chin.*
>
> *Next morning in court I was still in a haze,*
> *When the judge looked at me, he said, "Thirty days."*
> STREET SONG

52

AUTHORS AND JOURNALISTS

We don't have much use for poetry in Chicago, except in streetcar ads.
GEORGE HORACE LORIMER, THE SATURDAY EVENING POST

Actually in the second half of the nineteenth century, Chicago was as alert as Boston and New York to literary trends and had its own publishing house, Stone & Kimball, which, while it didn't publish much of local authors, had done well for Ibsen and Maeterlinck, George Santayana's first book of verse. On a more popular level, Eugene Field was writing a daily column, "Sharps and Flats," which later made column writing a career for many. ("May Field's sin in pioneering modern columnists be forgiven"—Carl Sandburg to the author.) He hung out with literary cronies, fellow journalists, and solid drinkers at McClurg's Book Store in the red-brick building at Monroe and Wabash. Their corner of the shop was labeled "Saints and Sinners Corner," because they were often joined by a Reverend Frank Gunsaulus. ("People don't have names the way they used to"—Ben Hecht.) The reverend had even written a novel, *Monk and Knight.* One listener to the corner later said of it, "Just talk; no Greek Gods clutching their members in drunken orgies."

Slanderous talk was at Billy Boyle's Chop House, where the tougher reporters gathered. From here, after a reaffirmation of life by whiskey, it was a good walk to the Press Club to meet Melville E. Stone of the *Daily News*. Here literature took a back seat to fantastic sunset-to-dawn poker games. The wrecks of careers piled up at the Press Club like shells at a clambake.

The celebrated and prosperous journalists were often members. George Ade hung out here; his *Fables in Slang* made him the Damon Runyon of his day. Booth Tarkington, if in town, would be at the bar with friends, fighting a failing battle with drink and blindness; Opie Read, publisher of the Chicago weekly, *The Arkansas Traveler*. He wrote a best seller, *The Jucklins*, that sold a million copies, but at railroad newsstands. The club was irrelevant to major events and mockings.

The genteel tradition was maintained by a Chicago group that went by the name of The Little Room. It met Friday afternoons over tea and watercress sandwiches, and also chewed Ibsen and Shaw. Here was to be heard Harriet Monroe, who brought a new interest in poetry to Chicago and then to the English-speaking world. Poets, too, now forgotten, like Wallace Rice, William Vaughn Moody, novelists Hamlin Garland, George Barr McCutcheon (a wow with *Graustark*, the cloak and sword epic), his brother, the splendid cartoonist John McCutcheon, Floyd Dell, and a top-ranking, much neglected novelist, Henry Blake Fuller, now in full eclipse, but well worth reading. Effusive, serene, knowledgeable, a Chicago Henry James.

Fuller was an exotic for Chicago. He had been published first at fifteen. A homosexual maneuvering in a society where he had to keep his private emotions well hidden, he wrote excellent novels about the city. His *The Cliff Dwellers* made an impression on the big-time critics in the East. It was one of the first novels that wrote of the thousands upon thousands who lived in and worked in the new tall buildings, some called them skyscrapers, that were beginning to appear in Chicago and in the nation. The tedious and redundant tensions of such a life were to lead to early themes of Sinclair Lewis.

America was not yet ready for realists, and Fuller wrote most of his later books with European settings. His last novel, *The Procession*—slightly disguised—was on a daring homosexual theme but created little attention. Coming back after the turn of the century from Europe, Fuller became the spark of the Cliff Dwellers, not named after his novel, but after Southwest Indian dwellings. The group existed on the top floor of Orchestra Hall.

Chicago also produced Frank Baum's *The Wonderful Wizard of Oz*, aided with pictures by local artist, Arthur Denslow. The magazine, *The Dial*, was shaped here, to become a worldwide messenger of the best poetry: Pound, Eliot, Joyce, D. H. Lawrence, and others. Soon on the horizon would come Carl Sandburg, Maxwell Bodenheim, and riotous reporters in a desultory hunt for fame. Charles MacArthur, Ben Hecht, also roaring editors of violent city rooms creating a whole bawdy school of hairy journalism: loud, romantic, and not too accurate. One city editor would quote Aeschylus, "Take heart, suffering when it climbs highest lasts but a little time."

The giant who matured in Chicago was Theodore Dreiser. He had first come there in 1884, as a boy, when his brother Paul Dresser (he had changed his name) was twenty-three and a blackfaced singer and songwriter with the Wizard Oil Troupe, a medicine show that toured the outskirts of Chicago and the surrounding countryside. Later Paul was end man for the Thatcher, Primrose and West Minstrel Show, always a citywide favorite. *The Dresser Song Book* was in print, and Teddy Dreiser was to help his brother with some lyrics for songs.

Dreiser had come to Chicago with his three sisters, Mame, Emma, and Theresa, two of whose life stories he would use as his models in *Sister Carrie* and *Jennie Gerhardt*. In 1884 they were all living in a Chicago flat, and Dreiser was a cashboy in a Madison Avenue dry-goods store.

Emma met L. A. Hopkins (in the novel *Sister Carrie*, George Hurstwood, of a truly swell saloon), the cashier at Chapin & Gore's fancy downtown bar. He was a suave, respected man-about-town, married and seemingly settled in his way of life. He stole thirty-five hundred dollars from the firm's safe, and he and Emma Dreiser eloped to Montreal, two people feeling that the life of contemplation is not enough. For Hopkins it was full ruin. The town took the affair with a shrug, but the newspapers built it up into a Chicago scandal. Hopkins returned all of the money by mail, all but eight hundred dollars already spent. The couple moved on to New York

City where they ran a low boardinghouse, renting rooms to whores. Such is the basic material of *Sister Carrie*.

In Dreiser's adolescence, this runaway sister made a great impression on him, but for him there was as yet only low-paid, miserable work. In 1887, when he was sixteen, he had odd jobs: a Halsted Street dishwasher, duty in a hardware store cleaning old stoves; he was a stock boy and sized canvases for artists.

Paul Dresser was a shiny success; all Chicago was singing his hit song, "I Believe It If My Mother Told Me."

When Dreiser was nineteen, he worked in the office of a real-estate man, Asa Conklin on Ogden Avenue, for three dollars a week. A year later he drove a laundry truck for Munger Brothers on Madison Avenue. Dreiser was piling up impressions of Chicago that would make his picture of the city and its people of before the turn of the century into solid, unique literature, with a writing style as lyrical as a flat trolley wheel.

By 1892, Dreiser, aching to write, had talked himself into a job on a fourth-rate newspaper, the *Chicago Daily Globe*. He covered convention meetings, interviewed passing celebrities at the Palmer House, Grand Pacific, the Richelieu, saw how the prominent, the rich, the self-inflated lived the good fat life of women, wine, gourmet food, dressed to the nines. He met men like Brand Whitlock, George Ade, who had made it in Chicago. What fine privilege was theirs, he thought. His copy editor on the paper, John Milo Maxwell, gave him a hint of the self-indulgent, greedy world he now faced. "Life, Teddy, is a goddamn stinking treacherous game, and nine hundred and ninety-nine men out of a thousand, are bastards." But this did not answer Teddy's tough metaphysical questions.

When Grover Cleveland was nominated in Chicago for President, Maxwell shrugged it off. "All politics are corrupt—heroes are only successful thieves." But what more was there beyond some stoic acceptance of mortality? Dreiser listened; he was still a lanky country boy, a bit chinless, puffy-lipped, adrift in the city; he was a cartoonist image at six feet and a half inch tall, thin as a walking cane, weighing but 137 pounds. He watched in wonder the World's Fair buildings going up in Jackson Park. He had his sexual hang-ups, dreams of impossible gratifications. He tried to think clearly of what he read at the Newberry Library: Hardy, Balzac, Herbert Spencer. He saw life as amoral rather than immoral. His work as a Chicago reporter made him sense that most conventional morality, as proclaimed by the Armours, Pullmans, Carnegies, was a fraud. Every living creature, busy Chicago seemed to say, is a victim of fate, all of them—Mrs. Leslie Carter, Mrs. Potter Palmer, Hinky Dink, Bathhouse John, even the great Charles Yerkes. Yerkes, a wily predator, pursued women (as Dreiser did), had fifteen lawyers at 150 thousand a year to protect him from his entanglements with women. (Dreiser was to write of him, "All life was . . . the strong preying on the weak," as Frank Cowperwood felt in *The Titan*.) Even the poor reporter eating his sixty-cent meal at Rectors, when he had the money, felt his own amoral drive. His final education was given him by the city editor, John T. McEnnis, a brilliant alcoholic. "Don't drink and don't get married whatever you do. A wife will be a big handicap. . . . Can you spare me a dollar for a pint?"

It was McEnnis—the price of a few pints was worth it—who got Dreiser a better job on the *St. Louis Globe-Democrat* at twenty dollars a week. Chicago was Dreiser's Yale and Harvard—as a whaling ship was Melville's—his education into the American scene. In 1912, when Dreiser came back to Chicago, he mingled with Edgar Lee Masters of the *Spoon River Anthology*. Dreiser wore his astrakhan-collared coat while viewing the literary revolt at Schogl's Restaurant, or at the Little Theatre in the Fine Arts Building on Michigan Boulevard, a theater founded by Maurice Browne, that played Shaw, Strindberg, Schnitzler—and had ideas from Stanislavski and Reinhardt. There Dreiser saw Kirah Markham star in *The Trojan Women*, and planned a seduction. And claimed a victory.

The Chicago of its literary flourishing was under the eyes of John Cowper Powys, an admitted voyeur, and Arthur Davison Ficke, a lawyer, poet, collector of Japanese prints. On the fringe, seeking admission, were shaggy Sherwood Anderson, Margaret Anderson (no relative) who would in her magazine, *Little Review*, publish part of Joyce's *Ulysses* and irk the Post Office Department. Margaret had no liking at all for Dreiser. "He could establish a quick sex sympathy . . . had no more wit than a cow." Some said they both showed interest in the same girl.

Mayor Funkhouser was the Chicago book and art censor. A

man of laconic idiocy, he arrested a dealer for selling a copy of the inane painting, *September Morn*. Dreiser, in a letter to the press, spoke out against such "pigmy, illiterate minds . . . A big city is not a teacup to be seasoned by old maids. Leave things be; the wilder the better for those who are strong enough to survive, and the future of Chicago will then be known by the great men it bred."

Dreiser had not had an easy time of it with his Chicago novels. He had spent seven months writing *Sister Carrie*, considered by many critics to be the best portrait of a real woman in our literature. Frank Norris, originally of Chicago, in 1900 a reader at Doubleday, had admired it when submitted and the firm had published it, after much misgivings. Only 456 copies of the book had been sold, and the author's royalties had come to $68.40.

Nor had Teddy Dreiser taken his newspaper editor's advice not to drink or to marry. Dreiser's first wife was the handicap, even if Dreiser was as wildly involved full time with various other women as his model Yerkes. (And he ended his life like so many American writers of great talent, a lush, as did Jack London, O. Henry, Tarkington, Sinclair Lewis, Fitzgerald, Hemingway, Faulkner. The mood of Ecclesiastes and the total absurdity of mankind—as writers saw it—leads but to the bottle.)

53

SILVER THROAT—W.J.B.

Not again!

AN EDITOR ON READING QUOTE FROM THE "CROSS OF GOLD" SPEECH
IN THIS TEXT

Chicago was a good city from which to launch a political career. Here, with a puritan bellicosity and the spiritual appeal to make an atheist weep, William Jennings Bryan made his beginnings, politically, with his famous articulated appeal to the dreams and hopes of the Middle Western farmer and the man on the street—his speech at the 1896 Democratic Convention in Chicago. There had been nothing like it before at political conventions, and nothing since. Perhaps this plea for silver coinage was the most electrifying moment in American politics:

"You shall not press down upon the brow of labor this crown of thorns, you shall not crucify mankind on a cross of gold!"

At that line, Bryan cast his arms straight out as if nailed to a cross. He dropped his arms, took one step back. There was no sound from the transfixed audience for several seconds. Then pandemonium filled the hall. A tremendous ovation began to swell. Bryan's supporters hoisted the thirty-six-year-old Congressman to their shoulders and paraded him about the hall. The band struck up a Sousa march.

The "Boy Orator of the Platte," "The Great Commoner," was on his way to fame and predilection to lost causes. The following day, July 10, 1896, he was nominated for President on the fifth ballot. He lost, as he also did in 1900 and 1908.

Bryan appealed to the simple people who sensed most politics had little honesty, and that little with the absurdities and deteriorations plainly seen in the actions of the elected officials who ran the city, and those who ran the nation. That hot July day in Chicago, when the young Bryan ended his speech on the silver coinage issue, a false hope went soaring with him; that moral indignation would purify the country and recover an old ideal.

It was at once clear to the powers in the land that William Jennings Bryan had to be destroyed. Three times they kept him from the White House. The methods of the first turnback of his try for the higher office pretty much set the pattern, even if the campaign of 1896 was the most cold-blooded in its attack on the democratic system; not to be seen with such muscle, naked power, until the big election money seized most of the media in the 1960s and 1970s.

Bryan was attacked at once by the respectable press as the rider of the "wave of the socialist revolution," an attack on the "rights of property" to ruin laborers, merchants, farmers, miners, and country lawyers: "this league of hell." Tumult, preparations to meet the threat; a death struggle, as the wheels of industry halted.

A great leader for free enterprise was Boss Mark Hanna, chairman of the Republican party, who it was noticed "showed an energy, a cool nerve for the great emergency that was akin to genius," levying huge assessments, $400,000 from the beef group, $250,000 from Standard Oil. "You make me think of a lot of scared hens," said Hanna at a meeting of industrialists. James Hill, the railroad magnate, changed political allegiance from the Democratic to Republican. "There is an epidemic craze among farmers and . . . those who receive wages or salaries," he wrote J. P. Morgan. The managers of the McKinley campaign "should get to work at once. . . . I will do anything or everything in my power to further the end we all have in view."

The Big Kill was on. Money poured out. Hill bought a newspaper, the *Daily Globe*, "to keep it from falling into the hands of the free-silver interests"; a Mr. Archbold sent money for a newspaper in the East. The *New York Sun, New York Tribune* joined in. Workmen were warned all employment would be forfeited should Bryan make it. Pamphlets by the million were circulated. On the eve of the election, the cities were decked with flags and a monstrous Republican parade took place from Wall Street; eighty thousand marchers against Bryan; one section, five thousand bankers and brokers, cheered for Pierpont Morgan. Before such an irresistible money force, brilliantly led by Hanna, Bryan went to decisive defeat. Hanna telegraphed McKinley: "God's in his Heaven—all's right with the world."

McKinley went on to meet the assassin's bullet, and Chicago meat-packers proceeded to prepare the poisoned beef that killed so many American soldiers in Cuba.

54

BLACK HAND, WHITE HAND

The land is full of bloody crimes, and the city is full of violence.
EZEKIEL 7:23

There is a sensitivity, an insistent cry of purity of purpose, in racial groups—the very word *racial* is a dirty word to some—their hackles rise when a historian mentions the ethnic background of a criminal. In New York City in the early 1970s, there was a league of Italian-Americans set up to protest mention of the Mafia or the Cosa Nostra as libel against them all—ironic, since the group was financed and led by the family of a man the FBI had identified as being the leader of a notorious Mafia family and its raffish assemblies in the East.

Crime knows no racial or national barriers; one has but to look at the evil record of those music-loving, schmaltzy, sentimental folk, the Germans in the twentieth century, whose horrible conduct in torture, extermination, and the slaughter of about twenty-five million men, women, and children, Jews, Russians, Frenchmen, gypsies, and others, is a blot on Teutonic *Kultur* never to be erased. And, as H. L. Mencken said, they were "the most civilized lovers of knowledge and music in Europe." So one must not look on the story of the Italian Black Hand, nor the later bootleg vice lords that emerged from it in Chicago, as committing an entire ethnic group to evil. The Black Hand gave an Italian tinge of *scandalo* way back around 1850. But it was active only among its own kind, in its own neighborhood, the Italian and Sicilian districts on Oak and West Taylor streets, and Grand and Wentworth avenues. Here in the odor of capocollo, polenta, and eggplant parmigiana, it existed.

For over three decades, the Black Hand as groups—rather than a society—brought terror to the vast majority of Italians in Chicago. Some estimates say the groups, with guerrilla ambush cunning, killed four hundred of their countrymen. Little Italy had a focal point, "Death Corner," where Milton and Oak streets met to the dealings in herbs, pasta, sauces, red wine, and old clothes. The crime groups worked with knife, with torture, bombs of nitro and gunpowder. One killer, known as Shotgun Man, is said to have knocked off about twelve of the thirty-eight Italians and Sicilians murdered in Little Italy in a period of fourteen months. In one record period of March 1911, in seventy-two hours, he methodically murdered four people. The law never caught up with him.

The Black Hand actually was made up of between seventy and eighty gangs of Italians when the twentieth century began. They had no main head, or interlocking organization, but continued to operate as independent units of terrorists in such categories as blackmail, kidnapping, and murder. There was no national or international organization as there is with the more modern Mafia. The Black Hand, as one unsigned criminologist report said, was only a *"modus operandi."* Cruelty needed no particular motive—it appears ingrained in human nature. To this add greed, and the Black Hand as trained by the gangsters of Italy and Sicily, the original Mafia and the Camorra. The term Black Hand came into use in American cities because the extortion texts usually contained a pen and ink drawing of a black hand, besides such primitive evil symbols as crosses, daggers, and skull and crossbones.

Locked into a society of simple Italians: laborers, shopkeepers, small merchants, speaking the new language poorly, or not at all (even their priests often did not speak English), the communities of the immigrants seemed trapped, victims of the most cruel and perverted of their own kind.

The Black Hand thrived on this isolation. The victim had to be someone who had money and property; and frugal, hardworking Italians, with some sense of merchandising, loan sharking, produce-marketing or real estate, could pile up some small and even large fortunes. The danger came when an Italian bought a house or building, or his wife wore a diamond—all sure signs he had made money and was ripe for plucking. He was then sent a letter asking for money. And warnings, if it was not forthcoming, that his home or shop or business would be given the attention of a black powder bomb or dynamite.

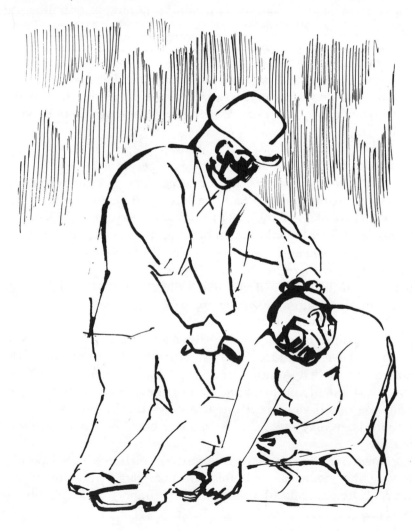

The next step—if refused—was to ask again for payment, and if this was ignored, the murder often followed, by dagger or shotgun. A lesson for all to remember. The sums asked for were large for their time and the conditions of the Italian community: one thousand to five thousand dollars. One author of some of the Black Hand's demands, a Joseph Gentile, was arrested at his house on Racine Avenue among his collection of pistols, sawed-off shotguns (for close work to create a horrible blasting wound and easy to carry under a coat), and dynamite for bombings. Also a letter addressed to an Italian victim named Silvani. Translated from the original Italian, most likely by some reporter, but retaining its odd illiterate rhythms, it read as follows:

"Most gentle Mr. Silvani: Hoping that the present will not impress you much, you will be so good as to send me $2,000.00 if your life is dear to you. So I beg you warmly to put them on your door within four days. But if not, I swear this week's time not even the dust of your family will exist. With regards, believe me to be your friends . . ."

Other samples of Black Hand poison-pen prose:

"We all of us thank you for the success that has happened, but for your security do that which we have written in the first, and take good care of doing the exact things, and woe unto you people if you do not deliver the said sum, more than the past $1,000.00 at the stated place. If you don't . . . we will think of something else. If we will not succeed here in Chicago [we will find you] in the other parts even to hell. Even if you leave the city we will think to revenge ourselves with a severe vengeance."

Most direct was:

"You got some cash. I need $1,000.00. You place the $100.00 bills in an envelope and place it underneath a board at the northeast corner of Sixty-ninth Street and Euclid Avenue at eleven o'clock tonight. If you place the money there you will live. If you don't, you die. If you report this to the police, I'll kill you when I get out. They may save you the money, but they won't save you your life."

Noted one Chicago detective in a conversation with a reporter: "Paying the money did not free the poor dago from future demands. If he paid out a bundle of scratch [money] like a lamb, he was sure to be shook down again and again. Sell his horse and cart, the farm produce market, mortgage his barber chairs, hock the bambino's gold earrings; the pistol was always on his neck, and he'd pay and pay, and you couldn't get any of them garlic eaters to open their yaps and tell us who had put them in debt and made them so scared."

With the years, the Black Hand grew more demanding, more powerful and the innocent more terrified than the ancient Jews under the eye of a wrathful Jehovah. By 1915, in the first three months of that year, fifty-five bombs were set off, all to terrorize and get victims to pay off some blackmail. The *Daily News* figured that ten paid the Black Hand's demands at first asking, to one who held off until the bomb exploded. Italians who knew their fellow countrymen's outlay in payoffs figured that over a half-million dollars a year was extorted from Chicago Italians.

The murder score showed a wide activity: 1910, twenty-five Black Hand killings, all unsolved; 1912, thirty-three, 1914, forty-two. No one talked of this outside the Italian district; no one helped the police. Police raids led to many arrests but never to any really meaningful convictions. When in 1910, the police arrested 194 Sicilians, all known criminals, the entire group had to be set free as no one dared testify against them. No witnesses, no convictions; it was a crime system of irresistible simplicity.

City officials and saloon keepers who controlled ward votes managed to parole the rare criminal Italian who got convicted. No Black Hand under arrest had much to worry over. Anyone who was to come forward against him was marked for death, also all his relatives to the smallest child.

Nor did the judge, the jury, the D.A.'s staff escape threats on their lives, but these were not carried out. A witness against a Black Hand, even on the stand, would clam up if someone stood up in the court and waved a red handkerchief at him. Newspapers reported on how ingrown was the Italian sense of personally taking care of crimes among themselves in Chicago. In 1911, an Italian wanted for murder of an Italian was hunted by detectives. A police reporter wrote: "They succeeded in learning who the murderer was, but in spite of nets and traps, weeks passed in a vain hunt for him. Finally an Italian detective saw the 'wanted man' leave the home of the brother of the murdered man. When the police summoned the brother to explain the strange affair, he declared that the murderer had been wounded and that he and his family had shielded and nursed the wretch back to life in order to kill him and thus duly and personally avenge the death of the beloved brother."

As one Italian barber put it, "What good thisa justice when around the corner there can be death? A man now, he think he has learned to think, he is always thinking of his own dying, so why hurry thisa by talking 'bouta the Black Hand?"

Chicago Italians tried to abolish the Black Hand in 1907; businessmen, lawyers, doctors, others organized a White Hand Society to fight the Black one, which responded at once by threatening death to *all* White Hands. Italian detectives were put on the Chicago force, members of the police sent to Sicily and Italy to study old-country records of Black Hand suspects in Chicago, and to survey the whole system of blackmail and terror as imported into America. The main problem of the White Hand group was that the few killers and extortionists they helped send to prison were *also* usually valuable ward political vote herders, and so were soon paroled to continue their criminal ways and deliver at the polls election time.

By 1912, the White Hand announced it was "so discouraged by the lax administration of justice," that it was ineffectual, and soon it was dissolved.

The United States government in 1910 had stepped in to try its luck, using as an excuse—to clobber the Black Hand—the misuse of the U.S. Mail and Post Office Department, in sending Black Hand letters. About six Black Hand men were sent to the Federal pens and served their time, for the Chicago politicians didn't think it wise to meddle with Washington. None of these efforts stopped the blackmail and the killings—it was just noticed that no more letters went by mail. What finally stopped Black Hand activities was the United States government itself, giving them a bigger kind of crime to exploit, with huge rewards running into billions of dollars. By 1919, it was clear Prohibition was going to be in, and the drinking habits of the Chicago citizens as well as the rest of the nation would hardly change. The Black Hand survivors and their broods mostly went in for the luscious rewards of bootlegging, alcohol distilling, smuggling, needling near beer with ether for kicks, hijacking and hiring out as guns, sluggers, and bombers for the new lords of crime, mostly Italians who were to become notorious and nearly untouchable by the law in the twenties. They did kill each other with a belligerent generosity.

The bomb, at first black powder, then dynamite, that invention of the Nobel Peace Prize giver, seemed a special Chicago darling. The Black Hand certainly pioneered its use as a terror weapon.

A typical Black Hand family that later moved up into big-time crime was the Gennas. The father had brought his family—wife and many children—to Chicago from Marsala in Sicily, in 1894. He worked as a railroad section hand. When he and his wife died, while the children were still very young, his sons, Sam and Mike, Jim, Pete, and Angelo, worked their way up into Black Hand blackmailing to positions of power and terror in Little Italy. *E' sempre l'ore*—it is always the right time—was their motto. They supported the ward bosses who supported them for the Italians the Gennas would herd to the polls on election day. The Gennas were murderous extortionists, but the politicians protected them—let them run a gambling place, poolrooms, and a blind pig (illegal drinking place). Their front was a cheese and olive oil importing business—a pungent *opéra-bouffe* front. Sam and Mike were the killing and beating up unit of the organization. Dapper Angelo, known as "Tony the Gentleman," avoided the crass items of assassinations, reprisals, the rough handlings. The family *consigliere*, Tony, was the mind who planned things, and had his toenails manicured and painted at his suite in the Congress Hotel. He had a box at the opera. The only educated Genna, Tony had studied music, architecture, and he gave parties for singers and theater folk. He lived with his mistress, Gladys Bagwell, the daughter of a Baptist minister. She had been a nightclub pianist. (Tony died in her arms after being shot.)

The Gennas imported Sicilian bodyguards. One was Samuzzo "Samoots" Amatuna, who first had the idea of carrying a shotgun in his violin case. This was when he tried to kill the business agent of the Musicians' Union, of which Samuzzo was himself a member. A dandy in his own right, he owned two hundred monogrammed silk shirts. When a laundry scorched one of these prized shirts, for revenge or fastidiousness, Samoots shot the laundry wagon's horse dead, in full daylight. A reporter's notebook said: "As the Church didn't hold animals to have souls, Samoots was not held in mortal sin."

Orazio "The Scourge" Tropea was gifted with *il maloochio,* the Evil Eye, so feared by slum Italians they micturated in fear. Another member of the gang was *Il Cavaliere,* Giuseppe Nerone, alias Antonio Spano—also known as Joseph Pavia—graduate of the University of Palermo, it was claimed, where he taught mathematics, moonlighted in serious crime, and fled to Chicago. He passed as a great financial genius, but the Genna boys used him as a torpedo, a killer. (Joining the Capone mob later, he killed Tony the Gentleman with a shot in the back.)

A killer team, John Scalise and Albert Anselmi, one short and

the other tall, "the Mutt and Jeff of murderers," used to rub garlic on their bullets, causing talk that garlic was a poison when used on a bullet that would enter flesh. Science denies this, but most Chicagoans believed it to be true.

By the end of 1919, the Gennas—with no overwhelming resistance to change—were out of the Black Hand business, at least as their major endeavor. They were obtaining, through political contacts and Washington payoffs, a U.S. government license to handle industrial alcohol. We leave the Gennas here—some three of them to be gunned down by rivals in the twenties.

The Gennas believed in the old Italian saying, *Il tempo buono viene una volta solo*—the good time comes but once.

It was Black Hand explosive experts who taught others the power of the bombs, and soon two-thirds of all the bombings were not by Black Hand gangs at all. Bombs were used by rival gamblers for control of games and sites, bookmaking, poolrooms, and by racketeers preying on business firms for protection money, by politicians who wanted to toss a real scare into a rival. And often in labor and management relationships, with all of their turbulence and impetuous conflicts and betrayals.

Management, corporations, hired goon squads and gunmen and bombers to intimidate union organizers, and unions emphasized their rights with their own hard hitters and bombers that blew up plants. It was a mean and dirty business from both sides. Industry had the most money and their scabs, Pinkerton men, hired killers who did great damage protecting Rockefeller holdings—shooting down miners' families, men, women, children. Big Steel, Big Railroads, Big Meat-Packing took to importing to Chicago bargeloads of hoodlums from other cities to bust up unionizing attempts. The unions, as they grew stronger, killed strikebreakers, broke heads. With power came union dues, with dues came huge sums of money, pension funds, and with millions of dollars in sight, the gangsters invaded the unions and took over many as personal empires—organized Mafia fronts as laundry workers, cabdrivers, waiters, bartenders were formed into unions for mob gain, using killings, cripplings, and torture to silence members who wanted honest officials.

Bombs were also active in Chicago's racial terror. Blacks felt the thud of the iron pineapples going off. In January of 1919, thirty-two bombs went off in the black sections of Chicago, warnings for them not to press into the all-white neighborhoods. Serious race riots broke out in July; five days of bombings, beatings, and murders harassed the black ghettos.

Chicago had taken to bombs during World War I, with a relish that only sharpened the appetite for later, bigger use of the bomb in the alcohol wars. The bombers were not amateurs as were the bombers of the 1870s, who often mishandled dynamite and blew themselves up for social revolutionary reasons. The later bombers were professionals for pay—and the reason for their activities was money produced from terror. These gangs of mixed groups of bombers and sluggers were for hire with a naked immediacy.

Investigations showed that the bombing of four laundries took place among those whose "engineers" had been on a strike. This led to Andrew Kerr of the International Union of Steam and Operating Engineers, which led to Jim Sweeney's gang who were for hire for bombing, shooting, slugging. The gang included "Soup" Bartlett (soup was the name for nitro in bombing circles) who was the explosive expert for the group, and Con Shea, a labor agitator who had been a bomb tosser himself since the age of sixteen. Doctrinaires of violence rather than fanatics.

Records showed the union once ordered Sweeney to slug twenty-five people senseless, and he had laundry addresses, places which were to be blown in. When Sweeney and Bartlett went to Joliet prison, Joe Sangerman took over. He was "the directing genius of the bombing trust" (Illinois Crime Survey). Sangerman, rapacious, ambitious, was also the big boss of the Barbers' Union, and a manufacturer of barbers' supplies which every good union shop was more than encouraged to stock, or suffer miseries of bomber etiquette. Sangerman's union, under his leadership, was kept busy hiring bombers to blow up the shops that had any uncertainty about agreeing to union domination. Bombs were needed to keep shop owners in line, and when Sangerman's bombers were free, he'd hire them out to others who had need of a bomb placed to go off in the right doorway, shatter someone's plate glass, even shake up a few people. Loyalties and antipathies didn't bother Sangerman; he'd work for anyone.

Sangerman later confessed that he ran an expert bombing shop, having on his payroll skilled bombers, like a team of five men and one girl who gave satisfaction. He offered arbitrary sluggings and bombings at various rates, $50 to $700 for a good clean job, depending on time and size. George Matriscino, also known as Martin, was the big bomb handler, the star of the Sangerman stable, an expert whom other bombers looked up to as their inspiration. A Matriscino job was a masterwork. His bombs were black powder bombs, but if he ran into some difficulties, he always carried two sticks of dynamite in his coat pockets. George was a bit of a publicity hound and liked showing off his press clippings. Newspapermen found him good copy at times, hoping he would come to trial and star in a courtroom. But somehow George got into trouble with the Barbers' Union, and some of the officers of that impassioned group gunned him down.

That politicians used bombs to settle their own scores, a novel idea for which Chicago can take credit as a first. The Nineteenth Ward was worth fighting for; in graft and boodle it ran up a high score—and by 1916, Alderman John Powers was squared off with Anthony D'Andrea in a power face-off. Since 1888, the Nineteenth had been Powers' private domain, where he ran a popular saloon, took care of protecting the gamblers, the whores and thieves. His takes from payoffs were fabulous in a day when any alderman with his hand out, palm up, did well. Tony had a naked immediacy and saw no reason he shouldn't take over the ward as alderman.

Tony D'Andrea was an ex-convict, a big man in several unsavory Italian fraternal orders, and was popular as a labor union official. The *Tribune* listed as part of his record that he was an "unfrocked priest . . . former power in the old 'red light district' . . . released from the penitentiary after . . . thirteen months on a counterfeiting charge . . . also connected with a gang of Italian forgers and bank thieves."

Tony, despite this ludicrous attitude of the press, felt his record didn't bar him from city politics. He ran for county commissioner in 1914; no dice. In 1916, for alderman of the Nineteenth Ward, and guns were used. One of Powers' men, Frank Lombardi, was killed in a Taylor Street saloon; that looked undemocratic and again Tony lost. In 1919, still striving, Tony D'Andrea tried for the post as the Democratic party's representative to the Constitutional Convention, everything being voided for him by a reform group bringing up fifty-six voters who were on the poll sheets, but who took an oath they had *never* voted in that election. This subversion of ethics was blamed on Tony.

Tony had been elected president of the Unione Siciliana—a big Italian muscle group—and he also was boss of four additional labor unions. The first bomb—as Tony tried to show his power—went off on Alderman Powers' front porch. Then someone returned a bomb to a Blue Island hall where Tony D'Andrea's followers were holding a meeting. Five people were badly hurt. Shootings, stabbings were in order on both sides in a political power fight. Tony's followers were victims of two more bombs.

Alderman Powers—no plaster saint himself—issued a statement of Tony's ways with elections:

"Conditions in the Nineteenth Ward are terrible. Gunmen are patrolling the streets. I have received threats that I was to be 'bumped off' or kidnapped. Alderman Powers' house is guarded day and night. Our men have been met, threatened and slugged. Gunmen and cutthroats have been imported from New York and Buffalo for this campaign of intimidation. Owners of halls have been threatened with death or the destruction of their buildings if they rent their places to us."

Two more Powers men died. . . . Then, much later, in the early 1920s, Tony himself fell to an assassin with the now ritual sawed-off shotgun. Said one habitual criminal of Tony's old gang at his last arrest. "I tell you, you find anybody what's not using a sawed-off shotgun, but one of them long ones, and you got no pro, but one of them *amatoors*."

55

"COMPANY, GIRLS!"

No woman is worth money that will take money.
JOHN VANBRUGH, 1696

Why keep a cow when you can buy milk?
AMERICAN FOLK SAYING ON WHORING

Come crime, war, hard times, gang bombings, no matter; the whores continued to offer, the madams to repeat their cry of "Company, girls!" and offer to the caller with kinky ideas the delights of "Liberty Hall." When back in 1895, Carter Harrison, Jr., had been reelected, he gave orders to purify Clark Street where a new trolley line for the first time carried passengers into the vice district. Some madams moved away, bag and baggages, to the West Side, some to South Chicago, on Harbor Avenue, the Strand, Thirty-first Street. A lot of houses shifted to the neighborhood around Clark Street and South Dearborn, being greeted by eager landlords like ministers plenipotentiary of a foreign power.

Not that Clark Street became pure; you could still get a girl (or a middle-aged woman) and a five-cent whiskey (of sorts), and most of the rooming houses were able to convert to brothels.

When the mayor was in office for his fourth term, he again tackled Clark Street, his insight and perception a bit more polished.

401

Now he was also driving the whores from Custom House Place and Plymouth Place. The real low dives, those in Little Hell, and on the West Side, were not molested. The evil places like the Black Hole, The Jungle, continued in the trade of selling basic physical sensations.

Italian pimps had a sales talk of *"O, la bella puttana!"* The Jungle, an incoherent blot on civilization, was a dozen connecting shacks, owned mutually by a half-dozen saloonkeepers who stocked them with about one hundred women, poor drabs who, because they were usually high and incoherent and bouncy with a drug called "encaine" (a synthetic cocaine), were known as "air walkers." Prisoners of the shanties, they stood naked in doorways or windows in a paralytic hope to attract trade that paid them twenty-five cents or half a dollar for use of their bodies, and they in turn stole what they could from the guest—his shoes if he foolishly took them off.

Bessie Lane ran a house on South Peoria which had higher standards—of price anyway. Nothing under fifty cents. The real owner of the cathouse was Mrs. Lemuel Schlotter, who passed as a society matron in her grand home on the North Shore. When she was tried in court for having a sixteen-year-old girl working as a whore, the jury was told "There she was [Mrs. Schlotter] posing as a society woman and living high on money turned over to her by her agent." What told most against the society woman were her account books in which were kept the names of all guests entertained by the girls, prices, and dates. Delinquencies and vice make odd inventory of assets and income.

In one four-day period, the books showed that six girls survived 394 customers, the girls' fees, their share, $98.50. In five days, six girls had 206 men, and the prizewinning whore was one named Florence who took on 130 of that total; in one fast day, 45 guests. Florence's pay for the speed run was $32.50. Kitty, another girl, rung up for the same period a mild 76. Society's Mrs. Lemuel Schlotter was sentenced to prison for a term of one to fifteen years. She served only a few years.

In the first decade of this century, there were call girls and assignation flats on Michigan Avenue, and on the South Side.

Drug laws were as yet hardly what they are today (nor was the huge use of drugs by noncriminal classes). Eugene Hustion was

"King of the Cokies." ("People think I'm dead, but not if they look closely"), and his wife Lottie was "Queen of the Cokies." Lottie claimed to be a college graduate, painted pictures in oils, composed serious music, and had a flat on Dearborn Street full of fine needle-work, her own. The flat also had a stock of thirty pounds of cocaine and fifteen of morphine. The King's and Queen's salesmen covered the Levee whorehouses nightly, making customers and deliveries. As the popular song of "Cocaine Bill and Morphine Sue" put it:

> Cocaine Bill and Morphine Sue
> Strolling down the Avenue, two by two
> "Oh, honey, won't you have a little sniff
> On me, have a sniff on me."

> Said Sue to Bill, "It'll do no harm,
> If we both just have a little shot in the arm."
> Said Bill to Sue, "I can't refuse,
> 'Cause there's no more kick in this darned ol' booze."

> So they walked down First and they turned up Main,
> Looking for a place they could buy cocaine.
> They came to a drug store full of smoke,
> Where they saw a little sign sayin', "No more coke."

> Now in the graveyard on the hill,
> Lies the body of Cocaine Bill,
> And in a grave right by his side,
> Lies the body of his cocaine bride.

Vice was as thick as miasma on the Levee. One of the citizens of the district was known as the "Mayor of the Tenderloin." Pony Moore was a black gambler and crook who owned the Turf Exchange Saloon on Twenty-first Street. He was involved in a scheme by brothel keepers trying to frame the Everleigh sisters in the death of Marshall Field, Jr. Pony offered one of the Everleigh girls twenty thousand dollars to testify she had seen Minna Everleigh shoot the Field heir in their bordello. While it was accepted as a fact by many Chicago people, wise in the ways of the underworld, that young Field was shot and killed there, then taken out and "found in his own room at home, fatally injured while cleaning his gun," no one was sure as to who actually shot the young man. Overhearing the plot on the telephone (the first use of the popular instrument to make a dramatic plot point), Minna had a police lieutenant, on the grab from the Everleigh sisters, take Pony Moore aside and give him a good talking to, also a few threats. A few days later, Pony also lost the license to his saloon. The sisters were iron butterflies with what is now called clout.

Pony Moore's great desire was to pass for a white man. He tried to bleach his skin, which made him look like the gray-white belly of a blotched, long-dead mackerel. As for his head of kinky hair, he tried various hair straighteners, one of which turned it so green he had to shave his head. He was also a bit mad on the subject of changes of costumes and diamonds. Once at Saratoga, he changed all his attire down to his underwear every hour. His pride

among all his precious stones was the big diamond stud he wore in his shirt, which was made thief-proof by a bolt and tiny padlock. He felt he was giving élan to a milieu, but few took him seriously.

The impression the Everleigh sisters always gave of their brothel was that theirs was the only really high-class knocking house and voyeurs' heaven in the world. When in 1911, the mayor ordered their house closed for "its infamy, the audacious advertising of it . . ." Minna called in the press boys and made a little speech of farewell to the Levee. "Of course, if the Mayor says we must close, that settles it. What the Mayor says goes, as far as I am concerned. I'm not going to be sore about it, either. I never was a knocker, and nothing the police of this town can do will change my disposition. I'll close up the shop and walk out with a smile on my face. Nobody else around here is worrying either. If the ship sinks we're going down with a cheer and a good drink under our belts, anyway."

56

ALL AROUND TOWN

One could keep up with the doings of the madams and the pimps and the girls in the pages of their own newspaper, the *Chicago Street Gazette.*

ALL AROUND TOWN. THE BALL. Shang Andrews' fourth annual ball will take place at Meisner's Concordia Hall, on Twenty second street, between State and Wabash avenue on Tuesday evening, November 20, 1877. We make this early announcement in order to give all ample time to prepare for the great event.

THE MUSIC. The boss band of Chicago, led by the great and only Louis Lepetre, will furnish music for our ball.

NO "INVITATIONS." We shall send out no "invitations" by mail; but hereby invite all our friends to be present on the night of November 20. This is to avoid any mistakes that might unavoidably occur, for we cannot be expected to know everybody's name and address.

Mollie Waltermeyer has ordered a set of black gutta percha teeth, and when she gets them that tall dry goods man had better look out for his nose.

Jimmy Barton returned from the Hot Springs last Tuesday. He is no longer a partner of our friend Ike Batchelder.

Kate Severance picked up her duds last Saturday morning, and moved to the head of Congress street, on State.

Madame Metzger looms up in very good style, with a $200.00 cloak. Every landlady on the West Side envies her; and yet Dan did not buy it.

Behind all this gay, hard-boiled chatter there was often a grim debasement of the human condition. Judge John H. Lyle, in his memoirs, recalls a case from his early days as an alderman when "a youth living in my ward came to see me for help. His sixteen year old sister had been missing for weeks. She had sent a letter, postmarked St. Louis, stating that she was happy in a new job. The brother was sure something was wrong. His anguish stirred my sympathy.

"I hired a detective who found the girl in a bawdyhouse. He brought her back to Chicago. Her wretched condition supported her story. This beautiful high school student had gone into the Levee seeking a real estate office where she was to make a payment on the family home. She asked a man for directions. He persuaded her to enter a restaurant. A knockout drop was slipped into her coffee. She was taken to a resort where the man seduced her and then sold her to the keeper of a brothel for $200. Repeated use of drugs clouded her mind. She was used as a prostitute for several days and then resold for $400 to a bagnio in St. Louis."

Prostitution brought crime, lawbreaking created outlaws. The two-gun man appeared in the district known as Bloody Maxwell, in the person of Buff Higgins. He was as deadly with his two pistols as Gary Cooper or John Wayne appeared to be on film. By 1906, Buff's reputation was filled with specific sagas of violence close to films like *High Noon,* but seen from the criminal's side. The *Tribune* tried to debunk Buff Higgins as "an arrant coward at heart . . . who succeeded in being a bad man because of his readiness to use the revolver when things threatened to go against him." The revolver, usually a .45, was also all Billy the Kid, the Youngers, and the Daltons needed, that equalizer, be it Colt or Smith and Wesson.

The revolver seemed to slough off superficialities, get down to basics.

Higgins was one of hundreds of thousands who came from Ireland as children with memories of talk of the potato famine, of British indifference to the blight, or the Hibernian starvation. Buff (no other first name appears in print) was two in 1873, when his immigrant family appeared in the United States and settled in Chicago on Johnson Street. He learned to read and write at the Walsh School, and soon he was leading the Irish gangs in boys' street wars, concentrating on the Bohemians. At thirteen, Buff's schooling ended and he took to attacking, being a desperado, smashing windows, looting fruit stands, tossing bricks around, suffering the sour, vague, prejudiced malaise of slum adolescence. In his late teens he was already a figure of power, of envy, in the whorehouses, saloons, and the accepted boss man, as an audacious heist artist, of the Johnson Street gang, drinking potable spirits, talking over crimes. Robbery was their main game. Buff, with inherent cruelty, killed two men and shot and wounded several more, even gunning down three policemen but not fatally. When he was arrested, no one dared appear against him; shopkeepers, merchants were too terrorized to utter any complaints or desire to testify. Even badly wounded men refused to identify him as their assailant. He took some exuberant delights in discharging a pistol; Freudians might hint he was impotent.

In 1893, aided by Red Gary and Johnny Mortell, he burst into the house of Peter McCooey on Johnson Street, hunting potential loot. Peter was no innocent bystander, but a notorious killer, having done time for murdering a policeman but he had been paroled after two years by an odd Board of Pardons under pressure from someone higher up. McCooey, a light sleeper, came awake as Buff was going through his pants pockets. Buff, seeing the sleeper awake, shot him without a second's thought and fled. McCooey didn't live long, just long enough to name Buff Higgins as his killer, and the jury believed him.

They hanged Buff Higgins, aged twenty-three, in March, 1894, in Cook County Jail. A newspaper print of the event shows that many people attended the show inside the grand courtyard of the prison. Invited guests formed an audience as Buff, flanked by warden, priest, and hangman, stood making some last statement, hands tied behind his back and waiting for the final drop and the hoped-for, last, quick convulsions.

57

SPORTS AND FIRE

STRONG LANGUAGE ON THE STAGE.—*There is a growing tendency in the plays of recent date toward the use of language on the stage which should be summarily checked. Writers no longer confine themselves to the use of "the big, big d_____," which is freely scattered throughout "comic opera," as jingling burlesques are called, "farce comedies," and serious pieces. The name of the Deity is frequently profaned and now we are threatened with a fierce epidemic of "hell." The word is no longer hinted at but spoken with loud voiced distinction as though its use was some master stroke of wit. A recent case has been pointed out in which a play upon the first syllable of the name "Helen" is made use of under the pretense of humor—save the mark!—and in which one man tells another to "go to hell." In "Shore Acres," the chief charm of which is its simplicity and rustic truthfulness, "hell" again appears.*

ILLUSTRATED AMERICAN, 1893

The sporting set of Chicago, be they gamblers, loose ladies, or the sons and daughters of the department stores and packinghouse families, nearly all loved Washington Park Race Track. Attacked by blue noses, reformers, impervious to charges of fixed races, it managed to exist until 1905. The nineteenth century wound toward its end, and the tallyhos still moved down the boulevard toward the park (whip at salute position), horses in jingling gear trotting high, dropping golden apples, ladies with lacy sunshades, "that suggested a courtesan's drawers" (*Police Gazette*) sat on top, with the gentlemen in tall gray hats. There were wicker baskets in place holding the cold chicken, the sliced grouse sandwiches, the rare tidbits, and, usually, an ice bin with wine bottles cooling. The wide hats of the ladies, long plumes bobbing, were balanced by a man riding behind, blowing a long brass horn in some supreme bedazzlement.

They were often snobs. "The Chicago people have been at it again. Some of the flitch of bacon aristocrats who attend the races at Washington Park objected to the presence of Miss Lillian Russell, 'an actress,' in the clubhouse. The president of the racing association, who was a friend of Miss Russell's, at first refused to obey the dictates of his associates in the matter, but the wives and daughters made such a hubbub that the president was finally compelled to ask Miss Russell to be content with a box in the grand stand, and to henceforth abstain from showing herself in the clubhouse" (*Illustrated American*).

The gentry, the riffraff, loved the races, as did the solid sports from the gambling dens run by Curt Gunn; he, big-bodied in pepper-and-salt herringbone tweeds, and also "Colonel" Fagin, John W. Gates, better known as Bet-A-Million (he'd bet on which raindrop would first reach the bottom of a windowpane), and who also loved big betting on bridge-whist games. Gates liked to sit in on a three-day bridge game, usually running Saturday to Monday in the Rookery Building. Losses and winnings there of a hundred thousand dollars were said to be common.

For years the town talked of the time the American Whist Association came to town for a convention, and Curt Gunn and a pal played, as professionals, against Bet-a-Million Gates and a partner, as amateurs. It was a five-thousand-dollars-a-side match game. Gates's side won, the amateurs. About cardplayers, Gates claimed there were "three kinds of liars: liars, damn liars, and experts."

There was other gambling: on the stock exchange, the commodities market, where often a delicate precision was needed to keep one's senses. In the winter of 1897–1898, Joe Leiter tried to corner the wheat futures contracts, to buy up all the wheat expected to be harvested. Joe was six feet tall, still in his twenties, and it seemed a good idea; his father was the partner of Marshall Field, a famous Chicago merchant, Levi Leiter, so Joe had money to get the scheme off the ground. He began to buy wheat futures. The deal was to buy cheap, hold, and when a shortage came, with Joe holding *all* the wheat, to sell out at inflated prices. A corner in wheat was the dream fantasy of many commodity brokers. The first Mr. Armour, the meat-packer, also had a way with commodities, and he ran Joe into a trap. He decided to bring in extra wheat. To ship in the extra millions of bushels to the market, he had the ice on the frozen-in Soo Canal dynamited in the dead of winter. Armour also

had millions more bushels on hand to throw on the market, stacked away in his huge warehouses on Goose Island.

Joe Leiter just underestimated the extra wheat supplies that someone out to wreck him could throw onto the market. When Armour hit him with cheaper wheat, Joe, caught in a naked immediacy, went down, lost six millions of his father's fortune. It took a couple of decades to get the thing through the courts, but the Leiters still had enough left to marry off a daughter to Lord Curzon.

But celebrities always remembered Chicago as a "grand town for fun," where the entremetteuse (procuress) had fine stock in trade. The giant Paul Dresser, brother of the novelist Dreiser, was still progressing. Paul with his eyes for the fancy whores, and his hit songs, "My Gal Sal," "On the Banks of the Wabash," and half a hundred now forgotten melodies. Nat Goodwin was the actor who married eight times, or was it nine times? Edouard de Rezke, visiting opera star, who liked to exercise on bike wheels, buffeted by a lakefront breeze, saying, "I no ride ze bee-ceecle in Czacago, ze wind too strong."

For the mob there was the terrifying grotesqueness of the Eden Musee Wax Works, a collection of demented faces, murderers, outlaws, scenes of gory crime, and a chamber of horrors. There was Frank Hall's Casino, Frank's Mirror Maze to drive you daffy and amaze the country folk. For "the girl hunters," the place to go was the Buckingham Dance Hall with its naughty girls and fancy hustlers—couples busy on a Mardi Gras night doing the cakewalk.

Union racketeering had already begun in the nineteenth century, and was reaching new highs in the late 1890s with M. B. "Skinny" Madden, a strangulating force to the city's progress. Skinny was owner and president of the Junior Steam-Fitters Union. Settling a simple strike cost a thousand dollars to be put in Skinny's pocket. A big strike call-off cost twenty thousand dollars. When the Federal Building cornerstone was laid, Skinny said a fine of five thousand dollars had to be paid. "That stone has been cut by non-union scabs." Skinny had a solid philosophy:

"Show me an honest man and I'll show you a goddamn fool."

He kept his union president's post by sheer nerve and hoodlum threats. His goon squeeze was deadly. He rose once at a meeting and announced blandly, "I propose I be elected president of this here union for life. All in favor, stand up."

Only a few steam fitters stood up.

Skinny said simply, "Now, then, if any sonofabitch wants to get up and vote *no,* just let him try it."

By 1900, he had tied up the city so tightly in a strike that hardly a brick or pipe wrench moved. When strikebreakers came in, both sides used murderous wrecking crews of thugs. Skinny's sluggers maimed and crippled hundreds. There were a few murders. But the truly classic age of gangster killings en masse was to come only in the 1920s.

In time, Skinny Madden was expelled from the American Federation of Labor, fined five hundred dollars for extortion in court. He retired, it was said, a millionaire.

Even with union racketeering, workers had dug the main channel of the gigantic Chicago Sanitary Canal, nearly thirty miles of it, a lot through solid rock and glacial muck. Over forty-two million cubic foot yards of earth were moved. Graft was there in plenty, for all contractors, payoffs to politicians, protection money. The citizens and taxpayers, aware of all this, howled in letters to the press, held meetings all to no avail. (The cartoonist, F. Opper, continued to draw the taxpayer as stripped nude, wearing an empty barrel for clothes.)

Meanwhile, Chicago played and gambled, made money or lived in slums, worked in sweatshops or hammered steers, skulls in packing plants. And always went to the theater. Fire laws could be avoided by bribing the fire inspectors, so sooner or later a great tragic theater fire had to come about. It came on December 30, 1903, when the town still hung with Christmas decor, and parents took their children to the shows.

The Iroquois Theatre was no ramshackle barn but one of the best. Chicago as a theater town had witnessed *Floradora* (including the famous sextet), *The Yankee Consul, Twelfth Night* with Viola Allen. Actors like Raymond Hitchcock appeared (he was to discover Cole Porter at a piano during a transatlantic crossing). Wilton Lackaye and other stars found the Chicago theater a good place to take bows in.

Eddie Foy, a wide-mouthed, lisping clown was playing the Iroquois in an extravaganza, *Mr. Bluebeard.* The Iroquois Theatre was new and, of course, "completely fireproof." Foy's show was a light happy thing, and that December matinee, parents and teachers had brought a great many children.

At 3:15 P.M., during the second act, as a double octet was singing away, a curl of smoke appeared from behind a scenery flat, and a red velvet curtain burst into a blaze. Most likely the fire had come from one of the overheated carbon arc lamps used for a moonlight effect. It shocked the audience like a seismic disturbance—into a first gasp of horror.

Then fire began to spread out in red tongues of flame, and Eddie Foy, eyes wide, mouth agape, stepped forward to the footlights. "Please, folks, just be quiet. There's *no* danger." It was a strange comic interlude going bad, he standing there in his grotesque costume, his face a mask of greasepaint. Backstage the cast, unrestrained in their fears, began to seek safety, and a stage door was banged open, a skylight somehow gave way, and so between open door and open ceiling, a fine draft was created that fed the fire like a furnace flue. Flames and clouds of smoke filled the stage and began to move out into the audience. The boxed-in interior of the theater was suddenly full of choking, screaming people, packing together on their feet into a panicked mass, all restraint gone—children screaming. People on the main floors had a little time for reaching the exits, but up in the balconies with aisles made too narrow, and conditions of exit overcomplicated, ways of escape were blocked, cut off.

The electric lights went out as wires were shorted, and inky darkness filled the auditorium; coughing and retching and the crunch of bodies took over. To the horror of the maddened crowd of children and adults, it was found exits were locked—the gates at stair landings were tightly chained to keep balcony people from getting down into the dress circle. No preparation had been made for emergency lights over exits, and draperies hid many exit points.

One alley wall of the theater had windows leading to fire escapes, but as these packed full almost at once, people struggling to descend met new crowds from other exits merging with theirs—all tried together to rush to the street below. Bodies seemed to explode and swarm and smother each other. Two hundred died in the angle of one staircase. Those trapped immovable on the fire escapes, as

doors burst open and shot out flames, became human torches. A few
planks were laid across the alley to another roof, and some smoldering people in burning clothes got across.

In fifteen minutes, fire crews were pouring tons of water into
the theater, seemingly unaware of the dead or dying still closely
packed in the place. When the firemen and others fought their way
into the interior, they found a scene from woodcut illustrations to
Dante's *Inferno*. A few hard-guy reporters fainted. Dead and dying
bodies were dragged out and laid in rows on marble-topped tables.
Those surely dead were wrapped in blankets patterned in series
along the curb.

Five hundred ninety-six human beings died at the Iroquois
that December afternoon, crushed, burned, trampled, stomped flat,
suffocated. One reporter wrote, "Five bushels of women's purses
were picked up . . . two barrels of slippers."

George Fife, employed in Doberman's Lincoln Avenue saloon,
wrote a dirge, a poem telling the story:

> *The Theatre was crowded*
> *With a gay and happy throng*
> *Of people who had come to see*
> *The play and hear the song.*
> *When what is this that strikes the ear*
> *In accents rising higher:*
> *The crowd sits back with horror thrilled*
> *As someone hollers "Fire!"*

Thrilled was hardly the proper word.

> *Oh! the terrible Iroquois fire,*
> *The terrible Iroquois fire!*
> *There's many a broken heart tonight*
> *On account of the Iroquois fire.*

There were, of course, the usual investigations and committees
of investigation, while bodies still lay in the morgues unknown, or
unrecognizable. Undertakers, as George Ade said, "immune to
human grief," held for ransom the remains of unidentified bodies.

"As usual, undertakers show no mercy during mass horror, some even raised prices," the press reported.

The mayor said he had sent warnings, and the manager shrugged them off. "I thought everything was all right!" It wasn't. Building and fire inspectors had failed to inspect, or worse, had taken a bit of graft. Building inspectors accepted bribes as low as a set of free tickets. When important people, theater managers, were indicted, including the mayor, Clarence Darrow, the great liberal cynic, pleaded, with a rueful shrug, for them in court, "It is not just to lay the sins of a generation upon the shoulders of the few."

Those who suffered most after the fire were the actors, for people shunned the Chicago theaters, plays closed, even a nonstop run of *Ten Nights in a Bar-Room.*

58

THE CRIME WAVE

Ain't they all in cahoots?
Ain't it fifty-fifty all down the line?
CARL SANDBURG

One good thing about bribing the Chicago City Council was that it could be scientifically, mathematically figured out as to how much it would cost to pass on a city franchise or other favor. The *Chicago Record* in 1894 gave the box score. "The highest price ever paid for aldermanic votes was a few years ago when a measure giving valuable privileges to a railway corporation was passed in the face of public condemnation. There were four members of the Council who received 25,000 dollars each, and the others who voted for the ordinance, received 8,000 dollars each. An official who was instrumental in securing the passage of the measure received the largest amount ever given in Chicago for a service of this kind. He received 100,000 dollars in cash and two pieces of property. The property was afterwards sold for 111,000 dollars. In one of the latest 'boodle' attempts, the aldermen voting for a certain franchise were supposed to receive 5,000 dollars each. One of them, however, had been deceived and was to get only 3,500 dollars. When he learned that he had been 'frisked' of 1,500 dollars, he wept in anger and went over to the opposition, assisting in the final overthrow of the steal.

"The 5,000 dollars per vote is the high-water mark in the Council for the last four years. During 1891 and 1892 there were a dozen ordinances which brought their 'bits,' yet in one case the price went down to 300 dollars." These two years were among the most profitable ever known in criminal circles up till then. "When it becomes necessary to pass an ordinance over the Mayor's veto the cost is 25 percent more than usual."

There was also a going rate for protecting certain criminals; and ward bosses took care of the boys who helped pile up the votes.

By 1906 the crime rate and the horror and danger of walking some of the Chicago streets had reached a level to frighten even

some city officials and give them thought over their filet mignons aux truffles. Women were robbed and murdered on the streets of the North Side where police protection for the citizens had been cut down. Footpads, holdup artists, and hoodlums boldly moved about, knocking down passersby, using cruel force, unnecessary brutality, tying some victims to street poles and lampposts, slashing them with knives and razors. Stores and shops were broken into, looted, private homes invaded, and drinking led to torturing of householders. Rapes were common, and no woman was safe, not even with an escort. Women who resisted rape were often beaten to death. The city was becoming a paranoiac's fantasy.

This caused great shock to respectable people; it was *not* common at the turn of century for any huge invasion of crime to move against the well-to-do, the middle classes. In our time, with muggings, holding of hostages, black and white rumbles, bombings, the need for money for drugs, the breakdown of our inner cities, we accept as nearly normal what deeply shocked Chicago in 1906. ("Why don't they stay with their own?"—cry at a public meeting.)

For those times, the criminal record of a Chicago day was horrifying to the average citizen. Four or five murders, the average of seven suicides, often ten deaths from bombings. (The bomb was to be revived as a protest weapon of the social revolution in the 1970s.) In one six months' period, there were forty-four murders, twenty of the victims being women all raped before, or *after,* the slayings. When a Mrs. Frank C. Hollister "of social prominence" (the rape and murder of the poor received little press notice) was found in an ash heap behind a fence on Belden Avenue, raped, murdered with a noose of copper wire around her neck, her body sadistically shattered by dreadful blows, the city cried out in horror. Genteel apprehension became terror. People gave up their houses and moved into hotels, women stopped shopping even in the light of day. New locks for windows and doors were put in place, lights were kept burning all through the night. A sleeping city had nightmares. Gas meter readers were shot at when suspected of being rapists. A Cook County grand jury, checking the city's precarious existence, got to the nub of it: "such a brazen exhibition of lawlessness cannot continue without official connivance."

The *Tribune* printed the comment of the Board of Education's Mrs. W. Keough on the pursuit of women and "hitting them on the head with a piece of gas pipe seems to be the favorite sport of the Chicago man. The man lies in wait for his prey as an East Indian hunter awaits the approach of a tigress. It is considered rare evidence of sportsmanship to capture the prey near her home."

These repulsive practices, debasement, and deaths had attracted little attention (except by reformers) when they involved white female slaves brutalized in the brothels—but this new wave of crime against schoolgirls and matrons aroused middle-class morality.

Sexual debasement, the menacing of the well provided, caused loud bourgeois reactions. There were mass meetings, prominent citizens formed committees, five hundred new policemen were added to the force to give a sense of invulnerability to the home. Vigilante groups were formed, old pistols oiled, street patrols, private detectives, often strikebreaking goons, were armed, were hired. But the focal point of infection remained: those city officials who were in alliance with the criminals of Chicago, even protecting the amoral, homicidal psychopaths. The crime wave, with all the attention it got, simmered down. But it remained only subdued, ready to flare up again, a world of nearly invisible presences to most.

The Twenty-second Precinct was notorious for the district called Bloody Maxwell, centered around Maxwell Street, one mile by two miles in area—given to crime and harlotry with some appeal to prurience, active in licentiousness and debauchery to please Rome in its lowest decline. Dead Man's Corner was famous in the district, on Sangamon Street, where police and criminals had shot it out for many years, killing each other for a big score on each side.

Here were to begin some of the great ethnic gang wars of Chicago. In 1905 an Irish gang—"the wild micks, the mackerel-snappers"—led by the McGinnis boys, took on a Hunky Bohemian group for a deadly warfare. The youths were in their early teens, but had pistols and exchanged shots, hitting no one seriously on either side. They began to frisk grammar school boys—taking coins, watches, pens—before letting them attend classes. Parochialism—its isolation—the bigotry of immigrant priests—turned many boys to a hatred of Protestants, Jews, blacks.

The Irish hoodlums' domination of the district, however, was weakening. They had been the prime tough guys, the "Ikey" beaters, the knocker-downers of Polacks. But the Bohemians, the Jews, the Germans had been invading the section since the 1880s, and their own tough guys, in self-protection, many given to crime, began to equal the Irish in articulated toughness. Gangs began to come to power along ethnic and old-country nationalistic lines. The gangs of Johnson Street, Celtic in origin, had to fight to stay in existence with such groups as the Weiss gang. The Weisses began late in the year 1866, as six brothers and two sisters, and they married into, in time, the Renich family. The Renichs were ten sisters and two brothers, and by 1900 there were a hundred members of the Weiss-Renich gang dynasty maintaining a criminal discipline and efficiency. Usually about two dozen of the gang were serving time—long or short terms.

The *Tribune* in 1906 gave a good picture of the district. "Within its borders are to be found a greater variety of people and more different kinds of living than in any other similar district in the world. It is a division of the city composed of sections of dozens of Europeans and even Asiatic cities . . . the crime center of the country . . . Murderers, robbers and thieves of the worst kind are here born, reared and grow to maturity in numbers that far exceed the record of any similar district anywhere on the face of the globe. Reveling in the freedom which comes from inadequate police control, inspired by the traditions of criminals that have gone before in the district, living in many instances more like beasts than like human beings, hundreds and thousands of boys and men follow day after day and year after year in the bloody ways of crime. . . .

"Murders by the score, shooting and stabbing affrays by the hundreds, assaults, burglaries and robberies by the thousands—such is the crime record each year for this festering place of evil which lies a scant mile from the heart of great Chicago. . . . Murderers, robbers, burglars, thieves, pickpockets and criminals of all sorts are bred here with a facility that is appalling. . . . From Maxwell come some of the worst murderers, if not actually the worst, that Chicago has ever seen. From Maxwell come the smoothest robbers, burglars and thieves of all kinds, from Maxwell come the worst tough 'gangs.' In general, it may be safely said that no police district in the world turns out such skilled and successful criminals."

The mastermind of the Weiss gang was the original Mrs. Renich's sister, known as Eva the Cow, legally Eva Gussler. A booster (shoplifter) and dip (pickpocket), she was, as reported, "as skilled in her work as Paganini on the violin." Eva was a lady Fagin, and her pupils were the terror of the affluent big stores as they fragmented the inventory with a skill and a bravado only equaled by a plague of grasshoppers.

Another gang that depleted profits by their pilfering was the Valley Mob that worked out of Fifteenth Street. Their chiefs around 1900 were at first Hinie Miller and Jimmy Farley, but both went to prison in 1905. Red Bolton, with inspired audacity, took over, but his precarious forays, too, ended in prison for life, for murder. It was the turn of Paddy Ryan, or Paddy the Bear, a round, rough, little ball of a man—just five feet tall, over two hundred pounds in weight. He was given to dubious improvisations and was in turn assassinated by Walter the Runt Quinlan. It reads like a doomsday history of the fate of early English kings. In the coming years of the bootleggers, Walter the Runt was knocked off by the son of Paddy the Bear, one Paddy the Fox; somehow by that time one is almost into the world of Orwell's *Animal Farm*.

The youth of the criminal street gangs of Chicago—the tainted tots—shocked the city. The newspapers reported a boy of six arrested for a serious crime. Arrests of boys under sixteen and younger were common, as in dreary pilgrimages they went in and out of the station houses, led by a priest, or a parent holding on to an ear.

Bill Dulfer, sixteen, casually killed two men while holding up a saloon. He told the police, "I didn't even have to aim to hit 'em. . . . Just held a gun in each hand and let go. They both came down. I saw 'em fall, that was all I wanted. . . . I'm a killer, not a robber."

Like so many, Bill had passed the street corner salvationists and not listened to their offer.

I stand here on the corner
With my drum.
It brings to us the sinner
And the bum, bum.
They come to us from hovel
And from ditch.
And we march on to victory
Without hitch!

59

KING PULLMAN

Behind every great fortune there is a crime.
HONORÉ DE BALZAC, THE HUMAN COMEDY

The winter of 1893–1894 saw the Democratic political clubs setting up soup kitchens and free-lunch counters. The politicians were the only ones who needed the poor (as votes) or gave a damn about their welfare as the stock market crash produced one of the recurring financial panics. Unemployment, hunger stalked the streets of Chicago's poor and middle-class neighborhoods. Ten miles south of Chicago, George M. Pullman had created Pullman City, to build his palace cars and sleepers, a company town. He had insisted it would be a community free of "all that was ugly, discordant and demoralizing," which was translated into an immense reverence for Mr. Pullman, the workers accepting cuts in pay, never being loud voiced, joining unions, reading no labor newspapers, no one being critical of work loads.

Pullman City on a three-thousand-acre tract was ten years old and situated where Mr. Pullman felt that Lake Calumet (once called Douglas Frog Pond), and its healthy breezes, "would pro-

425

duce ten percent more work." The streets were named after great inventors: Stephenson, Watt, Fulton, Morse, Pullman (of course), and the hotel after a daughter, Florence. The Pullman Palace Car Company factory dominated the town with its tall clock tower for those who couldn't afford an alarm clock. Rents were high. What cost fifteen dollars a month in Chicago, cost eighteen dollars in Pullman City. Dreams and income for Pullman were in the final score incompatible.

Pullman City had been planned before the panic of 1893—and Mr. Pullman didn't approve of blaming the trusts as some newspapers did.

A great deal has been written and debated about the robber barons of the nineteenth century—perhaps too much to interest the modern reader. In those days of laissez-faire, with the nation feeling its oats after the Civil War, a conflict that turned a farming nation into a great industrial one, men with daring, cunning (and organizing skills), cold to the needs of the rest of the community, began to grasp the pattern for controlling huge corporations in steel, wheat, meat, railroads, oil—anything that could be merged into one great organization. And in a time of feeble, harassed unions, or none at all, to keep wages down, hours long. The new lords of production and distribution were also able—as Clarence Darrow and Lincoln Steffens pointed out again and again—shamelessly to buy Congressmen and judges to get the laws they needed to increase their holdings. It has been told in great detail by serious students, and earnest journalists called "muckrakers" by Teddy Roosevelt.

Chicago was prime robber baron territory and had its share of meat-packer barons, railroad pirates on a grand scale. They were men who, like Frick, Gould, Hanna, and Carnegie, enjoyed the control of power over giant holdings, vast profits, many ignoring or perverting the laws of their time. Called captains of industry, they were often honored and always feared. Some were pious churchgoers like the Armours, the Rockefellers ("God gave me my money." John D.), some were honest merchants but stern and aloof like the Fieldses. Others like Yerkes, who seized Chicago street transportation, were out-and-out thieves.

George Pullman, who arrived in Chicago in 1885 with six thousand dollars earned on business ventures, was one of the hardest and meanest of employers. Anyone searching the press, the public comments of the time, cannot find anything good said of him. A financial panic reported in the press seemed only to increase Pullman's sadistic greed:

> Wall Street is still in the throes of panic and apparently limitless depression. From the facility with which the securities —or rather insecurities—dealt in on 'Change give over half or three-quarters of their value, one would conclude that the commodities in reference are worth a trifle less than the paper they are written on. In the prevailing "slump" in the stock markets it is at once a lesson and a gratification to find that the stocks and bonds of the so-called Industrials or Trust concerns are the ones that most readily yield to attack. They are one and all rotten to the core: "Chicago Gas," "General Electric," "Whiskey," "Sugar"—one and all are the money-grubbing contrivances of rogues and swindlers who would better grace the lower-most tier of a penitentiary than the front seats in Church and in Synagogue where they show themselves so conspicuously on the first and last days of the week.
> NORTH AMERICAN NEWSERVICE

There was no "Pullman Car Trust"—Mr. Pullman owned most of the patents for his sleepers and parlor cars. Pullman City was practical—Mr. Pullman liked the word *practical*. His company was valued at $12,360,000, but for not *too* mysterious reasons was assessed on the tax records at $1,695,500.

At Pullman City, the sludge and muck of the sewage—an embarrassing, sticky treat—was pumped several miles away to a farm and used as fertilizer. The shops of the town were Pullman shops, the renters paid Pullman water taxes. There was a Pullman church for hire ("He wasn't a man to let you pray for free"—*The Call*, a socialist paper) and a Pullman school for the children. All saloons and beer parlors were banned, and the tired worker had to trudge for a beer to dives a mile away in Kensington. Five thousand families lived there, but only 250 could spare the three dollars yearly fee to take out books from the Pullman library. Church rent was charged to any creed desiring to salve souls. But, explained Pullman, "it was not intended . . . for the moral and spiritual welfare of the people, as it was for the artistic effect of the scene." Few preachers felt they could afford the church rent or the scenery.

As Pullman wages fell in 1893, rents did *not*. All debts due the company were taken from paychecks. Some workers were actually only getting seven cents a week in cash. Any delegates or committees of workers that came to talk to Pullman about conditions were fired on the spot, thrown the next day out of their homes. Pullman preferred the cringing, obsequious manner in workers. The men were leaning toward Eugene Debs's American Railroad Union and unwisely—being weak and fundless—went out on a wildcat strike. One thousand workers walked out. Pullman laid off a few hundred more to show he didn't give a damn. Debs felt the men had picked a bad time to beard Pullman.

City and government groups begged Pullman to arbitrate; the workers and their families were in a pitiful condition. Mark Hanna, the big wily political boss, said, "A man who won't meet his own men halfway is a damn fool!"

By June a boycott of all Pullman cars was called as Pullman continued firing anyone who tried to talk to him. The railroad unions refused to move trains. Twenty-four railroads combined in a group as The General Managers Association, saw this time as a grand chance to bust Debs's young railroad union, knock it dead. Conductors, most engineers, switchmen, did not support Debs; they felt they were above the one big union of gandy dancers, freight handlers, the pick-and-shovel railroad workers. Trouble began as some trains were stopped, and the state militia, three companies with bayonets and live ammo, were ordered out. To bring in the Federal government, the railroads had unneeded mail cars attached behind Pullman cars, crying out "the strikers were hurling insinuations against the U.S. Mail!" By July, the attorney general had injunctions out against the strikers for "interfering with the U.S. Mails and interstate commerce." It was all a mixture of naïveté, toughness, a fear of the working stiff. President Cleveland—overcompensating for some inner problem—ordered army troops into Chicago. The strikers didn't have a hope after that, facing military strikebreaking. The President of the United States put it on a businesslike basis. "We are confronted with a condition, not a theory." No one mentioned Pullman's theory that workers had no rights at all.

One hundred thousand men were starving and out in the cold

between New York and San Francisco. They were facing thugs, murderers, enrolled by the hundreds as deputy marshals. Said one governor, "They are desperados hired without any regard for their qualifications." Actually they had good qualifications as skull crackers and man-killers.

As the hungry men marched, the better people frowned on the idea of the poor demanding survival through group action—what the radicals were calling "group solidarity." The newspapers gave advice to the men on the move, such as this by the *Chicago Herald*: "There may have been hungry men in Saturday's demonstration, but they were not workingmen. The procession that made its way from the lake front to the City Hall, blocking the most important business streets of the city for the space of an hour, was made up of the shiftless and the disorderly. No honest or respectable workingmen were in those ranks. No honest or respectable workingman has time for any such anarchistic foolery. He has, or can find somewhere, work for his hands to do sufficient to provide him with food and shelter. Such gatherings as those upon the lake front and such processions have few if any American auxiliaries. Their spirit and their methods are entirely European. We have not been brought up to think that bread is a gift of government, to be had on demand. This idea is European in its origin, and mobs howling for bread, such as we have seen the past week, may be found periodically in Paris, in London, in Berlin and in Vienna. In this country the Government does not provide bread for any of its people. Every man is a sovereign by right of citizenship and finds his own bread. And he is usually industrious enough and faithful enough to find butter with it for himself and family, as well as many other comforts. No man need hunger or starve in America, but freedom from starvation can only be won by willingness to work. There are always openings of some kind for men who are willing to work. The idle and the shiftless are welcome nowhere. It is not by overturning carriages on the streets, by blocking traffic and inciting riots, that either work or bread can be won. Let honest workingmen keep away from these mobs. They will find no help through them."

Deputies in premeditated simplicity, to frighten the men and their families, began shooting in Pullman City; a bystander was killed and the police chief, John Brennan, charged "deputies are shooting innocent men and women." He also had his hands full arresting "deputies" recruited from the Levee who were breaking into loaded railroad cars and stealing the contents.

The well-to-do citizens mostly retreated into sanctimoniousness. The troops camped around Pullman City and in Chicago tried to escort a train from the stockyards. The strikers blocked them by overturning freight cars; they spiked the switches. After six blocks' progress the train was stopped. Executives and scabs began manning the trains and they were beaten, hit by showers of bricks. In many places freight cars were set on fire, but some of these, the police chief reported, "had been set by men hired by the railroads" to discredit Debs's union. Hungry, jobless men move in no subtle nuances; workers beat other workers.

War came to Grand Boulevard as three soldiers died when an artillery caisson being rushed around the city blew up, tossing ugly fragments of shells and metal into the parlors of some of the fine houses along the street. President Cleveland now ordered Federal troops to move in, in large numbers, clearly to act as strikebreakers, and keep the trains running. Debs knew this was full defeat. Cleveland was on the side of the railroads—and so on July 9, 1894, the strike was over, defeated, twelve men were dead, a half million dollars lost in damages. Debs and some others were sent to prison in excessive misuse of the courts—for what was called "violation of an injunction," even though Debs was defended by Clarence Darrow. Unions were the devil's work, made servile men confused.

Pullman was in a grandiose state of success—he had been backed by the U.S. Army, the White House. He celebrated by hiring new workers where he could, leaving a thousand families of men not rehired to starve. Pullman refused to aid the homeless and hungry. Losers win nothing. The city of Chicago was left with the task to feed and clothe the miserable, the best it could. The new workers at Pullman had to sign pledges they would *never* join a union. The nation mostly was pleased at the abating of workers in revolt. No wonder radicals like William Jennings Bryan were a menace with their appeal to the horny-handed.

"God needed George Pullman more than Chicago," a fired railroad worker said in a beer garden when three years later George

Pullman died. His dead body was more of a problem to his family than when it was alive. It was feared the dispossessed workers would in some way take their revenge on the corpse. Apprehension took fantastic patterns. As dusk fell, funeral services were held privately in the guarded Pullman mansion on Prairie Avenue. At twilight, a convoy rather than a funeral cortege left the house to deliver the casket to its final resting place at Graveland Cemetery. A great pit had been dug there—one as large as an average room. It was lined with reinforced concrete and steel, built up eighteen inches thick. The mahogany casket, lead lined, was then cloaked in tar paper and over that plastered with quick-drying asphalt, after which it was lowered into the yawning pit. It was guaranteed that the casket would be airtight and waterproof until Judgment Day. Concrete— more of it—was then poured in to make a solid, sealed-in immovable object of the casket. Did anyone wonder if Pullman *could* rise from this on Judgment Day? Over all this were laid lengths of steel rails, at right angles and bolted together. The rails were then also imbedded in more concrete. It took two days for the sweating contractors to finish the hiding away of George Pullman. Ambrose Bierce, when he heard of it, remarked, "It is clear the family in their bereavement was making sure the sonofabitch wasn't going to get up and come back."

The final sod cover of the burial pit had myrtles planted on it, hiding the tons of steel and concrete, the casket and its various wrappings. Perhaps it was just as well Pullman's resentful twin sons could not get at his remains. He left them just three thousand dollars a year, stating in his will that "Neither have developed a sense of responsibility requisite for the wise use of large properties and considerable sums of money." There is a story—unconfirmed—they said they would bring their dogs out there to piss on the grave site.

Pullman left a visible estate of twenty-one million dollars, and a bad feeling in simple people against all millionaires. Eugene Debs served his harsh time in Federal prison; no mercy sat for him in Washington. He remained a strange, saintlike figure in American labor, an alcoholic who could not help himself—always in frail health. The later successful union organizations and presidents were never to see, use, or want his like again, as they rose coarsely to arrogant abused power. And some made common cause with the Mafia, the racketeers, the gangsters. Some unions created leaders like David Beck and James Hoffa, both to be convicted and sent to prison.

Not all free enterprises were as stiff-necked, foolish as Pullman. Chicago took pride in its busy business scene, the size of its commercial projects. In the East Carnegie, Rockefeller, J. P. Morgan had early begun to seize, buy out, or destroy rivals from their Wall Street headquarters, initiate the idea of combines called "trusts" or "rings," fully to own, control, and inflate some needed product such as steel, glass, oil, gas, ice. The ideas moved west. Whiskey, the popular native tipple, be it rye or bourbon, came under the powerful grab of the Whisky Trust (or Ring) and woe to the Chicago distiller who refused to join. By 1889, about twelve whiskey distilleries were ruling at one time eighty-three plants, and profits were high, to "accumulate a surplus for purpose of contest with outsiders" (legal report). The Whisky Ring regulated the liquor business, decreeing where and how much liquor be made, enforcing decree, controlling alcohol. Only two large independents out of eighty distilleries resisted. One of them, the *Chicago Tribune* reported, had caught a spy of the combination tampering with the valves of their vats; then came offers of bribes if they would sell out. After that, the *Chicago Tribune* continued, the distillery became the scene of an explosion: "All the buildings in the neighbourhood were shaken and many panes of glass were broken. . . . There were 15,000 barrels of whisky stored under the roof that was torn open, and if these had been ignited a terrible fire would have been added to the effect of the explosion. A package of dynamite which had failed to explode, though the fuse had been lighted, was found on the premises by the Chicago police."

The Whisky Ring won out in Chicago as elsewhere, and today there remains a loose understanding among distillers and distributors that keeps whiskey prices high, and quality often poor.

The methods in those days of doing business were no more corrupt than today; the exploiters were only more careless of exposure at times, and lived in a cruder age, the days before hired publicity smoke screens and regulations (usually ineffective). We have assumed the so-called robber barons have ceased to exist. They haven't.

Whatever methods were then used, the majority of businessmen and speculators felt it was all good for Chicago and so good for the nation. In a public address in Chicago, in 1883, a United States Senator had exclaimed: "Never in human history was the creation of material wealth so easy and so marvelously abundant, its consolidation under the forms of . . . vast units of power . . . monopolies which absorb and withdraw individual and independent rivalries. Herein are dangers it will behoove us to gravely contemplate and consider what forces shall be summoned to counteract them."

It was a time of pressing out the small fellow to make things bigger. There is the story of the time one of the Steel and Iron trusts was being put together. A party of steelmen were on their way to Chicago after a buying trip. The men had been drinking and were in a good mood.

"There's a steel mill at the next station," said one. "Let's get off and buy it."

Past midnight they pulled the owner out of his bed and put pressure on him to sell.

"The plant is worth two hundred thousand dollars—but it is not for sale," he said.

"Never you mind about the goddamn price, we'll give you three hundred thousand dollars—five hundred thousand dollars."

It was all for the good of Chicago, the country, no matter how things got done. Mark Hanna, the genius of the Republican party strategy, he who found McKinley and was to make him President, and dead, wrote with outraged sensibilities to a Senator who was investigating one of the trusts: Standard Oil. "You have been in politics long enough to know that no man in public office owes the public anything."

It had been made clear to the politicians elected to public office that their best interests and welfare were with the moneymen. To control the officeholder, Collis P. Huntington felt it "a man's duty to go up and bribe."

The consumer, the buyer of the overpriced shoddy product of the trusts, often felt bilked. The worker felt exploited. Many of the men who had created the monopolies decided they could appear, as they aged, as public benefactors by giving money to charities. J. D. Rockefeller began to help the Baptist churches with funds. One Chicago non-Baptist minister joined the gold rush of the eager pastors to the Rockefeller gaping money bag. He was told, "But I am not of your church." "That doesn't matter," said the pastor, "your money is orthodox."

In and out of Chicago in his prime was James Hill, the amazing Western railroad leader. He, like so many managers of big business, feared the discontent of the workers and the demands they could make. Like Rockefeller, he sensed support of the churches would perhaps keep the rabble in order. The church, he decided, could be a splendid controlling force among the masses. Hill, a Protestant, donated a million dollars for a Roman Catholic theological seminary in St. Paul. He explained: "No nation can exist without a true religious spirit behind it. Laws that forbid teaching Christianity are the weakest things in our government. . . . I do not care what the denomination may be. . . . Look at the millions of foreigners pouring into this country to whom the Roman Catholic Church represents the only authority that they either fear or respect. What will be their social view, their political action, their moral status if that single controlling force should be removed?"

Added a spokesman, of Mr. Hill's aid to churches to keep the people under the eyes of their priests, "This is as much a matter of business as is the improvement of farm stock or the construction of a faultless railroad bed."

A great majority of the Chicago workers, in the stockyards, slaughtering houses, factories, building trades were Catholics. They were no match for the remarkable men of the eighties and nineties who created the great industries, the huge fortunes. The philosopher Veblen wrote of these men in his book *The Theory of Business Enterprise*: "The method was that of the ambush and the snare. Its ruling principle was cunning. Its object was to deceive, circumvent, ensnare, capture. Low animal cunning was succeeded by more refined kinds of cunning. The more important of these go by the names of business shrewdness, strategy and diplomacy, none of which differ from ordinary cunning in anything but the degree of adroitness by which the victim is outwitted."

TIDES OF REFORM

At twenty a man is full of fight and hope. He wants to reform the world. When he's seventy he still wants to reform the world, but he knows he can't.

CLARENCE DARROW—AUTOBIOGRAPHY

The problem with reform is that the people most involved, those who are the object of reform, don't want to be reformed. Also they claim many of the reformers are themselves full of some indispensable guilt which makes fanatics of them. The other paradox is that most Americans dislike reformers, claiming those citizens who are reformers are stained with a kind of lingering parochialism that is guilt and puritan anchored, and so are suspected of being more kill-joy than enemies of exacerbated licentiousness. Chicago felt reform was the Protestant ethic gone sour, and the Irish Catholics, the Italians—the major objects of reform—seemed to see obscure, insidious rhythms in desires for change to man's lower "unchangeable" nature. They saw in reform pathological hatred of anyone's rights of enjoying himself in his own way.

The reformers pictured Chicago as a voyeur's and hedonist's dream. All this pro and con was tied up with the money rewards for catering to pleasure-seekers, drinkers, gamblers. What the joy-seekers wanted was not merely an attitude of passive tolerance, but also the corrupt city officials to protect them. The newspapers could only moan as the *Tribune* did: "Chicago is gang-ridden to such extremes that the safety of life, property and happiness are only proverbs, and, like many proverbs, absolutely untrue, and the real facts are that life, property and happiness are only safe when they are protected by locality, strength of arm, or firearms. Chicago is infested by gangs of hoodlums to whom the law is a thing to mock at and by whom the revolver and bullet and the strong arm of the officer are the only things that are feared, and who, after dark in every locality, and through the day time in many localities, menace the decent citizen's life and belongings."

Added Mr. Dooley, "A fanatic is a man who does what he thinks th' Lord wud do if he knew the facts in th' case."

If many elected officials didn't do much beyond steal and aid criminals, there were reform movements, most of which failed when viewed with inherent skepticism. Even if some reformers gained office. Preachers cried out the loudest. Most were sincere. The Elmer Gantrys, and their hellfire and brimstone jabberwocky-howlers, gathered their fees and newspaper space and drifted off.

One of the most serious viewers-with-alarm was the English evangelist and showman, Gipsy Smith, who went after crime and vice in the South Side Levee with all his might in the fall of 1909.

He preached that he was going to lead an army of Christians to the whorehouses. Bernard Shaw was saying just then, "I've heard about Christianity but I've never met any Christians." The local entrenched ministers and priests, snug in their congregations and parishes, were against such rash, direct action. It could only result in "undesirable publicity," they announced, would only advertise what was sold on the Levee. Police Superintendent Leroy Stewart was rather incoherent and felt Smith's idea was "inherently vicious." Still he promised an escort of mounted police to those troublemaking Christians. Too bad, some citizens said, there were no lions to throw them to. Gipsy proclaimed he would expose sin so it could be destroyed and would the Chicago press please send journalists to report the march of the crusaders?

On October 18, the great meeting was held in the Seventh

Regiment Armory at Twenty-fourth Street and Wentworth Avenue, with much indiscriminate praise for virtue against vice. Prayers were rising among faded army banners of the Indian-pogroming
horse soldiers of the Western plains, and old cannon on display
seemed ready to fire a broadside on vice. Gipsy Smith ended his
prayer, led his followers down the aisle, out to Wentworth Avenue,
men and women, most of them in long black gowns, carrying
torches as yet unlit. Three brass bands took their places, the
mounted troop of police took up positions at the head of Chicago's
Pilgrims' Progress—and so the congregation moved off to the hiss of
shoe leather, as yet silent in their ideas of hope and Christian grace,
clothed in the absoluteness of their cause.

How many of them were there? No one is sure. The press said
three thousand, then reported again, twelve thousand. What is certain is the rowdy crowd that followed the marchers; it was huge and
had come along to see the fun. Nearly fifteen thousand mockers followed Gipsy Smith and his bands. At Twenty-second Street, Smith
lifted up his arms and the bands at last blared forth with "Where
He Leads Me I Will Follow." The godly marched past the whorehouses, the lewd saloons, the depraved cafés, crossing, recrossing the
Levee, singing, chanting, shouting prayers, giving voice to God to
redeem these sinners, to forgive, bring hope and repentance to the
breasts of the hookers, drabs, joy girls, madams, pimps, barflies, perverts, the owners of bagnios. Come, come to the faith's sweet sedative, the addiction to your Redeemer.

From the windows of parlor houses, creep joints, luxury bordellos of the Levee, the cheap grind houses, the whores stared and
watched. Some cheered and mocked, a few wept—no persons are
harmonious within themselves. Mostly they just stared. In front of
the House of All Nations and the Everleigh Club, the marchers got
to their knees among the horse litter and gutter dirt. They gave the
Lord's Prayer, recited the Twenty-third Psalm. The bands joined
in. Voices were then raised in that sentimental favorite, "Where Is
My Wandering Boy Tonight?" And if he was in bed with a harlot,
he may have sat up and reached for his pants to see what the com-
motion outside was all about. Divergent life-styles faced each other
that night, psychologically incompatible.

The last number sung was "Nearer My God to Thee," which
legend was also to say the band played on the deck of the White

Star liner *Titanic*. (Wrong, it played ragtime as the ship sank into the icy waters.)

Marching away in sobriety and gravity for their cause, the Christians made for the Alhambra Theatre at Archer Avenue and State Street. Here Gipsy Smith in rational imagery began a prayer service dedicated to the fallen woman, the sins of her voluptuous evil, "the sad, idle life of the fallen sister" for whom hell yawned in iridescent flame.

The Levee had taken the march silently—mostly. Saloons lowered their shades, put out their lights. Some jeered from the safety of the crowd, but in the main the sinners and their parasites just watched and listened. The sightseers who had come for some excitement seemed to start to drift away. But then a popular ragtime tune came from a knocking-shop piano, lights went up, gas and electric, doors began to swing open, music grew in volume. Laughter and the sound of corks popping signaled a return to life on the Levee, a return to the pleasures of the flesh. The Levee had come through its bath of prayer and virtue untouched. ("Now girls be intimate in your loving, but never familiar—when you must fart, lean your ass off the bed"—Nell Kimball.)

The visitors, sightseers, milled about, and the girls were back on their backs, bartenders were sweating as they filled glasses, poured bourbon, pickpockets were busy. A reporter was told: "It was the biggest night on record in the Levee. What them evangelists done was set off the biggest advertising turnout the madams had ever seen."

Gipsy Smith had made the vice district familiar to thousands of boys and teen-agers. One policeman in a bar reported they roamed the Levee, seeking, learning, "getting their cherry copped, joint blown, discovering the fun of nookie." Only a maudlin madam (according to a news story) could add with crocodile tears, "I was sorry to see so many nice young men down here for the first time."

The press didn't think much of the crusade, and jests were made about it. Most of the high-toned ministers said none of *their* people had been there. The evangelist in pious affirmation insisted, "Time will show that great good has been done."

In one way, Gipsy was right. He had done much to make more money for the brothels and saloons, bring in new trade. But as time passed, many people began to see that the invasion of Satan's Mile had been worth it. The Levee's world of whore and criminal was exposed to the city for all to see. And the sight of all those youths testing the lure of prostitutes sank in to parents, teachers, even to a few politicians. The lethargy of accepting the Levee was cracked—foreboding and disenchantment had set in.

"CLOSE THE LEVEE!"

A whore shouldn't have sales days.
NELL KIMBALL: HER LIFE AS AN AMERICAN MADAM

There were other marchers against the intolerable conditions. The Cook County Chapter of the Woman's Christian Temperance Union, three thousand strong, led by their president, Mrs. C. Hill, came in feathers, carrying banners, to parade downtown, to pack City Hall and shout at Mayor Fred Busse to enforce fully the Revised Municipal Code, to outlaw the running of whorehouses, places of assignation. What, they cried out, about that fine of two hundred dollars upon conviction? Mayor Busse, with smug grace, promised there would be a "full investigation." Mrs. Hill suggested he do a bit of praying "for divine guidance." Mr. Busse stiffly answered he would in his "own good time and place." Spiritual austerity had met sanguine politics.

In January 1910, a huge meeting representing six hundred congregations of the Federated Protestant Churches took place in the Central YMCA, in the odor of old locker-room basketball shoes. The Very Reverend Walter T. Sumner, dean of the Episcopal Cathedral of Saints Peter and Paul, introduced a resolution: "Resolved, that the Mayor of the City of Chicago be asked to appoint a Commission made up of men and women who command the respect and confidence of the public at large, this Commission to investigate thoroughly the conditions as they exist. With this knowledge obtained, let it map out such a course, as in its judgment, will bring about some relief from the frightful conditions which surround us. Taking this report as a basis, let us enlist the support of every civic, protective, philanthropic, social, commercial and religious body in the city to carry out the plans suggested. If the present administration feels that it cannot subscribe to such a plan, make the report the basis of a pledge from the political parties at the next election and make it the basis for an election issue. But first get the plan. The city press will be back of any sane movement to improve present conditions. The Church certainly is. Social settlements have been agitating and endeavoring to reach some decision. The general public is in a mood to listen."

The mayor, robust, expansive—and wary—expressed the opinion that the conditions incident to the vice problem in Chicago were better than they ever were within present-day memory. ("What he say?" "What he *mean?*") "But," he added, "we all want still better conditions *if* they can be had." The mayor was a master of triteness and irrelevance.

The Vice Commission created a fund of five thousand dollars to investigate vice and its divergent life-styles. Even thieves among the aldermen like John Powers, Hinky Dink, and Bathhouse John voted *yes* on that. ("What harm kin it do?")

The courts came alive, resonant with legal Latin. A judge ruled and issued an injunction restraining some people from opening a new whorehouse in South Chicago, reason not moral, but material: "the presence of an immoral resort is damaging to adjacent property." The city was wholesomely skeptical about anything that might depress real-estate values.

As for the underage boys and teen-agers come to puberty lubricating their libidos among loose women—the police came up with Twelve Commandments. ("Just ten were good enough for Moses," said one policeman who believed the law lived in the end of a club.) Twelve commandments it was, then, the police were ordered to see fully enforced among the lads.

1. Messenger and delivery boys, or any person over the age of three or under the age of eighteen years, shall not be permitted either in the district or to enter the premises (of whorehouses—[No three-year-old philanderers were reported]).

2. Harboring of inmates under legal age . . . If inmates under age are found, the house shall be suppressed, and it shall be definitely understood that this action will be taken in any and all cases where this law is violated.

3. Forcible detention. No person, regardless of age, shall be detained against his or her will, nor shall iron bars or other obstacles be permitted upon any exit.

4. No women without male escorts shall be permitted in a saloon. All soliciting of this nature to be vigorously suppressed.

5. Short skirts, transparent gowns or other improper attire shall not be permitted in the parlors, or public rooms. [No restriction against appearing naked was listed.]

6. Men will not be permitted to conduct or be domiciled in a house of prostitution or to loiter about the premises. Males evidently subsisting on the income of inmates shall be arrested as vagrants.

7. Soliciting in any form shall not be permitted, either on the streets, from doorways, from windows or in saloons.

8. Signs, lights, colors or devices, significant or conspicuous, indicative of the character of any premises occupied by a house of ill-repute, shall not be permitted. [A popular favor was a common steel screw attached to a disc lettered GOOD FOR ONE ——.]

9. Obscene exhibitions or pictures shall not be permitted.

10. Restricted districts. No house of ill-fame shall be permitted outside of certain restricted districts, or to be established within two blocks of any school, church, hospital, or public institution, or upon any street car line.

11. Doors. No swinging doors that permit of easy access or a view of the interior from the street shall be permitted. All resorts shall be provided with double doors which shall be kept closed.

12. No liquor to be permitted, sold, carried or given away . . . in any immoral place.

With added funds, in time, the investigation had a full picture of what was going on in Chicago, even the working of whores in the new nickelodeon movies showing John Bunny and Flora Finch, *The Great Train Robbery*, the first of the Charlie Chaplins and D. W. Griffiths.

By 1915, a report could point the finger of the reformers once more in the proper direction . . . "the fact that prostitution in this city is a *Commercialized Business* of large proportions with tremendous profits of more than Fifteen Million Dollars per year, controlled largely by men, not women. Separate the male exploiter from the problem, and we minimize its extent and abate its flagrant outward expression. . . . In juxtaposition with this group of professional male exploiters stand ostensibly respectable citizens, both men and women who are openly renting and leasing property for exorbitant sums, and thus sharing, through immorality of investments, the profits from this *Business*. . . . Evidence has been produced showing that a highly respected and honored company, in whose hands respectable citizens entrust their money, has apparently assumed the trusteeship of four of the vilest houses of ill-fame in the Twenty-second Street restricted district. Again, several wealthy and prominent business men, whose advice is sought in matters pertaining to the civic welfare and development of Chicago, are leasing their houses for this business. One of these men has six houses in a part of the district where the most disgusting and flagrant violations of the law and police rules occur. The court records show that practically no effort has been made during the past three years to prosecute agents and real estate owners who are leasing and renting property for immoral purposes. The law affecting these persons is a dead letter. . . . During the month of October an investigator visited sixty-five real estate agents and owners, most of whom were located in residential sections of the city, and in forty-four instances they offered to rent rooms and flats. In each instance the investigator stated she wanted to rent the premises for a 'sporting house.'

"In the second place the Commission believes that something can be done by law honestly and efficiently administered. Practically no attempt has been made in Chicago to enforce the present laws. Many inmates have left the houses and now live in flats, where they sell liquor under a government receipt, procured at a cost of twenty-five dollars. 'There are five hundred flats opened up on the South Side since May 1st,' an inspector states. 'There are three hundred and sixty flats with prostitution on Cottage Grove

Avenue and all over; that is, from Twenty-second Street south and east of State Street.' It is undoubtedly true that the result of the order has been to scatter the prostitutes over a wider territory. . . .

"There is quite a number of massage parlors, manicure establishments and Turkish baths, especially in the downtown district, which are in reality nothing but houses of prostitution of the most revolting and insidious type. . . .

"Assignation hotels are scattered all over the city, especially in the downtown district and on the West and North sides. Prostitutes in saloons and on the streets use these cheap places. . . . There are also a great many assignation rooms, especially on the North Side from the river to Chicago Avenue and on the side streets west of State. These rooms are used to the same extent as the hotels."

Some amazing figures were listed. The city had five thousand known prostitutes working actively in houses, about two thousand walking the streets. This took no count of semipros, the working girls who earned a bit on the side, hustling weekends and nights "as free-lance quim." A more realistic figure, most newspapers felt, was that about fifteen thousand women in part or full time were prostituting themselves in Chicago for gain. Bohemian and middle-class adultery and unmarried fornication were not counted. One whorehouse in two years, 1906–1908, using from twelve to twenty girls, serviced 179,599 male guests.

As for income, the money taken in from women and disorderly saloons, the figure was twenty-five million dollars (again one must recall this was money worth many times our present currency).

The Vice Commission report was sent to Mayor Busse and the tainted City Council—both with so many fragmented allegiances— and there was passed a resolution placing it "on file." The council said the report could be printed if done "without expense to the city." A four-hundred-page book was at last issued; the Post Office Department at once began barring it from the U.S. mails as containing obscene matter.

As always, when reform reared its earnest head, vice simmered down a bit, became a bit subservient: "don't make trouble." Some houses closed, others existed fairly silently, and were open for only special clients. Commissions grew in number, expanded strategies.

A Law and Order League, the Committee of Fifteen under Julius Rosenwald of Sears, Roebuck (which underpaid its girls, driving some of them to become whores), the packinghouse's Harold Swift (at whose plants women sat at sausage machines at low pay, fingers infected by chemically doctored meat, and whose daughters would rather go into the streets). Good-meaning men, but for whom charity did cover a multitude of industrial sins. The commissions and groups did have teeth, and dives and houses had to close.

Virginia Brooks organized the Chicago Welfare League marches through the streets—to get saloons to obey the city laws. She paraded to the tune of "Onward Christian Soldiers," with ministers, Boy Scouts, Girl Scouts, a band, the Epworth League, the Baptist Missionary School, the Moody Bible Institute: a procession five thousand strong with splendid impulses of aggression for the Lord's work, as they saw it. There were great raids in varied cadences of screams and oaths—closing of saloons and more houses. Warrants in one raid were issued for 135 saloonkeepers and owners. Reported the *Record Herald*, "Electric pianos stopped as if paralyzed. Bright lights went glimmering. Into the streets poured a crowd of half-dressed women, some with treasured belongings tied in tablecloths. Others were packing suitcases as they moved, and most of them were running, a majority not knowing where they were going, but anywhere to get out of the district. In front of a few of the more pretentious establishments automobiles suddenly appeared. Women soon loaded them."

The saloon- and brothel keepers did not react with resignation or disillusionment—they began to raise a fund of fifteen thousand dollars to buy the legislation they needed to save themselves. And to counterattack reformers, the homeless whores were told to move into the city to annoy the genteel districts. Get on your loudest clothes and more paint than usual and parade. Go to residence districts. Ring doorbells and apply for lodgings. Get rooms only in respectable neighborhoods. Don't accost men on the streets, but be out as much as possible. Frequent respectable cafés and make a splash.

Just what came of this no one was sure, but a lot of women got some exercise and views of parts of the city they hadn't had in years.

By 1914, the state's attorney was promising again to clean up the Levee, which was, he admitted, "worse than ever before, infested with the worst criminals in Chicago, a segregated district of pickpockets, gunmen, robbers and burglars."

On the Levee they were singing again:

> *Get six gamblers to carry my coffin*
> *Six whores to sing my song.*
> *Put a jazz band on my tail-gate*
> *To raise Hell as we go along.*
> "ST. JAMES INFIRMARY"

Vice and murder continued on the Levee because the politicians and police, as usual, also shared in the profits of crime in the city. It was mostly our old friends Hinky Dink and Bathhouse John the *Chicago Tribune* explained:

"There are three reasons why the tragedy of the Levee could not have been avoided. First, is Alderman 'Hinky Dink' Kenna . . . The Levee exists because it is by the denizens of the Levee that he rolls up the voting power which causes such men as Carter Harrison and Roger Sullivan [Democratic boss] to consult him as a political peer, and County Judge Owens to have him as a trimmer. Second, is 'Bathhouse' John Coughlin . . . Third, is Captain Michael Ryan of the Twenty-second Street Police Station. He is the Chief of Police of the First Ward. The 'Hink' put him there. The 'Hink' and the 'Bath' keep him there. He has been denounced as either notoriously corrupt or incompetent. But [ward heelers] Funkhouser, Dannenberg, Gleason [chief of police] and Hoyne, himself [state's attorney], cannot budge Ryan from that station. They have all tried and failed.

"When State's Attorney Wyman closed the Levee, there was one set of dividing lines he could not touch. They were the lines marking out the police district. Captain Ryan's instructions to his subordinates are their only instructions . . . Chief Gleason and First Deputy Schuettler may send the Funkhouser squads and the Dannenberg squads to make raids, but they cannot force Ryan to make raids. And no matter how many raids they make and how they show Ryan up, he is still on the job, in complete control of his precinct lines.

"In other cities the one 'ring' has been found to be a clique of gambling kings who ruled the situation; in Chicago the 'ring' is extended to the formation of a complete wheel.

"Ryan is the hub. His plainclothes policemen, his confidential men are the spokes, the dive owners and keepers controlling strings of saloons and resorts . . . travel along without interruption.

But more important than any or all of these parts—the one thing without which the wheel could not revolve—is the axle, and this axle is the 'little fellow' to every denizen of the district, or 'Hinky Dink.' Men in uniform in Ryan's district are told to keep their eyes straight, ignoring what is going on behind doors and windows, and watching only for disturbances in the street. They are told to do police duty as if the social evil did not exist around them."

> *Frankie and Johnny went walking,*
> *John in his brand new suit.*
> *Then, "Oh good Lawd," says Frankie,*
> *"Don't my Johnny look real cute!"*

BOOK SIX

SODOM BY THE LAKE

62

MAX AND THE COLONEL

Journalism consists of buying paper at two cents a pound and selling it at ten cents a pound.
CHARLES DANA, IN THE SUN

Strangest of the families of Chicago were the Annenbergs; by legal records shown to be in the world of sluggers and wrecking crews, ready with blows, and worse, for those newsboys who didn't behave as the circulation boss saw fit.

They had been born to a Jewish junk dealer, from Koenigsberg, East Prussia, and, on arriving, Chicago gave them their first sense of strength. They had sly qualifications to power, backed by muscle. There was Max Annenberg, circulation slugger for the *Chicago Tribune*, whose job it was to hire the thugs and hoodlums who saw that the *Tribune* got onto the best newsstands, and to see that the dealers who also sold the *other* Chicago newspapers didn't give them too much space up front. Max—proving that ambition for some is an insidious disease—directed the wars against the thugs and sluggers of the *other* papers. Max was a mighty force—with no condescending jocularity—using the crunch for the *Tribune*.

As Ben Hecht said, when I was first working on this book, "The owners of the *Tribune* like Max's slugging so much they never even held it against him he was a foreign born Heb. . . . Now that was no trivial reward from those proud goyim."

Max's brother was Moe Annenberg, who owned the horse players' and poolroom hustlers' bible, *The Daily Racing Form*, and Moe didn't please too many Philadelphians by his ideas as publisher of the *Inquirer*. Moe served two years in Federal prison for cheating the Collector of Internal Revenue. A nephew, the records show, murdered a girl while under the influence of drugs, and got off lightly. Moe's son ended up, as a British journalist wrote me, "in my opinion the most unpopular Ambassador to the Court of St. James since Joseph P. Kennedy."

Max, the *Chicago Tribune* warrior slugger, with tenacity and audacity, worked hard. He had left Hearst to work for the *Tribune* because Hearst in 1910 wanted him to travel and do a little circulation slugging for the other papers in the chain. But Max liked living in Chicago, that toddling town. It was where the action was. Max, once testifying in court, admitted the bloody wars broke out when the *Tribune* reduced its price a cent, to match Hearst's *Examiner*. The Hearst people, he said, "were instructed to go around in automobiles and slug anybody who cut their order . . . or would permit the *Tribune* to replace an *Examiner* . . . and give them to understand that they were not only *through* with the newspaper business, but that they were *through* on this earth."

"Did *you* hire any sluggers?" he was asked.

"Lemme see. I had Mossy Enright . . . Jim Regan, Walter Stephens and Arthur McBride . . . four well known sluggers . . . at one time in that battle there were sixty men . . . by boat of us . . . on boat sides."

"How long did this struggle continue in 1910, when you had thirty sluggers and the other fellow had thirty sluggers?"

"Oh . . . about two years, couple of years anyway."

"Was anybody arrested?"

"Not what I know of."

Max Annenberg found the *Tribune* with nearly 190,000 readers. With the solid aid of his sluggers, and muscle power, in eight years the *Tribune* was selling close to a half million copies a day. Became number one, because Max tried harder, and the paper was very readable. (Max modestly admitted, "You don't need no advertising in no other paper when you advertise in the *Tribune*.")

The *Tribune* had personality, pride, and a bloody history of violence. A Congressional committee investigated certain brutal actions in the Tribune Building (and did nothing about it), reporting it as "a favorite resort of criminals both before and after the outbreak of violence in 1910." The official testimony at the hearings is like dialogue in a later Warner Brothers movie of the Eddie Robinson, James Cagney period.

"What is the name of the man who was killed in the *Tribune* office?"

Editor James Keeley on the stand: "We killed a man . . ."

"When you say *we*, do you mean you participated?"

"Oh no . . . I was using *we* as representing the company . . . we killed a man, or a man was killed in an elevator shaft . . . he was beaten up, thrown down the elevator shaft and shot at. . . . He was on the mail floor."

"And he was beaten up before that happened . . . made unconscious, was he?"

"Some of that . . . I think the fellow that was after him jumped down on him . . . came down after him and shot at him."

"He shot at the man he had thrown down the elevator shaft first?"

"I think he did, Judge."

"He was never prosecuted . . . never arrested . . . never indicted . . . no prosecution . . . by either the *Tribune* or any of its officers? . . . Was the man who was thrown down the elevator shaft an employee of the *Tribune*?"

"I think he had been *until* that morning."

"Was the man thrown down the shaft by an employee of the *Tribune*?"

"He was . . . in the circulation department."

The editor then described the circulation sluggers as "wrecking crews . . . and as a matter of fact, in the last year, they, the other paper, had gangs of murderers out . . . cold blooded murderers, and there has been killing on both sides."

"You know Moss Enright?" [Moss was identified as a notorious underworld figure working for Max Annenberg.]

"When I found out who he was, I fired him."

"Did not Moss Enright say at the time he confessed to murdering [a rival slugger] . . . that he worked for the *Chicago Tribune?*"

"I don't know whether he said it. I said he did work for the *Tribune* at some period."

No personal involvement, violence, self-incrimination reached the publishing level.

The Max Annenberg terror went on; sluggers and wrecking crews made the Chicago newspaper wars as exciting and dangerous as rumors of a Great War brewing in Europe. Max in 1914 became a sort of pseudo roughhouse expert on international affairs. "France is a corrupt and immoral nation." (It even lacked circulation sluggers.) "Belgium is not much better." (In Chicago someone also shot civilian hostages, it was pointed out.) "But Germany is in the full bloom of health and power!" A chaotic world refused to listen to Max, and Chicago was pro-French—mostly pro-British.

Max's publisher, Robert Rutherford McCormick, had to see this great war Max was talking of. The colonel, as he came to be known to fame, in evocative fervor went to visit the Russian front, where he admitted he wondered if he had "the physical courage to go on to the battlefield . . . [I] had been steeped as fully as any other in the cult of cowardice which has been such a distinct departure of modern American intellectual thought . . . Now we are to visit the place where the wine of death is spilled." (Along the way to the wine testing, he described an officers' lunch in the Russian trenches as "all kinds of good things to eat . . . caviar, sardines, cheese, canned lobster, cake, more caviar, radishes, cold meat.")

The colonel kept up a strange emotional reaction and equilibrium in his reporting for Chicago readers. Death, to gourmet dainties for lunch, are of equal interest to him. Summing it up for the readers with a poetic naïve amorality, "I have tasted the wine of death and its flavor will be forever in my throat."

Death, yes, he could rub against—in facile sentiment—but the foreign born at home he couldn't swallow. "The newly arrived immigrants . . . in event of invasion thousands and thousands of them will . . . join the invaders . . . none bound to defend the country . . . With what enthusiasm does anyone think that the American people would rush to arms to drive back an invader of the seaboard?" The colonel (National Guard) did not trust even the native born in the Eastern establishment as being fully American.

His cousin, Joseph Medill Patterson—the other side of the

coin—was a bit of a radical, and he went even further, attacking the *entire* scene. "Our country is inferior to other countries in many, if not most of the higher arts of civilization . . . a land of loafers. . . . We are rich, fat, soft, and easy pickings for any gunman among the nations." And like another and later gloom-sayer, Charles Lindbergh, Patterson admitted the Germans were the ones to watch—had a better *Kultur* in battle. "I do not think the German idea can be beaten in this war."

But when the bugles blew "Over There," Patterson went into World War I to do his duty, pocketing the German idea. He became a captain in the Rainbow Division, fought three months on the Lorraine front, was at Champagne under Giraud, and in action in the second battle of the Marne, also in Saint-Mihiel and the Argonne. He had a dynamic promiscuity for battle.

Colonel McCormick, too, went back to sniff—not too closely—at the wine of death. He was a spurred, booted, polished member of General John J. Pershing's staff. He became a real colonel, with a Distinguished Service Medal, and a citation for "organizing ability, unusual executive ability, and ["oddly," thought his fellow officers] of sound judgement."

The officers who had to serve with him found he gave them "the willies." Said one: "I can't imagine McCormick ever doing a kind thing for anyone. . . . He knew democracy had got out of hand in Russia, and he was afraid democracy would get out of hand here." His love of democracy did not extend to anyone patting his German wolfhound, Rajah. He issued strict orders forbidding any soldier to act friendly with the creature. "That's *my* dog!"

Meanwhile, back in Chicago, the *Tribune*, with its aggravating potentialities, was making millions of dollars that had to be invested. One scheme was to start a tabloid newspaper in New York City, "which didn't deserve any better." It was a huge, tasteless success among the lip-moving readers from the start. However, fourteen million dollars were lost supporting a failure, *Liberty Magazine*. Still there was enough for the solid dream of stone spires to arise in Chicago, almost a demonic spree in building for all eyes to look up to. A contest for the planned building was held—the winning design would have delighted a Borgia, a Medici. The Tribune Tower. Raymond Hood and John Mead Howells designed it, a thirty-six-story Gothic skyscraper on Michigan Avenue just north of the Chicago River bridge—to stand as the solid, material symbol of "the World's Greatest Newspaper." Some found it a maniacal, imbecilic growth. The genius among Chicago architects, Louis Sullivan, was hardly impressed. He saw it as a copious nervous disorder in stone and steel, and he dug deeply into the fantasy of Colonel McCormick's mind. In a report he wrote, he identified it for what it was. "It is an imaginary structure—not imaginative. Starting with false premises, it was doomed to false conclusions . . . it savors of the nursery where children bet imaginary millions."

Colonel McCormick, however, felt he had anchored himself, with its encrustation, to the grandeurs of the past. He wrote in an editorial, "Words cannot describe the beauty of the Taj Mahal. Man fails to voice the true impression of the magnitude of the Great Pyramid . . . To appreciate the symphony in stone which is Tribune Tower, you must see it, live in the same community with it."

Carl Sandburg is said to have remarked, "He might not share his dog, but you could look at his building" (Elliot Paul).

If the colonel couldn't get chunks of the Taj Mahal or the Pyramid to embellish his tower, he did insert stones that he claimed came from the Parthenon, the Great Wall of China, Notre-Dame de Paris, and, best of all, a bit of rubble from the Alamo. So from the crepuscular decay of the past, he adorned his walls.

A carved inscription in the lobby warned that the colonel had his eye on the rascals and soft livers in Washington. "THE NEWSPAPER IS AN INSTITUTION . . . TO . . . FURNISH THAT CHECK UPON GOVERNMENT WHICH NO CONSTITUTION HAS BEEN ABLE TO PROVIDE."

"*That*," Edgar Lee Masters said at first viewing the inscription, "puts Jefferson in his place."

Other names appear in the official history of the newspaper. "Homer would have liked to work on the *Tribune*. So would Horace, with his whimsicality; Herodotus, with his wealth of incident. So would Balzac, Addison, Samuel Johnson, Dickens, Hardy, Kipling, and Mark Twain."

One brash visitor from California, signing a special guest book, added, "You left off Max Annenberg."

To keep the McCormick name for vital, odd living up to snuff, there was Edith Rockefeller McCormick—daughter of John D. Rockefeller, *and* daughter-in-law of old Cyrus. Her husband Harold helped bring Mary Garden, Galli-Curci, Tito Schipa to the Chicago Opera Company. Edith divorced him, and he had a vitality gland operation—some claim monkey testicles—and, as we've noted, married the Polish "opera star," Ganna Walska. Edith had an ermine cape of 275 skins that spread like a tent and a plum-colored Rolls-Royce with two men on the box in plum-colored outfits. Also about a million dollars in jewels. She amazed her Chicago guests at dinners she gave in the Egyptian style, by announcing, "I am the reincarnation of Seti I, the child wife of Tutankhamen . . . it was a lock of my successor's hair that was found in the tomb." Later she gave James Joyce a thousand francs a month to ease his lot.

No matter what their philosophies or attitudes, the newspapers loved politics and crime, war or social events; to them Chicago, nearly always with a high wind blowing, was on its way to greatness. A cortex of action, in mean or grandiose style. The ore boats continued to come regularly from the Menominee, Gogebic, and Mesabi iron ranges, and crime and poverty existed as usual in regions back of the Yards. Orators spoke out in Bug House Square on topics of the crime of ostentation and wealth, controversial events; like new cults and old godheads. A sign read: *Jesus Saves!* ("But not like Marshall Field's," added some graffiti philosopher.)

The critics came, and the visitors, and said foolish things at times. Max Beerbohm, the sly elf of Edwardian England, added his own appraisal of the city. "In Chicago . . . little value is set on bricks and mortar. A fire enjoyed; then the buildings are reproduced and burned down again in leisure." As if to bear him out, the Chicago Historical Society displayed what might be the bell that hung around the neck of Mrs. O'Leary's cow. Might be.

What was clear and true was the growth of the city. Way back in 1860, its population has been estimated at 109,290. A decade later, at 298,977. In 1880, it was 503,185, ten years later, 1,440,850. By 1900, the population had risen to 1,698,575, and by 1910, to 2,185,283. In 1919, it was climbing to 2,781,705.

Three hundred and fifty thousand men from Illinois had gone

to World War I, and up from the South had come sixty-five thousand blacks to help expand the Black Belt to near bursting, so that during the war years, 1917 into 1919, twenty-five bombings of the black section had taken place—bigotry trying to keep them from expanding the boundaries.

The streets had changed from mud, cobblestones, to smooth paving—the horses were still there but in retreat as the primitive Packards, Simplexes, Pierce-Arrows were being outnumbered by the tin lizzie of Model T design, Henry Ford's people's car, the flivver and the Ford jokes that went with it. Gone were the spacious barouches, ladies with parasols up, India shawls, girls wearing hoops.

And visitors were still trying to figure out the city, making statements of their own confusion and bafflement. Julian Street, the novelist, was to break into wild language as he tried to measure the city.

"Chicago is stupefying. It knows no rules, and I know none by which to judge it. It stands apart from all the cities of the world, isolated by its own individuality, an Olympian freak, a fable, an allegory, an incomprehensible phenomenon, a prodigious paradox in which youth and maturity, brute strength and soaring spirit are harmoniously confused."

As for the history of violence in the early generation of Annenbergs, even in the 1970s it made news, and a film, *Jennifer on My Mind*. As the *Los Angeles Times* review reported:

> Roger L. Simon, whose novel "Heir" is the basis for the film, [was] inspired by the true-life case of Robert Friede, a 25-year-old heir to the Annenberg publishing empire, and aristocratic and wealthy 19-year-old Celeste Crenshaw, whose drug-wracked corpse was found in the trunk of Friede's car in New York on Feb. 7, 1966.

63

VIA CHICAGO—FLY COAST TO COAST
IN 49 DAYS

Birds can fly
And why can't I?
"DARIUS GREEN AND HIS FLYING MACHINE"

Almost no one recalls a soft drink, a grape juice drink, that Armour & Co. of Chicago had on the market in 1911. It was called Vin Fiz, and, because of it, Armour helped sponsor the first coast-to-coast flight by a flying machine, promoting the drink by naming one plane trying for the event the Vin Fiz.

The Chicago American, one of the Hearst newspapers, joined in with others in the chain in offering fifty thousand dollars to the flier who would first make it coast to coast with a stopover in Chicago. In 1911 the flying machine, not yet called the aeroplane by most (*airplane* came even later), was a risky device.

So between Armour's grape juice drink and the hunt for news headlines, Chicago could claim its place as a pioneer in the history of aviation.

The newspapers of before World War I always had a hearty head of steam up, always offering prize money to get people to break their necks. No one objected when William Randolph Hearst

461

was offering fifty thousand dollars for the first man to fly "coast to coast in less than thirty days." One who heard was Cal Rodgers, Calbraith Perry Rodgers.

In September of 1911, he was one of the raffish fliers who were out to try for the prize money. He was flying a Wright Brothers plane, the Model Ex biplane with a thirty-two-foot wingspan, a four-cylinder job that hoped for thirty-five horsepower. It had a water-cooled engine, two wooden propellers—a plane with a top speed, the Chicago press claimed, of fifty-five miles an hour. No exquisite detail—just a kite and motor. It was simple in design, flimsy in build, and had no throttle, so there were just two speeds, roaring along and stop. Levers controlled the wing warp that steered the plane before an age of ailerons. There was a flat, armless, wooden seat for the pilot, who was out in the open and with no wind protection. With the expectation of many crashes, a windshield would

have been a kind of hari-kari. In those days a flier, to have luck, first had to believe in it.

Armour & Co. talked of *its* flier and *its* drink. Cal Rodgers was thirty-two years old, too big for a flier in the shoddy canvas bird, being six feet four, and carrying two hundred pounds of himself around. He inspired respect rather than confidence. (To add to his handicaps, Cal was nearly stone-deaf, perhaps from all the exhibition flying done around Chicago—among other places—in open planes, near loud hammering motors.) To keep his teeth from jarring loose, he usually flew with a cigar in his mouth, and he had learned the trick of lighting it in the air. His father had been a cavalry officer who had died in the Indian wars in Wyoming Territory, his patrol hit not by a Sioux war party, but by lightning.

Armour & Co. as sponsors tried to keep Vin Fiz up front. To repair and replace parts and motors, Cal was going to be accompanied by a special cross-country railroad train advertising the drink —an engine and three cars lettered with the title Vin Fiz. The Armour train car was painted white and carried an extra plane, an auto (a Palmer-Singer), tools, and spare parts. There was also an observation car and a dining and Pullman car. Comfortable if not sumptuous, it could outdistance the plane *if* not held back. The train was for servicing the flier and the plane, as well as to carry Cal's wife, his mother, and a naval officer cousin, a repair crew, and Charlie Taylor, a Wright Brothers plane mechanic, *and* cases of Vin Fiz. Nobody expected an easy flight. The Armour people had officially named the plane the *Vin Fiz Flier*, and would pay Cal five dollars a mile for every mile he flew. While paying the cost of the special train, the packing company drew the line at laying out any cash for spare parts, repairs, gasoline, and oil. Cal's reward would come if he won Hearst's fifty thousand dollars.

So beside a sea of wrinkling jade, on September 18, at Sheepshead Bay, Long Island, a Southern belle dribbled a bottle of the grape juice mixture on the wooden skids—wheels added (smashing the bottle on the *Vin Fiz Flier* might have wrecked it). That commercial absurdity done, Cal Rodgers was handed a four-leaf clover. He climbed up on the plane's seat and lit a cigar, lowered his goggles from his cap (with its peak in the back), and signaled to start the engine. It sounded like an articulated saxophone. The two wooden props in back—it was a pusher plane—began to churn the air.

His route was simple—catch-as-catch-can—New York to California, via Chicago, home of his sponsor. It had to be done in thirty days. Two rivals, Fowler and Ward (first names not given in press story) were already off, or rather one was repairing a fresh wreck, the other had run into a barbed-wire fence, but they would both limp on. Fame, fortune, catastrophe, even death could lie ahead.

But the cigar was drawing well, and Cal got his plane into the air, scattering the crowd. He circled Coney Island, dropping leaflets explaining the goodness of Chicago's wonder brew, *Vin Fiz, the Ideal Grape Drink, Sold Everywhere*, made by Armour & Co. The *New York Journal*, a Hearst newspaper, wrote of the start as the "most daring and spectacular feat in aviation that the country or even the world has ever known." A bit premature, it seemed to some, as they watched the clumsy machine struggle off. Cal flew over Brooklyn at a height of eight hundred feet, then to the East River past the Brooklyn Bridge. Below was the battleship *Connecticut*, heading for the Brooklyn Navy Yard. Some teacup reader on the Hearst's *American* mused on the plane over the battle wagon and of coming things in the air. He saw "an age that may speed the doom of the battleship for all time." People suspected that, like most newspapermen, he drank.

Cal was the first man over New York and from there went on to New Jersey to pick up his train—steam up, waiting on the Erie tracks. Then he winged on to Middletown, New York. Cal had flown eighty-four miles in one hundred and five minutes.

On takeoff the next day, trying to avoid some power lines, he sideswiped a tree, turned over, and smashed into a chicken coop. The plane, standing on its nose, was a mess, and Cal had a bleeding scalp wound. Repaired—man and plane—with a fresh cigar and a bandaged head, Cal flew the ruptured plane to Hancock, New York, in seventy-eight minutes for the ninety-five miles. Several wrecks later—he and the plane in continual repair—he moved on to Chicago.

Flying was stormy as one of those grand Hoosier thunderstorms came up, streaks of heat lightning etching the sky. Rain began to flog Cal, unprotected as he was in his seat open to the sky, and he tried to shield his magneto from the wet. He was forced down by the storm, off course a bit. He was annoyed but unshattered.

Moving on, Cal failed in a takeoff when, against most rules of flying, he tried to get into the air downwind. He missed two trees and some telegraph wires, but hit a rise in the ground with one wing, and with a crash of wire, canvas, and frame, the plane wrecked itself for the third time and was ready to be rebuilt again by the train crew.

With luck and pure gut, by October 8 the *Vin Fiz* was in Chicago, three weeks after Cal Rodgers' start and a thousand miles of flying done (only about twenty-four hours of this was actual flying time in the air). He had two days to reach California or lose out on the fifty-thousand-dollar prize for flying coast to coast in thirty days or less. He knew that was a lost dream. In departing Chicago he said, "Los Angeles and the Pacific Ocean, prize or no prize, that's where I am bound."

Two days later, carrying his safety almost in his teeth like a mother cat her kitten, Cal was over Marshall, Missouri. By now the Hearst money was out of sight. He was in his second month of flying the continent. He went on to Kansas City, Muskogee, Oklahoma, to McAlester. Then to the State Fair at Dallas, near which city an angry eagle flew alongside the *Vin Fiz*, circled it, and was about to make a diving attack on the ship but changed its mind, perhaps feeling the thing was not edible, or too large to carry off to its nest.

More crashes, more repairs, wires to Chicago from merchants to keep shipping Vin Fiz.

Over California there was an explosion of the engine, peppering Cal with metal fragments from a dissolving cylinder. Wounded, bleeding, hot metal shards smoking, he managed a glide down to Imperial Junction where a local doctor worked on him for two hours, removing metal slivers from his body. (The Chicago press reports, among others, were too polite to mention his ass looked like a pincushion.)

The engine was a total wreck, and so the first discarded engine had to be placed back in the plane. Disheveled, his enthusiasm more drunken purpose than hope, Cal flew on.

Over Banning, California, the old engine began acting up; its spark plugs, like ancient teeth, were loose in their metal gums, the radiator leaking and spewing boiling water. It was patched up again, but no sooner was the plane in the air than a gas line broke.

On November 5, somehow, Cal Rodgers landed at 4:08 P.M., at Tournament Park in Pasadena (a park to become the Rose Bowl). Here, officially, the trip was to end; perhaps the Chicago grape juice makers were unaware Pasadena is *not* in sight of the Pacific Ocean.

"Pasadena citizens," recalled an old newspaperman I had lunch with, "are more flag-prone to visible patriotism than most. They wrapped Cal in a huge American flag close to smothering. And guarded by the Keystone Cops of the town, he was hauled to the Hotel Maryland. Tradition said he dug into a big rare steak and onions, but the truth was it was just a glass of milk (not Vin Fiz) and crackers. He was game but bushed. Cal made a little speech I always loved him for. 'Glad this trip is over. Not in this business because I like it, but because of the money I can make from it. Personally now, I'd rather be in an automobile with a good driver.' Vin Fiz was passed around."

Cal Rodgers had taken forty-nine days to get from New York to Pasadena, but actually had been in the air only three days and a little over ten hours. His average speed was just over fifty miles an hour. In all he had covered, by a shaky count, 4,230 miles, more or less. It was a bravura performance, people felt, with little future.

Cal knew he still hadn't reached the Pacific. So after a week's rest he took off again and headed west, to Long Beach. He didn't get there. He crashed halfway to the sea, wrecked himself in a field, the plane again a ruin. Cal was pulled out, battered and unconscious, his ankle broken. It was a month before he could fly again in the repaired plane. He went to it on crutches, crablike, to the re-patched *Vin Fiz*. He got aboard and headed once more for Long Beach and blue water.

Thousands were waiting on the shore as he came down onto the sand and taxied to wet his wheels and skids in the salt Pacific. Calbraith Perry Rodgers had made epic air history, ocean to ocean. And who today in Chicago remembers? Even Vin Fiz, the Ideal Drink, made by Armour & Co., lost out to insipid colas, cokes (called "dopes" in those days).

In April, 1912, Cal Rodgers took off for a run around the

beach. He headed out to sea, and just offshore a flock of sea gulls rose before him, and his plane plowed into them before he knew it, their feathers flying. Down went the plane. They got Cal Rodgers out of the wreck, his neck broken, and he was stone cold.

In the Chicago main office of Armour & Co., from some old file, they will show you the color posters advertising their long-forgotten foray into the soft-drink business with Vin Fiz, and pictures of Cal Rodgers and the plane named after their drink. When I asked one old clerk how the drink had tasted, he shook his head. "My father said like Chicago River sludge and old horseshoes. If there was grape juice in it, he claimed, it lost out."

64

THE LIFE AND DEATH OF
BIG JIM COLOSIMO

Love has pitched her mansion in the place of excrement.
WILLIAM BUTLER YEATS

What the world accepts for greatness is the individual who can take control, rule carte blanche, be able to face the extremity of suffering and debasement in others. Act as an implicit anarchist morally, be a homicidal psychopath if driven to dominate by force. Such a man was Jim Colosimo who, with little fear of consequences, was isolated in a sense of invulnerability because of his close ties with the law, the government of Chicago, the political powers. He, pimp and crime boss, operated in safety on deceit and manipulation by those who were elected to public office. He helped make the city's politics contemptible by his control of thousands of votes.

Already the future of Chicago's criminal gyrations was being seeded. Big Jim Colosimo, the first of the big-shot Italians to become a citywide power, ran two whorehouses, the Victoria and the Saratoga. The Saratoga on Twenty-third Street was managed by a young New York hoodlum Colosimo had imported in 1908, one Johnny Torrio (who was to import Alphonse Capone to Chicago). The Victoria was named after Big Jim's first wife, Victoria Moresco.

Big Jim Colosimo represented the old Italian criminal world of the Mustache Petes, cartooned as men with huge, hairy upper lips curled at the ends; who before they entered crime were mocked often as organ-grinders with a monkey, makers of home-produced wine, loving the bambinos and the pasta. Jim's progress was to point directly to the later patterns of the twenties, the mob rule of Capone.

Jim Colosimo was ten years old when his father emigrated from the old country and brought the boy to the city, and in Chicago Jim, with tenacity, was to live for nearly forty years, exist grandly in the whorehouse section of the South Side. The Levee was his empire of vice, his life, and he began there as a newsboy with an eye for extra little earnings, not all legit. He was also a bootblack and, in his late teens, a pickpocket, a pimp with six girls handing in their earnings to him. By the time he was twenty-five, he was a Black Hand blackmailer, doing very well in extorting money from well-off Italians of Chicago. The irony of this is that when *he* became a crime boss, the Black Hand blackmailed *him*, and Colosimo often paid off. Several times he was to fight back, himself killing three Black Hand members, his organization murdering a few more. But until the end of his life, Colosimo, in a sinister *tableau vivant*, is said to have paid off the Black Hand men who came too close to carrying out their threats on his life.

By 1900, Colosimo was in trouble with the police—some obscure point of a double cross—and he was forced to give up his whores and his Black Handing and take a lowly job as a Chicago street cleaner in an age when the horse still ruled the streets, and to most people the work was mordantly amusing. Always a man with an eye for the main chance, Colosimo soon became foreman of a street-cleaning crew and soon had his men organized into a social and athletic club. This slowly changed from just smoking strong, black, Italian cigars and drinking Chianti into a labor union of sorts that could deliver blocks of votes to the political machine of the First Ward alderman, Hinky Dink Kenna. The sweepers' union went with tragic inevitability under the control of the criminal, Dago Mike Carrozzo, and Big Jim became a Democratic precinct captain. Which meant no policeman would arrest him, just wink at any infraction of the law that someone higher up had not objected to. Such was, as one letter writer put it, "the moral hypocrisy of elections in our city."

When Big Jim, in 1902, married Victoria Moresco, she was already the proud madam of a house on Armour Street, and soon they were joint owners of another brothel and also of Colosimo's Café on Wabash Avenue. The café was the popular place for slumming rich folk to come and see the underworld at play and at their drinking. The malaise of the criminal was a thrill for bored Lake Forest conformists.

Big Jim expanded into white slavery ("You gotta wholesale them cunts"—Ben Hecht) and into political power, as the number of the votes he could deliver on election day grew in size. (Of each $2 Big Jim's whores earned, he took $1.20 away from them—Elliot Paul.)

Jim, ponce and murderer, was what was called in family circles, "a good son," and he could afford it. His income from immoral ways of making money from crime, the bodies of women, political know-how, was fifty thousand dollars a month, a huge sum of money in the early days of this century when money was not yet inflated, "as if printed on snowflakes" (Elliot Paul).

Big Jim, with a palliative compulsion, liked to spread his wealth around. The house he built for his father was impressive, but not as impressive as the gaudy monster he built for himself and Victoria. He had taste and, as someone said, "*all* of it bad." He piled the house full of all the expensive trash the antique dealers could unload on him. ("An antique is anything worthless from the past; like last week; a rich fool will pay for it a hundred times what it is worth and show it off." William Kite, *c.* 1925.)

Big Jim was a family man and good to any poor relative, with handouts and minor jobs in whorehouses and joints. Big Jim lived in style with hired help in uniforms, free of anarchy and indiscipline at home. When the auto was a status symbol, he had two chauffeurs in livery and the biggest monster of a motorcar available on the market. He was big, raffish, full of prurient malevolence, and he liked to show off his well-fed bulk in white linen suits and as a setting for his diamonds. Belts, cuff links, shirtfront, waistcoat, belt suspenders, all had diamonds set in them someplace. He was a famous fence, buying hot diamonds from thieves, and he carried little bags of the gems with him, handling and fingering the diamonds; he caressed them like a rosary.

It is rather extraordinary that a murderer, a white slaver, Black Hand blackmailer such as Jim Colosimo could attract the best people in Chicago, famous visitors to the city, to his Colosimo's Café. Not only the Potter Palmers, the Marshall Fields, but a late-supper group might have Al Jolson, John Barrymore, George M. Cohan, and Sophie Tucker (her singing, with *gestures*, of "Angle Worm Wiggle" caused her arrest by the Chicago cops). The Chicago Civic Opera Company always had a table held for them by opera-lover Big Jim Colosimo, for the opera patrons and such stars as Luisa Tetrazzini, Mary Garden, Titta Ruffo, Amelita Galli-Curci, Conductor Cleofonte Campanini, and John McCormack. Whatever inchoate mystique Big Jim had for the rich and respectable, they came like kittens to catnip.

Mixed with these social and artistic names would be, seated at nearby tables, Mike de Pike Heitler, the master pimp; Mike Merlo, boss of the criminal section of the Unione Siciliane: hoods "Izzy the Rat" Buchalsky and "Monkey Face" Genker; the Black Hand boss, Vincenzo "Sunny Jim" Cosmano; and other underworld crime figures of mindless energy, and a few with sinister brains. Often present, as if watching their progeny, were the First Ward aldermen, Hinky Dink and Bathhouse John.

Colosimo's Café had opened in 1910, at 2126 Wabash Avenue, featuring star singers and dancers, beautiful prancing chorus girls, and early jass (as then spelled) bands. The chef was the famous Antonio Caesarino, delighting gourmets and filling gourmands. The wine cellar was properly stocked: Haut-Brion, Clos Vougeot, Lafite. Cheese fanciers said its imported smells were rare and strong.

Colosimo's Café, as reported by the press, was the pride of the Levee, and the Gold Coast, Lake Forest quality, the theater and opera stars, came peeking into the vice district ("and what wasn't engaged in vice on the Levee didn't hardly exist") for a sight of the ponces, criminals, and whores of the Levee—and the folk rubbernecked right back.

The café was gaudy, but splendid, with much gold paint and mahogany-and-glass bar, green velvet walls. It made good newspaper copy. Crystal chandeliers hung like huge white bunches of grapes from the robin's-egg blue ceiling, a ceiling painted with "a mural of bare-assed seraphim playing around among woolly clouds." The dance floor could rise or fall on hydraulic lifts at the press of a button, and mirrors and hangings were plentiful "to show the place had cost a packet" (*Billboard* magazine). Tuxedos were much in evidence on the dance floor, and, as the waltz of the 1900s gave way to the Great War's bunny hug, the turkey trot, grizzly bear, the Castle Walk, the music became "Dardenella" and "Could She Yacki, Hacki, Wicki, Wachi, Woo?"

There were no closing hours, midnight being the start of the true high hour of festivities at the café. Many people went home bleary-eyed, if not entirely sloshed, at a dawn that came up like Carl Sandburg's fog "on little cat feet."

All the while on the second floor of the café, gambling went on, card games, dice, faro, chuck-a-luck, whatever a guest desired, except a guarantee of winning.

Big Jim liked being the host at the café, parading, showing off his diamonds, talking of his rare coins, yards of morocco-bound books (unopened), chinoiserie, bronzes, and marbles. To losers, he was known as The Bank, handing out loans from a wallet thick with thousand-dollar bills. Yet few of the guests could not be aware that his real income came from white slavery and whorehouses (with a take of six hundred thousand dollars a year).

It wasn't all easy going, as he ruled with promise, perversity, and cruelty. In 1914, Mayor Harrison, Jr., pressured by forces of reformers, took away the license of the Wabash Avenue café. But when Big Bill Thompson came in as mayor, back came the license with all the rest of a remorseless corruption. Big Bill opened an era. He was a pal to looters, a man who worked with criminals directly, who made it clear he would do his duty, and the gangsters would not work too hard on *his* side of the street. As Big Bill expressed it, "I may not be smart, but I'm smart enough to follow in the steps of the guys that made success." If he couldn't give the city good government, he could give it advice, offer folk myth naïveté as facts, and treat the English as an enemy. "Throw away your hammer and get a horn. . . . I promise to biff King George on the snoot. . . . Shall your taxes be spent to make your children hate George Washington and love the King?"

Big Bill Thompson's reward was a pal's tribute from Samuel Insull, a high-class Chicago society figure, opera lover, *and* a thief working the utility rackets. "Mr. Mayor . . . you are a veritable reincarnation of Abraham Lincoln, a Father Abraham come to earth again."

Colosimo wasted no time on such prose, such poignant hang-ups. He began to take over control of the call flats and the assignation houses, and their fronts, the cafés and dance halls. He collected a huge underworld fund to fight the city's Morals Division. His political position was solid, and by 1915 he was king of the South Side brothels and its prostitutes. In part he flourished because the gangster is, to many, the symbolic fantasy of a bored society, the infantile dream to seize with cruelty, hunt prey.

If Big Jim was a dealer in women's flesh, he was also a victim of it. In that hulk of meanness, dishonesty, of scatological outbursts, there also existed a spark that could fall in love. Approaching fifty, he divorced the predatory, discreet madam, Victoria, paid her off with fifty thousand dollars. He married a young show girl (and church singer), Dale Winter, who had been left stranded in penniless anguish in Chicago. She had gone to work for Colosimo in his Wabash Avenue café, and affirming impulses were exchanged. They had been married in Crown Point, Indiana, and three weeks later were back in Chicago. A week after that, Colosimo, said to be carrying a hundred and fifty thousand dollars (never found), was assassinated in the lobby of his café, a bullet sent directly into the back of his head.

The city was surprised how many political figures helped bury Big Jim. The Illinois Crime Survey tried to explain the interplay of crime and practical politics: "Politics in the river wards, and among common people elsewhere as well, is a feudal relationship. The feudal system was one that was based not on law but upon personal loyalties. Politics tends, therefore, to become a *feudal system*. Gangs, also, are organized on a feudal basis—that is, upon loyalties, upon friendships, and above all, upon dependability. That is one reason why politicians and criminal gangs understand one another so well. Politics, particularly ward politics, is carried on in a smaller more intimate world than that which makes and defines the law. Government seeks to be equal, impartial, formal. Friendships run counter to the impartiality of formal government; and, vice versa, formal government cuts across the ties of friendship. Professional politicians have always recognized the importance, even when they were not moved by real sentiment, of participating with their friends and neighbours in the ceremonies marking the crises of life—christenings, marriages, and deaths. In the great funerals, the presence of the political boss attests the sincerity and the personal character of the friendship for the deceased, and this marks him as an intimate in life and death."

Bathhouse John, before the casket was closed, knelt, recited Hail Marys and the Catholic prayer for the dead. Ike Bloom delivered the eulogy. "There wasn't a piker's hair in Big Jim's head. Whatever game he played, he shot straight. He wasn't greedy. There could be dozens of others getting theirs. The more the merrier as far as he was concerned. He had what a lot of us haven't got —class. He brought the society swells and the millionaires into the red-light district. It helped everybody, and a lot of places kept alive on Colosimo's overflow. Big Jim never bilked a pal or turned down a good guy *and* he always kept his mouth shut."

Bathhouse John tried to get Judge John H. Lyle, Republican alderman, to be a pallbearer. He declined.

"Jim wasn't a bad fellow," the Dink told a reporter. "You know what he did? He fixed up an old farmhouse for broken-down whores. They rested up and got back into shape and he never charged them a cent."

"Now that he's dead, who's going to run this convalescent camp?"

"Oh, Jim sold it. Some of the girls ran away after they got back on their feet. Jim got sore, said they didn't have no gratitude. . . . No matter what he may have been in the past, no matter what his faults, Jim was my friend and I am going to his funeral."

Big Jim's exaggerated funeral—he died in bad taste as he had lived in bad taste—set the pattern for all the gangster burials of the next twenty years. Over six thousand people showed up for this show (and the first version of that now old joke appeared at the event: "Give people what they want and you'll always get a crowd"). One thousand beribboned marchers of the First Ward Democratic Club were there in their best toppers, derbies, and cutaway coats. In front were Bathhouse John and Hinky Dink, for whom the dead man had delivered thousands of votes, many of them frauds. The whoremaster's casket had among its honorary pallbearers three judges, a member of Congress, nine aldermen, an assistant state's attorney, led by several limousines chock-full with flowers. And side by side with the honorable pallbearers such kill-ers, rapists, white slavers, ponces, and pimps as Johnny Torrio (who masterminded the assassination of Big Jim, his boss), Ike Bloom, Andy Craig, Jakie Adler; discreet curtains hid Cadillacs filled with madams, procurers, boozy whores.

Wrote the *Tribune*: "It is a tribute to power, regardless of the source or justice of that power. . . . It is a strange commentary on our system of law and justice."

The funeral was like a stretched-out painting by Hieronymus Bosch; paranoid fantasy made real. Archbishop George Mundelein refused a last resting place for Big Jim in a Catholic cemetery, *not* because Colosimo was a brothel keeper, debaucher of young girls, lived an indigenous life of crime, *or* because he had murdered peo-ple almost with an intense hilarity—no, *but* because Colosimo was a divorced man.

As for *who* did the actual murder? Torrio had his friend and chief murdered by Frankie Uale, a professional gun imported from New York for ten thousand dollars for the hit. And while Frankie was identified as being present at the time of the killing, by a café porter, the porter in terror refused later to identify the killer. Frankie Uale was head of the Unione Siciliana, of which, ironi-cally, Big Jim had been one of the founders.

Torrio had a shrewd sense of self-preservation and self-scru-tiny. Colosimo, it seemed to him, was spending too much time with his broad, Dale Winters, while Torrio was expanding their crime empire by wholesale bribing and corruption of county officials for vice rights. Colosimo, as "Mr. Big," was taking most of the in-creased income. It was mere bookkeeping logic to Torrio to remove Big Jim from the accounts.

And what did Big Jim leave behind besides thousands of dol-lars' worth of dying funeral flowers? When he died he was supposed to have five hundred thousand dollars in cash and diamonds, his home, the Wabash café, interests in shady enterprises. The gang-ster's lawyer announced he had been able to find forty thousand dollars' worth of precious gems. Gossip in newspaper offices always insisted that Colosimo had a hundred and fifty thousand dollars in his pockets at the time of the killing. Neither wife, Victoria or Dale, claimed any of Colosimo's estate. No one knows why not. Eventually it went to his father. The *Daily News* wrote that "the loss [of Jim's suspected millions] was due to his paying tribute to the Black Hand."

Tax and estate lawyers disagree, privately. In an interview for this book, declared one of the most prominent tax lawyers and experts on the rules of the Internal Revenue: "The grapevine, my father told me, was there were millions of dollars hidden away—in cash and diamonds. A smart cookie like Jim doesn't spend his life on the take and end up with a fistful of polished popcorn. Who got it? My guess, Johnny Torrio. When, he, Johnny, recovered from an assassination try, he sold out to Capone: breweries, cafés, cathouses —and left Chicago with thirty untaxed million, at least—some of that was maybe Big Jim's stashed fortune." Then the lawyer surprised me by quoting the Book of Job. "He shall fly away as a dream, and shall not be found."

The funerals of hoodlum chiefs—inspired by the grandeur of Big Jim's last show—became more and more garish and expensive. On flowers alone, twenty thousand dollars could be spent, often sent by the murderers with such a spelled-out floral message as: DEAR DEPARTED FRIEND.

The Rolls-Royce of funerals was most likely Dean O'Banion's, an early assassinated gang boss, whose casket alone amazed the *Tribune*. "It was equipped with solid silver and bronze double walls, inner-sealed and air-tight, with a heavy plate glass above, and a couch of white satin below, with tufted cushion extra for his left hand to rest on.

"At the corners of the casket are solid silver posts, carved in wonderful designs. Modest is the dignified silver gray of the casket, content with the austere glory of the carved silver post at its corners, and broken only by a scroll across one side. . . .

"Silver angels stood at the head and feet with their heads bowed in the light of the ten candles that burned in the solid golden candlesticks they held in their hands. . . . And over it all the perfume of flowers.

"But vying with that perfume was the fragrance of perfumed women, wrapped in furs from ears to ankles, who tiptoed down the aisle, escorted by soft-stepping, tailored gentlemen with black shining pompadours.

"And, softly treading, deftly changing places, were more well-formed gentlemen in tailored garments, with square, blue-steel jaws and shifting glances. They were the sentinels.

"In the soft light of the candles at the head of the $10,000 casket sat Mrs. O'Banion, a picture of patient sorrow."

For three days the body "lay in state" in Sbarbaro's funeral chapel, powder burns, bullet holes hidden by the embalmer, a rosary clasped in the hands, "soft tapered hands which could finger an automatic so effectively." The marble slab beneath the casket was inscribed, "Suffer little children to come unto me." One attending gangster wondered, "What he want with the kids?" (Ben Hecht).

65

THE WHITE SOX BASEBALL SCANDAL

Play not for gain, but sport. Who plays for more . . . stakes his heart.
GEORGE HERBERT, 1663

While most baseball fans and sportsmen who follow the game accept Abner Doubleday as the inventor or the popularizer of the American game of baseball, that is not a fact but a myth. Its true forefather was English—cricket and the old game of rounders, and by 1786 as "baste ball." It was tough enough to be banned at Princeton. From 1820 to 1833 it was played in Eastern cities as the Town Ball Game. In 1845, one Alexander Cartwright, in New York City, set down the basic official rules that were to be followed by the players from then on. The next year the first game of record, by his rules, was played in Hoboken, New Jersey, the New York Nine defeating the Knickerbockers, 23 to 1, in four full innings. The first professional ball team appeared in 1869, as the Cincinnati Red Stockings. From such evolutionary beginnings, the big leagues emerged into an affluent business, so that by 1919 baseball was one of the native popular sports, taking in millions at the gate; and that, too, was the year a cabal of gamblers rigged a World Series.

Not only the sports world was shocked to complete hysteria or disbelief, but all of the population of the country that had heard of baseball and followed some favorite team. The novel, *The Great Gatsby*, by F. Scott Fitzgerald, took time from the sexual doings among the sportsmen and society of Long Island to bring the disintegration of sporting honor and integrity into the book:

> Gatsby hesitated then added coolly: "He's the man who fixed the World Series back in 1919."
> "Fixed the World Series?" I repeated.
> The idea staggered me. I remembered, of course, that the World Series had been fixed in 1919, but if I had thought of it at all I would have thought of it as a thing that merely *happened*, the end of some inevitable chain. It never occurred to me that one man could start to play with the faith of fifty million people—with the singlemindedness of a burglar blowing a safe.
> "How did he happen to do that?" I asked after a minute.
> "He just saw the opportunity."

The World Series, with what appeared an untrammeled innocence, opened that year in Cincinnati on October 1 to a sizzler of a day, a humid eighty-three degrees. The city was all decked in bunting, with bands playing, as it enjoyed its first World Series with a flourish. The Reds, under manager Pat Moran, were heroes. Seats for the first two games were all gone, and ticket speculators were scalping the public at fifty dollars for a pair. The town was jumping as if at a popular lynching, hotels were packed, whiskey flasks in evidence as many people took a snort, and the growlers of beer and kegs of the stuff were foaming in private suites. In the hot, fecund summer, the sky was a Reckett's Blue, and iron hooves and flivvers hit the road.

The Hotel Sinton, the best hotel in town, had its big lobbies full of flashy locals, Babbitts, rubes, Chicago big shots and gamblers—all looking like a mob in the films of D. W. Griffith, then very popular. If you knew your celebrities, there was George M. Cohan, brilliant, witty, the author of "It's a Grand Old Flag," which was being parodied that day as "It's a Grand Old Ball Game." Some pointed out handsome, snow-crested, Senator Warren G. Harding, glad-handing and eyeing the women, who added to the disquiet and fervor around the ballplayers and the sports reporters. Among the sportswriters was a thin, balding, ironic-mouthed young man, Ring Lardner, who called ballplayers "ivory" and considered them mighty-muscled cretins, proof against the intrusion of original thought. He was to write the baseball classics, *You Know Me Al* and *Alibi Ike*. Modestly accepting introductions and admirers was Christy Mathewson, once the great star pitcher, a hero to farm boys or tomboys grown up in voluminous skirts.

Damon Runyon, still a sportswriter and not yet the Homer of guys and dolls, filed a Hearst Syndicate report of the rowdy happy doings:

"The streets of old Cincy have been packed for hours. People get up before breakfast in these parts. The thoroughfares leading to Redland Field have been echoing to the tramp of feet, the honk of auto horns since daylight. It is said that some people kept watch and ward at the ballpark all night long. Might as well stay there as any place in this town. They would have had the same amount of excitement. Flocks of jitneys go squeaking through the streets. This is the heart of the jitney belt. A jitney is the easiest thing obtainable in Cincy. A drink is next . . . Cincy is a dry town—as dry as the Atlantic Ocean."

It was before the yammering age of radio and television, but thousands of miles of wires were ready to carry the details of the national game to tens of thousands of scoreboards set up in every major city and town. The crowds came early to Redland Park. Just over thirty thousand perspiring fans packed the park, chomped peanuts, guzzled pop, chewed hotdogs. The local folk were proud of winning the right to play in a World Series, but not many had much hope of winning against the powerful Chicago White Sox, of taking the "World Serious," as Ring Lardner reported it. That, most agreed, would be an imprudent naïveté by folk from a section where the corn grew tallest.

The White Sox had the star players, the mighty throwers, the sockers of the horsehide with the oak and hickory shafts, fielders, base holders, quick as Doc Holiday on the draw. Eddie Cicotte had pitched twenty-nine winning games that season, lost only seven, and people spoke of his famous knuckle ball with awe. "Why it would fool Houdini himself," it was stated in a sports story in the *Chicago Tribune*. Catcher was the respected Ray Schalk, third base was held by George "Buck" Weaver, who laughed it up and was like a panther after balls hit anywhere near him. Shortstop was Charles "Swede" Risberg, a huge man of inexhaustible toughness and able to catch anything. On second base there was Eddie Collins (one of the few who didn't have a nickname—all the great ball-players were supposed to have an Elk's Club barroom nickname). Eddie was always listed by sportswriters as "the greatest infielder of the game." On first was Arnold "Chick" Gandil. "Shoeless Joe" Jackson not only held left field but was "a mighty man swinging at the ball with the old wagon tongue." Oscar "Happy" Felsch controlled center field "like a feudal dukedom." Right field was the domain of John "Shano" Collins, all-around man and better than most. Such were the Chicago team stars, and it was no use betting against them or their fellow players. But the people who were loyal to their team did bet.

When the umpire yelled "Play ball!" who was aware that schemes to rig the results, to throw the Series, smoldered in the eyes of eight White Sox ballplayers? To think so was like a five-year-old questioning that Betsy Ross made the flag, or that Washington axed a cherry tree.

To understand the complex, almost surreal way this all came about, we can begin with a gambler, bookmaker, wisenheimer, a sport around the shady sides of the sports world who knew the smell of sweaty socks, rubbing liniment, frowzy locker rooms, chewing-to-bacco-stained teeth, and who lived among the ghosts of cheap cigars offered freely in return for information. His name was Joseph Sullivan, but he was always called "Sport" Sullivan. Three weeks before the opening game of the Series, he was in Boston calling at the Hotel Buckminster. He asked to be connected with the room of Chick Gandil. Chick had been a fighter, was six feet two, had played pro ball for fourteen years. He was thirty-one, and he saw the day a few years ahead when he'd be out of big-time baseball. Chick had no education. Most looked upon him as a big hick, yet he had a native cunning, a poor white's greed. When he first met Sullivan, a sport who knew people like George M. Cohan and millionaires who smoked dollar "Hevanner" cigars, men like Harry Sinclair, the oilman, Chick was impressed, wondered how one got so rich.

Sullivan went to Chick's room, and there Chick put it to him friendly and on the level. As first baseman of the White Sox, Chick had a proposition for Sport Sullivan. Simply stated, he could convince enough of his pals on the team to throw the Series to the team favored to lose—the Reds. "I think, Sport, we can put it in the bag. And we want eighty thousand dollars for it."

Sullivan kept his amazement under control. Chick had said he trusted Sullivan, and had put it to him because he knew his good friend, Sport, could come up with that kind of big money from the gamblers he knew. Sullivan remained poker-faced, said he would sure think it over. He didn't mind breaking the law, he told Chick, but the fixing of a *whole* World Series! Now who would have thought it could be done? And could it?

Of course there had been scandals before in baseball. Hints of one or two tossed games. But a whole Series?

Chick explained that the epic dimensions and daring of the idea had thrown Sport off balance. It wouldn't be hard to make an easy catch seem lost, just out of reach, *or* an outfielder tearing his heart out as he seemed unable to catch up with the ball, *or* the shortstop moving just inches off from a hard grounder. And a pitcher, with one or two on, what if suddenly his control failed and someone socked one over the walls, bringing in three runs? Who could prove he had let the batter hit it? Sport shrugged—*who indeed?*

The newspapers had printed warnings for years: things on the pro ball fields were not all clean, not since our All-American Boys' fun at their village skills had been raised to a national interest. An upper New York State paper had written their local club had better "fold up if they can't play a square game." And soon after professional baseball got started, a St. Louis weekly had stated: "Baseball, as a professional pastime, has seen its best days in St. Louis. The amount of crooked work is indeed startling, and the game will undoubtedly meet the same fate elsewhere unless some extra strong means are taken to prevent it."

Chick Gandil had not suddenly come up with his brilliant idea, but in his rube way had been brooding on it for some time. Could he swing a Series with nine or six other players, or less? Would the boys come along? Charlie Comiskey, Chicago owner of the White Sox, was a mean and greedy bastard; every guy who played for him said so. Charlie might love baseball, have designed

Comiskey Park for his team's games, but he still was a penny-pinching dog, a Simon Legree to his ball team. His excuse was that the war in 1918 had cut down the number of paying customers at the gate, and so he had to drop ballplayers' salaries for their own survival. Yet everyone knew this was a crock of horse apples—attendance was big at the games and topped all the records at Comiskey Park. It was a great team, and every fan who liked the game wanted to see the White Sox in action. Comiskey continued to bear down on the players. "Kid" Gleason, in his first year as manager of the team, had it out with Comiskey. But the owner refused to talk about the players' salaries or even about better treatment. Most of his stars got less than six thousand dollars a year, and pro baseball as it was (and remains) was slave labor under contracts favoring the owners. Ballplayers were just muscle meat to be sold or kept, farmed out or fired, with players having little rights to make proper demands or decide their destinies. (Players on other teams, men not nearly as good as the White Sox stars, often got twelve thousand dollars a season.) That lack of sensibilities on Comiskey's part burned Chick up. There were no pensions, and the cheapskate owner allowed them only three dollars a day for meals on the road, and ballplayers have huge appetites.

Chick had put the idea of throwing the Series to his buddy, Eddie Cicotte. Eddie had deep money troubles: a fat mortgage on his new farm in Michigan, and a family that liked to do things as befitting folk connected with the league-leading White Sox. Eddie shook his head. Too risky. Chick said he could name his own price; the kingpin gamblers, the hoi polloi of odds takers, would meet it.

Eddie felt he was being exploited by bankers pressing for mortgage payments. So one night, as a rattling Pullman car took the team to Boston, Eddie Cicotte gave in. "Chick, I'll do it. For ten thousand dollars. But cash *before* the Series begins." Chick nodded and was off. He began to recruit his baseball Benedict Arnolds. Another pitcher was needed; Eddie and Claud "Lefty" Williams would most likely pitch the five out of nine games the Series would most likely run. Also willingly in came "Swede" Risberg, Fred McMullin, a reserve infielder. Now to convince Buck Weaver, Shoeless Joe Jackson, Happy Felsch. That would do it.

On September 21, 1919, the eight chosen were in Chick Gandil's room at the Ansonia, in Chicago, their heads together, talking things out. Chick explained that Sport Sullivan would get them the eighty thousand dollars. They would be paid off *before* the first game. As to what games would be thrown, that depended on how the gamblers wanted to juggle the odds. The blame for this betrayal was put on the shoulders of Charles Albert Comiskey, the skinflint owner. All agreed he was a no-good, Uncle Tom Show whip-boss, a tyrant.

All this was true, the men pointed out. Williams and Risberg were getting only three thousand dollars a season. Comiskey had given all of them the contracts and hadn't let them argue; they could take it or lump it. If they left the team, they couldn't play pro ball anyplace. They belonged body and soul to Massa Comiskey, a minor gripe being he didn't wash their dirty, sweaty uniforms too often, and the dog-wagon food you could get on three bucks a day wasn't at all like the fancy chow Comiskey set out for the sportswriters: steaks *that* thick from Kansas City, Kentucky sour mash bourbon, tables loaded with roasts, whole turkeys, lake whitefish, mountain trout, all prepared by Charlie Comiskey's private chef. Charlie was acting like Louis XV while Paris starved. Charlie, all greed, "was a blasphemous sonofabitch and Charlie didn't even keep his promises" (Ring Lardner to author).

Eddie Cicotte was promised in 1917 a bonus of ten thousand dollars *if* he won thirty games. But clever Charlie had Eddie benched as the player came close to that payoff figure. The owner was a morass of deceit. He had promised fine bonuses to the team if it won the league pennant that year. And with what did he pay off? "A case of cheap horsepiss-tasting champagne for the whole team— that was all" (Ring Lardner).

The players were also betrayed by most of the sportswriters and newspapermen who were fattened and fed by the owner, likkered at club expense, rode like lords in the owner's Pullmans and ate the fine food railroads in those days of Fred Harvey provided. To most players, the sportswriters were shaggy drunks and hotel lobby Don Juans; the ballplayers to them were dismal clodhoppers who had muscles and a good eye. A ballplayer didn't hand out H. Uppmann cigars, prime bourbon, or pheasant and those Caycee packinghouse steaks. (As Ben Hecht was to put it to me one day talking over the White Sox scandal, "The soul and integrity of most sportswriters could be bought for anything from a free haircut to a quick one in the hay with some depot waitress, who kept her silver-dollar fees in her mouth while she went through the gestures of l'amour without removing her chewing gum.")

The meeting with Chick broke up, the boys agreeing they would wait and see how much the gamblers were interested in the whole idea. There were little ambiguities of character among them as players, and much fear.

The complexity of the bribing of the White Sox has to be followed closely from now on, for the cast, from the gamblers' side, is rather large, like a full-dress production of *Guys and Dolls*. A man called William Thomas Burns now entered the picture; he had once played baseball and was usually called just "Sleepy Bill" Burns. He had a habit of taking a quick snooze while waiting on the dugout bench for his turn at bat. He feared holdup men and carried a huge Colt .45 which he called a "hawgleg" and stashed under his pillow. Sleepy Bill came from Texas, and when he left baseball in 1917, he went sniffing after oil as a wildcatter. He became a fairly rich man with incredible speed, as one did or didn't do in Texas. He spoke of oil leases, spudding-in, rotary drills, gushers, salt domes, and barrels-per-day. Sleepy Bill became no Rockefeller, but he had enough to be comfortable and live in style.

Sleepy Bill, rambunctuous and at liberty, came north to see his old buddies play, and in the lobby of the Ansonia glad-handed his old friend, Eddie Cicotte. Sport Sullivan must have already made some move to try out the fix on the sporting people, for Sleepy Bill asked at once, "Is it true about throwin' the Series?" Eddie shrugged—well you know there is always some kind of talk going round. Sleepy Bill sensed at once something was being cooked up, and he told Eddie, "Make no commitment till you hear from me." Sleepy Bill had an ex-fighter friend named Billy Maherg, in Philadelphia, who had gambler connections and could raise money.

So the cast grew larger on the gambler side. Sport Sullivan, Sleepy Bill Burns, and Billy Maherg coming up from Philly. Deceits and pretensions were about to take over.

66

HOW TO RIG A WORLD SERIES

Chance is a word devoid of sense; nothing can exist without a cause.
VOLTAIRE

It is hard to recall what baseball meant in a time when the dubious media of radio and television had not yet overwhelmed the population with dozens of sports pouring out of the air, smothering interest by surfeit and blurring the eyes by an overplenty of baseball, football, basketball, golf, and other sports.

Few small-town people then ever saw a big professional ball game. But most followed it in print. When a World Series came along, those prosperous people who could get to a Series were like pilgrims going to Mecca. The shock of the Chicago team scandal when it broke later fell on a more naïve nation, a more trusting world.

To pick up our story: as the gamblers gathered to prepare the fix, we are back to an idiot's drama of a fortuitous, bungled plot—plotting no novelist would dare invent.

(It might better be explained here that all of this section of the book is based on grand jury hearings and a search of old records and reports. All dialogue is as recorded.)

Cicotte and Gandil put their scheme to Sleepy Bill and Maherg. They felt now there was a real interest, and they wanted a flat hundred thousand dollars to throw the World Series. The hoarse bird note of greed, a vulture sound, was in their voices as they made their demand.

Soon Sport Sullivan, and Sleepy Bill and his prizefighter—independent of each other—were talking to gamblers to back the swindle, but were failing. No one really felt the Series *could* be fixed; "it was all crapper talk." Maherg, after failing to raise the payoff money, said there was only one man who had the loot and might back the fix: "Arnold Rothstein!"

It was a name that in 1919 was notorious, famous, and a bit of a mystery. Rothstein was a sportsman who raced nags on the tracks, horses, some felt, that were a little bit off color. Rothstein had moved in on Saratoga as a horse-owning man and gambler. He was a flashy, pallid, Broadway type, seen with all kinds of women and all kinds of Broadway characters, from gangsters to judges, actors and actresses, as a pal and feeder of sportswriters, and those who were soon to become big-shot bootleggers, that rise of the early Black Hand of Italian gangster and blackmail societies, into what was to become the powerful Mafia syndicates of the twenties through to the seventies.

Arnold was not a nice man. He was full of illicit habits, an abominable carnivore. He had appeared from a childhood of poverty in the East Side of New York, from an honest family. His father, Abraham Rothstein, had come up the hard way and, in the year of the White Sox rigging, had been given a big testimonial dinner as reward for a garment-industry arbitration. It was a festive event, not, it appears, attended by Arnold, but graced by justice of the United States Supreme Court, Louis D. Brandeis, and the governor of the state of New York, the Honorable Alfred E. Smith.

Arnold Rothstein feared neither the law nor a fierce, possessive Yahweh. He was one of the brightest of the many Rothstein children and had been a hard character as a boy. A poor student, too, except for figures, sums about money, gains and percentages, and then his interest was aroused. At school he began to take over street crap games, and by the age of puberty he was already a seasoned gambler who knew odds and percentages, and some dishonest ways to shade them in his favor. He saw that, with care and the proper pocketful of greenbacks, a crafty player could make money by not betting against the laws of percentages. Arnold stole from his father, hocked the family gold watch at times, but always got it back from his winnings before it was missed. He accepted life as ambushes and betrayals.

When he had a few thousand in winnings set aside, he became a loan shark, lending at five percent (mild compared to the five hundred percent of the Mafia today or the interest charged by auto dealers or bank credit costs).

Tammany Hall, the powerful political system that stole the city blind, liked the young thieves and hoodlums, gamblers, other slick types on their side to help rig elections. Rothstein moved up to meet the top men, the prizefighters, jockeys like Tod Sloan, who had pulled the king of England's horse in the running of the English Derby. Also he met the political bosses who could do favors for favors done.

So, politically protected, Rothstein ran gambling houses, and at Saratoga he spent over a hundred thousand dollars converting a mansion into a plush gambling house. Fortunes were lost there by Harry Sinclair, Charlie Stoneham, owner of the New York Giants ball team, Sam Rosoff, who built subways and took care of the Tammany boys in turn, Nick the Greek, whose true name was Nick Dandolis. Rothstein was said to be a millionaire "a few times over" from his gambling houses' income. But he remained ravenous for bigger gains, for new angles. "Arnold had moxie."

And now he could, he was told, fix the coming World Series. He was at the Jamaica Race Track when Sleepy Bill Burns and Maherg introduced themselves to him, mentioned some mutual friend who could vouch for them as being okay. They had a proposition for him, they said. Rothstein replied, *no*, he was busy, tied up in other directions. They insisted he listen. Maybe he said he'd see them later in the restaurant at the track. They were so blatantly earnest they might have something. But let them suffer a bit more.

Now entered another character in the gamblers' cast of actors. Rothstein had a hanger-on, Abe Attell, who had once been a featherweight boxing champion of the world—by fair means or foul.

Known as "Little Champ," Abe had won nearly four hundred fights, and at 116 pounds was still quick and alert to anything that might help Abe Attell. As with Pontius Pilate, truth was a jesting matter to Little Champ. His fights were often fixed, it was claimed, he letting a fighter stay upright until a certain round on which the gamblers had bet the fight would end. The New York Boxing Commission suspended Little Champ from boxing in the state. He retired in time, always looking with unctuous geniality for an easy thing. Rothstein liked the little fellow, and they were often together at the big crap games always going on in the Metropole Hotel in Times Square, where the national big-time sports and their dupes gathered to play for high stakes.

At the track Rothstein told Little Champ to see what the two characters wanted from him. Abe had a cabalistic nose for a good setup. Little Champ asked Sleepy Bill and friend what was up, and they put the proposition to him. Enough White Sox ballplayers were in on it to throw the Series for eighty thousand dollars. Rothstein could put up the money and take it from there, betting on a sure thing. They would take a small cut for their share.

When Rothstein was told later, he shook his head. "I just don't think it will work." Sleepy Bill waylaid Rothstein in a hotel lobby and put it to him direct. How could it miss with him, A.R., running things? Rothstein again shook his head. "In my opinion, for whatever it's worth, it can't work."

Little Champ thought things over. Three days before the Series began, he decided he'd take on the fix himself and con Sleepy Bill to go along with a little lie: "Arnold has changed his mind. He'll go in on it."

Sleepy Bill phoned Eddie Cicotte, and the White Sox pitcher said he'd wait and see how things went, *if* Rothstein was on the level about the payment in advance. Cicotte had the surface truculence of a nervous schemer.

Back into the picture this time stepped Sport Sullivan, who had first been told there could be a fix. Sport called at Rothstein's Riverside Drive home. They had known each other for some time. Sport told him how Chick Gandil had first come to him with the idea of a fix, and he, Sport, was sure it could be carried out with Rothstein's help. The boys would become committed and the gamblers would press them hard to stay involved. Rothstein felt better

about the idea coming from a gambler like Sport. With a self-depre-
catory smile, he said he'd think about it.

Enter one more actor now, Nat Evans, one of Rothstein's gambling partners. Rothstein told Evans to go to Chicago with Sport
Sullivan and talk to the boys—but under the name of "Mr.
Brown," not Evans. The drama was getting as filled with gamblers
as an Elizabethan stage with bodies.

Sport and "Mr. Brown" got to Chicago and met Gandil at the
Warner Hotel. Sport explained that Gandil had "given his word"
the players would be paid to throw the Series for the sum mentioned. Brown shrugged. "His *word?*" followed by the doubt of a
short laugh. "That's not much collateral for eighty grand." He said
he'd talk to his money people and let Gandil know. A pathetic disenchantment was overtaking Chick Gandil.

Rothstein had sniffed out Little Champ's own game, but he let
it ride. He was going to work with Sport Sullivan as his contact with
the boys. He told "Brown" Evans to take the forty thousand dollars
he gave him to Sport, and Sport would pay the players. The second
forty thousand dollars he would put in the safe of the Hotel Congress in Chicago, and if the boys carried on as they should, Sport
would use it to pay off the ballplayers. He had other things to do—
like getting down all the bets he could, very big bets on the Cincinnati Reds.

Rothstein began to contact his pigeons that he was making
book on the Series. He got his pal Harry F. Sinclair to bet $90,000
at good odds on the White Sox. Another pigeon was Nick the
Greek, whom Rothstein had done out of $250,000 in dice and cards
the year before. Now Nick was broke and felt he could touch Rothstein for a loan. Rothstein said why not, and passed $25,000 to Nick
the Greek, then offered him a sure thing as a tip. "Put it on the Cincinnati Reds for the Series."

In all, Rothstein put out $270,000 betting on the Reds. He had
a million or so more to bet, but felt at this stage of the fix he was not
too sure it would work out all the way in his favor. He didn't want
any self-commiseration over having gone in too far.

Mr. Brown handed Rothstein's $40,000 over to Sport Sullivan
to smooth the way to the White Sox ballplayers: forty $1000 bills.
Sport slyly put $29,000 of this money down as a bet on the Reds,

and, as talk had already started about some kind of a fix, the odds which had been 7 to 5 were now even money, and he had to take it at that.

Having cheated the ballplayers out of $30,000 in bribes, he gave Gandil only a $10,000 down payment. "Brown is goddamn sore the odds are dropping. He thinks one of your players has leaked something out. . . . You guys maybe got a deal with somebody else?"

Chick Gandil felt it was best to give the $10,000 to Cicotte to hold his interest, since the pitcher would have the hardest part of the sellout work to do in an actual game. Eddie Cicotte sewed the bills into the lining of a jacket, quivering at the uniqueness of having such a fortune in his possession.

Charlie Comiskey felt good. "Crookedness and baseball do not mix. . . . This year, 1919, is the greatest season of them all." Meanwhile to the innocent, for some strange reason, the odds remained even. Yet the White Sox should have been odds-on favorites to snatch the Series. George M. Cohan told Little Champ he had $30,000 down on Chicago. Little Champ said, "A tip from Little Champ, *switch* sides." Little Champ could still give advice. There was a ground swell of gossip. Something *was* wrong with the Series about to be played, but no one seemed to know just what.

Sleepy Bill still believed Little Champ was going to produce the $100,000 from Rothstein to pay the players to fix the Series. Little Champ said untruthfully that he had $100,000 from Rothstein, but that he would only pay it out $20,000 after *each* game, to keep the ballplayers in line. One lost game, $20,000 each.

The players, thinking Little Champ was also acting for Rothstein, decided to throw the first two games. Cicotte and Lefty Williams would be pitching; they were keyed up, but had never heard of such an expression as a traumatic experience.

The day of the game the betting was heavy, and the Cincinnati bettors were backing their team, and the even-money betting held. The day was hot, the crowd wild, and the ball game was a disaster for the White Sox. Somehow they seemed to be having a bad day of bad breaks. Cicotte, whom some claimed to be "the best pitcher in the world," was not up to snuff. He was out there trying hard, they said, but somehow it wasn't winning the game. That and a few seemingly hard-luck plays and the Reds won the first game of the Series. Score, 9 to 1. A clobbering, all agreed.

Back in the hotel, Sleepy Bill wanted to know from Sport *where* was the money to pay off the ballplayers? The boys had made it clear no more games would be thrown if the rest of the money wasn't on the line. Sleepy Bill had to tell the boys to carry on, the money would show up. It wasn't there—that was the basic deficiency.

However, the boys were in the noose. To collect, even if later, they had to go on with the deal. Meanwhile Charlie Comiskey was sweating at the rumor of a fix; it was louder now, though no real facts had yet surfaced. Still there was nasty talk among the wise guys, the sports. Charlie ran to the president of the National League, John Heydler, got him out of his hotel bed, explained there was "talk" of a betrayal but *no* proof. He had heard it and he wanted the president to know about it. Heydler just said, "Impossible! You just can't fix a World Series, Commy!" However the thing was serious, it had to be alleviated, ventilated, and the two went to the president of the American League, Byron Bancroft Johnson at 3 A.M. Heydler told him of Charlie's fears of the spreading rumor. Johnson, no friend of Comiskey, said, "That's the yelp of a beaten cur! Good night!" And he showed them the door. Charlie went off feeling insulted, but also a bit relieved. At least he had spoken about the gossip and was in the clear. If Johnson didn't want to commiserate with him—to hell with him.

Little Champ kept the ballplayers in line by showing them a fake telegram from Rothstein:

AM WIRING YOUR TWENTY GRAND. A.R.

Sleepy Bill, as a friend of the players, checked with the telegraph office. No telegram from Rothstein had come in for Little Champ Attell. The odds, once 8 to 5 against the White Sox, now where 5 to 4, and Rothstein was worried. It was too easy; winning two in a row was ruining the odds. Suppose some backsliding sinner talked? Still he bet heavily, added $85,000 for the Cincinnati Reds to win the Series (not just individual games) in case there was a double double cross on that day's game. *Something* was cockeyed on the Chicago end. With Sport Sullivan, Sleepy Bill, and his sidekick there, and Little Champ again in his good graces, and his own man Mr. Brown there—he should know all the angles. It was just that too many gamblers watching the fixed ballplayers were too many cooks in the broth, to mix a metaphor, as Rothstein often did. The fix was overproduced, overcast.

67

THE SICK WORLD SERIES

It's no sin to cheat a cheater.
GEORGE ADE

The boys stayed fixed, in hopes of the sight of money. They lost the second game to the Reds, 4 to 2. Little Champ and his gamblers seemed to have thousands as they counted their winning bets. Sleepy Bill wanted $40,000 to pay off the players. He was to get a ten-percent cut for handling the deal. Little Champ handed him $10,000, said, "That will have to do for the boys for a while."

"Not enough!"

"It's all they can have," said Little Champ.

"There's eight of 'em. They'll not accept."

"They'll take it," said Little Champ, expert on sport-fixing.

When Sleepy Bill brought the money to Chick Gandil, the player howled, "A goddamn double cross!"

Among themselves they talked—to even the odds, maybe they should win the third game, which would be played on the team's home grounds in Chicago at Comiskey Park.

Rumors were growing heads, and the heads were growing new

heads. Some sportswriters like Ring Lardner had taken the rumors seriously. He put it to Cicotte, "How come the first two games were so lousy?" Cicotte said, "I just was off form." On the train the doubting Lardner thought and boozed, and studied the players and sportswriters, boozed some more, and swayed toward his seat singing:

> "I'm forever blowing ball games,
> Pretty ball games in the air.
> I come from Chi
> I hardly try
> Just go to bat and fade and die;
> Fortune's coming my way,
> That's why I don't care.
> I'm forever blowing ball games,
> And the gamblers treat us fair."

It got a good laugh.

Next morning in Chicago the players told Sleepy Bill they were also throwing the third game. Little Champ wasn't too sure the boys weren't trying to pull a fast one, sore about not getting their full payment. Sleepy Bill Burns and his partner Maherg believed them. They put everything they had or could borrow on the White Sox to lose the third game.

Comiskey Park was a riot of color, a bedlam of sound from the hyperthyroid crowd as the third game, in which the White Sox could redeem themselves, began. Chick and his boys had lied to Sleepy Bill. They were angry and they were double-crossing the gamblers to show they could not be pushed too far. They won, 3 to 0.

It was the finish for Sleepy Bill. He had made $12,000 betting on the first two games, and now had dropped it all and more. Little Champ, who hadn't relied on Sleepy Bill's information, said sadly about the deceitful boys, "I don't trust them ballplayers no more."

As contact man, going to see the ballplayers, Sleepy Bill told them Little Champ wasn't *too* angry, even if he had lost a lot. "You hurt him bad, I guess."

The players didn't seem sad about that. Sleepy Bill said, "He's got twenty grand for you."

"Where is it?"

Sleepy Bill said, "He wants to see you score before he hands it over to you."

"Same old crap," said Lefty Williams.

Sleepy Bill, feeling short of cash, asked for his cut on the $10,000 he had gotten for them.

"Sorry, Bill, it's all out on bets."

Jumpy and confused, Sleepy Bill screamed, "I want my share. Give me a grand or I'll tell *everything!*"

The boys just shrugged, and Sleepy Bill went out and got drunk. So did his partner—both wondering how they had been aced out of the fix and were left big losers.

In New York Sport Sullivan told Rothstein everything was going along just jim-dandy. He didn't explain he had held out $30,000 from the players' bribes and had given them only $10,000. The fix wasn't as solid as it looked, but Sport was a master technician at the double cross, a virtuoso.

The next morning Sport called Chick Gandil to go ahead as planned; to show his good faith he was wiring $20,000 at once. Also Chick was to tell the boys there was $40,000 more held in the Congress Hotel safe for them. Sport Sullivan now had the problem of getting his hands on $20,000 to wire to Chicago before the fourth game started. Calling long distance to his gambling connections, he managed to get the money together and sent it off just before the game. Result: Cincinnati 2, White Sox 0.

Chick counted the $20,000 in new $1000 bills that some faceless man had silently delivered to him. He divided up what had been collected; $5000 to Swede Risberg, the same to Hap Felsch, and the same each to Lefty Williams and Shoeless Joe Jackson. Cicotte already had $10,000 from the first payoff.

It looked like rain for tomorrow's game, the fifth. Gleason, the White Sox manager, was giving it the old try with the sportswriters. He was an honest man and he was as puzzled as they were. Like the ball-club owner, Gleason was no dope. He, too, must have been wondering if the rumors were on the level. But as manager he had to put a good face, a taciturn facade on it.

"Luck favored the Reds. They would never have scored on Cicotte if it hadn't been for his own two errors. Cincy didn't hit him half as hard as Ring was hit. Cicotte threw his own game away . . . it was nothing but hard luck that beat the White Sox."

Most of the reporters had what was apathetically called "a loyalty to the sport." Also they were freeloaders on the management and expected the good life to continue—so why bother with rumor-ridden conjecture? But Ring Lardner was of a different metal. He had no great respect for the human race, which he saw as Swift's Yahoos, and he had the dark taste of the wary pessimist in his mouth when it came to charting the honor, grace, and humane hope in the average slob that made up the world. Lardner's picture of mankind may have been grim, as his fiction shows, but he never had any reason to change his opinions as he slowly drank his way to oblivion, wary of the human species and the ambiguities of existence.

Now he wrote as the fifth game was about to be played in the morning: "As for today's game, they was a scribe downtown this AM saying that 2 men asked who was going to pitch today and the scribe said Cicotte and 1 of the men said you are crazy as Cicotte has such a sore arm that he can't wash the back of his neck. So when we come out to the park this scribe told me about it and I said they wasn't nothing in the rules of today's game that required Cicotte to wash the back of his neck. 'Well,' said the other expert, 'the man was just speaking figurative and meant that Eddie had a sore arm.' 'Well,' I said, 'if he has only one sore arm he can still wash the back of his neck as I only use 1 even when I am going to a party.'

" 'The back of your neck looks like it,' said the other expert. 'Yes,' I said. 'But what is the differents or not about Cicotte only having 1 sore arm as he only pitches with 1 arm.' 'Yes, you bum, but that is the arm that the man said was sore.' "

Williams would pitch and Hap Felsch would try to make an easy catch look like something that just got away, letting runs score. The White Sox lost. In the press box another serious, honest sportswriter, Hugh Fullerton, was angry. The White Sox hadn't scored in twenty-two innings of play in the Series. Poor Gleason, the manager, had to explain things again. Meanwhile, the bribed players were making it clear to the gamblers. They got the news to Sport Sullivan: $20,000 more on the line or there would be no lost game in Cincinnati in the morning.

All the while Kid Gleason was sweating to the press: "Something is wrong. I don't know what it is. The team that won the pennant for me this summer would have made about fifteen hits off Eller in August. It wasn't the same team that faced him today. The Sox are in a terrible batting slump. It is the worst slump a team ever had."

"Man," Montaigne had written, "is frivolous, complicated, changeful and elusive as flowing water"—all these centuries before there was baseball. At the moment, man was changeful. Gleason put in Dickie Kerr to pitch, and the White Sox won, 5 to 4. So the Series stood 4 games to 2; the White Sox had to win the next three games in a nine-game Series to take the Series. Eddie Cicotte was to pitch the game of October 8. With no payment in sight, Eddie pitched a brilliant game and the White Sox won, 4 to 1.

Arnold Rothstein was beginning to wonder how his front men were running things in Chicago. He sent for Sport Sullivan for an explanation of just how the fix was going wrong. He felt the ballplayers were "just a bunch of dumb rubes . . . who agreed to work for peanuts." So what was wrong? He ordered Sullivan to see that the Series ended with the White Sox losing the game from the first inning. No use dragging it out to make it look good. Did Sullivan understand? He said he did.

Sport, desolate in disquiet, was in trouble. He had "his ass in a sling" and was no longer in control of the ballplayers. Rothstein was a hard man to finagle—he had muscle he could hire if he found out that Sport's greed had bollixed things up. Sullivan figured maybe he, too, could use muscle. (Chicago already had its hoodlum gangs; Prohibition was beginning to breed hijacking, alkey-distilling, the hideousness of mob rule, rub-out, and ride-taking.)

Sport got in touch by phone with a hoodlum mobster known only as Harry F., told him Lefty Williams, the pitcher, had a wife, and Williams wouldn't want any harm to come to her. So—why not? Sport would send Harry F. $500 right away for a little job he wanted done.

Thirty-three thousand people were expected to pack Comiskey Park for the game the next day. The drama was turning sinister with a gritty lucidity. That night Lefty Williams and his wife had gone out to dinner. As they returned to their hotel, a man wearing a hard dicer—as the derby was known in Chicago—watched them.

He was smoking a cigar. He nodded to Lefty, said could he have a private word, excuse us, Mrs. Williams, for a minute? He put it right to Lefty; he was to lose the next game. *No* arguments. Lefty, faced with some abdication of reality, pulled away, but the hood held him in an iron grasp. Forget the money, the hood said; nobody was going to get anything more. But something *could* and *would* happen to Williams' wife there if he didn't lose that game.

Williams was speechless. He hadn't expected any of this crazy business to turn deadly, to involve his family, his wife. It was like a bad movie. He just stood there, a yokel ballplayer. The man in the derby added, "Do it in the first inning. Blow up in that first inning." He said it serenely, without smugness, as Williams was later to recall.

Williams and his wife returned to their hotel. We have no record of their conversation. He did not, however, expose the Series fix to her, or the threat of the repulsive man in the derby.

The game the next morning was played before a huge crowd. Williams, his face furrowed and pensive, was way off, and Gleason began to warm up two other pitchers in the bullpen. The Reds scored three runs, four hits, three homers in fifteen pitches, and only one out. A gambler said, "It's the biggest first inning you ever saw." The inning ended 5 to 0. The game went on in catastrophe for the White Sox. In the imbecile end it was a final 10 to 5. A World Series in absurdities and senseless bad faith had been successfully rigged! Gamblers made millions, the public lost millions; baseball was never again the pure and honest American game. It would become bigger and bigger business, set up controls and judgments, and with radio and television coverage take its place as a giant American industry, still run with highly paid slave labor. But after this strange foray into crime, it would never again wear the clean garments of integrity and sportsmanship. It was always to remain somewhat suspect. One could imagine faceless people making plans in some secret place, the gloom punctuated only by gleaming cigar ends.

The most pathetic figure was that of Kid Gleason, the White Sox manager, crying out to the sportswriters in the locker room after the last game—like some ancient Greek betrayed by destiny and the gods, wondering at the prevailing fates that had done this to him: "Those Reds haven't any business beating us! We played worse baseball in all but a couple of games than we played all year. I don't know yet what was the matter. Something was wrong. I didn't like the betting odds. I wish nobody had ever bet a dollar on the team!"

As for owner Charlie Comiskey, when faced by questioning sportswriter Hugh Fullerton, Charlie realized now his players had sold him out. He spoke out in his rage: "They are seven [he meant eight] boys who will never play ball on this team again!"

The reporter went to work on the long task of exposing the scandal, but he was maligned by the sports magazines as a muckraker. As for the players in the plot, Sport Sullivan managed to get a final $40,000 for them. He himself had made $50,000 on the side in bets. The Swede got $10,000 of that in a last payoff. Chick Gandil, after some other small payments, in the end kept $35,000 for himself.

In time a grand jury would investigate the throwing of the World Series of 1919, indict the eight. Most of the ballplayers involved would testify, some confess. It made the entire front-page headlines of the newspapers:

The New York Times

EIGHT WHITE SOX PLAYERS ARE INDICTED
ON CHARGE OF FIXING 1919 WORLD SERIES:
Cicotte got $10,000 and Jackson $5,000

COMISKEY SUSPENDS THEM

Promises to Run Them Out of Baseball
if Found Guilty

TWO OF PLAYERS CONFESS

Cicotte and Jackson Tell of Their Work
in Throwing Games to Cincinnati

BOTH ARE HELD IN CUSTODY

Prosecutor Says More Players Will Be Indicted
and Gamblers Brought to Task

Yankee Owners Give Praise to Comiskey
And Offer Him Use of
Their Whole Team

Sleepy Bill Burns testified in detail. But it was all playacting in an inherent emptiness of legal patter. Rothstein and his lawyers confused everything. Baseball officials muttered their tones. Judges, juries, and the press made a mad, perceptibly tilted mess of everything. The jury, those twelve fairly decent and too simple men, still believing in the good clean game, came in with their verdict. A cheer went up. The ballplayers were *all* found "Not guilty!"

A defense attorney (Shakespeare had suggested "Let us begin by hanging all lawyers") with a straight face said, "The verdict is a complete vindication of the most mistreated ballplayers in history."

Commented *The New York Times*: "The Chicago White Sox are once more whiter than snow. A jury has said that they are not guilty, so that settles that. The Court instructed the jury to determine whether the defendants intended to defraud the public and others and not merely to throw ball games. To the lay mind, this sounds very much like asking whether the defendant intended to murder his victim or merely to cut his head off!"

Arnold Rothstein—for other crimes—was shot at a poker game being played for high stakes at the Park Central Hotel in New York City. The police suspected another gambler, George McManus, of firing the fatal shot, but the dying Arnold Rothstein refused to say who had shot him and why. Avarice and caution held him until the end.

The ballplayers who were found not guilty went on to play ball in outlaw or semipro baseball clubs for a few years. The one line from the whole affair that entered American folklore was spoken after the first grand jury hearing, when Shoeless Joe Jackson had just made a full confession. As Jackson departed from the grand jury room, a small boy clutched his sleeve, tagged after him.

"Say it ain't so, Joe," he pleaded. "Say it ain't so."

"Kid, I'm afraid it is."

68

1919

For Chicago it was the time of counting the wear and tear of the city as the boys came back from the training camps and the A.E.F., of news of them dying of the influenza epidemic in the army huts. It was a war done with at the Great Lakes Naval Station. But somehow the lights had gone out on the slogan "To make the world safe for democracy." There was the hope that the young men shivering in their khaki overcoats would find jobs, women, homes. (Jay Gatsby, George F. Babbitt were already making connections.) The year 1919 came in freezing cold along the Loop, on the lakefront; for many it was a time when the world had lost its heroic couplets. In the whorehouses, over the gamblers' tables, the easy wartime money was gone, and in curtained store fronts, gypsy fingers laid out the tarot pack of cards ("a dark man . . . cross water . . . good fortune . . . twenty-five cents, please").

The saloons along the Levee were full ("I traded my Croix de Guerre for a pint of Panther Sweat") and so were the flophouses.

507

Along the Gold Coast and up in Lake Forest, the gentry were garaging their Pierce-Arrows and Stutz Bearcats—were loading their cellars with good hooch and wines—the real McCoy—and preparing to live by the silver cocktail shaker and a Fourteen Points Peace Mr. Wilson was going to make, and something to be called the League of Nations. Well, that meant peace forever, they said at the Chicago Club—and no more fortunes in munition stocks. Buy General Motors, and what are the grain and hog bellies futures listings for on LaSalle Street commodities? Austere audacity or wait for a Republican President?

Melancholy and nostalgia sat on Chicago that cold New Year's Day of 1919. The city was back from its wartime dizzy ride —back to its games of fatality and chance. Not all the men involved with crime in Chicago were Italians in 1919 when Prohibition went into effect. A.B., who once drove for Bugs Moran, remembered for me his upbringing.

He, an Irish kid in the tough wards, soon learned he was different from the other kids if only because he was Irish and they were not. And an Irish Catholic kid soon got to sense he was a lot different. The knowing came slowly. But suddenly it was there. He heard remarks that shocked him, and then he realized not everyone south of the Loop went to Mass, had holy pictures and crucifixes in the house, believed in the pope's infallibility, knew what was Holy Communion, the Sacrament of the Holy Eucharist. Lots of killers carried holy medals, murdered at night, went to Confession in the morning.

"For me it was even at my worst—the Church was real, as normal as breathing. I not only accepted Faith, I relished it, was devoted to it. To us Chicago Irish trying to make a place for ourselves in a hard-ass city that was new to our parents and grandparents, the Church, it was the solid rock that sustained us. As a kid I was hungry, dirty, but not lost or wandering. I belonged, really belonged, see? The Communion of the Saints was a living bond among all us members of the Church. I was serious on Septuagesima Sunday and on the first day of Lent; for me Ash Wednesday was really the message the old priest recited: 'Remember man thou art dust and unto dust thou shalt return.' And we'd go out and roll drunks and gang-bang some dame.

"But then in fear of God, I'd shiver and see myself dissolving into a handful of earth. But being young, death was something that happened only to other people, you know, in some other place. Unless one was *very* old, and then I'd carry the tools for the priest, his oil and his scarf—we'd come to bring the Extreme Unction, to help, as my mother would say, when sober, 'Someone we loved slip into the eternal grace and happiness of God.'

"Even hijacking, whoring, gambling—away from the Church, I knew we were different. Some of the other hoods I knew, Black Protestants, mocked the holy medals we wore, they never crossed themselves when passing a church, they took holy names in vain as a curse, not thinking what they were doing. And if they became vocal with rumors that some bigots were passing on about nuns, priests or the Pope, why we had a brannigan, see, a mean fight. So in a way my Faith kept me in condition and developed my right uppercut, helped with a cosh I kept handy.

"In the main, I remember my boyhood Faith as being part of the mick and dago families in the church, the smell of incense and the Latin, with the young priest still rolling his Rs in the Dublin way. And me and my friends assisting in the Mass, not feeling silly at all in my gown and lace, and good with the feeling that in this house of God, I was sheltered, protected, and sure that devotion to Him and to Mary set the way for Man's Redemption, and I'd try and think of me being in a state of grace.

"We weren't good boys, we choir kids, we horsed around and pinched each other and often the good father in charge of us would only be doing his duty to give us a mean knock on the head. He had a hard fist and said we'd end up in prison—some of us did.

"I felt good in being a Catholic. When in the Holy Communion I knew the truth of This is My Body, This is My Blood. I was aware when just a kid that to miss Mass without a reason, like say chicken pox or two broken legs, was a mortal sin, and I was thankful on Epiphany for those gifts I got, and not resentful for those I didn't get. I'd hear the deacon sing out: *'Lumen Christi'* and we all answering, 'Thanks be to God.' But somehow it didn't prevent our stealing—and worse. Much worse.

"We were not, in or out of church, goody-goody boys, and the priests and nuns had their hands full with us. And they weren't the holy waxworks, the pious folk the movies often show them as. They were hard, they were overworked, they were scared of us. They were folk my mother said were dedicated to renouncing a great deal of what we saw as the good times of life. They may have had lots of human failings, and could give you the back of the hand across your yap as well as lead you to the remission of mortal sin by the Sacrament of Penance as an Act of Contrition. When I was a kid, Catholics were still not accepted in some places. Our lives were hard and bare-assed—everybody nearly got drunk a lot.

"The trouble with Chi when I was growing up in the time of World War I was that being honest on our block starved you; your old man got drunk on payday after a week of cow-shit shoveling for Armour, or my mother putting in time at a sausage-stuffing machine. You ever smell a broad, no matter if they could wash up, that has been doing ten hours pushing crap into yards of gut?

"So when easy money come along for a gink like me—lookout for a crap game, or driving a beer truck for Bugs—all we wide guys we took. And my sis—Katherine, a girl that was gang-banged at fourteen in a cellar. What the hell, Katie said, why work like a slave as a housemaid for eight bucks a week and stupped by the old man, when she could turn a trick in the back room of any saloon, and later a speak, or be part of a setup to take the wartime shipyard workers, country jakes, first time in a silk shirt, let loose with pay in their poke in a big city?

"No there was nothing to going right, like the priest wanted, not when you saw your mother and father rolling drunk and tearing at each other, and every year, or sooner, another stinking kid brought howling into our three-room flat, with no hot water and the john in the hallway and me brothers stealing coal and boxes to keep warm with one stove.

"Where the Church failed us was not giving us something besides Mass and warnings—give us here in the city, like say no bedbugs in the wallpaper, and let us have strawberry shortcake, and clothes that nobody's three brothers had worn before you. Savvy? But I didn't drop out of church—like most of me pals who went into the rackets. No matter how I whored around or got boozed up, I went to church from time to time. I'd come home Easter, slip some dough to me mother, the smelly kids with running noses something for Christmas. It's no malarkey when I tell you I felt I was better than the hoods I ran around with, because I believed in God, even if he'd boil me alive for a million years. I don't know, I guess I felt with so much hell on earth, he'd skip it up there, sorta parole me."

"So I carried my Faith with me, with my Smith and Wesson. I could always find a church someplace, an old priest in faded surplice to serve the Mass, wise-looking, kind of worn, full of wrinkles with years, or a young father eager and full of feisty ideas he'd get me to see things right and everything would work out. And I prayed: 'Into Thy hands, oh, Lord, I commend my spirit.'

"I came to see that sin is not a condition, but as they said, a personal thing, knowing, see, transgressing God's law. In the Fall and Redemption I came around to original sin through the fall of the first man. It was sure good to be able to confess, to be in a state of grace, to know that no matter where I would run for it, or be, there was an altar and a priest who would bring me under the Triptych of the Kingdom. Yeah, I *took that* serious. Now I'm an old man, but it still figures.

"There were guys, dames, ones in the rackets I admired who were my pals, who didn't feel as I did. Didn't have a faith. I wondered how they managed when me, with the Faith, had times of despair, of dark hating hours. Well, I survived, you can see that. I survived because of my Faith, and a lot of luck. I was aware of facing, as some people never are, the four problems of life—existence, pain, evil and death; I read a lot in my two stretches in stir, and I tried no long-hair con on myself.

"Like all young punks living high at times, I was aware of the body, see—and the bodies of others. I was darn human; I was in part, you know, biological? I knew Saint Paul had said, 'It is better to marry than to burn.' I sure believed that marriage was established by the command of God, for Christ had placed it among his sacraments. Well, I fucked that up—my marriage—never mind. So there was in me, even in 1919, a conflict between what I was as a human being, and what I am as a soul. The flesh and the spirit had some mighty fancy wrestling matches. Oh, brother. I never solved them as a man; maybe I have since as a Christian. Somebody spared me—of the thirty, forty hoods I ran with over the years, all are dead, died young but me and Joey up in the laughing farm, and what's his name in Congress?"

69

LAST OF THE GOLD DUST TWINS

Chicago the jazz baby—the reeking, cinder-ridden, joyous Baptist strong-hold, Chicago the chewing gum center of the world, the bleating slant-headed rendez-vous of sociopaths and pants makers—in the name of the seven Holy Imperishable Arts, Chicago salutes you.
BEN HECHT, CHICAGO LITERARY TIMES

The riverboat jazz had been—like some soiled yet lambent jewels—coming north to Chicago since 1900. By 1917, when the New Orleans sporting-house district, Storyville, was closed, and the horn men came upriver to shiver in the cold of the lake shore, the sound of their music had begun to seep into the roadhouses, and then into the first speakeasies. There was King Oliver who brought a kid named Louis Armstrong, and a piano girl, Lil Hardin, to Chi, and then there was Bix, Leon Bismark Beiderbecke, and the Wolverines and what was to be the Chicago Style; while kids were trying on "Livery Stable Blues," white side men listening to King Oliver's Creole Jass Band (not jazz) playing "The Royal Garden Blues," "Dippermouth," "High Society." It was jazz at the De Luxe Cafe on the South Side, and the first white sounds, as early as 1915, that of Tom Brown's Syncopated Novelty Orchestra at the Vista Gardens.

None of this sat too well with two old men, getting older, losing

513

hold, remembering too often old glories and ancient victories. There was still the First Ward, and still the Democratic party and elections to steal, floaters to vote, and cigars to smoke when the tallies were in and the swindle done. Only it was the younger men now who took orders from upstairs directly. They paid just a lot of lip service and gave too much lip to the Bathhouse and the Dink, who, still making gestures of judicious manipulating and fearing final oblivion, fought any idea they were obsolete—or their gregarious nineteenth-century life-style out of step.

It seems fitting to end this book on the Chicago that began its saga on these pages with the Civil War, and has come round to the final last echoes of World War I, with the Bathhouse and Hinky Dink. Beyond this point, it's another Chicago, one of the contemporary Stonehenges later coughing in smog and welfare check whiskey. A Chicago, 1920–1970, is too much written about. But there is time in some mockery of Apollonian majesty, for these two characters to take last bow; come on Bathhouse and Hinky Dink.

By 1919, they were beginning to slip from power like a Mack Sennett Keystone Kop on a banana peel. But they had their memories, the time Bathhouse stood up in the City Council and asked for a law to construct a twelve-foot stone and brick wall around the city's cemeteries—it would do no harm to the dead, and get felicitous approval from the masons and bricklayers' unions, and those who sold bricks and building supplies.

"Cemeteries are base places at best," pointed out the Bathhouse in an interview. "They have a deadening effect on the neighbourhoods. . . . What's the use of spoiling a whole neighbourhood by having a job lot of woozy tombstones . . . it might be a good idea to sell space to advertisers." So today most Chicago cemeteries have those twelve-foot walls, but *not* yet the advertising for armpit spray or sozzled gasoline.

When Bathhouse ran for reelection, it wasn't ever on a reform ticket. Howled the Christian Endeavour Society and the Committee of Fifteen, issuing a statement worthy of later racists and Birchers, "The Hinky Dinks, Bathhouse Johns, Jew Kids, Polack Bens, Jim Colosimos, and Mike the Greeks must go. . . . It's a war to the finish!"

But as a state legislator, Tom McNally, beholden to Bathhouse John, put it, "If our Bathhouse Jawn was to put on a tin star and went and reported to the YMCA every time Maggie got a can of beer, and wouldn't let Tom and Pat or Dave drink what he wanted to, he would be the summer idol of the reformers. Or if he went and blew on every 4-11-44 policy game that he seen goin' on in basements, they would receive him with open arms. But, gents, he ain't that kind. He don't stick his nose where he ain't wanted. If you want a drink before twelve or after twelve, go to it, says Jawn, so long as you don't disturb yer neighbours."

Bathhouse could only order his followers to unrestraint and resiliency: "Be gentlemen, like you always are, an' carry yer standard bearer's motto: HONESTY AND NO SLANDER." As an admirer put it, "Election time, Bathhouse John is loose as a goose."

He won again by 2605 votes. Bathhouse always won. He helped carry Mayor Harrison to victory again with him, and the mayor asked, "Why with everybody against me, why was it I won?"

Bathhouse John smiled and said in his best basso profundo: "Well, Mr. Mayor, I'd say you won because of the public satisfaction with the well-known honesty which has caricatured your every administration."

Mayor Harrison, Jr., knew how much the two aldermen, the Dink and Bathhouse, meant to him. He wrote of Bathhouse in a book he put together that the alderman ". . . he would have travelled far and high as a leader of men . . . human it is, too prone to dismiss as beneath contempt a type of man who . . . is not to be blamed altogether for his derelictions."

Of Hinky Dink he said, "Mike Kenna, with all his faults and failings . . . a fine fellow, a good husband who led the quietest of lives, devoted to the home circle. . . . I never once knew him to lie. Our cards were always on the table face up, nothing ever held out." It is hard to discredit dishonest men who helped elect you and kept you in office for five terms. Politicians have that touch of genius of never reaching that saturation point where they can admit a follower is a thief and worse.

The two aldermen were so confident of victory at times that they cut the cost of buying a man's vote to fifty cents, and one election to fifteen cents a head. This brought revolt from the drifters and floaters and bums. One Tom McKenna, a flophouse resident, led an insurrection against price cutting. "Don't remember how much I got [last time] 'cause I was too drunk. . . . But now they ast us to register fer fifteen cents. And they're gettin' so strict, I can't register more than in two places. Hell, that's a poor day's pay, only thirty cents, beer and soup. Me, I'm holdin' out all day . . . half a dozen of us guys gotta stick together and make a proposition. They'll have to come 'round."

By late noon, Hinky Dink gave in to the rebels—when the *other* side, the Republicans, were offering twenty-five cents a vote. The Dink met their price; no use risking any inconclusiveness of results. As a ward worker put it, "Some of them sots and geeks aren't honest. You pay for their vote, buy it—and what happens? they go crooked—take from the other side too!"

Hinky Dink and Bathhouse wasted no time in orgies of vituperation; what cut the mustard was delivering the votes. Always they delivered the largest plurality for Harrison than any of the city's thirty-five wards. The *Tribune* would announce another victory sourly.

CARTER HARRISON ELECTED

THE SAME OLD FRAUDS IN RIVER WARDS

HINKY DINK LEADS THE RAIDS

William Randolph Hearst, who himself at one time had political hopes, printed his opinion of the same event: "Harrison's election means a new clean Democracy in Illinois."

Mr. Dooley paid little attention to remarks others made on elections, but did comment that, "Manny a man that cuddent direct ye to the dhrug store on th' corner whin he was thirty will get a respectful hearin' whin age has further impaired his mind."

With Prohibition, the Italian gangsters took over most of the paying off of the city officials for favors on lawbreaking, brothels, gambling. They went on buying judges, courts, police, even a reporter or two. This meant Bathhouse and the Dink lost out more and more and even stood aside, as long as the big shots let them stay on as aldermen, no matter how grandiose the looting, how remorseless the new corrupters.

Bathhouse John was going broke. Racehorses, bad investments

in corn crops and the steer market were protagonists who beat him. He tried to raise pigs by feeding them the city's garbage which he got delivered free, but the pigs became tubercular in prurient malevolence, died before Swift or Armour could make their end profitable.

Even Bathhouse John Coughlin's fame as a native, top-hatted poet faded as the press exposed him and claimed he never wrote or was the author of such ebullient dandies as

TO A HOD CARRIER

Tis not a ladder of fame he climbs
This rugged man of bricks and mortar;
The mason gets six for laying the bricks
While the hod carrier gets but two and a quarter.

It was excruciatingly mean to print he was not the true author of all of the famous Bathhouse poems. Gossip hinted it was a reporter on the *Tribune* named John Kelley who was the true creator. Kelley, the secret bard, it was who wrote such classics as "Ode to a Bathtub," "Why Did They Build the Lovely Lake So Close to the Horrible Shore?" "Suds and Spuds," "Farewell to the Wellington Hotel," "They're Tearing Up Clark Street Again" . . . and the classic "When the Moonbeams Kiss the Roses in the Glow of Eventide." Even "She Sleeps at the Side of the Drainage Canal" was lost to Bathhouse; it was as if Shakespeare had to see *Hamlet* slip away to the queen's jester.

There was work still to be done. Chicago had seen blacks by the thousands come north to the South End of the First Ward. And all were Republicans, carrying the icon of Abe Lincoln. The Dink and Bathhouse converted many of these black folk to the Democratic party by silver dollars, beer, and an edge into the gravy of the vice games. The Dink still had his free-lunch Exchange, his flophouse. The bums and others would line up every morning at the Exchange, each with a tin pail to get his portion of Rub-of-the-Brush. This was a huge vat filled with all the revolting, mixed, saloon's drippings of beer, bourbon, Scotch, ale, wine, and everything else that would flow down a drain of a bar into a bucket. Each man got his little pail of these alcoholic slops and was contented to sit sipping it in the park, or along the curb, until it was time for the noontime free lunch. Prohibition soon closed the Exchange. The saloons sadly gave away their big glass schooners as mementos; sixteen inches across the bowl, eight inches high, three pounds eight ounces empty, inside four and a half inches in diameter, four inches deep, and holding a pint and nine fluid ounces of foaming beer.

In November of 1910, Bathhouse's wife, Mary Coughlin, died, and Bathhouse looked older as a widower. In time he set up some woman in the lingerie business, and is said to have coined the phrase, "At my age they don't have to be beautiful, just patient." Other aging Don Juans have claimed it since.

The Dink, with no saloon, ran a little bit of a social club, disguised as a cigar store, with pictures of the great potentates of political power from the past on the walls. He was a very rich man, but that didn't matter when the incisive cadence of power was slipping away. Bathhouse was getting a bit stained, the good clothes needed dry cleaning, his 250 pounds now was no tailor's model. But the color of the vests, the height of the collars, the polka-dot ties were still those of a dude from another era.

His stable of horses broke Bathhouse. The sense of the insecurity of life hemmed him in. He would still hum and sing an old favorite of the days when the First Ward balls were popular.

> 'Twas at a fancy ball last night
> I was the fairest belle
> Among the nice young fellas was
> An eighteen caret swell.
> He won me heart, he won me hand
> While dancin' in the Waltz.

He couldn't admit the old days were gone, the great houses built by the first millionaires growing shabby and being turned into homes for nuns or drunk cures, and the fine paneling of Indiana walnut and Michigan white pine being painted over. And always at his back the new gang lords to deceive and threaten. It was all introverted lunacy, and since the Great War, he, who had been a combination of the Artful Dodger and the wily Odysseus ("that's what the newspaper fella printed"), had become a stained clown. A long way from the time all orders on how the Levee was to act and behave came from Coughlin and Kenna through them fellas Ike Bloom and Solly Friedman. Brothel keepers were compelled to place insurance with a company owned by Bathhouse; ordered to buy all their liquor from Freiberg's in which Bathhouse owned a half interest; they were given a list of four grocery stores at which to buy their food supplies. The Levee, the ward then, *was* Coughlin and Kenna, accused of grafting and collecting by every newspaper in Chicago, every reform organization. But none of that ever reached prosecution. They had followed the advice of William Mason, afterward United States Senator. Mason told Bathhouse John: "Stick to the small stuff and let the big stuff alone." The stuff had paid enough to buy a racing stable, sixty horses, a country estate, a private zoo in Colorado.

He refused to accept any idea his life had been shoddy. He insisted in interviews it had been a great life. "I enjoyed every minute of it. There was one thing wrong—Lady Luck played me false."

As for Hinky Dink, he tried to impress on the newer aldermen he still ran the First Ward; in righteous tenacity he insisted to reporters, "It's an absolute lie that I deliver any of the vote by fraud. I go 'round election day mornings and see the clerks and judges are on duty. I preach to them to be honest. . . . I got the cleanest and most respectable ward in the city." All the same, the Dink's vote buyers were still asking strangers, "You vote yet, son? You wanta make fifty cents?"

"But I voted in another precinct," said a *Tribune* reporter so approached. The vote buyer felt that was a superficial excuse. "I voted six times today, an' I'm gonna vote four times more. That'll be five dollars for the day's work."

When the Municipal Voters' League wrote that Bathhouse John was "voting for the good of the city," for some reason Bathhouse took umbrage. "This endorsement by the MVL is just *too* much!" roared Bathhouse.

"You oughta sue 'em," suggested Hinky Dink, dead pan.

A reputation for honestly helping the city could ruin an alderman: it was nothing short of idiocy to be endorsed by the MVL in the First Ward.

Better to forget it and join the last of the old boys in a speakeasy and sing an old favorite. There was so much time for singing now.

> Oh, the night that Paddy Murphy died, I never shall forget,
> We all got stink-in' drunk that night and some ain't sober yet.
> But the on-ly thing we did that night that filled my heart with fear:
> We took the ice right off the corpse and put it in the beer.
> Wo, ho, ho,
> That's how we paid our re-spects to Pad-dy Murphy.
> That's how we showed our hon-or and our pride.
> That's how we paid our re-spects to Paddy Murphy on that night that
>   Pad-dy died.

The petty political tasks Bathhouse now had to perform were small ones. One boss of the council put it directly to Bathhouse John and the others . . . "You go along with us, or you don't get a can of garbage moved out of yer ward till hell freezes over."

Bathhouse saw to it the garbage was collected properly in the First Ward. "A man has a duty to his con-stit-u-ents."

Feed bills for his racehorses fell due and he couldn't pay. He couldn't raise the cash for the entry fee for his racing stable. He wandered in incoherent anguish. He was given a dinner by some jesters and decorated as the Knight of the Bath. He gained weight, ballooned out, and his clothes were no longer that of the Levee's Beau Brummel. Everyone he had come to power with was gone, all but Hinky Dink, the indestructible. The Dink was "still full of piss and vinegar," he told barflies.

Bathhouse became ill, and after weeks of misty fantasy, divergent mutterings, he died in the Lexington Hotel. When the lawyers got through with his estate, there was almost nothing left; the racehorses were sold for a fraction of what Bathhouse John Coughlin had paid for them. His debts ran to fifty-six thousand dollars.

Hinky Dink Mike Kenna was eighty years old. He was very rich, and he was going blind. But the Democratic party still needed him to implement and expedite—now that Bathhouse was gone. Needed him in the City Council. He went back, coming out of his rooms in the old Auditorium Hotel like an ancient turtle, blinking in melancholy slowness in the sun. He attended a few meetings, a cigar held in his old jaws, spitting recklessly in all directions, and then he faded from the scene into solitary indifference, to that moribund ennui of the very old. What use the holy medals, scapulars, rosaries?

In the obituaries of the last of the old-time political buffalo herd, one reporter—as the story was told by Elliot Paul—added a line from Thomas Browne's *Religio Medici*, first printed in 1642.

"The lives, not only of men, but of Commonwealths and the whole world, run not upon a helix that still enlargeth; but on a circle where, arriving to their meridian, they decline in obscurity, and fall under the horizon again."

The city editor blue-penciled it. "The readers, if they want philosophy, let 'em read the funnies—like Mutt and Jeff . . . and the Katzenjammer Kids."

A PERSONAL EPILOGUE

The last time I stood in old Dearborn Station at Polk and Dearborn, the air age was about to claim us. It was in the early 1940s, a day of raging winter storm, snow falling like goose down, a wind whipping it along past emerald and ruby-lit signal towers, rows of ice-blue tracks, men in earmuffed caps moving baggage carts, piling up carloads of mail as they stopped to beat mittens together, collect around a metal basket of burning coke.

I stood looking out, waiting for the *Super-Chief* to be made ready and back in toward me for loading. I was standing with John Barrymore, coat flung over his shoulders, and Sinclair Lewis, waiting to continue our journeys westward to sunshine and the then still clean air. We had come on from the East, come in the night on a marvelous roadbed and a club car properly serviced.

The three of us were travelers who loved Chicago, where we had visited, adventured, and been entertained, often for long stays, since our boyhood. Barrymore, in decline, had been touring in a dismally wretched play, *My Dear Children.* A play he had saved nightly by inventing his own dialogue, often carrying on a conversation with his Chicago audiences. I had worked with him, written texts he had done for radio. Sinclair Lewis I had known since 1937, when I was supposed to aid him in the art background, the research for a novel about an American genius, a painter, a book that was never written.

The searing cold entered the vast railroad station, even though the steam heat hissed in radiators around us. In those days there was no through train from coast to coast. One emerged at Union Station, at Jackson and Adams, into summer heat or winter fury from the *20th Century Limited,* or *The General,* collected baggage, found a redcap, was hustled into a taxi and shuttled crosstown to the already decaying Dearborn Station. Usually between trains one had to wait from four to eight hours to connect with the Santa Fe *Chief,* or *The City of San Francisco.* One could pass time by going to the Palmer House to try whatever gourmet delights one might find there in the thirties and forties, when the lake whitefish was as yet unpolluted. Or one could throw poker dice with the house girls in various bars. However, with family along, there was the air-conditioned Paramount, where a band leader named Paul Asche always seemed in residence. Or go out to the Field Museum, or the Art Institute and enjoy again the early Picasso clowns, the marvelous Seurat, and, if you were known, inspect some of the world-famous Buckingham collection of rare Japanese prints.

There was often enough time for Marshall Field's big store, larger than ever, Kroch's bookstore, an art gallery or so. Then back to Dearborn Station to board in the smell of train grease, Cracker Jack, and humanity moving toward the waiting train, the redcaps accepting coins, and on board the white-coated waiters, herds of them it seemed, already setting the linen-covered tables in the dining car; ready to serve those excellent meals at leisure and in detail. Not the slop offered the airline passenger out of Midway (formerly Chicago Air Port). "Air-carried warmed-over garbage" (Tallulah Bankhead).

But in the fury of that Chicago winter day, the Arctic wind coming down from Canada and the Pole and across the lake and

Loop, a snowstorm of the quality Chicago was famous for, there was nothing much to do but remain in the station and wait.

Barrymore took a full pint of Jim Beam from his tailored English overcoat, a garment well cut but a bit travel-worn, and offered, "A libation, gents?" We passed the bottle one to the other and took invigorating sips.

Barrymore smacked his lips and made a hand gesture over-elegantly. "Chicago was always a great theater town. But discriminating. You couldn't give *them* the peasant doss we fed the torpid natives of the hinterlands."

Sinclair Lewis, the scar tissue of his face scarlet in the cold, nodded. "Was always the dream city for us yokels at the whistle stops and jerkwater depots. Chicago was where my father went to medical conventions, and the village sports and garter-snappers went for sinning. As for the highbrow hounds, they lapped up Chicago opera and theater, and what they reported to us rubes as *culture.*"

"My sister Ethel, and Lionel always said that here the audiences were warmer. True . . . How they would have loved my Hamlet. Or did I play it here? Memory fades, you know."

We agreed to that, and neither Lewis nor I could remember if John Barrymore had brought his Hamlet to Chicago.

"Ah, well, it was the women of this stockyard Venusburg I remember best." He lifted the worn but still fairly unique profile to better advantage and smiled. "The prewar beauties of me youth, 1910, 1912. And later the dancing of the Castle Walk as I romantically swayed to Victor Herbert. . . . In the barbaric twenties the city was still vital, yet it had grown older, as did those *so* kind, accommodating ladies . . .

> *"Beauty is but a flower*
> *Which wrinkles will devour*
> *Brightness falls from the air*
> *Queens have died young and fair."*

Lewis and I sipped Jim Beam and admired the recitation of the Thomas Nashe verse. It did fit the mood. They were not young anymore. In Europe there was a dreadful war. Solid values, the actor said, seemed lost; gentility, grace, mortally wounded. He and

Lewis had known an earlier Chicago. I was aware nothing grows more untrustworthy than nostalgia, as we talked of old eating places, grand hostesses, theaters with Sarah Bernhardt, Lillian Russell, famous poker games at the Seneca Hotel, the grand bordellos on the Levee, the Samuel Insull days of fabulous opera with Mary Garden always on her "last tour." Naturally we remembered the gang wars and Prohibition gin, the voice of Big Bill Thompson, and the images of Al Scarface, and *who* did kill Jake Lingle? Days, nights of pageants and fairs, food served on flaming swords. Lewis spoke, too, of the dead from the just gone past. "Poets, thieves, journalists, bankers, Cicero con men, ladies who held literary salons on Lake Shore Drive, old hedonists who remembered Nell Kimball, the Everleigh sisters. Talk of real-estate values, grain-market speculators."

John Barrymore nodded. "That time a noted gangster and vice lord was killed by falling off his horse in a Chicago park, and his merry men *merrily* executed the steed, put it on the spot—as the expression was—with their pistols."

That Chicago was gone. Yes, with King Oliver's jazz, Bix, the Wolverines, and John Held's flappers.

The public-address system overhead, scientifically adjusted so one heard hardly anything but static and slurred vowels, announced that the Santa Fe *Super-Chief* was now loading. Sinclair Lewis put the empty pint into a litter container; Barrymore, with the fixed leer of his Svengali, followed two giggling girls toward the waiting train; the wind and snow punished us all the way to the Pullmans.

By the summer of 1972 my transportation to the city was airborne. Returning from Paris I was flying now in the belly of one of those uncomfortable, oversized monsters, with its banal movies in which the sound hardly ever functioned, and the food, even in first class, was worse than ever. We made our approach to O'Hare International Airport, and I saw a city I knew, yet also a city strangling in suburbs that was moving away from my memory of it. The Chicago Circle Campus, the "Big John" Hancock erection (local wit), U.S. Gypsum's space-eating decor—so much new architectural chic. Shaped like ax wedges, snorkels, piled-up pancakes. As we slowed speed, flaps down, I wanted to say *I accept you—I accept you*

. . . But *I don't* have to *respect you* as I once did the Leiter Flats, Louis H. Sullivan's home on Park Avenue, Henry Richardson's Marshall Field's warehouse (razed in 1930), Cyrus McCormick's Rush Street Victorian residence. I had to admire the new Wacker Drive, the already obsolete Union Station that had gone up in 1924. But I disliked the greedy bulk of the Merchandise Mart, and for the Jane Addams Housing Project, I could only hope for the best. From the air, most of the city was scarred with cubist shapes made of stone and glass and steel. And "who could ever forgive the dirty scientific work done under the grandstands *there* at Stagg Field that in 1940 produced the Doomsday Bomb?" (Ben Hecht).

The flophouses of West Madison, Canal, and North Clark streets I knew were still there below me, full of drifters, winos, the dispossessed, and the Chinese were still crowded around Wentworth Avenue and Cermak Road. As for the yippies, the protesters, grass smokers, women libbers—were they past their high peak of revolt, those bloody convention nights of 1968—Mayor Daley's police putsch on students, dropouts advocating brown rice and organic kale? And peace!

When we landed at O'Hare and I rode into the city, picked up by a friend for an appearance on the television talk show of a popular Chicago figure, it took a warming-up period for me to tune in again on the hurry of Chicago streets, the forms of the surviving, old, soiled buildings, the pigeons still besmirching nineteenth-century historic bronze. All this was ignored by Afro hairdos, the hot pants chicks. Billboards shouted with their images of beer, autos, and the features of the loser-who-won, running again for the highest office. Chicago in the 1970s had gone beyond the "Century of Progress," 1933–1934, that I had attended. As for the lectures I had given in the past at the city's colleges, my talks of recollections of Hemingway, Faulkner, La Stein, Dos Passos, and *always* in those days the jazz age hero, Fitzgerald, the writers were now classics, read or unread, brushed aside by one professor I remember at the University of Chicago—in shoulder-length hair and General Burnside earlocks—as "romantics in a dimming past, filled with self-pity and the boozy egos of expatriates, their voices having *little* to say to us."

"Chicago remains as it always was—*if* you look for it," said the man with whose family I was spending the weekend. (He was a pollution-control biologist.) They lived in a rehabilitated three-story private house on Lincoln Avenue in Old Town, with two children, one dog, and double locks.

That night trying to sleep—I was fighting off an attack of the Old Nostalgia—I decided that Euripides had been right: "The first requisite to happiness is that a man be born in a famous city." And as I dozed off, I was again on a luxury train leaving Chicago, and the famous Nobel Prize novelist with me was ordering highballs and the great actor was reciting a benediction, as he called it, to the city with a verse by Herrick, our train moving fast, seeking escape to more open country.

Great cities seldom rest; if there are none
To invade from far; they'll find worse foes at home.

It had been, it was, a great city. It had been invaded but had swallowed and survived its invaders; yes, even its home-grown foes.

INDEX

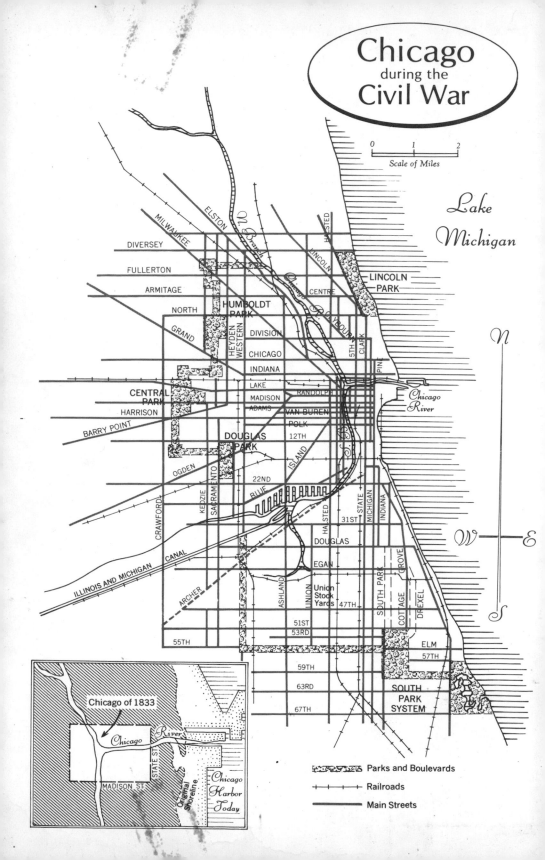